A History of Brazil

A History of Brazil

THIRD EDITION

E. Bradford Burns

Columbia University Press
NEW YORK

Columbia University Press
New York   Chichester, West Sussex

Copyright © 1993 Columbia University Press

Library of Congress Cataloging-in-Publication Data

Burns, E. Bradford.
     A history of Brazil / E. Bradford Burns. — 3rd ed.
          p.   cm.
     Includes bibliographical references and index.
     ISBN 0–231–07954–0
     ISBN 0–231–07955–9 (pbk.)
     1. Brazil—History.   I. Title.
     F2521.B89   1993
     981—dc20   93–12216
                                                 CIP

Casebound editions of Columbia University Press books are printed on permanent
and durable acid-free paper.

Printed in the United States of America

c 10 9 8 7 6 5 4 3 2 1

In history we only point to the dominant figures, those who destroyed or constructed, leaving behind a trail of blood or a ray of light. We do not remember whose shoulders bore them, the courage of the masses which gave them their strength, the collective mind which exalted their minds, the unknown hands which pointed out to them the ideal which only the most fortunate attained. And often the unknown person is the one whose cooperation was the most vital in bringing about the great event.

—João Capistrano de Abreu, 1889

A people cannot be free if they do not control their own sources of wealth, produce their own food, and direct their own industry and commerce.

—Alberto Tôrres, 1914

The entire structure of our colonial society was rural. That fact is essential to understanding our development until the fall of the monarchy or more precisely until the abolition of slavery. 1888 divides two epochs, the most decisive year in our evolution as a people. From that moment Brazilian life shifted from one pole to another, the transition to urbanization which only after 1888 plays a decisive role.

—Sérgio Buarque de Holanda, 1936

We espouse a nationalism based upon our aspirations for economic development. The proper nationalism for Brazil seeks to elevate our country to the level of the developed countries of the world so that it can speak as an equal without subservience, without fear, and without any feeling of inferiority.

—Juscelino Kubitschek, 1956

A mestizo culture is taking shape, so powerful and innate in every Brazilian that in time it will become the true national consciousness, and even the children of immigrant fathers and mothers, first-generation Brazilians, will be cultural mestizos by the time they are grown up.

—Jorge Amado, 1969

We have two countries here under one flag, one constitution, and one language. One part of Brazil is in the twentieth century, with high technology computers and satellite launches. And, beside that, we have another country where people are eating lizards to survive.

—Wilson Braga, 1985

Contents

List of Illustrations

Maps

Acknowledgments

More than two decades have passed since the first edition of *A History of Brazil* was published. Almost three decades have passed since I taught my first course on the history of Brazil. During that time, this text has changed; my teaching has changed; the students have changed. Surprisingly, I find the Brazil I know personally has not changed all that much. I seem to find more continuity in Brazil than I perceive in my historical views of it. The three editions of this book reflect these evolving views. Certainly this third edition dwells more on historical continuities than the previous two.

This text evolved largely through the course I teach on Brazilian history. In 1964, 5 students enrolled; in 1992, there were 250. The students across those years contributed significantly to my knowledge as well as to the shaping of this history of Brazil. Their perceptive questions as well as insights helped me sharpen my perspective. Our discussions formed the basis for this text, and its outline reflects the contours of the course.

The major advantage of specializing in the history of Brazil is the opportunity to travel there. Anyone who has visited Brazil understands the attraction of that nation and its people. My travels and research have taken me just about

everywhere anyone might want to go in that vast land. The facility of access to Brazilian museums, libraries, and archives—public and private—and the generosity of Brazilians in sharing their resources enhanced the pleasures of research and study. I extend my warmest thanks to those institutions and people. They have made my visits to their country delightful, rewarding, and memorable experiences.

For the information, facts, and interpretations set forth in this history of Brazil, I bear responsibility. Whatever errors exist also bear my imprint.

E. Bradford Burns
Muscatine, Iowa
April, 1993

A History of Brazil

Introduction

Brazil, the affable and amiable giant, attracts attention. It excites the imagination. It dazzles the beholder. The intensity of the light, the brightness of the color, the richness of the vegetation, the vastness of the landscape, the beauty of the people combine to make a seductive sight few have been able to resist. The alternating simplicity and complexity of the land and its inhabitants further intrigue any who delve even shallowly beneath that alluring surface. It has always been so.

Not immune to the attractions of the land, the Portuguese who discovered, explored, and settled Brazil saw it as a terrestrial paradise. The first description of the newly discovered domain spoke of it as "so well favored that if it were rightly cultivated it would yield everything." A Jesuit father, dazzled by what he saw, wrote back to the metropolis in 1560, "If there is paradise here on earth, I would say it is in Brazil." A chronicler later in that century prophesied, "This land is capable of becoming a great empire." The Brazilians expressed equal confidence. In the first history of Brazil, written in 1627, Frei Vicente do Salvador confided, "This will be a great kingdom." The enthusiasm continued. In the history published by Sebastião da Rocha Pita in 1730, that Bahian rhapsodized, "Brazil is the earthly paradise regained." Within

a century, one Brazilian poet, Francisco de São Carlos, had reversed the comparison. In his long poem *A Assunção,* he depicted Paradise in terms that made it sound strikingly similar to Brazil.

The attractions of Brazil did not go unnoticed by other Europeans. At various times, the French, Dutch, and English sought their fortunes in Brazil. Indeed, the British presence was a major economic reality of the nineteenth century.

Although throughout much of the nineteenth and twentieth centuries Brazil attracted only limited and sporadic attention from the United States, the years since World War II witnessed a burgeoning interest and concern on the part of the North Americans. U.S. investments in Brazil during this century rose spectacularly. When it became evident by the late 1950s that Brazil would exercise a major international role not only in the Western Hemisphere but on a global scale as well, U.S. government leaders, military officials, scholars, and businessmen rushed to learn more about the South American giant. President John F. Kennedy reminded his listeners that one had only to glance at a world map to appreciate the geopolitical importance of Brazil.

North Americans glanced at that map. They focused attention on the Portuguese-speaking people of South America. As one consequence, studies of Brazil, popular and erudite, cascaded off the presses. This history, now in its third edition, testifies to that reality.

Brazil offers a fascinating history. It records the dramatic struggles for survival against natural elements, for independence from foreign domination, and for the creation of a viable national state. Most impressive, it reveals the transference of European ideas and institutions to South America where, albeit challenged and influenced by the Indians and Africans, they tenaciously took root and flourished. They prevailed over the centuries, providing an astonishing continuity to the flow of Brazilian history. For anyone interested in the history of the nations of the New World, Brazil offers valuable points of comparison, as well as significant contrasts, with Spanish America and Anglo-America. While the nations of the New World might not have a common history, they do share

some common historical experiences. Europeans arrived in the Americas during an era of rapid commercial expansion. Throughout this hemisphere, they encountered and confronted Indians whose civilizations varied widely. Exploration, conquest, and settlement challenged the English, Spanish, and Portuguese and elicited different responses from each of them. They transplanted European institutions to the Western Hemisphere, and those institutions' adaptation and growth here took various courses. The Europeans hoped to resolve the pressing labor shortages by coercing the natives to work for them and, where that failed, by importing legions of African slaves. The metropolises all tried—once again with differing degrees of success—to impose mercantilism on their American domains. Within a span of less than half a century, colonies from New England to the Viceroyalty of the Plata revolted, threw off their European yoke, and entered the community of nations. The struggles to establish national states, to develop economically, and to assert self-identity absorbed the energies of the newly independent peoples.

In the course of their growth, the colonies and then the nations of the New World often responded quite differently to similar stimuli. The English in North America and the Spaniards in Argentina fought the Indians, in effect excluding them, while the Spaniards in Mexico incorporated them as an integral part of the colony. The Peruvians bitterly debated in the early nineteenth century the type of government they wanted; the Brazilians quietly coronated the resident Braganza prince as their emperor. The North Americans and Brazilians expanded westward, incorporating territory claimed by others; the Bolivians, Ecuadoreans, and Venezuelans ignored their hinterlands. The military played a predominant role in the first half-century of Peruvian independence, while during approximately the same years the military of Chile and Brazil exercised minimal influence.

Within the framework of hemispheric experiences, Brazil displayed some unique characteristics. For example, in the nineteenth century, its changes from a colony to an independent empire, from a monarchy to a republic, and from a slaveholding society to a free society occurred essentially

without violence, thus giving it an evolutionary character rare in the New World. Further, its ability to homogenize the three diverse racial elements into a single society on such an immense scale aroused the world's admiration. Although not free of racial tensions and inequities, Brazil nonetheless serves as one of the best examples of extensive miscegenation and racial harmony. It would seem to have much to teach the rest of the world on the difficult topic of racial relations. Thanks to the varied racial contributions, Brazil boasts a unique civilization. Indeed, on that fascinating level alone, it merits study. Certainly Brazil provides many useful insights into the problems faced by a nation whose governments have been determined to "modernize," that is, to recreate their nation after the image of Western Europe or the United States. No one disputes that Brazil possesses all the elements to facilitate economic development. The economic reality—that development thus far has eluded Brazil—constitutes one more cogent reason to study it.

The Visconde do Pôrto Alegre once remarked, "To know the biographies of all the outstanding men of a period is to know the history of those times." Much of Brazil's historiography reflects that view. A later nineteenth-century Brazilian historian, João Capistrano de Abreu, suggested an alternative approach to history: the study of ordinary people and their contributions to the historical process. The unnamed too deserve their place in history. It was not only princes, prelates, and politicians who built Brazil, but also the anonymous *bandeirantes* who explored, conquered, and opened up vast tracts of the interior, the forgotten black slaves upon whose skill and muscle the growth of Brazil depended, and the ignored women who provided the sinew and cohesion of society.

Heroes appear as they must, but they serve to illustrate and to particularize the broad trends of their times. Often historians of Brazil emphasize the individual and slight those broader trends. As a refreshing change, Capistrano de Abreu, whose *Capítulos de História Colonial* ranks as the most perceptive history of colonial Brazil, prided himself on being able to write the history of Brazil without a single reference to Tiradentes, the overly eulogized precursor of indepen-

dence. His works emancipated the study of Brazilian history from its overreliance on the biographies of the great and on political events to pay at least equal attention to social, cultural, and economic movements. Indeed, Brazil is far too complex for its history to be treated as a political chronicle.

Among the many themes that constitute Brazilian history some deserve particular attention in order to highlight the significance of modern Brazil. Territorial expansion—the real epic and major accomplishment of the past—commands a priority. Capistrano de Abreu singled this theme out as the dominant one of the colonial period, but its importance extends into the early twentieth century as well. The Luso-Brazilians swept across the South American continent from the Atlantic coast to the foothills of the Andes. Missionaries, cattle herders, and gold prospectors made good the seemingly exaggerated claims of the explorers.

The continuous fusion of European, African, and Amerindian populations into a homogeneous society is a second important theme. Thanks to the peaceful and thorough amalgamation of the three races in the tropics a unique civilization emerged and flourished.

A third theme is political evolution from colony to viceroyalty to kingdom to empire to republic. This process continues in the twentieth century in the drive to democratize Brazil, a goal more the ideal of selected intellectuals and the aspiration of the masses than a reality. Seemingly the period 1945–64 witnessed some effort and some success in the realization of that goal. But in the mid-1960s the effort at democratization was dashed against the rocks of economic realities. The fearful privileged classes and foreign interests pushed the military to seize the government and rule for their benefit. A return to democracy in 1985, a formality that effectively marginalized the majority, has failed to dissipate economic frustrations.

Urbanization, yet another significant historical theme, got under way in the eighteenth century, spurred by the discovery of gold and increasing commerce. The opening decade of that century had not ended before the first urban-rural clash occurred. Antagonisms have not abated. In the last

half of the nineteenth century the cities emerged as a major force, and thereafter they shaped the course of Brazilian growth. Within the cities, both modernization and industrialization took place, becoming significant forces in the shaping of Brazilian history by the end of the nineteenth century, and accentuating the differences between the cities and the more traditionally oriented countryside. Nationalism, a force that can be considered seriously in the twentieth century, is also nurtured in an urban environment. Urbanization, modernization, industrialization, and nationalism mutually interact, and their combined strength accelerates the rate of change. By the end of the nineteenth century, dynamic new groups appeared in Brazilian society in sufficient numbers to play influential roles: industrialists, European immigrants, a middle class, and a proletariat. The middle class, coopted by and supportive of the economic, political, and social elites, exercised a major influence over events in the twentieth century.

As elsewhere in the underdeveloped world, a desire for change pervades contemporary Brazil. The masses now understand the difference between their own afflictions and the affluence of the privileged few. Fully aware of that difference, they seek to diminish it by improving their own conditions. To do so means to challenge the past, those conservative, oligarchical, and paternalistic traditions, patterns, and institutions which have governed Brazil for so long. The challenge intensifies.

Bitterly opposed to each other are those who strive to maintain the old structures and those who struggle to destroy them. Change and continuity provide the dialectic and drama of modern Brazil. In the opinion of the eminent Brazilian historian José Honório Rodrigues, "The struggle which is now taking place is not between liberals and conservatives, it is between progressive reformers and counter-reformers." He affirms that two principal characteristics of the Brazilian people are a desire for progress and an optimism about the future.

It takes a strong dose of faith and courage to be optimistic in the face of alarming conditions. As this text will point out, illiteracy remains high, wages low, nutritional levels min-

imal, under- and unemployment endemic. The social and economic statistics forge a harsh reality at the close of the twentieth century and present a gloomy picture. When the American visitor Herbert H. Smith surveyed Brazil at the opening of the last decade of the empire, he remarked, "If ten American travellers were asked to give their views of Brazil, we would hear ten different opinions, grading all the way from paradise to despair." Neither "paradise" nor "despair" should be emphasized to the exclusion of the other.

Despite many handicaps, growth in Brazil has been steady if perhaps slow and erratic. Brazil has maintained its unity in the face of every obstacle, emancipated its slaves without civil war, evolved from a monarchy to a republic without bloodshed, and laid the foundations for a modern and industrial society. The ever diversifying economy is no longer a simple extractive one. The illiteracy rate has fallen gradually. The nation has shown that it can exercise greater independence in its international relations. The population in general is becoming aware of those advancements, is proud of them, and is enticed by the mystique of a greater Brazil that will provide a fuller life for all. In the past centuries, Brazil has had more than enough prognosticators who foresaw a brilliant future for the country, often very unrealistically. It is not the task of the historian to dispense prognostications, but no historian who has followed Brazil's versatile adaptation and its bold resolution of some of its problems can fail to be affected by some Brazilians' enthusiasm and optimism about the future of their country.

Chapter One

Interactions:
New Challenges
and Continuities

The recorded history of Brazil began with the arrival of the Portuguese. The sudden discovery of unknown land in the West surprised the experienced sailors. What they saw impressed them. They puzzled over the Indian, unlike the African and Asian they already knew, and they marveled over the lush tropical coast. The new arrivals aroused the curiosity of the indigenous Americans and also must have fired their suspicions. Although generally peaceful, the first encounters challenged both the natives and the intruders to revise their views of their environments and their world. For both, they heralded a new age, new ideas, and a new order.

The land promised the Portuguese much, but the natives traded reluctantly. To exploit the potential wealth and to protect the extensive coastline from foreign interlopers, the Portuguese resolved to settle Brazil. They thus began their largest colonizing effort and in the process transferred Portuguese civilization to a South American environment.

The Land

On any global map, Brazil stands out. It is huge, the world's fifth largest nation. It dominates South America and the South Atlantic, and geopolitical realities confer on it a prominent international role. Occupying nearly half of South America, it stretches from the Atlantic in the east to the Andes in the west, from the Guiana Highland in the north to the Plata Basin in the south. Most of this territory lies in the tropics. In a certain sense this subcontinent of 3,200,000 square miles is an island surrounded by the Atlantic Ocean and the Amazon and Plata river networks, for those fluvial systems reach inland from the ocean like giant, clutching hands whose fingers come within a few miles of touching each other in the west of Brazil. (See Map 1, Brazil, Showing States and Their Capitals, and Map 2, Rivers of Brazil.)

The Atlantic, bathing 4,600 miles of coastline, serves as the highway to the world, carrying immigrants and merchants, capital and ideas to Brazil and bearing the products of the land away. The obvious importance of that vital connection has exerted a powerful influence on the formation of Brazil. For one thing, the Portuguese and their American descendants preferred to remain close to the sea. In the picturesque language of a seventeenth-century historian, "They cling crablike to the beaches." Unlike Hernando Cortés in Mexico, they never performed the symbolic act of burning their ships.

That coastal belt is narrow. North of the Amazon it confronts the Guiana Highland, gently rounded hills with stumps of eroded mountains. South of the Amazon it is pressed between the ocean and the Brazilian Highland. Between Salvador and Pôrto Alegre the shore is bordered by a steep, wall-like escarpment. Some deep bays, such as Todos os Santos, Vitória, and Guanabara afford excellent harbors. A few rivers provide possible routes of penetration inland. South of Santa Catarina the coastal barrier gives way to lowlands.

It was this luxuriant coastal plain that led some Europeans during the early years of exploration to believe they had

Map 1. Brazil, Showing States and Their Capitals

located, at long last, the elusive earthly paradise. The learned Jesuit missionary Manuel da Nóbrega reported in the mid-sixteenth century on the pleasant climate, neither hot nor cold, on the ever green foliage, and on the abundance of nature that provided a large variety of fruits, fish, and animals. His descriptions match perfectly those given of the terrestrial paradise by medieval scholars. To Nóbrega's way of thinking, the Creator had made of Brazil a showpiece. Foreigners and Brazilians alike agree. The varied geography provides an always dramatic backdrop for the historical drama.

Westward, beyond the plain and the escarpment, stretches an extensive and uneven plateau, comprising roughly five-eighths of the national territory. Of the two extravagant river networks draining the interior, the Plata system is the less important. Only the upper reaches of the Paraná and Paraguay penetrate Brazilian territory, thereby linking Brazil with Paraguay, Argentina, and Uruguay. Historically they have served as important highways of commerce and routes of communication with the interior.

Unquestionably, the dominant river is the Amazon—referred to very aptly and descriptively in Portuguese as the "river-sea"—the largest river in volume in the world, with fourteen times the volume of the Mississippi. In places it is impossible to see from shore to shore and over a good part of its course it averages one hundred feet in depth. Running eastward from its source eighteen thousand feet above sea level in the Andes, it is joined from both the north and south as it rushes across the continent by more than two hundred branches, some of them mighty confluents. Together this majestic river and its tributaries provide twenty-five thousand miles of navigable water. Small ocean-going vessels can navigate as far inland as Iquitos, Peru, some twenty-three hundred miles from the sea, where the river is already two thousand feet wide. This entire network of rivers furnished the means of penetrating both the north and far west of Brazil.

The magnitude of the river always has excited the imaginations of those who traveled on it since Francisco de Orellana first discovered and descended it in his expedition of 1541–1542. William Lewis Herndon, who made a similar jour-

Map 2. Rivers of Brazil with Amazon and La Plata Networks.

Map 3. Comparative Size of Brazil. (The boundaries of Brazil easily encompass all the European countries.)

ney down the river a little over three centuries later, marveled, as many had before and would thereafter: "The march of the great river in its silent grandeur was sublime, but in the untamed might of its turbid waters, as they cut away its bank and tore down the gigantic denizens of the forest it was awful. I was reminded of our Mississippi at its topmost flood."

In order to better study this vast, diverse land, geographers have divided it into several more or less cohesive regions. Although the number of these regions depends on the criteria of classification each geographer employs, one of the most commonly used divisions, by the National Council of Statistics of the Brazilian Institute of Geography and Statistics, designates five regions: the North, which includes the Amazon Basin, the southern slopes of the Guiana Highland, and the northern slopes of the Brazilian Highland; the Northeast, whose principal characteristic is the arid *sertão*, although there are also forested coastlands and rich coastal sugarlands; the East, historically important because it contains the two old capitals of Salvador and Rio de Janeiro, and economically important for its fertile lands that produce more of the country's agricultural output than any other region; the South, a temperate zone extending from São Paulo to Rio Grande do Sul, essentially a region of high plateaus; and the Center West, a huge, underpopulated region, whose high plains support isolated mountain ranges.

From the time of first discoverers until the present, the potential of this immense area has impressed all who have considered it. The epithet "Land of the Future" was fastened on Brazil early in its history and remains to taunt its inhabitants. The challenge of the land has been all the greater because of the relatively few humans who have inhabited it.

The Indian

Various estimates place the number of Indians inhabiting Brazil at the opening of the sixteenth century at somewhere between two and four million. Whichever estimate one favors, that vast area of South America was strikingly under-

populated. In fact, large parts of it were uninhabited. The ancestors of the indigenous population probably migrated to the Western Hemisphere from Asia over forty thousand years ago. Most evidence seems to indicate that they crossed from one continent to the other at the Bering Strait, slowly moved southward, and dispersed through North and South America.

In the immensity of Brazil those few groups of Indians fragmented into innumerable small tribes. For general purposes of classification, the Portuguese tended at first to divide the diverse tribes into two categories: the Tupí-Guaraní and those once called the Tapuya. The Tupí predominated along the Amazon and in the coastal area from the mouth of Amazon to that of the Plata under a variety of tribal names. They spoke related languages, later referred to by the Portuguese as the "língua geral," which gave a very superficial cohesion to them. Located more in the interior, although in some places found along the coast as well, were the Tapuyas. They spoke various languages that seemed to exhibit little or no apparent relationship to one another. All the Indian groups shared a few physical characteristics. They tended to be short in stature, to be bronze in skin color, and to have straight, black hair. Beyond that their physiognomy varied considerably.

Modern anthropologists have abandoned the earlier classification of the Indians as Tupí or Tapuya. Although they emphasize the heterogeneity of the indigenous peoples, they suggest, for purposes of convenience and simplicity, another classification dividing the natives into two main groupings: Tropical Forest cultures—inhabitants of rainforest areas, dependent primarily on agriculture and fishing—and Marginal cultures—inhabitants of the plains and arid plateaus, dependent on hunting, fishing, and gathering.

Because of their predominance along the coast, the Tupí tribesmen—a major component of the Tropical Forest cultures—were the first natives the Europeans encountered and, for a long span, the only major Indian group with which the new arrivals maintained sustained contact. The Tupí, willingly or unwillingly, wittingly or unwittingly, facilitated the European adaptation to the new land, and this group appears to

be the single most important native element contributing to the early formation of a Brazilian civilization. The anthropologist Charles Wagley concluded, "the Indian heritage of Brazil is, then, in the main a Tupí heritage."

The Tupí tribes tended to be very loosely organized, with populations estimated at between four and eight hundred. Their small and temporary villages, often surrounded by a crude wooden stockade, were, when possible, located along a riverbank. The Indians lived communally in large thatched huts, approximately 250 to 300 feet long and 30 to 50 feet wide, in which they strung their hammocks in extended family or lineage groups of as many as one hundred persons. Patrilineal kinship was central to their societal organization. They usually practiced monogamy, but polygamy was not unknown. Most of the tribes had at least a nominal chief, although some seemed to recognize a leader only in time of war, and a few seemed to have no conception of a leader. Some tribes had councils of warriors or groups of respected elders, or both, who met with the chief to advise him on important matters.

More often than not the shaman, or medicine man, was the most important and powerful tribal figure. He communed with the spirits, proffered advice, and prescribed medicines. The religions abounded with good and evil spirits. Thunder, wind, rain, the sun, the moon—in short, nature—received major attention. The Tupí demonstrated a dread of forest spirits who could bring sickness, misfortune, and defeat in warfare. Because the spirits displayed a fondness for the night and prowled about under cover of darkness, the Tupí stayed close to the fireside after sundown. Part of their rich mythology still lives in Brazilian folklore. Still told, for example, are the tales of Saci-perere, the one-legged Indian who creates mischief; of Iracema, the captivating beauty with long green hair and a seductive voice, who lures young warriors into the depths of the waters; and of Uirapurú, the Amazonian bird that gives happiness in love. Less romantic aspects of tribal rites included ritual cannibalism. Prisoners taken in battle were pampered while being fattened. Later they were ceremonially clubbed to death, cooked, and eaten. Anthropolo-

gists heatedly debate how far cannibalism extended beyond ritualism.

Constant warfare provided the tribes with frequent opportunities to capture prisoners. The warrior with his bow and arrow, spear, club, or blowgun held a place of high esteem.

Warfare, however frequent it might have been, occupied only a part of the Tupí male's time. The men also hunted and fished. They cleared away the forest to plant crops. Nearly every year during the dry season, the men cut down trees, bushes, and vines, waited until they had dried, and then burned them. The burning destroyed the thin humus and the soil was quickly exhausted. Hence it was constantly necessary to clear new land, and eventually the village moved in order to be near virgin soil. In general, although not always exclusively, the women took charge of planting and harvesting crops and of collecting and preparing the food. Manioc was the principal cultivated crop. With a wide variety of uses, it served mainly as a flour. Maize, beans, yams, peppers, squash, sweet potatoes, tobacco, pineapples, and occasionally cotton were the other cultivated crops. Forest fruits were collected. The self-sufficient tribes produced, gathered, and hunted food for themselves, not for trade. They attached scant importance to surpluses. The Tupí made ceramics, wove baskets, and developed loom weaving.

To the first Europeans who observed them, those Indians seemed to live an idyllic life. The tropics required virtually no clothing. Generally nude, the Indians developed the art of body ornamentation and painted elaborate geometric designs on themselves. Into their noses, lips, and ears they inserted stone and wooden artifacts. Feathers from colorful forest birds provided an additional decorative touch. Their gay, nude appearance prompted the Europeans to think of them as innocent children of nature. The first chronicler of Brazil, Pero Vaz de Caminha, marveled to the king of Portugal, "Sire, the innocence of Adam himself was not greater than these people's." On the basis of information about Brazil and its natives provided by French colonist Durand de Villegaignon, who was in the Guanabara Bay region between 1555 and 1559,

Montaigne wrote *Des Coches*. He advanced the theory of natural human goodness, a condition to which primitive peoples—in this case the Tupí—corresponded more closely than others. Repeated contacts with the Indians caused later chroniclers to tell quite a different tale: one in which the Indians emerged as villains, brutes who desperately needed the civilizing hand of Europe.

The Europeans failed to appreciate the harmony of the Indians with their environment and the high degree of their self-sufficiency. Indeed, the Indians' economic behavior contrasted sharply with the capitalistic motivations of their "discoverers." The Indians maintained a communal or reciprocal attitude toward production and consumption. The notion of private ownership hardly existed, and nature was to be revered, not exploited. Tribal status did not derive from material affluence, and economic considerations were less important than kinship, social dictates, religion, and community. The Europeans never succeeded in comprehending these Indian values.

The Indians had adapted well to their tropical environment and had much to teach the European invaders about the utilization of the land, its rivers, its forests, and their products.

The European

As the sixteenth century approached those European invaders were not far off. Europe, on the eve of a commercial revolution, searched for new trade and new lands. Portugal led that quest.

A crossroads of many peoples—Iberians, Celts, Phoenicians, Greeks, Carthaginians, Romans, Visigoths, and Moslems—Portugal mingled many cultures. From that mixture, the first modern European nation emerged. To assert its independence, Portugal had to free itself of both Moslem control and Castilian claims. In 1139, Afonso Henriques of the house of Burgundy used, for the first time, the title "King of Portugal," a title officially recognized in 1179 by the pope,

then the arbiter of such matters. The struggle to expel the Moslems from Portugal lasted until 1250, when their remaining armies were driven from the Algarve region in the south. Neighboring Castile then conceded recognition of Portugal's claim to the Algarve and the national boundaries were delineated much as they remain today. The task of consolidating the state fell to King Denis, whose long reign, 1279–1325, marked the emergence of the truly modern national state. Desiring to create a stronger secular state, he challenged the Roman Catholic Church by curtailing its land holdings. His success encouraged the growth of the relatively weak State at the expense of the more powerful Church. Furthermore, he substituted Portuguese for Latin as the official language of government.

In the fifteenth century, Portugal became Europe's foremost sea power. Lusitania (as the Romans named that province of their empire perched on the westernmost tip of continental Europe) was well situated for its maritime role. Most of the region's sparse populace, less than a million in the fifteenth century, inhabited the coastal area. They faced the great, gray, open sea and nearby Africa.

At that time European knowledge of the world beyond the Continent was vague and contradictory. Educated men accepted the idea that the earth was a sphere. Norsemen had reached some unknown world beyond the seas. The travels of Marco Polo in Asia at the end of the thirteenth century had excited considerable speculation and interest. Knowledge of Africa was imperfect, limited to northern Africa only. Primitive navigational aids, frail ships, and fear of the unknown had kept men off the high seas and confined to European waters. In Portugal, however, there developed an urge to venture and expand into distant and either little-explored or totally unknown regions. By the end of the fourteenth century, the nation was at relative peace: the state had been consolidated; internal struggles had ended; foreign threats were not imminent. Thus Portugal could turn its attention outward, and the Portuguese initiated their overseas expansion in Africa, with the conquest in 1415 of strategic Ceuta, guardian of the opening to the Mediterranean.

In a society dominated by the Church, religious motives
for expansion played at least a superficially important role.
The Lusitanians hoped to defeat the enemies of their faith in
Africa and to carry the word of God to that continent. Commercial reasons for expansion were probably even more compelling. Direct trade with the fabled Orient via an all-water
route would break the Italian commercial monopoly and bring
cascades of riches to Portugal. Lisbon as the entrepot of Eastern pepper, cinnamon, ginger, nutmegs, cloves, tapestries,
and porcelains created a vision of wealth alluring to people
of all classes.

The first to understand fully that the ocean was not a
barrier but a vast highway of commerce, Prince Henry (1394–
1460), known as "the Navigator" to English writers, was a
confirmed landlubber. That provident prince, significant as
the symbol of Portuguese expansion, surrounded himself with
navigators, cosmographers, and maritime scholars at his residence on Sagres Peninsula, the harshly beautiful westernmost tip of Portugal. Listening to the expert advice of his
day, he defined Portugal's policy of exploration: systematic
voyages outward, each based on the intelligence collected
from the former voyager and each traveling beyond its predecessor.

The improvements in geographic, astronomical, and navigational knowledge which characterized a century of accelerating sea-borne activity facilitated the task of the men of
Sagres. Throughout the fifteenth century, improved, practical
charts, the *portolani*, kept the sailors abreast of the latest
maritime experience and were reasonably accurate in showing distances and coastal configurations. Through careful study,
the heavens became a guide to the navigator out of sight of
the land. Stars, particularly the North Star, were observed in
order to take latitude fixes. Later the experts learned to calculate latitude by observing the sun's zenith north or south
of the equator at noon. For that, tables of the sun's declina-
tion were carefully worked out. Still with no means of finding
longitude, the navigators continued to rely on dead reckon-
ing, but with a firmer knowledge of latitude and the help of
improved charts that calculation was made both easier and

more accurate. The compass, in use before 1300, continued to undergo refinements. The astrolabe, which permitted the navigator to take a fix on a celestial body, was cumbersome and tended to work far better ashore than aboard a rocking ship. Nonetheless, it was helpful for determining latitude. The invention of the quadrant in the fifteenth century faciliated taking sightings, usually on the North Star, to enable the navigator to locate the ship's latitude. Though inventors of neither the compass, the astrolabe, or the quadrant, the Portuguese were the first Europeans to experiment with their use on the open seas. Their mastery of the science of ocean navigation made them tutors to the rest of maritime Europe in the fifteenth and sixteenth centuries. In a moment of great maritime triumph, the Portuguese launched the caravel, a ship that could tack, and thus sail against the wind. As a direct consequence of those improvements and with the encouragement of Prince Henry, the Lusitanians sailed farther and farther out to sea and away from their base. In 1488, Bartolomeu Dias rounded the Cape of Good Hope and pointed the way to a water route to India.

The Lusitanians were shaken momentarily in 1492 when Columbus reported—mistakenly—to João II that he had reached India by sailing west, sad news to a Portugal on the verge of reaching Asia by circumnavigating Africa. Both Spain and Portugal jealously guarded their sea lanes and each feared the incursion of the other. War threatened until diplomacy triumphed. At Tordesillas in 1494, representatives of the two monarchs agreed to divide the world. An imaginary line was established, running pole to pole 370 leagues west of the Cape Verde Islands. The agreement gave Portugal everything discovered 180 degrees to the east of that line and Spain everything 180 degrees to the west. Then, within the half of the world reserved for Portugal, Vasco da Gama discovered the long-sought water route to India, when his protracted voyage in 1497–1499 joined East and West for the first time by sea. It was a profitable discovery. The cargo he brought back to Lisbon repaid sixty times over the original cost of the expedition, and the new lucrative trade promised to enrich the realm.

In the decades following the return of Vasco da Gama, Portuguese vessels appeared in the most distant ports. The monarchs abandoned the agricultural policies of the past to become merchants. Indeed, under Manuel I (1495–1521), the commercial interests of the kingdom became inextricably intertwined with national interests. Along the distant coasts of Africa and Asia, the Portuguese eagerly established their commercial—not colonial—empire. Trade attracted them rather than settlement. Lisbon and other Portuguese ports served as great warehouses through which the trade of three continents passed, to the delight and profit of the Portuguese. They succeeded in setting up a global trading empire in the sixteenth century and reaped substantial rewards from the crown's maritime policies.

Within a short period of far less than a century, the Portuguese seaman landed on three distant continents bearing a cross in one hand and carrying a market basket in the other; when the native inhabitants challenged him, he readily substituted sword and lance for both. As a hearty, robust, adventurous, and resourceful knight-errant with the whole world as his stage, it was little wonder that he believed in his privileged and special position. In the most admirable fashion, the Portuguese seafarer proved himself to be adaptable in both time and space. And nowhere was he more adaptable than in Brazil.

Discovery and Challenges

Manuel I appointed Pedro Alvares Cabral to command the fleet being prepared to follow up the discovery made by Vasco da Gama. Amid colorful pageantry and with the kingdom's best wishes, thirteen ships with twelve hundred men sailed from the mouth of the Tagus River on March 8, 1500. The voyage to India began routinely. Then, on the 20th of April, the sailors unexpectedly sighted weeds and reeds in the ocean and an occasional bird in the sky. Two days later, at 17° south latitude, land unexpectedly appeared in the west. Cautiously the fleet approached the coast. After landing to

explore, the curious Cabral claimed the newly discovered island (for so he thought it) for his sovereign. Then he spent a week reconnoitering the coast. Before continuing to Asia, Cabral dispatched news of his find to the king in a literate and highly descriptive letter written by the scribe Pero Vaz de Caminha. That letter is the official chronicle of the birth of Brazil, although that was not the first name the new land bore. Cabral christened it Ilha de Vera Cruz, and it was also known as Terra or Provincia de Santa Cruz. But none of those names entered into popular usage. The merchants who were soon attracted to the plentiful stands of brazilwood, the source of an excellent red dye, called it *Terra do Brasil,* and the name Brazil quickly gained popular acceptance. That name first appeared on a map in 1511.

At first the Portuguese imagined that Brazil would be a convenient way station for the India fleets, but winds, currents, and distances made that impossible. As a matter of fact, between 1500 and 1730 only about twenty ships, all separated from main India fleets by some extraordinary circumstance, took shelter in Brazilian ports. On the other hand, Brazil strategically provided excellent flank protection for the vital and profitable sea lane to the East. Brazil initially served as a sentinel.

Of the native reaction to the arrival of the bearded, white adventurers, no account exists. The Indians at first were shy—but not astonished. They maintained a certain distance between themselves and the strangers, reluctant at first to receive the *degredados* (those criminals exiled to serve their sentences) who were ordered to live among them to learn their languages. Later, an increasing number of *degredados,* deserters, and shipwrecked men found their way into Indian tribes where they apparently flourished. Some of them became almost legendary figures. They sired an army of mestizo offspring, exerted a powerful influence over the Indians in their areas, and later helped the Portuguese establish their first colonies. They adapted perfectly—and it would seem happily—to their new surroundings. According to João Capistrano de Abreu, Brazil's foremost historian of the colonial period, each became "morally a mestizo."

Expeditions with the dual purpose of trade and exploration followed the discovery. Although the extent of those activities during the early years remains undetermined, it would appear that within a decade after its discovery the coast had been at least cursorily explored, and a few trading posts had been established to traffic in the lucrative brazilwood. During those first decades dyewood was an easy export, since it grew abundantly along the coast from Rio Grande do Norte to Rio de Janeiro. The Crown established a monopoly over its exploitation and eagerly sold its rights to merchants. Fernão de Noronha was the first to buy the contract and in 1503 he dispatched ships to fetch the dyewood. The ship captains bartered with the Indians, exchanging trinkets for the brazilwood they cut. The welcome the new European textile industries accorded the red dye spurred that trade, and by the end of the sixteenth century about a hundred ships sailed annually from Brazil to Lisbon loaded with the wood. When the coastal stands were gradually exhausted it became necessary to search inland.

The handsome profits from the brazilwood trade not only enticed Lisbon merchants to pursue it but awoke the interest of foreigners as well. As the era of commercial expansion got underway, other Europeans resented and challenged the Iberian claims to international trade monopolies. Increasing numbers of French ships explored the extensive Brazilian coastline in open challenge to Portuguese claims. To discourage the interlopers, the Crown ordered a coastguard detachment to Brazil from 1516 to 1519 and again from 1526 to 1528. Those tiny fleets found it impossible to police effectively the three thousand-mile coastline with its innumerable coves, bays, and inlets. When diplomacy and coastal patrols failed to eliminate the French threat to Brazil, and hence to the Asian sea lane it guarded, King João III (1521–1555) decided upon a third method: colonization. Colonization was a novel undertaking in the Portuguese commercial empire. Up until that time, with the notable exception of the Atlantic islands, the Portuguese preferred simply to establish trading posts. Nonetheless, the monarch sent Martim Afonso de Sousa with five ships, four hundred crewmen and colonists, seeds, plants,

and domestic animals to establish one or more colonies and, in the process, to destroy French trade and explore the coast. After reconnoitering the coast from Pernambuco to the Plata, Martim Afonso founded the settlement of São Vicente in 1532 in the area near present-day Santos. A chapel, a small governmental headquarters, two tiny fortresses, and quarters for the men were built. Using the broad powers delegated to him by the king, the captain appointed municipal officers and distributed land. Wheat, grape vines, and sugarcane were planted; cattle were introduced; the first sugar mill was put into operation in 1533. On the plateau above São Vicente, those first colonists founded a second small settlement, Piratininga, the future São Paulo. They constituted the first permanent settlements in Portuguese America.

Martim Afonso established the pattern of land distribution to be followed thereafter. Because Brazil was vast and the colonists few, he distributed the land with lavish generosity. In Portugal, quite to the contrary since 1375, the king sparingly parceled out the *sesmarias,* the traditional, individual land grants, so that no one person would receive more than he could effectively cultivate. Martim Afonso ignored such a precaution, and set a precedent followed thereafter in colonial Brazil. As one consequence, the good coastal land was quickly divided into immense sugar plantations, and not many more decades elapsed before huge *sesmarias* for cattle ranches in the interior put much of the backlands under claim as well. Grants along the coast of twenty to fifty square miles of land were common, and in the interior they frequently encompassed areas ten to twenty times that size. Realizing that the gigantic estates created a type of semifeudalism in practice, if not in name, and that they kept most of the best land fallow and hence unproductive, the king belatedly tried to reverse the course. Repeatedly promulgated decrees—in 1695, single *sesmarias* were limited to four leagues by one league in size; in 1697, they were reduced to three by one; in 1699, all land not under cultivation was to be expropriated, and so on throughout the eighteenth century—sought vainly to limit the size of the estates. Late in the eighteenth century one of the viceroys, the Marquês de Lavradio, complained

bitterly that those huge estates, poorly managed and only partially cultivated, retarded the development of Brazil. He pointed to the unused fields held by their owners as symbols of prestige, while at the same time he noted that farmers petitioned him for land to till. Some of the captaincies had to import the food they were perfectly capable of producing themselves. The *latifundia* (large estates) originated at the birth of the colony and remained a dominant characteristic of Brazil thereafter.

Patterns for the Future

Brazil challenged the Portuguese commercial empire. The Indians proved to be at best reluctant and unreliable traders. The French scoffed at Lusitanian claims of exclusivity. The Portuguese government realized that, in order to keep Brazil and carry on trade with it, it would have to colonize on a much broader scale. Yet, the Crown, already overextended in Asia and Africa, had no resources to do so. In view of that, the king resolved to implement the donatary system used successfully in the Atlantic islands. Given enormous territory and broad powers, each donee bore the responsibility to colonize his own captaincy at private expense. Between 1534 and 1536, João III divided Portuguese America into fifteen captaincies distributed among twelve donees. Each averaged fifty leagues in width and extended inland to the nebulous Tordesillas line. Those land grants, inalienable except by transmittal by inheritance to the oldest son, brought to the New World some of the residue of a feudalism long on the wane on the Iberian peninsula. In effect, the donatary system interposed between the king and his subjects a hierarchy of landlords who enjoyed certain attributes of government: they could tax, impose law and justice, make appointments, and distribute the land in their captaincies in *sesmarias*. Like the medieval vassal required to render military service to his lord in return for his fief, the donees were expected to defend their captaincies from attack and thus to hold Brazil in the name of the monarch. Some characteristics of feudalism were

undeniably present, although, of course, it was a long way from the classical feudalism of the Middle Ages. Those who would minimize the charge that the donatary system introduced feudalism into Brazil argue that the king, at least in theory, did fix, limit, and regulate the powers of each donee and that the captaincies were expected to engage in imperial trade rather than pursue the self-sufficient household economy of the medieval manor. In one sense surely, the donees were capitalists investing their money in the New World with the expectation of reaping handsome profits. Thus, despite vestigial feudal characteristics, the captaincies were supposed to be partially linked to the emerging capitalist system as well.

Few of the donees rose to the challenge confronting them. Representatives of the minor nobility and middle class, their incomes from Asian ventures, governmental salaries, or landholdings proved inadequate to cover the expense of the services demanded. As a group, they lacked the experience and ability as well as the capital to execute their heavy responsibilities. Furthermore, they confronted a hostile, untamed—indeed, unknown—environment. Lack of discipline among the colonists, Indian attacks, and French harassment compounded the difficulties. A majority of the captaincies failed. Only two of them, Pernambuco and São Vicente, achieved prosperity.

Pernambuco was by far the richest and most important of the sixteenth-century captaincies. The captaincy closest to Portugal, it offered extensive stands of brazilwood along the coast and excellent soil, the *massapê*, for sugarcane. The intelligent and aggressive donee, Duarte Coelho, took advantage of the presence of Vasco Lucena, a Portuguese who had lived for years among the local Indians and knew their language well, to avoid many of the wars with the native population that decimated other colonies. He understood the importance of commercial crops and ordered cotton, tobacco, and sugarcane planted at once. He proudly reported to the king, "We have extensive fields planted with sugar cane. The people here have all worked as hard as possible and I have given them all the aid possible and soon we will complete a very large and excellent sugar mill." By mid-century, fifty

mills were producing enough sugar to load annually forty to fifty ships for Europe. By 1580 Coelho's son was the richest man in Brazil and one of the wealthiest in the empire. In Pernambuco the operation of an agricultural colony for profit enjoyed its greatest success.

The São Vicente captaincy, initially established by Martim Afonso de Sousa, also flourished, with sugar the basis for prosperity. Families of Italian sugar growers from the Madeira Islands immigrated to that southern captaincy bringing much needed agricultural and technical skills. By 1545 the colony possessed six sugar mills. Together Pernambuco and São Vicente implanted the sugar industry in Brazil. Likewise they accounted for much of the brazilwood trade. The first to cultivate the soil of the New World on a commercial basis, the two captaincies proved that profitable agricultural colonies could be established far from the motherland and could provide a relatively constant source of wealth for crown, landowner, shipowner, and merchant, a novel concept for midsixteenth century Europe and one which did not go unobserved. Spurred first by the examples of rich mines in Spanish America and then by lucrative agricultural settlements in Portuguese America, Europe moved to change its far-flung trading routes into more complex overseas mining, agricultural, and commercial empires. Such a move resulted from and reinforced Europe's adoption of modern capitalism.

However, those two prosperous captaincies were exceptions to a general trend all too evident in the rest of Brazil. The other captaincies were reduced in a short time to a sad spectacle, as their surviving colonists degenerated into a demoralized lot. Bickering and insubordinate, they engaged in smuggling and other criminal activities. Moreover, French interlopers continued to violate the coast with impunity. The captaincy system had failed to produce the expected results.

After studying the unhappy situation in his overseas domain, King João III concluded that a centralized administration was needed to coordinate further colonization, to provide effective protection, to unify the execution of justice, to collect taxes properly, and to prohibit French contraband trade. He thus intended to limit the independence as well as

the powers of the donees. In 1548 he bought back the captaincy of Bahia to make it a crown captaincy, seat of the new general government for Brazil. He appointed Tomé de Sousa, a loyal soldier who had served him well in Africa and India, as the first governor-general in charge of all civil and military administration. The king also named a *provedor-mor,* a chief treasurer, and an *ouvidor-geral,* a chief justice to assist de Sousa. One thousand soldiers, government officials, carpenters, masons, artisans, and colonists accompanied the new governor-general to South America.

The fleet of six ships dropped anchor in the splendid Bay of Todos os Santos on March 29, 1549. Caramurú, the white adventurer who had settled in Bahia, presented himself to offer assistance and to guarantee the cooperation of the local Indians. Tomé de Sousa set about constructing the new capital, giving form and substance to the central government. Scattered along the extensive coast were approximately fifteen Portuguese settlements. De Sousa dispatched the chief justice and the chief treasurer to the various captaincies in an effort to eliminate abuses and to regularize administration. He himself paid a prolonged visit to the South. To accelerate economic development, he generously distributed *sesmarias,* imported cattle from the Cape Verde Islands, and encouraged the construction of more sugar mills. The Indians reluctantly provided the labor force during the early decades of the colony. The governor-general was particularly concerned with the regulation of that labor force—an obvious source of wealth for the colony—and with the welfare, particularly the Christian indoctrination, of the Indians. After all, the monarch had written specifically in his orders to Tomé de Sousa, "The principal reason motivating my decision to settle the land of Brazil was in order that the people of that land might be converted to our Holy Catholic Faith." To fulfill Portugal's obligations to those natives, de Sousa relied heavily on the Jesuits.

The official party of 1549 included six Jesuits under the leadership of Manuel da Nóbrega. True, clerics had accompanied all the expeditions to Portuguese America from the visit of Cabral onward, the Franciscans being particularly evi-

dent in those early decades. But until 1549 the Church played a minor role in Brazil. With some exceptions, the clergy attended more to the affairs of the Portuguese colonists than to the Christianization of the Indians. The king desired to propagate the Catholic faith in the New World and chose the Jesuits to be his instruments. Only 128 Jesuits arrived between 1549 and 1598, but with exceptional zeal they left a lasting imprint on the new land. They carried European church-centered civilization to the Indians and nurtured it in the tropics by establishing—and for two hundred years maintaining—the best educational facilities of the colony. In a very real sense they conquered Brazil spiritually.

To be Portuguese was to be Roman Catholic. The populace embraced the Catholic faith unquestioningly, and, whether understanding its dogmas or not, defended it devotedly. The Luso-Brazilians were born, reared, married, and buried Catholics. The Church pervaded every aspect of their lives. The king defended the faith within his realm, in return for which the pope conferred royal patronage upon the Crown, temporarily in 1515 and permanently in 1551. Holding power in all but purely spiritual matters, the king collected the tithe and decided how it was to be spent, appointed (and at times recalled) the bishops, priests, and other officials, authorized the construction of new churches, determined the boundaries of the bishoprics, and—of great significance—approved and transmitted papal messages—or refused to.

To the degree that Portuguese control expanded in the New World, so did that of the Roman Catholic church. The establishment of the general government of Brazil was followed in 1551 by the creation of the bishopric of Brazil. Previously Brazil had belonged to the diocese of Funchal in the Azores. Fittingly, the bishop resided in Salvador alongside the governor-general. In 1676, the archbishopric of Brazil was created with Salvador as the metropolitan see. Two new bishoprics, Rio de Janeiro and Pernambuco, were established at the same time. By the end of the eighteenth century, four others existed: Pará, Maranhão, São Paulo, and Mariana (Minas Gerais). Throughout the colonial period—indeed, until 1907—Salvador remained the religious capital of Brazil. Its arch-

bishop headed the Roman Catholic church in Brazil, and the religious orders maintained their principal representatives there. The Church structure in Brazil, with its well-defined hierarchy, its regular and secular clergy, its bishoprics and parishes, followed perfectly the European model.

The African bishoprics of São Tomé and Angola also were suffragan to the archbishop of Bahia. The Church in Angola depended heavily on Brazil. Serafim Leite, distinguished historian of the Jesuits in Brazil, affirmed, "The evangelization of Angola was in the hands of the Jesuits of Portuguese America." Actually the ecclesiastical traffic moved both ways. A few Jesuits crossed from Angola to Brazil, and some Portuguese born in Angola moved to Brazil to study in Jesuit colleges. A number of Brazilian Jesuits mastered African languages, a skill that most of those from Angola already had, so that they could catechize the newly arrived black slaves.

The Jesuits have already been singled out as the most important religious order contributing to the formation and development of Brazil, but they were by no means the only representatives of the regular clergy. The Franciscans had been the first to reach Brazil, and they too played an important role. The Capuchins, Benedictines, and Carmelites were all represented in Brazil before the end of the sixteenth century. The Crown hesitated to sanction the building of convents for nuns in Brazil, feeling that the relatively few women in the colony should be encouraged to become wives and mothers rather than virginal recluses. Not until 1665 did the king grant permission for the establishment of a convent, and authorization for a second did not come until seventy years later. By the mid-eighteenth century, a half-dozen convents could be found in the major coastal cities.

Of major importance for Brazil were the *irmandades*, voluntary associations of the faithful that became an integral part of colonial social life. They built handsome churches, merrily celebrated the feast days of patron saints, and dutifully maintained charitable institutions such as hospitals and orphanages. Indeed, works of charity, education, and social assistance compose some of the noblest chapters of the history of the Roman Catholic church in Brazil.

The Church maintained as careful a vigil as possible over its flock in Brazil. Nonetheless, some examples of moral corruption among the clergy provided bawdy gossip for colonial ears. Backsliders—especially Jewish converts, the New Christians—could expect to account for themselves before the Inquisition. As an institution it was never established in Brazil, but it operated there through the bishops and through three visitations: to Salvador da Bahia and Olinda, 1591–1595; to Salvador, 1681; and to Belém, 1763–1769. Still, the hand of the Inquisition rested lightly on Brazil, where a liberal degree of toleration developed.

A major challenge to the Church was the conversion of the Indians. The Jesuits, under the skilled and dedicated leadership of Manuel da Nóbrega and José de Anchieta, rose to meet that challenge. They deemed it wisest to gather the nomadic natives into villages, the *aldeias*, where they could more easily be instructed, Christianized, and protected under the watchful eye of the Church. Some would add that the *aldeia* system facilitated the exploitation of Indian labor. The system permitted the maximum use of the few regular clergy in Brazil: usually one or two brothers administered each village and in that way supervised many Indians. Each *aldeia* centered on a church, built of course by the indigenous converts themselves. Around it were a school, living quarters, and warehouses. The ringing of church bells awoke the neophytes each day, summoning them to Mass. Then, singing hymns along the way, they marched outside the village to cultivate the fields. The brothers taught reading, writing, and the mastering of useful trades to the young and able. Indian sculptors, painters, masons, carpenters, bakers, and locksmiths, among others, were soon practicing their trades. Many of the villages achieved a high degree of self-sufficiency, and most sold some of their products to outside markets. Although the brothers administered the missions through various Indians whom they appointed to office and invested with the customary symbols of that office, the churchmen, in the final analysis, rigidly controlled the lives of their charges. It was not a simple figure of speech when they spoke of the neophytes as "their children," for that was exactly how they

regarded them. Under their guidance, the Indians contributed to the imperial economy, worshiped as Roman Catholics, dressed like Europeans, mastered European trades, and paid homage to the king in Lisbon. Thus, those touched by the *aldeia* system were brought by the determined hand of the missionaries within the pale of empire.

To increase the base of economic prosperity, the governors-general encouraged agriculture in general, and sugar cultivation in particular. The number of sugar mills multiplied, particularly in the captaincies of São Vicente, Rio de Janeiro, Espírito Santo, Bahia, and Pernambuco, where the huge sugar plantations and mills quickly became powerful agricultural, industrial, and social organizations. The labor shortage continued to harass the colony. At first the only readily available workers, the Indians proved to be unsatisfactory plantation hands. The Portuguese tried three methods to incorporate the Indians as laborers into their agricultural system: first as slaves, second as a type of indigenous "peasantry" through detribalization and acculturation in the *aldeias*, and third as wage earners slowly integrated into the capitalist system. The controversy over Indian labor sparked acrimonious debates between the Jesuits and the planters. The vocal Jesuits—and the Church in general—regarded the enslavement of the Indians as contrary to the Christian intentions of the king and intensified efforts to save them both physically and spiritually by gathering them into the villages. The planters loudly criticized that interference with their labor supply. In the end, all the methods used to incorporate the Indians failed. The Indians refused to surrender their life style for the inexplicable work demanded by the Portuguese, work that had few if any rewards for them. The gap between the communal, self-sufficient Indians and the capitalistic Portuguese could not be bridged.

Internal concerns gave way before external threats. Governor Mem de Sá devoted much of his attention and resources to the perennial French threat. In 1555, Vice-Admiral Durand de Villegaignon founded France Antarctique around Guanabara Bay, an area rich in brazilwood. The French presence there isolated São Vicente from the rest of Brazil. Mem

de Sá attacked the invaders on several occasions. On March 1, 1565, he established Rio de Janeiro as a base from which to fight the stubborn French, and, after a prolonged siege, expelled them in 1567. After the defeat of the French, Rio de Janeiro grew rapidly in size and importance, partly because of its excellent harbor and partly because of the sugar industry which prospered on the fertile soil of the region. The Crown manifested its delight with the accomplishments of Mem de Sá's administration by retaining him as governor-general long after his four-year appointment expired in 1562. He stayed on until he died in office a decade later.

The last of the Aviz kings died in 1580, after which the Spanish monarchs ruled Spain and Portugal jointly for sixty years. By then, however, the patterns of colonial Brazil already had been well established. The economic and social domination by large estates and their owners, agriculture for export, subservience and exploitation of labor, and responsiveness to European demands—characteristics well implanted during the period from 1530 to 1560—held sway. If anything, the long years of Spanish rule fortified them.

Chapter Two
The Colonial Experience

Brazil's official colonial apprenticeship lasted more than three centuries. Social amalgamation, territorial expansion, and economic and political dependency characterized the South American colony during that long era. Portugal imposed its language, religion, and institutions, and during the last half of the sixteenth century they sent roots deep into the Brazilian soil and soul. Although other influences wrought some modifications over the following centuries, the Portuguese language and Roman Catholicism remain dominant, while the institutions, subject to differing nomenclatures and embracing superficial changes, display a startling degree of historical continuity. They still shape the present.

Social Amalgamation

The Portuguese adapted quickly to the new environment, whose geography and climate approximated those they had encountered in their extensive travels in other parts of the world. They evidenced a flexibility, both physical and psychological, that seemed to make them sufficiently malleable to learn from the conquered. In the case of Brazil, the blending

of the Lusitanian and Amerindian cultures was facilitated by the favorable attitudes of both toward miscegenation.

The Portuguese monarchs customarily sent out on their global expeditions a combination of soldiers, adventurers, and petty criminals condemned to exile. The Portuguese female was noticeably rare during the first century of Brazilian history. Her scarcity conferred a sexual license on the conquerors, already well acquainted with Moorish, African, and Asian women. The Indian women submitted to the desires of the European males. Men like Caramurú attested to the Iberian potency by siring villages of miscegenated offspring. As a result, there appeared almost at once a "new race," the *mameluco* or *caboclo*, a blend of European and Indian well adapted physically and psychologically to the land. Drawing the essential from the diverse cultures of both parents, the "new race" accelerated the amalgamation of the two civilizations.

The Indians provided more than sexual gratification: they facilitated Portuguese adjustment to the new land. They taught the invaders the best methods of hunting and fishing, the value of the drugs the forests offered, the quickest way to clear the lands, and the methods of cultivating the crops of the New World. They introduced them to new foods such as the manioc, soon the dietary staple of the Luso-Brazilians. The Lusitanians quickly adopted the light boats skillfully navigated by the Indians on the inland waters. They copied the methods used by the Indians to build simple, serviceable structures. In time, Portuguese domestic architecture underwent some significant modifications in the tropics: the severity and exclusiveness of the Portuguese house gave way to the open, outwardly oriented Brazilian residence with its extensive veranda communicating with the world. Another concession to the tropics was the universal adoption of the Indian hammock. One early arrival noted his delight with the hammock in these words: "Would you believe that a man could sleep suspended in a net in the air like a bunch of hanging grapes? Here this is the common thing. I slept on a mattress but my doctor advised me to sleep in a net. I tried it, and I will never again be able to sleep in a bed, so comfort-

able is the rest one gets in the net." Words from various Indian tongues, such as *hamaka* (hammock), *tobako* (tobacco), *manioca* (manioc), and *typyoca* (tapioca), slipped into the Portuguese language (and, subsequently, into English as well). In the seventeenth century, the Luso-Brazilians began to substitute Indian for Portuguese place-names in geographic nomenclature. A modern dictionary, *Pequeno Dicionário Brasileiro,* lists some twenty thousand words of Indian origin. In truth, the Europeans depended heavily on the Indian during the early decades of settlement in order to accommodate successfully to the novel conditions. Thomas Turner, an Englishman who lived in Brazil for two years at the end of the sixteenth century, summed up that dependence in his observation: "The Indian is a fish in the Sea, and a Foxe in the Woods, and without them a Christian is neither for pleasure or profit fit for life or living."

The newly arrived also depended on the Indians as the labor force in the growing colony. The Portuguese, for their part, revealed a reluctance to engage in common labor and a persistence in forcing others to do it for them. Under increasing pressure that soon resulted in enslavement, the Indians paddled canoes filled with Portuguese along the rivers; guided them through the interior; planted, tended, and harvested their sugar, tobacco, and cotton; and waited upon them in their homes. They were the instruments by which wealth was created in the new colony and, as such, indispensable to the Europeans.

The Crown, eager to see the Indians brought within the pale of the empire as Christianized subjects, resisted their enslavement. The papal grant authenticating Portuguese territorial claims had made it clear that the monarch must Christianize, civilize, and protect the Indians, a responsibility the kings took very seriously. At great expense, missionaries were dispatched to preach to the heathen, to convert them, and to induce them to live in villages under the guidance and protection of Church and Crown. The Jesuits were the most active of the religious groups fulfilling those obligations. They ardently defended the Indians and rigorously prodded the royal conscience. In their concern, the Jesuits took their defense

of the Indians directly to the king to whom they vividly reported the mistreatment and enslavement of his American subjects. The planters dispatched to the court their own representatives who emphasized the barbaric nature of the Indians, their indolence and refusal to work without coercion. Unfortunately we do not have records of the Indian view, but their predilections to flee Portuguese colonization indicate their rejection of labor demands. The debate over the role and place of the Indian within the empire, much like the one already underway in Spain, raged for several centuries.

By and large the monarchs sympathized with the Jesuits' case. As early as 1511, King Manuel I had ruled that no one was to harm his Indian subjects upon pain of the same punishment as if he had injured a European. In his instructions to the first governor-general of Brazil, King João III called for tolerance, understanding, and forgiveness toward the Indians. Relations with them were above all else to be peaceful so they might more easily be Christianized. Permission was granted, however, to enslave any Indians who fought against the Portuguese, a provision that offered a gaping loophole through which the colonists could obtain their native slaves. Predictably the colonists righteously swore that their Indian slaves had been taken in a "just war." The Mesa da Consciência e Ordens (Board of Conscience and Orders), a religious council in Lisbon, handled, in theory at any rate, questions arising from the interpretation of these laws, and one of the thorniest questions before it was to determine which slaves were held justly and which unjustly. It rigorously declared that peaceful Indians living in harmony with the Portuguese could not be enslaved. Theoretically the law punished any planters found guilty of unjustly holding Indians as slaves.

The theological and judicial debate over the enslavement reached its first climax during the reign of the devoutly religious King Sebastião (1557–1578). In 1570 he prohibited the enslavement of any Indians except those taken prisoner in a just war. King Philip II in 1595 confirmed that decree and reduced the term of slavery for prisoners to ten years. In 1605 and again in 1609 King Philip III went even further. He declared that all Indians, whether Christian or heathen, were by

nature free, could not be forced to work, and must be paid for their work when they volunteered it. Strong pressures from the planters, including riots in Brazil, induced him to modify his position in 1611 in order to permit once again the enslavement of war prisoners, a concession much abused. The high death rate among the Indians exposed to European demands and diseases, their retreat into the interior, their amalgamation into the new Brazilian society through miscegenation, and the increasing importation of Africans to meet the growing labor needs of the colony did more to solve the complex question of Indian-European relations than did all the altruistic but impractical or ignored legislation of the Portuguese kings.

The final word on European-Indian relations came from the authoritative Sebastião José de Carvalho e Melo, better known by his title, the Marquês de Pombal, an enlightened but despotic ruler of the Portuguese empire in the name of José I from 1750 to 1777. That prime minister expelled the most tenacious protectors of the Indians, the Jesuits, in 1759, accusing them, among other things, of isolating the Indians and thereby inhibiting their incorporation into the empire. Pursuing the centuries-old desire to incorporate the Indians into the empire, he raised them to the rank of equality with all the king's other subjects. A new law guaranteed the personal freedom of each Indian (who thereafter received a Portuguese surname and was required to speak Portuguese). Henceforth, each Indian village was to have a school where Portuguese was taught rather than the native language. To assimilate the Indians more quickly, Pombal decreed that any Portuguese who married an Indian would improve his (or her) chances of preferment and promotion. Under severe penalty, he forbade the use of any pejorative adjectives or nouns to describe a person's mixed Indo-Portuguese background. He hoped through that varied legislation to make the Indian an integral and active participant in Brazilian life. In at least one way he partially accomplished that goal. To the degree that Pombal broke down the Indians' isolation and made them a part of the empire, he integrated the North, where the majority of the remaining Indians could be found in the late eigh-

teenth century, into the rest of the colony, an accomplishment that helped to insure the future unity of Brazil. Of course, practically speaking, whatever the intention of those laws, they simply facilitated the exploitation of the Indians.

The planters soon realized that the Indian was not a satisfactory answer to the labor problem. At the same time, the rapid growth of the sugar industry sent the demand for workers soaring, thereby intensifying the labor shortage. The planters soon focused on Africa as the most likely source for labor. Blacks had been imported into Portugal at least as early as 1433, and by the mid-sixteenth century the Portuguese were well acquainted with the West African coast and its inhabitants. The blacks proved well adapted to the tasks required by the colonists. Furthermore, the troublesome reservations about using Indians as slaves rarely extended to the use of Africans. For those reasons a forced migration of millions of Africans began in the mid-sixteenth century and continued apace until 1850. It is believed that the first black people directly imported from Africa arrived in Brazil in 1538. In that year a ship of Jorge Lopes Bixorda, an experienced and well-known slave trader, unloaded its human cargo from Guinea. One Jesuit father wrote from Pernambuco in 1552, "There are in this captaincy a great number of slaves, both Indian and African." Thereafter a deluge of slaves poured out of Africa.

Once the traffic became well established, the cargo of blacks moved uninterruptedly across the Atlantic. Brazil sent its tobacco, sugar, manioc, beans, flour, spirits, cloth, and sweetmeats eastward in exchange for the slaves and, to a lesser extent, for palm oil, rice, ivory, gold, and the products of Asia. The trade between Angola and Brazil reached such proportions that the former became practically a dependency of the latter. The Portuguese historian Jaime Cortesão affirmed, "Angola was during the seventeenth and eighteenth centuries a Portuguese province of Brazil." At one point in the mid-seventeenth century, from 1658 to 1666, two successive governors of Angola, João Fernandes Vieira and André Vidal de Negreiros, were Brazilians. By the close of the eighteenth century, the merchants of Rio de Janeiro alone were

dispatching some twenty-four ships a year to that African colony. The direct trade route was not the only one followed. About a half-dozen European nations, principal among which were Portugal and the Netherlands, used a triangular route: European goods to Africa, African slaves to Brazil, Brazilian sugar to Europe. By whatever means they came, the number of Africans imported was staggering. A conservative estimate of the number of blacks surviving the Atlantic crossing to Brazil, over the span of three centuries, was about 3.5 million. By centuries, the estimated numbers were: sixteenth, 100,000; seventeenth, 600,000; eighteenth, 1,300,000; nineteenth, 1,600,000. Thus, the Portuguese imported into Brazil more blacks than the Indians they found there.

The African origins of Brazil's slaves were extremely varied. They came from Guinea, Dahomey, Nigeria, Ghana, Cape Verde, São Tomé, Angola, the Congo, Mozambique, and many other parts of Africa. Precise origins are difficult to ascertain because of the mixing of the slaves in Brazil as well as miscegenation with whites and Indians, and because the government in 1890 ordered destroyed many official records relating to slavery. A study of African cultures surviving in Brazil enables anthropologists to identify three major contributors to Brazilian society. The first are the Sudanese groups of which the Yoruba and Dahoman predominated. They originated in the African areas that later became Liberia, Nigeria, Ghana, and Dahomey. Although scattered throughout Brazil, the Yorubas seemed to be concentrated principally in Bahia; the Dahomans, in Bahia and Maranhão. The slave buyers considered these Sudanese blacks particularly desirable because they were tall, strong, brave, intelligent, and reputed to be hard-working and good-natured. The Mohammedanized Guinea-Sudanese groups composed the second classification of African contributors. Those Malé blacks, of whom the Hausa were probably the best known, were found mainly in Bahia. They followed the austere precepts of their religion. Some of them were literate in Arabic, and they possessed numerous skills, including much-appreciated gold-mining techniques. Among slave-owners they had the reputation of being intelligent and industrious but somewhat sullen, resentful, and

rebellious in captivity. The Bantu from Angola, the Congo, and Mozambique were the third group of contributors. They were found principally in Rio de Janeiro and Minas Gerais. Regarded as peaceful and adaptable, they knew how to work metals, weave, and make pottery. They also tended livestock and farmed.

Africans could be found in every part of the colony, with the greatest concentrations in Maranhão, Pernambuco, Bahia, and Rio de Janeiro, where they worked at various agricultural tasks, and in Minas Gerais, where they mined gold and diamonds. With the exception, then, of Minas Gerais, they exerted their greatest influence in the coastal areas and their presence and influence were less obvious in the interior.

The African contribution to Brazilian evolution was great and varied. The cooks introduced into the diet new staples such as red peppers, black beans, and okra and new culinary concoctions such as *caruru* and *vatapá,* and into the kitchen new utensils such as the wooden spoon and the mortar and pestle. The "mammies" who raised all the children of the planter told them stories of African origin and sang them songs of that continent. The children in their formative years were intimately exposed to the pronunciation, habits, and ideas of the Africans. The lady of the mansion chose favored black women to be her companions, and they amused her with tales and songs of Africa. The plantation house was a logical place for African and European cultures to meet and mingle. Before too many decades had passed, African cultural traits were easily visible in the colony's dress, music, dance, and religion. On one level a syncretized Afro-Brazilian religion developed, known as *Candomblé* in Bahia, *Xangó* in Pernambuco, and *Macumba* in Rio de Janeiro. On another level, the Afro-Brazilians softened some of the asperity of Roman Catholicism. They enlivened church festivals, drawing them out into the street to commemorate the patron saint's day and adding folk plays and dances of a religious nature rooted in syncretism.

Doubtless the Africans' major contribution was their labor. Their muscles supported Brazilian civilization. They did much more than simply work in the fields. They brought with them, or learned in the New World, many skills essential to

the growth of Brazil. They were the carpenters, painters, masons, jewelers, sculptors, locksmiths, tailors, cobblers, and bakers. They made technical contributions in metallurgy, mining, cattle-raising, and agriculture. In the judgment of Prince Johan Maurits, the famed viceroy of Dutch Brazil, "It is not possible to effect anything in Brazil without slaves . . . and they cannot be dispensed with upon any consideration whatsoever; if anyone feels that this is wrong, it is a futile scruple."

The Africans helped explore and conquer the interior and defend Brazil from attack. In times of war, they were the soldiers who fought the hostile Indians or the foreign invaders. Black regiments under black leaders—notably the much-praised Henrique Dias—struggled against the Dutch in the seventeenth century. When the French sacked Rio de Janeiro in 1711, the governor of Minas Gerais rushed to the aid of the city with fifteen hundred horsemen and six thousand armed Afro-Brazilians. They were an indispensable ingredient of colonial Brazil. In truth, the conquest, settlement, and growth of Brazil were Afro-European joint ventures.

Few Europeans felt slavery was wrong. Portuguese law sanctioned it. The attorney-general of the state of Maranhão, Manuel Guedes Aranha, expressed a typical view in 1654, when he wrote, "It is a known fact that different men are fitted for different things: we [the whites] are meant to introduce religion among them [Indians and Africans]; and they to serve us, hunt for us, fish for us, work for us." Such a classic statement of racism constituted the core of European imperialism for centuries. Always solicitous of the welfare of the Indians and uncertain of the morality of their enslavement, the Roman Catholic Church accepted African slavery so long as the blacks were Christianized. However, a few voices—principally from the Jesuits—did eventually speak up in defense of the Afro-Brazilians. In the seventeenth century, the humane Padre Antônio Vieira on several occasions denounced brutal punishments and abuse of the black slaves. During one famed sermon, he cried emotionally,

O inhuman traffic in which the merchandise is men! Few masters, many slaves; masters richly dressed, slaves despised and

naked; masters banqueting, slaves dying of hunger; masters swimming in gold and silver, slaves loaded down with irons; masters treating their slaves like brutes, slaves in fear and awe of their masters as if they were gods; masters present at a whipping, standing like statues of might and tyranny, slaves prostrated, their hands strapped behind their backs, like debased emblems of servitude.

Peradventure these men are not our brothers?

Were these souls not redeemed with the blood of the same Christ? Are not these bodies born and do they not die like ours? Do they not breathe the same air? Does not the same sky cover them? Are they not warmed by the same sun?

Vieira even went so far during some sermons as to question the institution of slavery itself. On one such occasion, he asked rhetorically "Can there be a greater want of understanding, or a greater error of judgment between men and men than for me to think that I must be your master because I was born farther away from the sun, and that you must be my slave because you were born nearer to it?" He must have startled many of his listeners with the remark, "An Ethiope if he be cleansed in the waters of the Congo is clean, but he is not white; but if cleansed in the water of baptism, he is both."

In the opening years of the eighteenth century, both André João Antonil and Jorge Benci wrote to urge better treatment of the black slaves. For its part, the Crown promulgated edicts in 1688, 1698, and 1714 against their maltreatment. They had no enduring effect. In 1761, Pombal liberated all the slaves in Portugal, but slavery, the very sinew of the mercantile economy, continued in Brazil without any real protest except from the slaves themselves.

On occasion the slaves rebelled, killed their masters, and set fire to the plantations, both buildings and fields. More often, they simply disappeared into the trackless interior where they sometimes established small settlements known as *quilombos*. Of the many *quilombos* established in Portuguese America—and scholars still have not directed sufficient attention to this topic to allow even a calculated estimate of their size or number—the longest-lived and largest was the famous Palmares in the interior of Alagoas. There, through-

1630 - 95

out most of the seventeenth century, a pseudo-African state with a population of approximately twenty thousand flourished. Palmares is significant as the major attempt by the blacks in Brazil to organize a state with African traditions. To the Luso-Brazilians the *quilombo* challenged established order because the blacks enticed other slaves to flee the plantations and join them, a threat to an already tight labor supply. Furthermore, the lands Palmares occupied blocked westward agrarian expansion. Repeated campaigns against the stronghold failed. Between 1672 and 1694, Palmares withstood an average of one Portuguese expedition every fifteen months. Finally a combination of dissension within the *quilombo* and the royal government's use of ruthless and persistent Paulista *bandeirantes* destroyed it at the end of the seventeenth century. Throughout the colonial period—for that matter well into the national period—the threat of slave rebellion hung ominously in the air, causing the plantation owners and even the city dwellers uneasy hours.

The miscegenation characteristic of Portuguese-Indian relations also characterized Indian-African and Portuguese-African relations. Within their permissive slave society, the white men of the plantation houses took full advantage of the black women. As a consequence, a mulatto population appeared early and grew rapidly. The population of Salvador da Bahia, in the heart of rich sugar and tobacco country, in 1803 very well exemplified that miscegenation. In an estimated population of 100,000, approximately 30,000 were white, another 30,000 mulatto, and the remainder black. Of Brazil's approximately 3.5 million inhabitants in 1818, only about a third could be classified—very liberally—as white, 500,000 as mulatto, and about 2 million as black. With good reason, one Portuguese observed, "Brazil has the body of America and the soul of Africa."

Of the three groups contributing to the increasingly homogeneous nature of Brazilian society, only the Indians declined in number and, hence, in importance and influence during the colonial period. The European and African influx continued. Of course European immigration never approximated the numbers forcefully sent from Africa. In the late

seventeenth century, the Lisbon government urged greater immigration of married Portuguese couples. It succeeded in persuading families from the Azores to settle in appreciable numbers in the extreme northern and southern regions.

The discovery of gold in the late seventeenth century lured greater numbers of Europeans to Brazil. Estimates indicate that the population of European stock increased tenfold during the eighteenth century.

The three groups, Indian, European, and African, lived and mixed together with, all factors considered, a minimum of friction, although the brutality of the experience for the Indians and Africans should not be dismissed. In the process three continents fused sexually, socially, linguistically, and culturally to form a nation much more homogeneous than any other of comparable size. A hybrid civilization emerged and so did a new type of person, the Brazilian, the compound product of extraordinary diverse elements. It would not be an exaggeration to affirm that this "new race" conquered the new land.

Territorial Expansion

The Luso-Brazilian sweep across the South American continent from the Atlantic to the Andes constituted one of the greatest epics of Brazilian history. Portugal responded defensively to foreign threats and interlopers in the New World by establishing tiny, isolated, agricultural nuclei along the coast. Olinda to the north, Salvador da Bahia in the center, and São Vicente to the south were the first settlements of strategic and commercial importance. Seaborne foreigners and the hostile Indians of the interior menaced those fragile settlements. The Crown's efforts to strengthen and to connect them meant that for many decades emphasis fell on coastal settlement to the neglect of inland expansion. At first the government even put legal restrictions on inland penetration. The foundation of Rio de Janeiro in 1565 helped to unite Salvador with the South, just as the establishment of São Cristóvão de Rio Sergipe in 1589 helped to unite the colonial

capital with the North. With the arrival of more colonists and the defeat of the resisting Indians, the area surrounding each of the settlements was conquered, settled, and incorporated into the agricultural economy of the colony.

From time to time some timid exploration filtered into the interior. Those *entradas* resulted from a curiosity to learn what the hinterland might offer and from a hope of discovering gold and other precious metals. Those expeditions also captured Indian slaves for the colonists.

At first the colony expanded faster in the North in direct response to increasing European pressures on Portugal either to occupy the coast it claimed or to forfeit it to others. The union of the two Iberian crowns between 1580 and 1640 eliminated early rivalry between Spain and Portugal over the territory between São Vicente and the Rio de la Plata. Also, in the South there was no brazilwood, a natural product much sought after by the French, English, and Dutch, who hovered along the northern coast because of its abundant stands of brazilwood, as well as its fertile land favorable to sugar cultivation. The presence of these Europeans motivated the Portuguese to expand in their direction. Engaged in such "defensive colonization," the Portuguese founded one settlement after another, each north of the last one, until they established Belém, in 1616, on the Amazon River.

The newly founded settlements of São Luís do Maranhão and Belém were isolated on the northern coast far from the Cape of São Roque, where the coast suddenly turns southward. It soon became apparent that because of winds and sea currents these settlers could communicate more readily with Lisbon than with Salvador. Accordingly, when the Crown appointed a judge for São Luís in 1619, it ruled that appeals should be made directly to Lisbon rather than to Salvador. Two years later, the king created the state of Maranhão (as contrasted with the state of Brazil) composed of Maranhão, Pará, Amazonas, and, for a time, parts of Ceará and Piauí. The new state had a modest birth. Settlement consisted only of four forts, one in Ceará, the others at São Luís, Belém, and at the mouth of the Amazon, with minuscule villages at their side. The first governor, Francisco Coelho de Carvalho, gen-

erously distributed the land in *sesmarias,* by then a well established practice throughout Brazil, and created six hereditary captaincies with the hope that their donees would encourage immigration. Growth, however, was slow. The white population of the state numbered only two thousand in 1700. In 1677 the bishopric of Maranhão was erected, suffragan to the archbishop of Lisbon. The seat of the government moved to Belém in 1737 because of the increasing importance of the Amazon River. The northern coast, for a long time neglected and then later only weakly held, tempted the expanding European powers.

The French were the most serious threat to Portugal's claims in the sixteenth and early seventeenth centuries. After their expulsion from Rio de Janeiro in 1567, they turned their attention to the North. From Paraíba to the Amazon they traded with the Indians whom they urged to oppose the Portuguese. In 1612, a French expedition under the command of Ravardière began to colonize Maranhão. The Portuguese reacted by sending expeditions against the French interlopers in 1614 and 1615. After their expulsion in 1615, the French ceased to be a major threat to Portuguese hegemony in this part of the New World. True, Jean-François du Clerc attacked Rio de Janeiro in 1710 and Duguay-Trouin captured and plundered that city the following year, but those were isolated attacks little related to colonization. France maintained its claims to Amapá, the territory between the Amazon and Oiapoque rivers, until 1900 when an arbiter recognized the Brazilian claims as valid. The English made some annoying and costly raids on the coastal settlements in the late sixteenth century. James I magnanimously bestowed some land grants in northern Brazil upon nobles of his court, but they made no serious effort to colonize. The final and major foreign threat came from the Dutch during the seventeenth century.

The Dutch knew Brazil. During some periods, Dutch bottoms carried over half the trade between Brazil and Portugal. Before 1591, ships of any flag could trade in Brazilian ports so long as they were cleared from a Portuguese port first. Those ships carried away Brazilian products after paying

the required taxes and duties and calling at Lisbon for clearance. Traditionally the Dutch and Portuguese had gotten along well together, but their amiable relationship ended when Philip of Spain ascended the Portuguese throne. The Dutch, fighting a protracted war for their independence from the Spanish Hapsburgs, were the sworn enemies of the Castilians. In the unification of the two kingdoms, Portugal inherited that quarrel. In 1585 and again in 1590, 1596, and 1599. Philip II ordered the seizure of all Dutch vessels in Portuguese ports and the imprisonment of their crews. The Dutch sought retaliation. They established a few trading posts along the lower Amazon in the early seventeenth century. However, the principal weapon of revenge was the Dutch West India Company, founded in 1621 to encourage colonization and commerce through conquest.

Lured by lucrative sugar exports and convinced that Portuguese America was the colony Philip held most weakly, the Dutch West India Company selected Brazil for its initial conquest. The Company's fleet first attacked Salvador, an excellent port well situated for future expansion, and carried it in 1624. The Luso-Brazilians expelled the Dutch the following year and repulsed two more attacks in 1627. The company then shifted its attention from the political center of the colony to its economic center, Pernambuco. Its forces appeared off Recife in 1630. After capturing that port, they began a conquest that at its height extended from the São Francisco River northward into Maranhão.

The Calvinist soldier and intellectual Johan Maurits of Nassau-Siegen presided over the most fruitful years of Dutch occupation, 1637 to 1644. Captivated by Brazil, the viceroy put to work some forty-six scholars, scientists, and artists to study and to depict the land. He typified the Dutch curiosity about the tropics, a curiosity that the Iberians hitherto had lacked. Hence it was the Dutch who made the first—and for a long time the only—scientific study of the tropics. Albert Eckhout painted magnificent canvasses portraying the Dutch colony. Willem Piso studied tropical diseases and their remedies. Georg Marcgraf made collections of fauna, flora, and rocks. The

Dutch maintained an aviary as well as zoological and botanical gardens. The first New World astronomical observatory and meteorological station were built in Recife.

Economic matters quite naturally commanded much of Maurits' attention as well. In an endeavor to avoid monoculture, he tried to make the colony self-supporting in foodstuffs. The company monopolized all trade in slaves, dyewoods, and munitions but permitted the inhabitants of the conquered colony to engage freely in all other trade. By reducing taxes and providing liberal credit terms to planters to rebuild ruined sugar mills and to buy slaves, the viceroy rehabilitated the sugar industry. Those were splendid years for the Netherlands. Indeed, 1641 marked the apogee of Dutch power in the Atlantic, with fur trading posts on the Hudson River, fortresses in Guiana, the possession of Curacao and Aruba, sugar colonies in Brazil, and slave-trading posts in Africa. Understanding the importance of slavery to sugar, the Dutch seized part of Angola to insure a labor supply for their Brazilian plantations.

Shortly after the departure of Maurits, the bitter guerrilla warfare raging for a decade and a half against the Dutch coalesced into an open campaign coordinated by Governor-General Antônio Telles da Silva from Salvador. Contacts between the leaders in Bahia and Pernambuco were made. André Vidal de Negreiros of Bahia met twice with João Fernandes Vieira, a wealthy mulatto planter who had collaborated with the Dutch until 1644, to promise that troops from Bahia would march overland to aid a rebellion in Pernambuco. Portuguese soldiers under Antônio Dias Cardoso, black and mulatto troops under Henrique Dias, and Indian levies under Felipe Camarão penetrated the hinterland of northeastern Brazil in early 1645, initiating their campaign to expel the "foreign heretic."

New developments in Europe complicated the conduct of the war against the Dutch in Brazil. With popular support, the Braganzas seized the Portuguese crown in 1640 and declared Portugal's independence of Spain. United by their mutual enmity toward Spain, Portugal and the Netherlands ceased hostilities toward each other in Europe. Portugal's determi-

nation to maintain its newly gained independence from Spain absorbed most of its attention and energy. The Brazilians, however, refused to come to terms with the Dutch and continued the struggle to expel them. *Mazombos* (whites born in Brazil), Afro-Brazilians, and Indians from all parts of the subcontinent joined ranks in the common campaign. Their victories at Guararapes in 1648 and 1649 proved their land superiority over the foreign invaders. The Brazilians even carried their attacks to Angola. First, they sent munitions, guns, and supplies to the Portuguese besieged in the interior of Angola. Then, Salvador Correia de Sá e Benavides, bearing the imposing title "Governor of Rio de Janeiro and Captain-General of the Kingdom of Angola," sailed from Guanabara Bay with two thousand men and recaptured Luanda from the Dutch, thus restoring Angola to the Crown. The "Restorer of Angola" then reopened the intensive trade between the two South Atlantic colonies. By that time Dutch Brazil was clearly in the process of decay. Constant interprovincial bickering in the Netherlands resulted in poor leadership and irresolute policy within the Dutch West India Company. In turn, the company neglected the colony and failed to pay the soldiers and sailors regularly. Their morale plummeted. By 1648 the Brazilians had reduced the Dutch to Recife and its immediate environs. However, as long as the Dutch controlled the sea, a stalemate resulted. At that point, Portugal reawakened to its need for Brazilian sugar, of which the Northeast was a primary producer, and took a more active interest in the colonial conflict. To break the impasse, Antônio Vieira suggested to the king that a Brazil Company be formed and given special privileges in the Luso-Brazilian trade, with the obligation that it build and equip a fleet of warships in Brazil. In 1649, the Brazil Company's first fleet sailed for the New World. The Dutch ships, undermanned, underprovisioned, and in lamentable condition, mutinied and returned home. Portugal for the first time took command of the seas. The outbreak of war between the Netherlands and England in 1652 sealed the fate of the Dutch in the South Atlantic. The Portuguese fleet blockaded Recife and completely isolated the demoralized Dutch garrison, which surrendered. By the terms of the capitulation

of Taborda on January 26, 1654, they left Brazil, and the Luso-Brazilians triumphantly entered Recife several days later.

The consequences of the Dutch presence in Brazil, and of the long war, were many and significant. Historians agree that "the reconquest" awoke the first national sentiments among the varied and scattered inhabitants of the sprawling colony. It helped to forge unity. The Brazilians, much more than the Portuguese, had fought the war and won the victory. They had defeated a major European maritime power, one that had in fact humbled Spain, once the occupier of Portugal. That achievement infused into the Brazilians a new pride that replaced their old feeling of inferiority before the Portuguese. Men of all regions, races, colors, and social positions had contributed in a united effort to the final victory, a feat that weakened former geographical, social, and color barriers. The protracted struggle had welded Brazil into an unprecedented psychological and social unity, so that its inhabitants thought of themselves, more than ever before, as Brazilians. The mercantile Dutch made Recife the first truly bourgeois commercial center of Brazil. They found it a village of 150 houses and left it a bustling port with over 2,000 houses. They created an urban, commercial class in contrast to and eventually in conflict with the traditional rural class. The defeat of the Dutch marked the end of any major overt foreign threat to northern Brazil. Full attention turned from the northern coast to the southern and to the vast interior. The government in Lisbon was particularly concerned about the South; the Brazilians, with the interior.

By the mid-seventeenth century both the Spaniards and the Portuguese understood the importance of the Rio de la Plata network. Spain wanted to control it to prevent any penetration into the silver-mining regions of Upper Peru, while Portugal coveted it in order to open up and to protect the southern interior of Brazil. The Portuguese colonization of the far South began in 1680 with the foundation of Colônia do Sacramento across the Plata estuary from Buenos Aires. The new settlement was far too isolated from the main body of Luso-Brazilian colonization to thrive, and the Spaniards immediately challenged it. The Luso-Brazilians established a

supply base in Santa Catarina in 1684 and a fortress in south-ern Rio Grande do Sul in 1737. From the points of that trian-gle, the Luso-Brazilians penetrated and colonized the South. In 1739, the Crown created the captaincy of Santa Catarina and in 1760, the captaincy of Rio Grande do São Pedro, which it elevated to the rank of captaincy-general and renamed Rio Grande do Sul in 1807. The struggle to dominate the Plata turned out to be as prolonged as it was bitter. The area approximately encompassing present-day Uruguay changed hands with bewildering frequency from 1680 until 1828, when the independent nation of Uruguay emerged, and no other area better symbolized the rivalry of the two Iberian monar-chies for empire. Thus foreign rivalry intensified Portugal's attention to the South, just as it had in the North. Because of that challenge, Lisbon took a very active interest in the explo-ration, colonization, and fortification of the area. The settle-ment of the North and South through official encouragement contrasted markedly with the inland penetration from the center captaincies, which was characterized by spontaneity and the near absence of official impetus.

Westward expansion during the seventeenth and eigh-teenth centuries, in many ways a direct continuation of the adventurous spirit that had carried the Portuguese to the four corners of the world, accounts for the phenomenal territorial growth of Brazil. It was also the first Brazilian epic. The Por-tuguese empire had been coastal; Portuguese expansion, mercantile. The *mazombos*, mulattoes, and mestizos led the way into the interior. Brazilian inland expansion had its timid beginnings in the sixteenth century, became the marked characteristic of the last half of the seventeenth and first half of the eighteenth centuries, and in certain phases lasted until the early twentieth century when Brazil acquired Acre, its westernmost state. That spectacular expansion resulted from the activities of hearty adventurers known as *bandeirantes*, a term derived from the Portuguese word for flag, *bandeira*. In medieval Portugal a *bandeira* signified a group of soldiers equal in size to a company and designated by a distinctive banner. The militia of São Paulo adopted the term and by extension it came to mean an expedition departing for the

interior. Participants in such expeditions were called *bandeirantes*.

All three races contributed to the bandeirante expansion. *Mamelucos,* the offspring of Indians and Portuguese, composed the majority of the rank and leadership of the expedition, but Afro-Brazilians—in their status as either slaves or freedmen—participated too. Mulattoes on occasion led some *bandeiras.* The *bandeirantes* adapted perfectly to the land and were inured to the hardships of the interior. Europe meant nothing to them; the virgin land engulfing them meant everything. They disdainfully turned their backs on the coast and plunged into the interior to seek wealth and power. Indian slaves, runaway black slaves, precious metals, and land were the forms of wealth they pursued. By exploring new territory, opening new routes of communication, and claiming new regions for the Crown they hoped for the rewards of royal recognition and preferment. Clearly they paid homage to their distant king, but on the other hand they expressed little if any allegiance to Portugal. As a matter of fact, their pursuit of freedom from colonial bureaucracy was a further impetus to their movement into the interior. Wrote a crown judge to the governor of São Paulo in 1736, "These Paulistas only concern themselves with making new discoveries so as to live free from the judges. And when they see that these follow them, they continue to make other discoveries in remote regions where one cannot pursue them owing to the great distance."

The *bandeirantes* traversed those immense distances mainly by foot or canoe. Travel by horseback was the exception. Rivers proved to be important routes into the *sertão* and became increasingly important in the eighteenth century. Where rivers did not exist, the *bandeirante* moved forward on foot. Barefooted, wearing simple, loose cotton trousers, sometimes with a cotton shirt and sometimes without, and with either a stocking cap or a broadbrimmed hat on his head, he carried a sword and pistols in his belt, a knife at his chest, a rifle slung over his shoulder and cartridge belts girded to his body. Many borrowed and mastered the bow and arrow of the Indians. Little wonder that this rugged and heavily

armed explorer filled the Indians with terror and gave pause to his enemies.

The land challenged the *bandeirantes*. They traversed inhospitable terrain and forded turbulent rivers. Swamps and dense forests mocked their efforts. Arid stretches taught them to bless those numerous, troublesome streams they had so recently cursed. And everywhere they encountered hunger, their one certain traveling companion. Game was scarce, and fruits, nuts, berries, and roots proved to be rare and coveted delicacies. The Indians possessed either meager rations or none at all. With great courage and no small amount of endurance the *bandeirantes* stoically met the challenge and triumphed.

The Paulistas, already separated from the coast by the Serra do Mar, were the most dedicated to the exploration of the interior, but they were not the only *bandeirantes*. Salvador, Recife, São Luís, and Belém all served as staging points for daring marches into the unknown.

In the sixteenth and early seventeenth centuries a series of local communications networks centered on each major settlement: São Vicente, Rio de Janeiro, Bahia, Olinda, and later São Luís and Belém. Their only common contact was via the Atlantic Ocean. *Bandeirante* expansion invalidated the sea lanes as the only common unifier and established inland routes, some by river, others by land, still others by both river and land, to connect the newly established settlements with the older coastal population nuclei. Such lines of communication developed during the last half of the seventeenth century and multiplied during the eighteenth century until, converging one with the other, they connected all the major settlements. Transportation over those radiating routes of communication was by canoe if by river and by mule train if by land. The mule trains, operating on regular schedules and charging fixed rates, consisted of twenty to fifty mules, each carrying approximately 250 pounds, and covering twenty to twenty-five miles a day. Where possible they halted at *ranchos,* establishments that quickly sprang up along the major routes to furnish provisions and rude shelter for both the mules and the *tropeiros,* or drivers. The *tropeiro* was a distinctive Brazil-

ian type. Rough and ready, he belonged to the same school as the *bandeirante* except that he also possessed a sense of business adventure and acumen. From the ports he distributed European merchandise throughout the interior; conversely he brought the products of the *sertão* to the coast for consumption or export. More than a mere merchant, he carried throughout Brazil ideas, expressions, news, and introductions to differing life styles. In short, he was a significant agent of national unity.

The navigators and their canoes played a similar role where the rivers made it possible. The usual dugout canoe, fifty to sixty feet long, five to six feet wide, and three to four feet deep, carried about twelve thousand pounds and a crew of eight who used short paddles and punting poles. The crews paddled by day and camped along the river banks at night. By the eighteenth century, fleets of canoes plied the inland waterways. They provided a cheap means of transportation. Since a small canoe usually carried the load of ten or eleven mules at about a third of the cost, canoe transportation was cheaper than mule transportation despite the more circuitous water routes. Those vital transportation networks that linked the various regions of Brazil were the by-product of the *bandeirantes'* explorations.

Economics motivated the *bandeirantes*. Like the Spanish conquistadores they marched into the *sertão* with the hope of finding riches. Here then, as elsewhere throughout the Western Hemisphere, the hope of discovering El Dorado enticed men into the unknown. The *bandeirantes* sought to capture Indians and sell them at a lucrative profit to the coastal planters or use them on their own plantations. The search for gold also impelled them. The *baneirantes* from São Vicente and São Paulo pushed southward, attracted by minor discoveries of alluvial gold. The foundation of Paranaguá (1648), São Francisco do Sul (1658), Florianópolis (1678), and Curitiba (1693) resulted from that pursuit of gold. Other *bandeirantes* from São Paulo, Rio de Janeiro, and Salvador moved westward, converging in Minas Gerais, in their pursuit of gold and other precious metals and stones. The continued quest for minerals drew them into Goiás, Mato Grosso, and Amazonia.

By the mid-seventeenth century, the *bandeirantes* were opening the Amazon to trade and settlement. In 1669, the Crown built Fort São José de Rio Negro at the point where the Rio Negro met the Solimões. That juncture became the first population center in the interior of the Amazon. Exploring the North were several other groups: official detachments of soldiers sent to expel Spanish interlopers; the *tropas de resgate,* those expeditions in search of Indian slaves; and the *sertanistas,* merchant adventurers seeking the wealth of the region. They sold cocoa, vanilla, spices, medicinal herbs, woods, fruits, nuts, and animal skins to Belém, other settlements, and the metropolis. Also very active in the Amazon, as elsewhere in the interior, were the missionaries. A kind of *bandeirante,* they too helped to explore, open up, and settle the interior. However, their motivations were quite different. They eagerly left the coastal settlements for the *sertão* in order to Christianize the Indians and to save them from the predatory slave-hunting *bandeirantes.* To the best that their limited numbers permitted, they persuaded the Indians to live within the protective confines of the church-oriented villages scattered throughout the interior from the Amazon to the Plata.

The consequences of the *bandeirante* expansion were enormous. Their explorations opened up the interior by pioneering routes of communication and transportation, supplying geographic information about huge areas which hitherto had remained blank on maps, and pacifying or decimating hostile Indians. In the wake of these explorations a variety of economic activities began that infused new wealth into the Portuguese empire. Gold, diamonds, and cattle were the most conspicuous contributions of the interior. Finally settlements sprang up in the newly opened areas. Some settlements owed their origin to a crossroads, a *rancho,* or a watering place; some to a gold lode or a diamond discovery; others to a natural stopping spot or transfer point along the waterways; and still others to a mission village or agglomerations of a military nature.

Bandeirante activity also contributed to Brazilian unity. From the seventeenth century onward, the Brazilians began

to demonstrate a remarkable mobility. Over the centuries it strengthened national unity. Through the interior people moved more freely from one region to another than they had among the population clusters of the coast. The waterways and paths eventually intertwined into an effective network binding the colony together. The mines of Minas Gerais, Goiás, and Mato Grosso beckoned to people from the entire length of the coast and mingled them together. Removed from the coast with its ties to Europe, the people who entered the *sertão* submerged themselves in the vastness of Brazil. They were forced to modify their European or pseudo-European ways to suit the terrain and the climate. They borrowed heavily from the Indians. Isolation transformed them into Brazilians. Brazil owes its territorial expansion to the *bandeirante*. The Treaty of Tordesillas had given the bulge of South America to Portugal. The union of the Spanish and Portuguese crowns between 1580 and 1640 had blurred the boundary lines between Spanish and Portuguese America. Spain, preoccupied on the West coast of South America with the mines of Peru, failed to block the Luso-Brazilian expansion except in the Plata area, the back-door route to the mines. Too late, the Spanish monarchs realized that by default they had forfeited half of South America to the Luso-Brazilians. In the mid-eighteenth century the situation on the Iberian peninsula—the Spanish monarch was married to a Portuguese princess and the heir to the Portuguese throne wed to a Spanish princess—favored a frank discussion of the South American boundaries based on real-politik. The two crowns agreed to redraw their South American boundaries. The Treaty of Madrid of 1750 officially abandoned the Tordesillas line in favor of two principles: 1) *uti possidetis,* that is ownership by occupation rather than by claim, and 2) the recognition of natural boundaries, that is the use of rivers, mountains, lakes, and other natural landmarks to mark the boundaries, rather than the use of the always controversial astronomical fixes. That was all very well, but then in violation of the principle of *uti possidetis* Spain got title to the Portuguese Colônia do Sacramento, which it regarded as a threat to its position in the Plata, and Portugal in turn received the Sete Povos das

Missões, Spanish Jesuit mission settlements along the eastern, or left bank, of the Uruguay River, which Portugal considered a threat to its control of Rio Grande do Sul. That authorized exchange of territories was the most unpopular aspect of the treaty. However, neither side surrendered those areas at that time.

The individual most responsible for the Portuguese success in the Treaty of Madrid was Alexandre de Gusmão, a Brazilian from Santos who had been educated at Coimbra University. He understood the importance of the principle of *uti possidetis* as the best means to gain legal recognition for *bandeirante* expansion, and he worked energetically for the incorporation of that principle into the treaty. Thanks to his efforts, the formal territorial outline of Brazil took legal shape; the boundaries between Spanish and Portuguese America ever after kept the approximate contours the Treaty of Madrid gave them.

Vigorous *bandeirante* activity had permitted Brazil to expand generously, except in the Plata region where the two Iberian empires struggled for control. The principle of *uti possidetis* injected into Portuguese diplomacy by a Brazilian provided the legal basis upon which Brazil based its boundaries thereafter. The Treaty of Madrid provided the model for future Portuguese and Brazilian claims. The lengthy frontiers enclosed an amazing variety of wealth that the Luso-Brazilians exploited almost indifferently during the colonial period.

Economic and Political Dependency

Portugal expanded overseas to enrich itself. The political and economic institutions imposed by Lisbon on Brazil pursued that singular goal. Portugal soon enough understood that Brazil was its prized possession and exploited it to the fullest extent possible. No rhetoric can disguise the economic and political realities: the colony existed for the benefit of the motherland.

"Brazil can sustain itself with its ports closed and without the aid of any other land," boasted Frei Vicente do Salvador

in 1627 in his history of Brazil. The boast was not entirely idle. A look at a map readily indicates why. The very size of the colony and the kaleidoscopic variety of its geography seem to insure a sufficiently diverse range of natural wealth to fulfill the boast.

Reverses in Asia during the last half of the sixteenth century caused the metropolis to focus its economic attention on a hitherto neglected Brazil. Thereafter, Portugal depended ever more heavily on Brazil to supply a variety of raw materials that were marketed profitably in Europe to the temporary relief of royal and commercial coffers. Brazilwood, sugar, tobacco, cotton, hides, Amazonian drugs, gold, and diamonds were some of the most important natural products the young colony offered to the Old World. Agriculture was the principal source of wealth. Mining, although more glamorous and prized, was but an interlude and, in comparison to agriculture, a secondary producer of wealth. However, whether from the soil or subsoil, Brazil produced lavishly. During many years the products of Brazil constituted approximately two-thirds of Portugal's export trade with foreign countries.

The abundance of economic possibilities may well have been a curse as well as a blessing since it permitted, indeed encouraged, an economic dilettantism that handicapped orderly development. Despite a dazzling potential, the economy never diversified. To an extraordinary degree, it became and remained export-oriented, devoting much of its capital, technology, labor, and lands to products for sale abroad. More often than not, it relied for its well-being on a single natural product whose sale abroad dictated the course of colonial prosperity. If the product sold well, the colony prospered; if not, stagnation and misery engulfed it. External demand decided the colonial well-being, a dependence exaggerated by stubborn reliance on one major export. The colony exercised no authority over its own economic destiny. Lisbon did. Nor did the Luso-Brazilians ever achieve any notable efficiency in the exploitation of any of those natural products with which generous Nature endowed them. With haphazard, old-fashioned, and inefficient methods, they exploited one natural product until some other area of the

world eager to share the profits outproduced and undersold the Brazilians through the employment of more efficient methods. Then the Brazilians, after some hesitation and considerable economic stress, turned to yet another natural product. Those economic cycles with their sharp alternations between prosperity and poverty began with brazilwood, and continued through sugar, tobacco, cotton, cocoa, rubber, and coffee. From the beginning, extreme economic fluctuation has been a major characteristic of the Brazilian economy and a powerful influence on the course of Brazilian history.

The agricultural structure contributed to the preservation of those cycles. The huge plantations and ranches, owned by relatively few and often employing large numbers of slaves, sought to supply to the international market on as large a scale as possible the tropical product most in demand. Quick and large profits were the goal. Agriculture was thoroughly speculative. Those capitalistic pursuits were carried out within a semifeudal framework.

The large estate, the *fazenda* based on a generous sesmaria, could be considered as some remote vestige of the medieval manor. The estate owner, truly the lord of the manor, was a patriarchal chief who ruled family, servants, slaves, and even neighbors—unless they were large estate owners like himself—with absolute authority. The great size of the estate, its isolation from royal officials, and the relative weakness of local bureaucrats all strengthened his power. Furthermore, the estate chaplain and local parish priest orbited around him like satellites, lending the prestige of the Catholic church to augment his authority. From the shaded veranda of his house, because naturally the "big house" was the focal point of the estate's activity, the patriarch oversaw the land, listened to petitions, dispensed justice, and in general held court. Those large and often well-furnished houses sat in the midst of barns, stables, carriage houses, warehouses, workshops, and slaves' quarters. As far as possible the estate was self-contained. Carpenters, blacksmiths, bakers, seamstresses, candlemakers, and a host of skilled and semiskilled slaves satisfied nearly all the simple, local demands. Need for contact with the world beyond the estate's boundaries was minimal.

A rough road led to the next estate and the nearest village. Occasionally a *tropeiro* appeared to peddle his wares. More important, the road provided a means of transporting the estate's principal crop to the nearest port, which the patriarch and part of his family visited from time to time to purchase from the outside world a few luxury items for themselves. The rural economy consisted of much more than the patriarch, *latifundia,* slavery, and export crops. Yet, those features dominated, characterized Brazilian agriculture, and shaped much of the colony's social and economic life.

Although these patriarchal estates could be found in sugar, tobacco, cotton, and, to a lesser extent, cattle country, the sugar plantation as it developed along the coast from Pernambuco to São Paulo became the best-known and perhaps most typical example of them. During its earliest years, roughly between 1530 and 1560, the sugar industry acquired well-delineated and seemingly unalterable characteristics: large plantations that underused or failed to cultivate most of their lands, emphasis on a single crop, reliance on slave labor, export orientation, and dependency on foreign markets. Together they established a firm economic pattern and not just for the colonial period. The pattern's longevity can only amaze the observer, who recognizes in it a continuity that not only shaped the economy for nearly half a millennium but imprisoned it.

From the mid-sixteenth to mid-seventeenth centuries, Brazil supplied Europe with nearly all its sugar, a lucrative export encouraged by the Crown with tax exemptions, monopoly privileges, guarantees against court attachment of production facilities, and patents of nobility. Despite some obvious hardships—an untamed physical environment, hostile Indians, marauding European interlopers, high freight rates, and a chronic labor shortage—sugar quickly became the major crop. By 1600 sugar production exceeded 65 million pounds a year, a tenfold increase during the previous quarter-century. By that time sugar yielded more profit to Portugal than all its exotic trade with India, and the Europeans living in Brazil enjoyed a higher per capita income than their counterparts back home. Governor-General Diogo de Meneses did

not exaggerate when he observed to the king in 1609 that sugar provided the real wealth of the empire. The number of mills increased rapidly: in 1550 there were 70 mills; in 1584, 115; in 1612, 179; in 1627, 230; and in 1711 the number had grown to 528.

The sugar industry was complex. The large sugar-plantation owner, the *senhor de engenho,* leased most of his land to small contractors, known as *lavradores,* for a portion of their crops. With his own slaves, the *lavrador* planted the cane (one planting sufficed for several years), cut it, and transported it by ox cart to the mill. The average *lavrador* produced one to two thousand cartloads of cane a year. To do so, he needed twenty able-bodied slaves. The *senhor de engenho* possessed all the complex and expensive machinery to grind and process the cane. So large was the operation that his mill, turned by oxen, horses, or water, and all its adjacent buildings resembled a small village. He employed fifteen to twenty Portuguese overseers and technicians and approximately one hundred slaves. A mill of that size could expect to produce between 110 and 125 tons of sugar per year. The final product was divided between the *senhor de engenho* and the *lavrador,* the former receiving three-fifths to two-thirds and the latter one-third to two-fifths.

Between 1650 and 1715, increased competition from European colonies in the Caribbean caused Brazil's income from sugar to decline by two-thirds. Shortly after their expulsion, the Dutch, assiduous students of every aspect of the sugar industry in northeastern Brazil, established large-scale plantations in the Caribbean. Their efficient organization, use of new equipment, extensive financial resources, and favorable geographic position closer to the European markets meant that they could produce well and sell cheaply. France and England imitated the Dutch example in the Caribbean islands. The competition bode ill for Brazil's economy. Brazilian sugar lost most of its European markets. An increasing world supply of sugar lowered the price. By the last quarter of the seventeenth century Brazil's economy was in its doldrums. Despite the wide fluctuations in price and demand, however, sugar remained a major industry. Plunging to new lows in the 1760s

and 1770s, the sugar industry revived later in the eighteenth century, when rebellion shook the Caribbean, particularly Haiti, reducing supplies for the European market. The consequent rise in sugar prices rekindled Luso-Brazilian interest in the crop, and Brazilians began to look methodically and scientifically at its production and problems. Sugar merited the attention: it made up approximately three-fifths of Brazil's exports during the colonial period.

After Caribbean competition had sent the Brazilian sugar economy into a tailspin, and while the economic future looked most somber, the *bandeirantes* discovered gold in Minas Gerais. The cry of *gold*, in 1695, reverberated throughout the empire. People with visions of El Dorado dancing before them descended upon the mines from every direction.

Rowdy, raucous lawlessness characterized the mining camps. Boomtowns sprang up overnight. From practically zero in 1695, the population of Minas Gerais (the General Mines) zoomed to thirty thousand by 1709 and reached a half-million by the end of the century. The increase of population and importance of the southeastern interior prompted the government to create the captaincy of São Paulo and Minas Gerais in 1710. Minas Gerais became a separate captaincy in 1720. In the beginning most energy went into the search for gold. Little thought was given to agriculture, with the result that food was both scarce and expensive.

For the task before them, the Luso-Brazilians possessed scant mining knowledge. They lagged far behind the Spaniards in mining techniques. The prospectors sought out the alluvial gold in riverbeds or, secondarily, worked the riverbanks and shallow deposits in the neighboring hillsides. Subterranean mining was not common. With the price of slaves rising, the miners had few excess funds to spend on mining equipment and would not have known how to use it, had they been able to buy it. The government in Lisbon enacted a mining code in 1702 but failed to recruit and dispatch any mining experts to the interior of Brazil to bring a modicum of order and efficiency to the careless miners. The government was not so tardy about collecting the "royal fifth," a crown tax of 20 percent of the gold mined. The government erected

a complicated bureaucratic apparatus to insure payment of the fifth and to eliminate any smuggling, but, no matter how elaborate the precautions, it never succeeded in outwitting the crafty miners who made fine arts of smuggling and of dodging taxes.

The mania for gold propelled the *bandeirantes* farther west. In 1718 they discovered gold in Cuiabá, Mato Grosso, a seven months' river journey from São Paulo. The diggings were shallow there, and they were exhausted more rapidly than those in Minas Gerais, but that did not prevent a rush into Mato Grosso to exploit the new finds. By 1726, Cuiabá had burgeoned into a town of 7,000, of whom 2,600 were slaves. In 1725, Goiás witnessed the discovery of gold and the familiar pattern of rush and boom ensued. In recognition of the development of those western areas, the Crown created the captaincy of Goiás in 1744 and of Mato Grosso in 1748.

In the midst of such euphoria some prospectors found diamonds, first reported to Lisbon in 1729, in a section of Minas Gerais lacking in gold deposits. The government immediately isolated and thereafter rigorously regulated the diamond district, centered around Tijuco (Diamantina), to protect the small and easily satiated market. Later, other more limited finds were made in São Paulo, Bahia, and Goiás. In 1771, Pombal put the mines directly under the Crown's control in order to eliminate smuggling and maintain high prices. The total production of diamonds during the century after their discovery is estimated as being in excess of three million carats. As in gold mining, smuggling abounded so that such an estimate must be given considerable latitude.

Mineral production increased yearly until 1760, the year of maximum output and the culmination of twenty years of intensive expansion. Over the eighteenth century approximately two million pounds of gold were produced legally, which meant that Brazil provided approximately 80 percent of the world's gold supply in that century. During the century mining absorbed the attention of both the population and the government. However, despite promise and appearance, the mines never provided more than a façade of wealth. The gold and diamonds slipped through the fingers of the Brazilians

and Portuguese into the hands of the northern Europeans, particularly the English, who sold manufactured goods to Portugal. In truth agriculture did more to develop Brazil. The average per capita income from the sugar industry, for example, was considerably higher than that from mining at a corresponding stage.

As was inevitable in the hectic boom of mining, disappointments and failures predominated. A few struck it rich, and in the growing urban centers such as São João del-Rei, Sabará, Mariana, Tijuco, and Ouro Prêto, extraordinarily handsome civil and religious architecture testified to a measure of prosperity. Ouro Prêto, the capital of Minas Gerais, exemplified the flowering of rococo art in Brazil. Its thirteen churches, various government buildings, graceful fountains, and many two-storied houses, scattered picturesquely over the hills upon which the city rests, still recall the splendor of that city during its decades of greatest activity. In contrast with the rest of the captaincies in the eighteenth century, an essentially urban society characterized Minas Gerais. A small class of exalted governmental officials and successful miners and merchants dressed elegantly, furnished their residences with European luxuries, attended local theatres, and even read and discussed the latest French, English, and Portuguese books.

The consequences of the discovery of gold and diamonds were impressive, both for the colony and the metropolis. The discovery, coming at the precise moment when Portugal's economic situation was in decline, seemed, on the surface, to have saved the economy. Wealth poured into Lisbon to be misspent on extravagances. In reality, the gold simply paused briefly in Lisbon on its way to London and other European commercial centers. It has been observed with some sagacity and a little exaggeration that Brazilian gold mined by African slaves financed English industrialization. In 1703 Portugal had signed the Treaty of Methuen with England, agreeing to buy British manufactured goods in return for English importation of its wine and agricultural products. The balance of trade quickly tipped in England's favor, and Brazilian gold paid the growing deficit. Freely spending Brazilian

wealth, the Portuguese let the Industrial Revolution bypass them, and the influx of gold masked for some generations the unfortunate consequences of this position: economic stagnation, thwarted development, and dependence on the English. For Brazil, that situation meant double dependency. The South American colony was not only economically subservient to the mother country in true mercantilist fashion but, since Portugal exercised an ever-diminishing degree of economic independence under expanding English domination, also found its destiny increasingly shaped in London rather than in Lisbon.

Throughout the Portuguese empire, the influx of gold drove prices up. The miners evinced a willingness to pay almost anything for slaves, cattle, agricultural produce, and European products. The Portuguese in the metropolis were hardly more careful. Inflation menaced the imperial economy. In the long run, the gold enriched neither Portugal nor Brazil; to the contrary, it added to their impoverishment.

Gold also contributed to absolutism in eighteenth-century Portugal. Prior to that century the king, whether it pleased him or not, had to convene the *Côrtes* (parliament) in order to obtain money. When the *Côrtes* adjourned in 1697, the monarchs did not summon it into session again until the rebellion in 1820 led to its convocation. The monarchs had no reason to request money since the royal fifth from the mines kept the exchequer properly filled. Gold thus contributed to despotism and prevented five generations of Luso-Brazilians from getting any legislative experience, however limited it might have been.

In Brazil, the discovery shifted the colony's population. Traditionally the inhabitants had clung to the coast, with the region between Bahia and Pernambuco being the most heavily populated. The discovery dislodged significant numbers of coastal dwellers who were enticed into the interior by dreams of wealth. The heady news of gold strikes also encouraged immigration from the motherland directly to the interior. Slaves were diverted from their usual coastal destinations to the gold fields. The resultant acute labor shortage along the coast aggravated the agricultural decline already well under way. In

general, attention shifted from the Northeast to the Southeast and the transference of the colonial capital from Salvador to Rio de Janeiro in 1763 was dramatic proof of that change.

Mining served as an impetus to urbanization. New towns sprang up with each discovery of gold. Commercial activities intensified in the Southeast with the resultant increase of the bourgeois class. More government officials arrived to oversee the minting, protection, and shipment of the gold and diamonds. Whereas in the seventeenth century 4 cities and 37 towns were founded, the eighteenth century witnessed the creation of 3 cities and 118 towns.

The rising importance of gold exports significantly altered the carefully balanced relationship between the *mazombos* and the Portuguese by divesting the Brazilians of some of the local economic autonomy they had enjoyed, an ending of benign neglect if nothing else. As exemplified in the sugar economy, the *mazombo* planter elite oversaw the planting of the cane, production of sugar, and preparation of sugar exports, while the Portuguese merchants, maritime interests, and bureaucrats marketed it abroad, a harmonious division of labor profitable to both parties. Such harmony burst before the inundation of gold and diamonds. The Crown believed those precious metals and stones to be too valuable to allow the continuation of the division between production and international marketing so well delineated in agriculture. Portuguese adventurers arrived in large numbers to search for gold; soldiers and bureaucrats invaded Brazil to protect the Crown's interests and monopolies. In short, the Brazilian elite found itself shoved aside in the gold and diamond rushes. The Portuguese violated regional authority, local prerogatives, and *mazombo* interests, much to the disgust of the Brazilians. The collapse of the division of labor and greater intrusion of the Portuguese bureaucracy alienated many of the Brazilian elite and would contribute mightily to the causes leading to Brazil's independence.

After 1760, economic stagnation set in. A native crop, Brazilian cotton, provided an exception to the trend. Maranhão first exported the crop but soon Pernambuco, Bahia, and Rio de Janeiro grew it for sale abroad. Much simpler than

sugar production, cotton required far less capital. By the end of the eighteenth century a typical cotton plantation employed fifty slaves and produced around 64,000 pounds of unseparated cotton a year. Production reached its peak during the early decades of the nineteenth century when the United States, because of President Jefferson's embargo policy, and then because of war with Great Britain, failed to supply the European cotton market, creating a vacuum that Brazil eagerly filled. In those years, cotton accounted for a fifth to a quarter of Brazil's exports.

Tobacco was a third important crop, used widely in trade with Africa and, after the Dutch popularized its use, with Europe. In fact, the fine quality of the Brazilian leaf made it sought after even in distant Asia. Although its cultivation spread from Sergipe to São Paulo, tobacco production centered in Bahia. The crop had a social as well as an economic significance: small farmers could cultivate it profitably. Tobacco production required no elaborate equipment, just a shed in which to cure the leaf. With minimal labor needs, it employed few workers. Here then was a lucrative crop the less substantial farmers could raise for export.

To a more limited extent, cocoa, rice, and indigo were also produced for export. For home consumption, the farmers planted wheat, beans, potatoes, a variety of vegetables, and fruits. Indigenous foods such as corn, the sweet potato, manioc, *palmitos,* the Brazilian banana, *cajú,* the pineapple, and myriad other domestic fruits were available in the marketplaces. They contributed some variety to the local diet but did not figure significantly in overseas commerce.

One other economic activity, cattle raising, exercised an influence over the growth of Brazil that far transcended the economic sphere. Martim Afonso de Sousa introduced cattle into Brazil between 1531 and 1533, and Tomé de Sousa brought more in 1549. Cattle arrived regularly thereafter. The earliest cattle centers were São Vicente, Bahia, and Pernambuco. Cattle ranches accounted to a large extent for the settlement of the long coast between Bahia and Pernambuco during the last half of the sixteenth century.

In a certain sense, the cattle industry grew as a response

to the needs of the sugar industry. In the third quarter of the sixteenth century, the sugar plantations and the cattle ranches occupied much the same territory. The meat provided an important source of food for the plantations with their relatively large numbers of workers. The oxen served as draft animals to haul firewood, essential for the processing of sugar cane; more often than not they also turned the grinders in the sugar mills. They were equally indispensable in clearing, planting, and harvesting the fields. As cattle breeding expanded quickly in the second half of the sixteenth century, the Portuguese government forbade it within ten leagues of the coast in order to protect the precious sugar lands and to reserve them exclusively for cane cultivation. That decision exiled the cattle industry into the interior, where it continued to flourish.

Cattle herds often followed close on the heels of the *bandeirantes*, moving thus ever deeper into the *sertão*. There the *vaqueiro*, the sinewy cowboy of mixed Indian, African, and European blood, settled and held the frontier. At times he also contributed to its expansion. The *vaqueiro* was often the first line of defense against the hostile Indians. He either killed or drove them into the hinterland or, at times, incorporated them into the cattle frontier. Cattle herding was the one task in which the Indians participated with gusto, and they contributed skills and blood to the formation of the *vaqueiro*. A visitor to the interior of Maranhão described the *vaqueiro* dressed "in pants and shirt of rough cotton and eating and sleeping on a dried oxen hide spread on the ground," and characterized him as "hospitable, easy-going, and willing to help . . . with a rustic coarseness but sincere and full of good faith."

The constantly expanding cattle industry, notable for its insatiable need for large areas of land, radiated outward into the sertão from Pernambuco, Bahia, and São Vicente. Pernambuco was an exceptionally active nucleus of expansion. The industry penetrated the far South from Minas Gerais and São Paulo, crossing the southern valleys and plains into Paraná and Rio Grande do Sul. In the far South, a second type of cattleman appeared: the gaucho, a combination of Span-

iard, Portuguese, and Indian. Also an accomplished horseman, he spent long periods in the saddle, controlling the
herds with his skillful use of the lasso and *bolas*.

In addition to expanding and settling vast stretches of
the interior, the cattlemen contributed to colonial unification.
The mobile nature of their product meant that they could
walk it to market, and this they did on long cattle drives. With
herds of one hundred to one thousand head, they ambled
north, south, east, or west, wherever the market beckoned.
Their long drives opened new communication routes and
connected widely dispersed areas. Since Maranhão raised
large herds of cattle which sold well in Brazil, the cattle industry served as an economic link important for the eventual
union of the states of Maranhão and Brazil. Along the most
trampled routes, hamlets sprang up near watering holes, river-
fording spots, and mountain passes. An entire new business,
cattle fattening, developed near the markets. Other businessmen bought and sold cattle. Obviously the industry was much
more than regional in scope. Unlike sugar, mining, or other
economic pursuits, it operated on a colony-wide basis, linking the sertão with the coast, the North with the South.

Furthermore, the cattle industry linked the two principal
economic activities of the colony: the production of sugar
and gold. The cattlemen circulated freely between the sugar
and gold producers, selling to one or to the other or to both.
The most obvious physical link between the regional economies of the Northeast and the Southeast, which is to say
between sugar and gold, was the São Francisco River. It flows
south to north, from the goldfields to the sugar lands. Its
valley was also one of the centers of the cattle culture from
which cattle moved north or south with equal ease. The gold
mining industry with its heavy demands and enticing payments for food hastened the development of that valley. By
the early eighteenth century, it was so well settled that a
traveler easily passed along its entire 1,500-mile course by
going from house to house, never over a day's journey apart.
The demands of the miners also gave impetus to cattle and
mule raising in the South. For generations those animals had
fetched minimal prices, but after 1695 prices rose spectacu-

larly. Drives northward became regular events. During the eighteenth century at the fair of Sorocaba in São Paulo over 200,000 head of cattle from the South were sold biannually. The plodding hooves of thousands of cattle and mules broke down the barriers between the far South and the rest of Brazil to facilitate its integration into the colony.

Cattle ranches varied in size. None, of course, were small, but some reached staggering proportions. The vast ranch of Diaz d'Avila by all accounts surpassed most European states in size. Established in the late sixteenth century in northern Bahia, it centered on the São Francisco and extended endlessly into the sertão. The first step in starting a ranch was to build a house for the rancher and corrals to break the cattle and keep them tame. Around the rancher's house gardens were laid out, and fields were cultivated to provide food for the owner, his cowboys, and his other workers. When necessary, the rancher ordered the burning of trees, bushes, or other growth to create pastures for the cattle. Not even the smallest ranch began with less than two hundred or three hundred head of cattle. The rancher strove to keep a herd of between one thousand and two thousand cattle. In addition, he needed horses to help round up the cattle and for the drives. A small ranch could get by with twenty-five or thirty horses, but a well-run ranch required between fifty and sixty.

The ranches for the most part maintained the neofeudalistic atmosphere characteristic of the coastal plantations. The owners when at all prosperous had the power, prestige, and wealth to qualify for the ranks of the colonial aristocracy. Even more isolated from the centers of colonial government than their coastal plantation counterparts, they more often than not exercised complete authority over their subordinates. Still, in direct contrast to the coastal owners, the cattlemen could and often did provide some variance from the more rigid hierarchical system characteristic of the sugar industry. Some scholars choose to emphasize certain democratic features at work or latent in cattle raising. It would seem that often the ranch owners were closer to their workers, who were relatively few in number, and on occasion even worked right along with them, sharing the monotony of the

long drive, the hazards of branding the cattle, and the limited diet of meat and milk (or maté in the South). Slavery was not a widespread institution in the cattlelands. As a means of payment to his vaqueiros, the rancher customarily shared the newborn calves with them. Every four or five years the cowboys were entitled to take one out of every four newly born calves. In that way it was possible for the ambitious vaqueiro to start his own herd. Since the industry required little investment—no special equipment or machinery, no barns, no silos—some of the cowboys were able to move into the entrepreneurial class. Thus from one point of view a certain—if in practice limited—social and economic mobility was more evident in the cattle industry than in any other of the colony's economic activities.

The cattle industry was far more important in the long run than the short. It provided essential support for other economic sectors but contributed only slightly to colonial exports. The Brazilians exported no fresh meat; they exported hides as wrappers for tobacco or maté as well as in consignments to European shoemakers. Income from those exports was insignificant in comparison with income from sugar, gold, cotton, and tobacco exports.

Despite wide fluctuations, the Brazilian economy grew and its trade expanded. Belém, São Luís, Recife, Bahia, and Rio de Janeiro—particularly the last three—were the principal ports through which passed increasing amounts of goods. Direct trade with Africa flourished, and coastal trade thrived. The excellent port of Salvador illustrated the bustling colonial commerce. By the close of the eighteenth century, well-plied routes radiated from Salvador to Europe and Africa and along the nearly four thousand-mile coast. An average of fifty ships a year crossed between Salvador and Oporto and Lisbon, bringing European and Asian manufactured goods, wine, flour, codfish, butter, cheese, and salt to Brazil, and carrying sugar, spirits, cotton, tobacco, coffee, woods, gums, balsams, and medicinal roots to the Old World. From Africa ships discharged slaves, wax, and gold dust in exchange for alcohol, tobacco, and coarse, printed textiles from Portugal. Small coastal trading vessels, averaging about 250 tons, filled the

harbor. Salvador traded extensively with the South, particularly the Plata region, sending sugar, rum, earthenware, and
European goods in exchange for silver, jerked beef, and hides.

Portugal proved to be tardy and relaxed in codifying its
imperial mercantile policy, which took shape as much by
chance as by design. It hoped to obtain from Brazil a variety
of products that could not be produced at home and to sell
the surpluses to other European nations. The object, of course,
was to maintain exports in excess of imports, the desired
"commercial balance." In all ways, Brazil was expected to be
a source of wealth to the metropolis. Royal officials looked
upon the colony as a great "milch cow," which could be
exploited for the benefit of the Crown, the metropolis, and—
not least of all—the bureaucrats sent to the New World. As
Governor Silva Gama of Rio Grande do Sul unabashedly expressed it, "Nothing interests me more than the fiscal matters
of the Royal Treasury. To save on expenses as much as possible, diligently to collect all moneys owing to the Crown
without undue harm to its subjects, and to devise new ways
of increasing its revenue are the objects of my constant zeal."
Most officials maintained that attitude throughout the colonial period: they sought to enrich the metropolis through
exploitation and taxation of the colony. Also, not a few of
them sought to earn their fortunes during their tropical exile
in order to return to Portugal and live well.

Portugal's mercantilist policies took a variety of forms
over the centuries. One method, employed in an effort to
monopolize all Brazilian trade, was the convoy system. This
provided for annual fleets, protected by men-of-war, to and
from Brazil. However, the highly decentralized Portuguese
trade patterns—so unlike those of its Iberian neighbor—and
a shortage of both merchant ships and war ships reduced that
effort to a few halfhearted attempts made sporadically over
two-and-a-half centuries. In practice, foreigners blatantly
conducted a profitable contraband trade with Brazil. The economic companies, inspired by the Dutch and English India
companies, fared little better than the convoy system.

The government made various attempts to control the
economy. Monopolies flourished. Trade in Brazilwood, salt,

tobacco, diamonds, to mention a few commodities, felt at one time or another the hand of monopolistic bureaucracy. Taxes, many and varied, put special strains on the economy. There were the taxes on agricultural and pastoral products, known as the *dízimo,* or tithe, and the *quinto,* or fifth, levied on mineral products. Until the middle of the seventeenth century, the major source of income for the Crown was the tithe on sugar. After the discovery of gold, the *quinto* became the single major contributor to the treasury. The Crown taxed both the internal and the external commerce of its colony. Customs houses in the principal ports collected the duty on overseas trade. Stations at the most important river crossings and along the most frequented roads exacted tolls and taxed internal trade. The *entradas,* duties on merchandise, slaves, and cattle entering Minas Gerais, exemplified a special type of tax exacted by the royal government. The Brazilians paid a series of excise taxes on both locally produced and imported products classified as luxuries, such as wines, tobacco, and salt. A variety of legal fees, quitrents on Crown property, and "voluntary contributions" further enriched the royal coffers. Indeed, the complete list of taxes, duties, and fees would be a long one. One foreign observer remarked in 1809 "Taxes are laid where they fall heavy upon the lower classes, and none are levied where they could well be borne." The Crown did not always collect those taxes itself. Instead, it often used the Roman system of tax-farming and awarded a monopoly contract for a stipulated period, usually three years, in exchange for a fixed payment to the royal treasury.

Fearful that the colony might relax its efforts to produce the raw products most in demand in Europe, the royal officials kept a sharp eye peeled for unnecessary diversification of the economy. In the best mercantilistic manner, Portugal did not allow Brazil to produce anything that Portugal already produced or could furnish. With the exception of shipbuilding and sugar processing, the Crown disapproved of any manufacturing in Brazil. On the other hand, the Crown occasionally encouraged the production of new crops that would find a ready market in the metropolis or Europe. Though meeting with frequent frustrations, the Marquês de Lavradio,

viceroy from 1769 to 1779, diversified the economy slightly by promoting the production of indigo, rice, and wheat. Lack of imagination on the part of the Crown, the merchants (both in Portugal and America), and the local farmers probably did more to hinder economic diversification and growth than did stern mercantile decrees.

The Portuguese official who did most to codify and implement mercantilist policy was Pombal. He fully realized that Portugal's prosperity depended on the well-being of Brazil. A Brazil flourishing economically would provide a sound basis for Portugal's felicity. Under Physiocrat influence, he thought to survey scientifically the potential of Brazil as the basis for more exploitation. He hoped to strengthen, even diversify the economy.

The Brazilians did not docilely accept all the burdensome restrictions placed on them, and their protests reached Lisbon regularly. In particular, the municipal council chambers echoed with stormy debates, the results of which crossed the ocean as pleas or petitions to the monarch for one or another change. As the nineteenth century opened, educated *mazombos* wrote eloquent appeals for a modification of the mercantilist policy. The Brazilians also took action. A number of economic conflicts erupted into riots or rebellions that rent the otherwise tranquil air of the colony.

Minas Gerais was a hotbed of disturbances in the eighteenth century. As the mining rush got under way, the Paulistas with their Indian slaves resented the arrival of the Portuguese and coastal prospectors with their African slaves. The Paulistas regarded the "foreigners" or "outsiders" as interlopers on their gold claims and derisively referred to all of them as *"emboabas."* Rivalry between the leaders of the two factions erupted in late 1708 into open warfare, which ended with the defeat of the Paulistas the following year. Trouble simmered in the mining region, and in 1720 a popular rebellion against improved methods of tax collection broke out under the leadership of Felipe dos Santos. The colonial government quickly repressed it. The mundane subject of delinquent taxes and rumors of attempts to collect them sparked some romantic poets of Minas Gerais, in alliance with a few

planters, merchants, and clergymen, to plot in the name of independence. The plans came to naught in 1789 when the *Inconfidência*, as it has since been known in history, was revealed to the governor, who took swift action. The subsequent execution of the leader, Joaquim José da Silva Xavier, more picturesquely known by an epithet describing his profession as *Tirandentes*, "the Toothpuller," created a martyr for Brazilian independence.

Meanwhile, in the Northeast, the rural aristocracy with its seat in Olinda felt challenged by the nearby growing commercial center of Recife, a bustling port of some eight thousand inhabitants by the beginning of the eighteenth century. Most of the merchant class was Portuguese and more often than not those *mascates* (a pejorative term meaning "peddlers" that the Brazilians liberally employed) held the planters in debt. One contemporary anonymous writer complained, "They [the merchants] try only to get as much profit as possible in order to enrich themselves no matter what the cost to others, and they do not hesitate to extend credit one year to the planters so that the next they can demand all the income and profits of the sugar mills." The planters consequently resented the power of the merchants, accusing them of seeking "to destroy all that is noble." They sought to save themselves through direct trade with English and Dutch ships, a commercial activity forbidden by Portuguese mercantilist policy, and naturally opposed by the *mascates*. When the king elevated Recife to the rank of a city in 1710 and thus freed it from the political control of Olinda, the planters reacted by attacking and capturing the port. The following year the *mascates* rebelled against the forceful rule of the sugar aristocracy. A new governor dispatched from Lisbon to Pernambuco settled the War of the Mascates at the end of 1711 with a generous pardon for everyone. The sharp division between the Brazilian sugar aristocracy and the immigrant Portuguese commercial bourgeoisie lingered for nearly two centuries and precipitated periodical rural-urban clashes. The *mascates* served as a constant catalyst. At first they gave rise to or strengthened Brazilian nativism, later Brazilian nationalism. Indeed, even as early as the 1710–1711 disturbance, some

planters in their hostile reaction to the outsiders mentioned vaguely the possibility of creating some independent republic modeled on that of Venice.

Economic stagnation in the last third of the eighteenth century intensified the discontent already prevalent in Brazil. Exports declined. The gold fields had been exhausted and Portuguese technology was not sufficient to exploit the lodes which lay more deeply buried. Sugar sales were slow. Income declined. The only relief—temporary as it might have been— was provided by events far from Brazil over which it had neither control nor influence. The revolt of England's thirteen North American colonies disrupted customary trade between Europe and North America, providing Brazil, particularly Maranhão, the opportunity to sell rice and cotton in European markets usually dominated by North America. The slave revolt in Haiti beginning in 1791 destroyed the source of much of Europe's sugar supply. The amount and value of Brazil's sugar exports grew proportionately. But this sort of temporary recovery and prosperity simply underlined the vulnerability of Brazil's economy. Brazil enjoyed another period of prosperity before lapsing back into decline and lethargy in its never-ending cycle of sharp economic fluctuations exacerbated by export dependency.

Upon reviewing colonial Brazil's economy, two major and depressing conclusions emerge. On the one hand, colonial Brazil's economy fostered internal social inequity; on the other, it was a victim of external policies which implanted and nurtured dependency. The plantation economy required substantial wealth or access to capital. Thus, only a few could participate in and benefit from it, that is, the privileged with funds to invest. After receiving their *sesmarias*, they bought African slaves or recruited labor from the ranks of the poor and unskilled. They invested in sugar mills, warehouses, processing equipment, or whatever the plantation required to make it productive and profitable. The predominance of such a plantation economy accentuated the social, economic, and political differences between masters and slaves, patriarchs and laborers, and perpetuated class distinctions to the extent of creating caste implications. Very few could aspire to up-

ward mobility. The slaves and hired hands could hardly hope to become plantation owners, since even if they might acquire land the cost outlay for equipment was prohibitive. More likely, subsistence farming was the only option open to the manumitted blacks and free laborers—they could escape the labor control mechanisms. Peasants and small farmers did exist—they certainly contributed to the local and regional economies—but they rarely crossed the lines that separated them from the planters who enjoyed wealth, preferment, and power. The great gap between the privileged few and the huge humble majority was a fact of life in colonial Brazil that transcended economics and had profound social and political consequences as well.

Dependency meant that the Brazilian economic well-being, or lack of it, resulted from the consequences of decisions made far distant from South America, more often than not in Lisbon but increasingly in London as the Portuguese themselves became more dependent on the English. The dynamic sector of the Brazilian economy was exports and was thus subject to the fluctuations of European markets over which the Brazilians exercised no control. The emphasis on a single export increased Brazil's economic vulnerability and multiplied the effects of capricious demand and/or of successful competition. The structures and dynamics of the Portuguese empire worked to the economic detriment of Brazil by imposing insidious patterns of economic dependency. The cycle of market flunctuations was but one obvious symptom of that dependency. Pervasive poverty was another.

As a colony, Brazil also depended politically on Lisbon. The monarchs imposed institutions of political control that reflected Portuguese needs, European experiences, and imperial goals. Brazil constituted only one portion, albeit an immense one, of the global Portuguese empire. For three centuries, the New World colony evolved within that larger framework in which the various components interacted. Portuguese America inherited many practices perfected elsewhere in the empire and, likewise, it contributed to the development of other parts of the empire; in particular it was closely associated with Angola. Before the end of the six-

teenth century, Brazil emerged as Portugal's most valuable overseas possession. The mounting sugar profits and the subsequent discovery of gold confirmed its primary position. Still, until the royal house of Braganza moved its court from Lisbon to Rio de Janeiro in 1807, no special laws or institutions governed Brazil to distinguish it as a separate, distinct, or privileged entity within the larger empire.

In reviewing colonial Brazil's political evolution—the process of continuous advance from a simple to a complex political subordinate—over the course of three centuries, one finds that two general characteristics stand out. First, governmental control over Brazil grew stronger throughout the period, even though that process was erratic at times. By the advent of the nineteenth century, the king, his viceroy, and his governors exercised more power more effectively than at any previous time. Second, the political status of Brazil slowly improved throughout the course of three centuries. A central government under a governor-general, the personal representative of the king, began to exercise a modicum of authority in 1549 and brought some order and justice to the unhappy and generally ineffective rule of the donees in the captaincies. In 1646 the monarch elevated Brazil to the status of a principality, and thereafter the heir to the throne was known as the Prince of Brazil. After 1720 all the chiefs of government of Brazil bore the title "Viceroy." Finally, Prince-Regent João raised Brazil to the status of a kingdom in 1815, thus, at least in theory, putting it on an equal footing with Portugal within a politically absolutist empire.

The concept of government prevalent during the centuries when Portugal possessed Brazil differed markedly from that of our own time. An astute student of the Brazilian past, Caio Prado, referred to the Portuguese government as "an undivided whole." By this he meant that few of the subtleties of political science with which we must reckon today had yet come into being. There was neither division of power, nor any distinctions between branches of government. Church and state were practically one. All power rested in the hands of the monarch, who was the state. He made, interpreted, and executed the laws. On the one hand, he formulated the

general concepts that governed the empire, and on the other he decreed a staggering array of minutely detailed laws. He protected and governed the Church within his vast domains. Indeed, he ruled by divine right. The one overpowering constant, then, in imperial government was the monarch. The houses of Burgundy and Aviz centralized and strengthened royal power at the expense of the nobility and the Church. The Braganzas, heirs to that trend and witnesses to the example set by the neighboring Hapsburgs, exercised their jurisdiction and prerogatives as the supreme heads of the empire. Clearly the monarch was the unquestioned authority from which all power emanated. He spoke the final word. (Before Brazilian independence only one woman had ruled: Queen Maria I. In 1777, in the absence of a male heir, she ascended the throne and remained monarch, despite her later dementia, until her death in Rio de Janeiro in 1816.)

The rule of a vast and widespread empire, however, required administrative assistance, and over the centuries a number of governmental organs emerged to fill that need. For a long time those bodies handled both metropolitan and overseas matters in much the same way, without distinguishing between the two. The Portuguese law codes were the Ordenações Afonsinas, 1486–1514; the Ordenações Manuelinas, 1514–1603; and the Código Filipino of 1603—in full use in Brazil until 1823, and in partial use until 1917, when the Brazilian Civil Code was enacted. Though frequently amended and supplemented, they uniformly governed the entire empire regardless of their applicability. The monarch viewed sophistically—or, one might argue, naively—the unity of the Portuguese empire. Scattered and varied it might have been, but uniformity persisted. To an impressive degree the same officials moved uninhibitedly from one continent to another, thereby contributing to the unity, uniformity, and universality of the empire.

Naturally, as the empire expanded some administrative specialization had to develop; only then did home and overseas affairs occasionally fall to bureaus treating specifically one or the other. Still, the Crown never authorized a special body to handle Brazilian matters exclusively. Only in some

tax and Indian matters did the South American colony ever receive the individual attention its wealth and importance merited. Local administrators did become adept, however, in adapting the general imperial codes and fiats to suit the local scene. They had to. The third governor-general, Mem de Sá, remarked to the king, "This land ought not and cannot be ruled by the laws and customs of Portugal; if Your Highness was not quick to pardon it would be difficult to colonize Brazil." Such extralegal liberties were tolerated because of the great distance separating king and colony and, not infrequently, because of absolute necessity.

For about two centuries, colonial (and, therefore, Brazilian) affairs were handled through a royal secretary or a secretary of state who, after 1736, bore the title "Minister of Navy and Overseas." Men of this rank, selected because of loyal and often meritorious service, enjoyed unqualified royal confidence. They had direct access to the monarch's ear and were, of course, accountable only to him. They were assisted, in turn, by a variety of administrative organs that, in the practice of the age, excercised a mélange of consultative, executive, judicial, and fiscal functions. One of the most important of those bodies was the Overseas Council (*Conselho Ultramarino*), created by João IV in 1642. It was the evolutionary result of considerable experience, numbering among its distinguished predecessors the India Board (*Casa da India*) and the Council for India and Overseas Conquests (*Conselho da India e Conquistas Ultramarinas*). The latter, established in 1604, was particularly significant in Portuguese administrative history, because it separated for the first time the administration of overseas affairs from those of the metropolis. The president, secretary, and the three councillors of the Overseas Council usually had served in the colonies, and during its history its members included many who had resided in Brazil. The Council divided itself into standing committees to treat various military, administrative, judicial, and ecclesiastical matters. Its primary duty, however, was to advise the king. It showed greater concern with commercial matters than its predecessors, and its authority in such matters grew accordingly.

Other governmental organs continued to have dual metropolitan and colonial responsibilities. For example, the Treasury Council (*Conselho da Fazenda*), created in 1591 to replace the Treasury Supervisors (*Vedores da Fazenda*), administered public finances and the treasury; the Board of Conscience and Religious Orders (*Mesa da Consciência e Ordens*), established in 1532 by João III, advised the Crown on ecclesiastical and Indian matters; finally, the *Casa da Suplicação* served as a supreme court for many colonial judicial disputes. Together these bodies formed the principal bureaucratic apparatus that enabled the monarch to rule the scattered overseas domains.

In Brazil, representatives of the Crown administered that colony. At the apex stood the viceroy, "the shadow of the king." When it became evident that the donatory system was failing, the king dispatched a governor-general to centralize control of the colony. In particular, he saw to it that all taxes were properly collected, that the king's justice was enforced, and that the colony was militarily prepared to repel interlopers. Those governors-general were effective officials, or not, largely in proportion to their personal strengths and weaknesses. Those who were vigorous dominated the colony. Those who were weak found themselves almost unable to control the capital city, their powers eroded by ambitious bishops, captains-general, municipal councils, and important court justices. Between 1640 and 1718, three of the chiefs of state of Brazil, because of their high noble rank, bore the title "Viceroy." After 1720, all bore that title; by then their duties were more or less well defined by custom and law. In theory—and one must continually emphasize the frequent variance in these matters between theory and practice—the viceroys of the eighteenth century as a group were stronger and more effective administrators than their predecessors, with, of course, exceptions. Outstanding were the Conde de Sabugosa (1720–1735), the Marquês de Lavradio (1769–1779), and Luís de Vasconcelos e Sousa (1779–1790). The king's chief representative in Brazil served for an average term of six and one-half years in the sixteenth century, of three and one-half years in the seventeenth century, and of slightly less than six

years in the eighteenth century. Most were professional soldiers and members of the nobility.

The central government was located in Salvador da Bahia until 1763. By the early eighteenth century the capital boasted of a population of over one hundred thousand, making it, after Lisbon, the second city of the empire. The presence of the viceregal government, as well as the capital's location midway along the Brazilian coast and confronting Africa, lent considerable military importance to Salvador. The government dispatched soldiers from Salvador to replenish garrisons as far away as Colônia do Sacramento, or even Africa and Asia. Also, the city was the residence of the only archbishop in Portuguese America. The capital, furthermore, was a bustling port, the entrepôt of trade with Africa and Europe. Majestically situated on the ample All Saints Bay, Salvador stood on two levels: pressed between the bay and a sharp escarpment were the docks, warehouses, shipyards, and business houses; high above, crowning the escarpment, were the governmental offices, homes of the wealthy, and some of the finest religious buildings in the Western Hemisphere. Two immense public plazas graced the upper city. Surrounding one were the impressive Viceregal Palace, the Treasury, the building housing the municipal council (and the jail), and the High Court. The magnificent College of the Jesuits dominated the other plaza.

For military and economic reasons, in 1763 the Crown moved the seat of the viceroyalty from Salvador to Rio de Janeiro, another excellent and bustling port. An important vertex in the triangular South American–European–African trade and a staging point for contraband commerce in the Plata, Rio throbbed with activity. The Southeast had acquired new economic importance because of both mineral and agricultural exploitation. Rio de Janeiro afforded the viceroy closer scrutiny over the vital routes to and from the gold lodes of Minas Gerais. At the same time the economic importance of the Northeast diminished. Furthermore, after the Treaty of Taborda in 1654, foreign threats to the Northeast ended. (Thereafter it was the West Indies that attracted the attention

of the European maritime powers.) Portugal faced a new challenge in the far south of Brazil. Increasing tension with Spain after the founding of the Colônia do Sacramento in 1680 necessitated greater attention to and protection of claims in the Platine region. Rio de Janeiro was chosen to be the new capital, then, because in the eighteenth century it was geographically closer to this military threat, as well as to the economic activities of the colony. The city had been growing steadily, and the discovery of gold in the hinterlands and the arrival of the viceregal court accelerated that growth. It, too, could boast of imposing civil and religious architecture. Rio de Janeiro became a focal point for colonial wealth where a small, affluent class lived comfortably.

The governors-general and viceroys depended on a growing bureaucracy to carry out their primary functions of administering the colony, overseeing its military preparedness, dispensing the king's justice, and enforcing the taxes. Of greatest importance was the High Court (*Relação*), first established in Bahia in 1609 under the presidency of the governor-general. A second Relacão was established in Rio de Janeiro in 1752. Those courts primarily functioned as the highest law tribunals in Brazil from which there was limited appeal to the Casa da Suplicação in Lisbon. They also reviewed the conduct of all officials at the end of their terms at office and conducted whatever other investigations might be required. Secondarily they served as consultative and administrative organs. When the governor-general absented himself from the capital, the highest member of the court, the chancellor, usually governed in his place. The governor-general often requested the advice of the legally trained judges on a host of judicial and administrative matters. The magistrates who served in Brazil, at least between 1609 and 1759, were highly trained professionals who came from socially middle-rank groups. Between 1653 and 1753, at least ten Brazilian-born magistrates served on the Relação. Like other imperial officials, the magistrates served throughout the vast empire, and there existed a notable exchange of them between West Africa and Brazil. The Relação bore a certain resemblance to the

Audiencias of New Spain. Tax matters and the supervision of the treasury fell to the responsibility of another bureau, the Board of Revenue (*Junta da Fazenda*).

The government of the state of Maranhão was similar to that of the state of Brazil, only seemingly less well defined. Nor did the northern state develop the strength of the southern one. It depended even more heavily upon Lisbon. The king appointed a governor-general and a chief justice (ouvidor-mor). A slow growth and a scanty population negated the need for a high court, and none was authorized for Maranhào. In 1737, the capital was transferred from São Luís to Belém, an increasingly active port that for some time had been the effective center of the state. In recognition of the growing importance of the Amazon, in 1755 the king created the captaincy of São José do Rio Negro (the present-day Amazonas), subordinate to the captaincy of Pará. The newly founded town of Barcelos, several hundred miles up the Rio Negro, became the first capital of the subordinate captaincy.

Captaincies were the principal terriorial subdivisions of the two states. But the Crown regretted entrusting its New World territories to donees. In 1548, starting with Bahia, the monarch set out to reabsorb those hereditary captaincies, giving them the name of royal captaincies. That process was slow and erratic. Some the Crown purchased back from their owners; others it simply took over when they were abandoned or left without heirs. Yet at other times, reversing its own policies (as so often happened), it awarded new captaincies to private individuals, hoping thus to encourage settlement of distant or neglected regions. Thus policies alternated in a confusing manner over a period of two centuries. At the opening of the seventeenth century, eleven hereditary captaincies existed; ten new ones, five in each state, were created during that century. By the end of the seventeenth century the states of Brazil and Maranhão contained six each.

As representatives and appointees of the king, the governors and captains-general of the principal captaincies—and the governors or captains-major of the subordinate captaincies—carried out the same responsibilities on a regional scale that the governor-general or the viceroy carried out on the

colonial scale. The governor-general was to coordinate, harmonize, and oversee their efforts. Here, as in so many instances, theory and practice diverged. Distance, intrigues, the varying effectiveness of personalities, and the vagueness of the law often meant that the governor-general, and later the viceroy, exercised little authority over the various governors of the captaincies. In times of crisis, particularly those engendered by the fear of a foreign attack on a coastal city or of Spanish expansion in the South, the military authority of the governor-general or viceroy increased. His martial powers may well have been his strongest. Of course aggressive and assertive executives succeeded in extending their authority much further than their more reticent predecessors. In truth, the governor-general and his successor, the viceroy, never exercised the same degree of control or authority as did their counterparts in New Spain. For that matter, in remote corners of Brazil, the captain-general, governor-general, and king all seemed equally removed and theoretical. Considering the size of the colony, the scant number of small, scattered garrisons with a handful of soldiers, and the few royal officials (almost all of whom resided in a half-dozen coastal cities), the extent of metropolitan control over the colony was remarkable. The Crown maintained its authority and control principally through the power of legitimacy. The Brazilians accepted the system, seldom questioned it, and rarely challenged it. When they did question or challenge the system prior to the end of the eighteenth century, they quickly acceded to the forceful imposition of the royal will.

Royal control increased during the eighteenth century. The absolutist tendencies noticeable during the long reign of João V (1706–1750) found their instrument of perfection in the person of the Marquês de Pombal, who ruled through the weak José I from 1750 to 1777. Portuguese historians contradict one another in their treatment of that powerful prime minister, some praising him as a savior and others damning him as a madman. Brazilian historians have treated him more consistently. They gratefully acknowledge the contributions he made, indirect as some of them might be, to the formation of their country.

An ardent nationalist, Pombal hoped to strengthen his economically moribund country through better and fuller utilization of its colonies, the foremost of which unquestionably was Brazil. To better exploit Portuguese America, he sought to further centralize and standardize its government. He abolished the state of Maranhão in 1772 and incorporated it into the state of Brazil, creating for the first time, at least in theory, a single, unified Portuguese colony in the New World. After the unification of the two states, Pombal encouraged trade between them so that commerce would further cement political integration. Actually the paths the *bandeirantes* trod through the interior did more to further trade and communication between the areas than did the infrequent and tardy coastal communications. No matter how imperfect the union between the two might have been, it set the psychological tone that helped ensure the future unity of the empire of Brazil. An impatient enemy of the hereditary captaincies, the prime minister dissolved the remaining ones and brought them under direct royal control, with the minor exception of Itanhaém, a small private captaincy in the South which lasted until 1791. As a consequence, Brazil in 1800 consisted of the following principal captaincies: Grão Pará Maranhão, Ceará, Paraíba, Pernambuco, Bahia, Minas Gerais, Goiás, Mato Grosso, Rio de Janeiro, and São Paulo; and the following subordinate captaincies: São José do Rio Negro (Amazonas), Piauí, Rio Grande do Norte, Espírito Santo, Santa Catarina, and Rio Grande de São Pedro (Rio Grande do Sul).

As a further measure to fortify royal authority, Pombal expelled the Company of Jesus from the empire. He had long harbored suspicions that the Jesuits plotted against him and accused that powerful order of challenging the secular government. (Injudiciously they had criticized some of his economic schemes.) An attempt on the king's life provided him with the opportunity he sought to drive the "Black Robes" from the realm. In 1759, he ordered approximately six hundred of them to leave Brazil. Until that time, they had run most of the best schools in Brazil, and colonial education suffered severely after their expulsion. Furthermore, many Indian vil-

lages were left unadministered. This situation enabled Pombal to strengthen the government's hand in both education and the care of the Indians. For good or bad, he ended the isolation enforced upon them by the Jesuit villages. By requiring the Indians to speak Portuguese, dress like Europeans, and adopt useful trades and crafts, and by encouraging whites to intermarry with them he attempted to bring them within the Luso-Brazilian community. Many of his ideas were highly impractical. Yet by bridging some of the separation between the Indian and Luso-Brazilian communities he further unified the colony and modified one of the major differences between the North and the rest of Brazil. The *aldeia* system, however, by no means disappeared. In 1809, Henry Koster wrote about several *aldeias* he knew of in Ceará, one of which he visited and inspected. A priest lived in the former residence of the Jesuits and attended to the spiritual life of the Indians, while a white director oversaw their secular life. Koster noted, "If a proprietor of land is in want of workmen he applies to the director, who agrees for the price at which the daily labor is to be paid, and he commands one of his chief Indians to take so many men, and proceed with them to the estate for which they are hired. The laborers receive the money themselves, and expend it as they please; but the bargains thus made are usually below the regular price of labor." Even the power of Pombal could not eliminate all the exploitation of the Indians.

Pombal hoped to settle the boundaries with Spanish America. He favored the principle of *uti possidetis*. Because the Treaty of Madrid violated that principle in the Plata, he worked to annul it; this he accomplished in the Treaty of El Pardo in 1761. Brazilians, of course, have always appreciated Pombal's support of their maximum boundary claims, but their interests concerned the Marquês not at all. His interest in a larger Brazil lay in his hope for a richer Brazil, hence a more prosperous Portugal. Always, of course, it would be a Brazil subservient to the mother country. For that reason he tried to restrict the independence of the municipal governments but, although it is true that those local governments

exercised less freedom than they had in their heyday, the seventeenth century, they still continued to be active and important nuclei of local politics.

The municipal government was the one with which most Brazilians came into contact and the only one in which they participated to any degree. Governing much more than the town and its environs, each municipality extended to meet the boundaries of the next. In sparsely settled Brazil, the municipalities contained hundreds, often thousands, of square miles. European countries seemed dwarfs compared to some of those municipal giants.

The most important institution of local government was the *senado da câmara*, the municipal council. A restricted suffrage of the *homens bons*, which is to say the propertied class, elected two justices of the peace, three aldermen, and a procurator to office every three years. The presiding officer was a *juiz ordinário* (ordinary judge) if elected by the other councilmen, or a *juiz-de-fora* (outside judge) if sent by the Crown. By the end of the seventeenth century, the Crown was appointing a presiding officer in the most important towns and cities. The duties of the council varied. Meeting twice weekly, it meted out local justice, handled routine municipal business and local administration, and passed the necessary laws and regulations. The procurator executed those laws. In cooperation with the Church, the *senado* helped to oversee local charities. The municipality enjoyed its own sources of income: rents from city property, license fees for tradesmen, taxes on certain foodstuffs, charges for diverse services such as the verification of weights and measures, and fines.

Unlike their Spanish American counterpart, the *cabildo*, the *senados* exercised considerable independent power. Even after the king's *juizes* became presidents of the major *senados* and even after more limitations were placed on the final selection of the council members, they continued to display a remarkable independence. The *senado* of São Luís during the seventeenth century was particularly ambitious. So often did it summon the governor to appear before it that the king in 1677 ordered it to desist forthwith, reminding the councillors that the governor represented the Crown and could not

be ordered around. To protect their interest, the larger cities maintained a representative at the court in Lisbon as a sort of lobbyist.

As Brazil's foremost historian of the colonial period, João Capistrano de Abreu, has pointed out, the *senado* frequently served as an arena—the first one—for the struggles between the *mazombos,* the whites born in Brazil, and the *renóis,* the whites born in Portugal. The Portuguese officials, occupying all levels of government except the municipal, enforced the universal law of the empire. Their point of view was global. They saw Brazil as one part of a larger empire which existed for the grandeur of Portugal. The *mazombos* sitting on the municipal councils cared only for the local scene; their vision was restricted. It was, in short, Brazilian. They wanted to enforce those aspects of the laws beneficial to them, to their community, and, to a lesser extent, to Brazil. Those different perspectives gave rise to repeated clashes in which the *mazombos* did not always give ground to the *renóis.* In the seventeenth century, the *senados* repeatedly expelled Jesuits, judges, and even governors whom they considered unpopular or unsympathetic to local causes or situations.

One of the bitterest struggles was over the Indians. The *senados* of Belém, São Luís, Rio de Janeiro, and São Paulo, to mention only the most vitriolic, were locked in battle for decades with crown officials over the Indian question. The crown officials in alliance with the Jesuits attempted to enforce the altruistic policies of Lisbon. The *senados,* representatives of the local landed class, refused to surrender their native slaves. They succeeded in persuading the king to modify his policies. In that and myriad other matters they spoke out boldly in favor of local interests.

Furthermore the *senado* provided Brazilians with an opportunity to gain some governmental experience. During the first decades of colonization, qualified or even educated persons were rare, and often men of dubious reputation served on the *senado.* Later, the municipal government became the stronghold of the local aristocracy whose economic power lay in the land and whose political power in the *senado.* From those *senados* the landed gentry later rose directly to posi-

tions of national power. Membership in the *senados* was never self-perpetuating, here once again a contrast with the *cabildo*. In fact, the offices rotated rather freely among the *homens bons*. More than that, eventually some of the *senados* included representatives of the working-class guilds. In Salvador, for example, between the mid-seventeenth century and the early eighteenth century, four *procuradores dos mestres* exercised voting rights in matters related to crafts, trades, and the economic life of their city. The king suppressed the people's representatives in the Salvador *senado* in 1713, after they had incited the masses to demonstrate against a price increase in salt and a suggested 10 percent tax on imported goods. The *senado* in that city reflected changing social patterns in the colony. João V in 1740 ordered that the names of prominent businessmen and merchants be included on the electoral roles for the posts of aldermen. He thus confirmed that the business and commercial class was well established and qualified to hold public office. Later, when Pombal reformed the government's fiscal system, he did not hesitate to hire his accountants and financial officials from the local business and commercial community. Those changes denoted a certain social mobility that permitted members of the petite bourgeoisie to transcend barriers and enter the more privileged classes.

In times of crisis, the *senado da câmara* amplified its membership to become a *conselho geral,* a general council. On those occasions, local military, judicial, and ecclesiastical authorites, as well as representatives of the people, met with the *senado* to discuss the emergency at hand. Such a meeting took place in Rio de Janeiro in 1641 after the governor of the captaincy, Salvador de Sá, received word of the Portuguese declaration of independence from Spain. The general council discussed whether to acknowledge João IV as the king of Portugal and decided affirmatively.

A second institution of local government deserves mention because of its significant influence on political behavior: the regional militias. To command the local militia, the principal figure of prestige and power—usually the largest landowner—held the rank of *capitão-mor,* equivalent to a colo-

nelcy. He easily integrated the military assignment and its prestige with his already considerable powers as the local patriarch. Clearly the two positions complemented each other. In the absence of regularly constituted governmental officials in the hinterlands, those *capitães-mor* performed a variety of administrative and even judicial tasks. Obviously it was to their own interest to enforce law and order in their region and they did so to the benefit of local tranquillity. Their power varied widely and, as in so many cases, depended mainly on their own abilities and strengths, since the distant government could do little to help or hinder them. They often became local *caudilhos,* the precursors of the local *coroneis* who played significant political roles in the post-independence period.

Such, in the most general terms, was the structure of government under which the inhabitants of Brazil lived during more than three centuries. On the one hand, the great distances and the slowness of communication and travel allowed for considerable local autonomy and many irregularities. Thus, in practice, the Crown could hope to dictate only the broad outlines of policy, leaving interpretation and implementation up to colonial and local officials. On the other hand, the Crown exercised a number of checks and controls to limit the degree of latitude permitted to overseas personnel. In theory, at any rate, all the laws were formulated in Lisbon and only needed enforcement overseas. The king sent to Brazil only officials of unquestioned loyalty. He suspected that, at best, life in the colony increased in everyone "the spirit of ambition and the relaxation of virtues." For a long time he refused to appoint any Brazilians to high colonial posts; never did he appoint many, because of his suspicion of their loyalty. Later the Crown relaxed its policy and permitted a number of Brazilians to become judges, governors, and to fill other high offices in Brazil, as well as in other parts of the empire and in the metropolis itself. Even more Brazilians received appointments to lesser posts in Portuguese America.

Since so many officials—the viceroy, governors, bishops, treasury officials, etc.—had direct access to royal ears, considerable reporting and "tattling" occurred, making all over-

seas personnel cautious. Furthermore, those officials could expect at any time a *devassa, visitação,* or *correição,* an on-the-spot investigation to which all subordinates could be subjected. At the end of all terms of office, each administrator could expect a *residência,* a judicial inquiry into his public behavior. All those checks required an immense amount of paperwork, an abundantly evident attribute of all Luso-Brazilian bureaucracy. The multitude of lawyers, scribes, and notaries in all the major cities testified to the fascination of the Iberian mind with legal and bureaucratic matters.

Stronger in organization and authority than governmental institutions were the patriarchal plantation families. Those large, cohesive family units appeared at the inception of the sugar industry, and they grew together. As early as the mid-sixteenth century, a few of those family groups, like that of Duarte Coelho, proprietor of Pernambuco, were evident. Later, as their number increased, they could be found in all the rural areas. The paterfamilias dominated the household and the plantation, ruling with unquestioned authority. He and the other males of the household, through their polygamous activities, liberally expanded the basic family unit to include hosts of mestizo and mulatto children, verifying again that it was in and around the plantation house that European, Indian, and African cultures blended together most perfectly to create a Brazilian civilization. The traditional godparent relationship (*compadrio*) further ramified and reinforced the enlarged family structure. Profoundly Christian and emphatically patriarchal, those family units set the social tone and pattern for the entire colony. The strongest of these families formed a landed aristocracy that dominated the *senados da câmara* in the colonial period and the newly independent national government in the imperial period.

By the close of the eighteenth century Brazil was widely, if thinly, settled. Growing at a rate approximated at 1.9 percent annually, the population at that time was approximately 2.3 million, with Minas Gerais, Bahia, Pernambuco, Rio de Janeiro, and São Paulo, in that order, the most populous captaincies. The majority lived along the coast or in the fertile river valleys. The trend of migration to the interior acceler-

ated by the discovery of gold had abated by this time, and in many cases reversed, with some return of the population to the coast. Obviously hollow frontiers still characterized the land settlement.

Five different regions of settlement existed. The far North, which included the vast Amazon valley, was scantily settled, a few villages dotting the river banks and coast. In the cattle-lands of the *sertão* stretching from Maranhão to Minas Gerais, the mestizos dominated. The dry land and light vegetation grudgingly supported cattle, some horses, and a few sheep and goats. Ranches and hamlets were scattered over that vast interior with no concentration of settlement. The lush sugar coast extending from Maranhão to São Vicente included excellent ports and the largest cities in Brazil; the Afro-Brazilians prevailed in that more concentrated settlement. The mining regions of Minas Gerais, Goiás, and Mato Grosso exported gold and diamonds but retained enough wealth to create a few prosperous towns. Livestock, sugarcane, and agriculture played secondary economic roles in the region. The far South boasted of excellent agricultural and pastoral lands. Immigrants, white Europeans from the Azores, settled the coastal region. Their small family farms grew grapes, wheat, and olives. In contrast, *bandeirante* types migrated overland from São Paulo to colonize the interior of the South. There one encountered patriarchal cattle ranches and profitable mule- and horse-raising businesses.

Chapter Three

Nation Building

By the close of the eighteenth century Brazil was formed territorially, although later some minor changes occurred. The Brazilians as a people, a racial composite of Europeans, Indians, and Africans, already existed. Indeed, certain basic types—the gaucho, *vaqueiro, tropeiro, bandeirante, senhor do engenho*—stood out. A distinct psychology characterized the Brazilians. Some Brazilians articulated a desire to alter their relationship with Portugal, a desire from which independence eventually sprang. The first half of the nineteenth century marked a period of somewhat leisurely political change, most notably the evolution from colony to nation, superimposed upon the remarkable continuity of economic and social structures whose foundations were deeply rooted in the colonial past.

Psychological and Intellectual Formation of Nationhood

During the second century of colonization, the Brazilians began for the first time to think of themselves and their surroundings in introspective terms. In 1618 Ambrósio Fernandes Brandão made the first attempt to define or interpret

Brazil in his *Diálogos das Grandezas do Brasil* (Dialogues of the Greatness of Brazil). In doing so, he exhibited his devotion to the colony, chiding those *renóis* who came to Brazil to exploit it and return wealthy to the Iberian peninsula. Less than a decade later, in 1627, the Franciscan friar Vicente do Salvador, a native Brazilian, wrote the first history of Brazil that boasted of the colony's favorable position, gigantic size, profitable sugar industry, and, above all else, its enormous potential. Setting the pattern for future self-examination, those two contributed intellectually to the incipient nativism that, a century later, would engulf the elite. The Bahian Jesuit João Antônio Andreoni, writing under the nom de plume André João Antonil, initiated the eighteenth-century glorification of Brazil with his florid but highly informative *Cultura e Opulência do Brasil* (Culture and Opulence of Brazil), published in 1711 in Lisbon. Royal authorities promptly suppressed it. They reasoned that the treatise revealed too much—both to prying foreign eyes and to the mounting native egos—for Antonil sang a hymn of praise to the wealth of Brazil. *Cultura e Opulência* contained much less defensive explanation than *Os Diálogos* and was far more boastful.

Against that background of increasing nativism, that pride in and devotion to local surroundings, the intellectual life of Brazil accelerated as the colony became more urbanized in the eighteenth century. Growing in number and population, the urban centers brought together diverse peoples, exposing them to wider varieties of experiences, life styles, and opinions. Such a milieu encouraged the introduction, discussion, and circulation of ideas, facilitated by the construction of a new secular intellectual infrastructure that permitted the intellectuals to contribute significantly to change in the colony and, eventually, to the declaration of Brazil's independence.

That intellectual infrastructure consisted of such formally organized institutions as academies, schools, and public libraries, and of less formal but equally significant ones such as private libraries, bookdealers, and literary gatherings. The formal and informal institutions interconnected frequently,

buttressing and strengthening each other. The same intellectuals participated in all of them.

The foundation stone of the intellectual infrastructure
rested on the various academies that sprang up and flourished briefly in Salvador and Rio de Janeiro throughout the
eighteenth century. Six of them can be identified: Academia
Brasílica dos Esquecidos (Salvador, 1724–1725), Academia dos
Felizes (Rio de Janeiro, 1736–1740), Academia dos Selectos
(Rio de Janeiro, 1751–1752), Academia Brasílica dos Renasci-
dos (Salvador, 1758–1760), Academia Scientífica (Rio de Janeiro, 1772–1779), and Sociedade Literária (Rio de Janeiro,
1786–1790, and 1794). The academies provided the perfect
forum to ventilate the thoughts wafted westward from Europe. With a baroque flourish, the academicians introduced
and discussed a wide variety of ideas in their sessions. Devoting much of their time to environmental and botanical studies, they emphasized improvement of agriculture and exploitation of the natural wealth of Brazil, thereby demonstrating
their endorsement of the European physiocrat doctrines gaining popularity in Portugal. In general the Brazilian academies,
like their counterparts throughout the Western world during
the eighteenth century, sought and examined the body of
practical knowledge that might promote people's fuller utilization of, and adaptation to, their surroundings. In doing so,
they came to more fully appreciate the potential wealth of
Brazil; by their high praise of that potential many of the
savants contributed significantly to a spirit of nativism that the
cities nourished. Indeed, in the speeches made and poems
recited in the academies, it is possible to trace the development of a new Brazilian mentality: a profound psychological
change from a feeling of inferiority to Europeans to one of
equality or even superiority. Libraries, educational reforms,
the *tertúlias literárias* (private literary salons), and—finally, in
1808—the tardy arrival of the printing press sharpened the
new mentality.

The flow of new ideas into Brazil increased as the intellectual infrastructure expanded. The input of new ideas and
the construction of the infrastructure buttressed each other.

The more ideas that entered, the stronger the infrastructure became; and as the infrastructure strengthened, it became easier for ideas to migrate. The progress of intellectual change from adherence to more traditional ideas to acceptance of much of the thought associated with the Enlightenment took place over generations. The slowness of the process was by no means peculiar to the Luso-Brazilians; it was rather a testimony to the fact that people are more creatures of habit and tradition than of innovation and change.

Obviously, in this process the intellectuals themselves figure predominantly. It is difficult to define them precisely. We use *intellectuals* in a general sense to refer to all the educated elite: teachers, doctors, lawyers, bureaucrats, some military officers, merchants, and priests—those who engaged in literary conversations, read European authors, exposed themselves to new ideas or methods emanating from Europe, and concerned themselves with the world around them. A tiny group, their importance lay not in their size but in their ability to articulate, and in their location. They lived in the cities, near the decision-making process. Their skills in expressing their ideas cogently in public oratory, in the classroom, in conversation, and, later, in books and newspapers made them influential. Unlike their counterparts before the eighteenth century, they were increasingly less associated with the church, more secular in origin and orientation; above all else, in their professed devotion to reason they were prone to question some of the ideas and institutions that their predecessors had not only accepted but defended.

At the very core of the intellectual elite were the university graduates, or in some cases the ablest graduates of seminaries, *colégios,* and military schools. Brazilian students who had studied in Coimbra (more than three thousand Brazilians received degrees from that Portuguese university during the colonial period), Montpellier, and a few other European universities, brought back with them the latest thoughts, as well as a common experience that unified them. Colonial officials regarded them as propagators of seditious ideas. Those graduates began the construction of the secular intellectual infrastructure; as it grew it recruited more diverse elements into

the intellectuals' ranks. The intellectuals appear a *group* when contrasted with the rest of the population, but among themselves they held diverse opinions and manifested different life styles. They became increasingly divorced from the traditional rural patrician class; of course they were not associated with the slaves or peasants who made up the vast majority of the population. They occupied, then, a middle position between the two extremes of Brazilian society. The intellectuals played a number of significant roles in the late colonial period by ushering new ideas into the country, creating a flattering image of Brazil that was the basis of nativism, and voicing in a cogent and often literary fashion some of the major complaints of the colonials. Likewise, they suggested and championed some major reforms in the imperial system.

The intellectuals of the period understood, perhaps better than anyone else, the conditions of Brazil. They also knew, either through reading, conversation, or travel, about other areas of the world, particularly western Europe, whose progress and achievements they admired, envied, and hoped to emulate. Partial toward the "progressive" countries, they freely drew ideas from them. The vast difference between reality (Brazil as it was) and desire (Brazil as they wished it were) frustrated them and heightened their advocacy of change. Indeed, by the beginning of the nineteenth century, the intellectuals and the commercial class—both urban groups—were the foremost partisans of innovation. A convincing case can be made that those two groups were fundamental in bringing about Brazil's nominal independence in 1822. They provided much of its leadership.

The increasing pride of the Brazilians in themselves and in their beautiful land was a major characteristic of the colony during the early nineteenth century. Whereas formerly the Brazilians had only compared their land to paradise, in 1819 Francisco de São Carlos published a long poem, *A Assumção*, in which he pictured paradise as remarkably similar to Brazil. The Brazilian deputies to the Portuguese Côrtes in 1822 voiced their nativistic pride repeatedly with a frankness that widened the gap between them and the Portuguese. As one deputy reminded the assembly, "There is not a Brazilian who does

not boast of the great resources of his land; there is not a Brazilian who is not proud of the potential which Brazil has to be one of the first nations of the universe." The resources and potential of Brazil provided the major themes of a vibrant nativism.

Growing pride in Brazil, coupled with a knowledge of the enlightened thinking of the eighteenth century, prompted the intellectuals to criticize those aspects of the Portuguese imperial system they believed inimical to Brazil's well-being. Criticism, after all, constitutes one of the principal activities of intellectuals. By later standards their criticism would seem mild; indeed, the majority of the intellectuals appear to be moderates. Hipólito da Costa repeatedly emphasized in his newspaper *Correio Braziliense* the need for reform, not revolution, an observation with which succeeding generations of intellectuals concurred. However, as moderate as the intellectuals were in their suggestions and aspirations, they proved to be instrumental, given the climate of opinion favoring change, in discrediting enough traditional ideas so that change, indeed, took place.

Scattered and oblique at first, the criticism did not become pronounced until the later decades of the eighteenth century. It intensified during the early years of the nineteenth century and, although directed at many targets, economic, political, and social, perhaps economic complaints have been most familiar to subsequent generations.

The *inconfidências* of Minas Gerais (1789), Rio de Janeiro (1794), Bahia (1798), and Pernambuco (1801) and the rebellion in Pernambuco (1817) expressed festering political grievances in dramatic form and somewhat more precise language. Unlike the critics before them, the participants in the *inconfidências* and the rebellion were specific: they decried the Portuguese imperial system as repressive, preferred republican to monarchical institutions, and in general subscribed to the political doctrines popular at the time in France and the United States. The extent of republican sentiment has never been adequately measured, and assessments of it range broadly.

In addition to political complaints, the intellectuals voiced frequent economic criticism, prompted in part by the eco-

nomic doldrums of the late eighteenth century. Bewilderment over the widespread poverty in Brazil in the midst of potential wealth was best expressed in the pertinent question of Luís dos Santos Vilhena, a Portuguese who lived for twelve years in Bahia: "Why is a country so fecund in natural products, so rich in essence, so vast in extent, still inhibited by such a small number of settlers, most of them poor, and many of them half-starved?" He laid the blame on slave labor, *latifundia,* and obsolete agricultural methods. In doing so, he castigated the fundamental economic institutions of colonial Brazil. His discussions of the need for greater economic freedom and reform, of "hunger," "shortages," and "poverty" were indications of the nature and severity of the crisis into which the imperial system had plunged.

From Lisbon, the Brazilian José Joaquim da Cunha de Azeredo Coutinho commented on the imperial economy in three essays. In the first, he argued that any governmental regulation of the price of sugar would thwart the natural economic order, harming not only Brazil but, in the long run, Portugal itself. The second essay, following both nativistic and physiocrat traditions, analyzed the rich resources and potential of Brazil and proceeded to recommend policies that would permit the best utilization of them. Azeredo Coutinho emphasized frequently the physiocrat doctrine that agriculture was the true source of wealth; gold, a false wealth, instead of enriching the empire had impoverished it. Greater liberty, he reasoned, would help Brazilians tap their potential wealth. He called specifically for the abolition of the salt monopoly and the restrictions on forest industries, the granting of permission to manufacture in Brazil, and the allowance of freer trade outside the empire. A third essay correctly attributed Brazil's economic distress to an overemphasis on mining and a consequent neglect of agriculture. He urged Luso-Brazilians to take advantage of the new European technology to increase their economic efficiency. In the depressed economy of the period, Brazilians were receptive to there new economic ideas.

The essays suggested some far-reaching adjustments in the Brazilian economy but did not imply that they should be instituted by means other than reform within the empire. Like

most of his contemporaries, he preached neither revolution nor independence. Undoubtedly the importance of his three essays lay in that, for the first time, a series of basic economic reforms highly desired by Brazilians had been classified and clarified. Azeredo Coutinho wanted them to be carried out within the empire, but when they were not forthcoming from Portugal, Brazilians came to realize that only by taking control of their own destiny could change come about. Hence, by indicating a path to economic reform, Azeredo Coutinho's essays had the unexpected effect of increasing the Brazilians' desire to be economic masters in their own houses.

A third aspect of the intellectuals' criticism focused on pressing social problems. Slavery aroused some concern, although few advocated the outright abolition of the institution. The Bahian conspirators of 1798 seem to have been the only ones to favor so dramatic a remedy. An impressive, albeit limited, criticism of the harsh treatment of the slaves appeared. The *Idade d'ouro*, published in the heartland of the slave system, editorialized on June 16, 1812, on the necessity of eventually ending the slave trade.

Many of the deputies representing Brazil in the Côrtes in 1822 expressed strong opinions against slavery. Notably effective in his efforts to protect the nonwhite from discrimination—as well as in his nativistic defense of the Brazilian "family"—Cipriano José Barata de Almeida, a deputy from Bahia, reaching an emotional apogee in his oration before the *Côrtes*, declared

Mulattos, *cabras,* and *crioulos;* Indians, *mamelucos,* and mestizos are all our people, they are Portuguese; they are honorable and valuable citizens. Throughout history they have proven their value to Brazil, defending it, working for its prosperity whether it be in agriculture, commerce, or the arts. Those races have provided great heroes. . . . They are Portuguese citizens, the sons of Portuguese or Brazilians, even if they are illegitimate. Whatever their color, whatever their status, they were born in Brazil.

Much to its credit, the Côrtes voted unanimously to extend the suffrage to all freemen.

The harsh treatment accorded the Indians awakened the social conscience of some intellectuals. José Bonifácio, for one, defended the remaining original inhabitants. The ode he published in 1820 testified to his social concern. Some observed that the Roman Catholic church had failed to help the Indians because it had neither properly "civilized" them nor integrated them into the colony. Criticism of the Church's missions, the Church's Indian policy, and even its "indolent clergy" appeared in print.

A long editorial commentary appearing in the *Idade d'ouro* on May 29, 1812, in many ways summed up the criticism of the Brazilian intellectuals. Labeling the Portuguese "inert," it said, "The three centuries since discovery have not been well employed to construct the strong foundation Brazil now needs." The editor counseled the building of roads and an increase in immigration in order to improve conditions in the colony. The newspaper thanked Prince-Regent Dom João for the salutary reforms he had instituted and intimated that they should be expanded.

The intellectuals suggested those reforms they felt would benefit Brazil. Implied in their criticism or accompanying it, as the discussion above indicates, was a program of reform, most of it based on ideas emanting from those few nations whose government, culture, and/or economic success they most admired.

At this juncture, it is tempting to oversimplify, to point to one current of criticism and one program of reform, and to show how the first intensified as the second gained popularity over the course of a century. Events and emotions were far more complex, however. Varying intellectual trends moved forward and backward, intersected, and contradicted one another. Some intellectuals simply sought change within the system; others questioned the system itself and saw change as altering it. On one issue the intellectuals seemed unanimous: they insisted that Brazil's status within the empire be improved. They felt it imperative that the kingdom's overwhelming importance be recognized. After all, at the beginning of the nineteenth century, Brazil had a population larger than the metroplis, furnished approximately three-quarters of

the empire's exports, and boasted an economic potential far superior to that of any other part of the empire. In size, Brazil dwarfed the motherland. The inevitable clash between metropolis and colony on the issue of the colony's rising importance was postponed by the unexpected transfer of the court to Rio de Janerio in 1808. The return of the king to Lisbon in 1821 brought the issue to the forefront again.

To summarize the political reforms most frequently advocated, it can be said that on more than one occasion over this span of time intellectuals suggested the integration of the Indians and manumitted blacks into society, the unification of the sprawling territory by means of better roads, the promulgation of a constitution based on the concept of government as a social contract, a strengthening of Brazil's voice in the imperial government, and the enhancement of the roles of the legislature and judiciary. A few spoke out for the establishment of a republic. As for economic reforms, they favored free trade, industrialization, modernization of agriculture and mining, and an end to burdensome restrictions, monopolies, and taxes. Their social statements were much more nebulous. Isolated voices paid lip service to the concept of the equality of all men and talked in vague terms of improving the conditions of the Indians and the slaves; a few even spoke of ending the slave trade. They wanted personal liberties, civil freedom, and religious tolerance. Most emphatically, they proposed ambitious programs to reform and expand education. Such, then, in composite, was the ideology of change espoused by the intellectuals. It has never been fully implemented, but it set forth the goals of the reformers throughout the nineteenth century.

The influx of enlightened ideas and the growing economic discontent combined to promote rebellion. As already noted, the *inconfidência* Mineira resulted partly from a reaction to a threat of improved tax collection and partly from an imperfect comprehension of enlightened thought. The curious mixture of economics and idealism plunged the Mineiro elite into impractical plotting. The outcome was an abortive rebellion. Brazilian historians have given the *Inconfidência*

far greater significance than it seems to deserve. At best it revealed some romantic dreamers at work, but the plot itself never passed the hypothetical stage. Although they all thought in terms of independence, some of the conspirators were republicans, others monarchists; some advocated the abolition of slavery, others favored its retention. The plot is worthy of consideration only because it proves that many ideas of the Enlightenment penetrated the interior of Brazil sufficiently to arouse economic and political discontent.

Less discussed but perhaps more important, the Bahian conspiracy in 1798 provided the unique example of the penetration—imperfect as it may have been—of the Enlightenment into the thinking of the masses. Confronting his judges in Salvador at the close of the eighteenth century, the twenty-three-year-old soldier Lucas Dantas do Amorim Tôrres stated, "We want a republic in order to breathe freely because we live subjugated and because we're colored and we can't advance and if there was a republic there would be equality for everyone." More than boldness characterized his statement. Obviously, the young soldier had imbibed the thoughts of the Enlightenment; the revolution of ideas had reached him. Dantas was but one of a larger group of conspirators arrested in Salvador in 1798 for plotting against the Crown. By and large those conspirators were simple folk: soldiers, workmen, artisans, and so large a number of tailors that the movement sometimes bears the name "Conspiracy of the Tailors."

As in the case of Dantas, the testimony of the other defendants at the trial revealed that those representatives of the lower classes were acquainted with current European thought. Their accusations against Portugal were similar to those of the intellectuals of the time. In general, the conspirators favored independence, a republic, equal treatment of all men, abolition of slavery, and free trade. The Bahian rebels proposed changes far more profound than did other colonial dissidents before and after them. They were the only ones to strike at slavery, the institution that was the sinew and muscle of colonial Brazil. In some ways their desires harmonized with the Enlightenment more than the programs of the intellec-

tuals, who were compromised by their aspirations or their association with the interests of the colonial upper class or the Portuguese.

The Bahian conspiracy added the dimension of the common person, almost always overlooked, to the history of ideas in colonial Brazil. As Dias Tavares, a historian of Bahia, noted, "The Brazilian people rarely appear in the histories of Brazil, but in the revolutionary movement of 1798 they are the principal actors." The urban masses also acted on the ideas of the times. The influence of the intellectuals extended beyond the narrow confines of the elite.

In Recife a third conspiracy led to a rebellion in 1817. Some of the elite had read the latest European books and discussed the ideas wafted across the ocean from France and England. Bishop Azeredo Coutinho, already famed for his essays on economics, founded a seminary in Olinda in 1800 for the general education of the captaincy's youth. His seminary reflected much of the thought of the Enlightenment. Since French was taught there, the students had direct access to the primary literature of that intellectual movement. Some years later, in 1814, a Masonic lodge was established; discussions there frequently touched on republican ideas. The elite were fully cognizant of the successful revolutions in the United States and France, as well as of the holocaust enveloping much of Spanish America. Economic considerations also encouraged thoughts of rebellion. During the War of 1812 (between Great Britain and the United States) and for some years thereafter cotton from Pernambuco sold exceedingly well in Europe; planters realized as much as 500 percent profit on their shipments. Conscious of their renewed economic importance and hopeful that it would continue, the planters complained ever more bitterly about Portugal's bureaucratic restrictions on their activities. The antipathy between the Brazilians and Portuguese in the area continued unabated from the days of the War of the Mascates. A certain regional pride was involved in the conspiracy, which planned to establish a republic only in the Northeast. Word of the plot reached Governor Caetano Pinto, but his hesitation in arresting the

military officers implicated gave the rebels an opportunity to execute their plans. They captured the Governor and packed him off to Rio de Janeiro. The initial actions of the provisional government revealed much about the philosphy that had brought it to power. It abolished the brazilwood monopoly, all titles of nobility, class privileges, and some taxes. Rio de Janeiro reacted with unusual swiftness. The Royal Navy blockaded Recife as troops advanced on the city overland from Bahia. Under those military pressures the revolt collapsed. Less than three months after the republic was proclaimed, Pernambuco returned to the monarchical fold. It was the principal revolt of the colonial period and testified dramatically to the existence, and even the popularity, of republican ideology.

The cause of independence, timidly put forward by the *inconfidências* in Minas Gerais and Bahia and boldly proclaimed in Pernambuco, was best served by events far from the coasts of Portuguese America. Struggles in Europe brought about a political transformation of Brazil.

The Braganzas in Brazil

In the early nineteenth century, Portugal found itself caught between its traditional alliance with Great Britain and the demands of Napoleon, who was determined to close Europe's ports to English trade. Napoleon ordered Prince Regent João, ruling in the name of his demented mother, Maria I, to seal the Portuguese ports, confiscate British property, and arrest British subjects. The prince regent reluctantly agreed to close the ports but to nothing more, a decision that prompted Napoleon to invade Portugal. In late 1807 the army of General Andoche Junot marched on Lisbon. In view of those events the British minister, Lord Strangford, counseled João to move his court to Brazil. The approach of Junot negated any other alternatives in the prince's mind. In return for generous commercial privileges in Brazil, the British agreed to transport the royal family to the New World and to pre-

serve intact the Portuguese empire. On the day Junot entered Lisbon the Braganzas and their court sailed for their tropical destination.

Historians generally applaud João's decision to move his court to Brazil. The Brazilians lauded it. For their part, the Portuguese soon would complain that the Crown tarried too long overseas. The event remains unique in history: the Braganzas were the only European monarchs to rule an empire from one of the colonies rather than from the metropolis, the only royal family to set foot on its American domains.

The fleet was divided by a storm at sea, and most of the ships stopped first at Salvador da Bahia, while the rest sailed directly to Rio de Janeiro. João and the royal family were aboard those vessels that called at Salvador. Surprised, the inhabitants of the former colonial capital greeted their monarch on January 22, 1808 with joy and excitement. Their city scrubbed and festively decorated, the inhabitants, dressed in their finest attire, impatiently awaited the new course of history opening before them. Within a few days the Brazilians heard evidence of the changes in store. Already committed to permit the English to trade with Portuguese America, João listened attentively to a petition to throw open the ports to world trade and thereby end the rigorous Portuguese restrictions on and monopolies of external trade. In response, on January 28, the prince announced, "Royal Decrees and other Orders which until now prohibited trade between My Vassals and foreigners are suspended and without vigor." It was a significant economic step that at first glance seemed to abandon three hundred years of mercantilist policy. Some historians have enthusiastically deemed the decree the declaration of Brazil's economic independence, but that is a premature claim.

Some effects of the decree were immediate. In the following three years, Bahia increased its exports by 15 percent and its imports by 50 percent. Customs receipts at the five principal ports rose 20 percent. In the port of Rio de Janeiro there were 90 foreign ships in 1808 and 354 in 1820. Not surprisingly, vessels flying the English ensign predominated. By the end of 1808, about one hundred British merchants

resided in Rio de Janeiro. It is safe to conclude that after 1808 Brazil had little economic contact with Portugal. Great Britain rapidly and completely replaced the mother country in commerce, an economic reality officially recognized by the treaties of 1810. Skillfully negotiated by Strangford, these treaties set the maximum duty on British goods at 15 percent (the duty imposed on imports from Portugal itself were set at a minimum of 16 percent, and for other countries the minimum was 20 percent). They also conceded to the English a right to have their own judges in Brazilian and Portuguese ports. In short, it was economic capitulation, an acknowledgement of the shift of Brazilian dependence from Portugal to England. So, freed from Portuguese mercantilism in 1808, Brazil fell at once under the economic control of Great Britain, from whom the Brazilians bought most of their manufactured goods but to whom they sold only secondary amounts of their exports; this situation would prevail for over one hundred years. The Swedish minister in Rio de Janeiro reported to his government that the treaty made Brazil a colony of Great Britain.

The opening of the ports was followed on April 1, 1808, by a decree revoking all previous prohibitions on manufacturing. Some small textile factories were built in the decades that followed, and an infant iron and steel industry began. The steam engine made its maiden appearance in Brazil at this time. In 1815 Bahia boasted its first steam-driven sugar mill. Two years later Pernambuco also possessed one. By 1834, there were sixty-four of them in operation. To encourage such enterprises, the Crown appointed the Royal Committee of Commerce, Agriculture, Factories, and Navigation. Among other activities, it awarded prizes for the introduction of new crops. The establishment of the Bank of Brazil in 1808 in Rio de Janeiro, with branches in Salvador and São Paulo, further stimulated the economy. After centuries of steady but lethargic growth, Brazil's population increased by about one million in two decades. Table 3.1 indicates the growth as well as the approximate composition of the population.

The cultural changes wrought by the presence of the Crown metamorphosed the intellectual and professional life of Brazil. That was emphatically true of the capital. When the

Table 3.1 Population Figures and Components, 1798 and 1818

	1798	1818
Whites	1,000,000	1,040,000
Indians	250,000	250,000
Freedmen	225,000	585,000
Slaves	1,500,000	1,930,000
Total	2,975,000	3,805,000

court arrived it found a beautifully located but somnolent city of approximately sixty thousand inhabitants.

A foreign merchant and resident of Rio de Janeiro during the first year of the court's presence left a valuable socio-economic perspective of the city through his analysis of the inhabitants' employment. John Luccock estimated that there were 1,000 connected in various ways with the court, 1,000 holding public offices, 1,000 men who resided in the city but received their incomes either from their plantations or from shipping, 700 priests or religious people, 500 lawyers, 200 medical doctors, 40 wholesale merchants, 2,000 retail merchants, 4,000 clerks, apprentices, and commercial servants, 1,250 mechanics, 100 vendors, 300 fishermen, 1,000 soldiers of the line, 1,000 sailors belonging to the port, 1,000 free Afro-Brazilians, 12,000 slaves, and 4,000 housewives. The remainder of the population consisted of children. Within a decade after the arrival of the court, the city's population doubled. The influx of an estimated 24,000 Portuguese, a large contingent of Frenchmen and Englishmen, and some European diplomats lent a certain cosmopolitan air to the capital. The desperate need for institutes of higher learning was partially answered: in 1808 a naval academy was established and in 1810 a military academy, both of which offered courses in engineering and drawing; a medical school opened in Salvador in 1808 and another in Rio de Janeiro in 1810; likewise, courses in economics, in 1808, agriculture, in 1812, and chemistry, in 1817, were offered; a library of sixty thousand volumes was inaugurated in Rio de Janeiro in 1814. Indicating the fascination with French culture, the Crown invited a French cultural mission to Rio de Janeiro in 1816 and founded the French-staffed Academy of Fine Arts some years later. Most

remembered from that group of talented French instructors is the artist Jean Baptiste Debret, whose brush depicted memorable scenes of the epoch. Primary and secondary education received a badly needed impetus to grow and to improve. Law schools did not appear until 1827 when one was organized in São Paulo and a second in Olinda. After several abortive attempts in the eighteenth century, printing presses at last arrived and began to operate, principally in Rio de Janeiro, where the first newspaper, *Gazeta do Rio de Janeiro*, appeared in 1808, and in Salvador, which started to publish its first newspaper, *Idade d'Ouro do Brasil*, in 1811.

In addition to those cultural institutions, the colony also witnessed the establishment of myriad governmental bureaus, all new to Brazilian soil. The presence of the Crown centralized control of Brazil in Rio de Janeiro to a degree unattainable or even unthinkable in the viceregal period. That centralization of power served as a powerful force for the unification of Brazil. Two European visitors observed, "Even the more remote provinces of the infant kingdom, whose inhabitants, led by curiosity, interest, or private business, visited Rio de Janeiro, soon accustomed themselves to recognize that city as the capital, and to adopt the manners and modes of thinking, which, after the arrival of the court, struck them as European." Portuguese officials on all levels surrounded the prince regent. No Brazilian served as minister, nor was any chosen to sit on the Council of State, although they held posts on the secondary level and below. The metropolitans monopolized the government while the colonials financed it. Still, the Brazilians could not contain their pride, especially at the outset, in finding the fountainhead of the empire on their soil. Ignácio José de Macedo typified the elation of the Brazilians when he wrote:

In its colonial status, from which it had just emerged, Brazil was known only because of the products of an abundant Nature; and now with its new status within the Empire, it begins to be admired for its political products which foretell its future elevation and long life. The unexpected transference of the Monarchy brought a brilliant dawn to these dark horizons, as spectacular as that on the day

of its discovery. The new day of regeneration, an omen of brighter destinies, will bring long centuries of prosperity and glory.

Such emerging attitudes, accompanying an intensified nativism, a strengthened bureaucracy, and an increased centralization of political power in Rio de Janeiro, prepared Brazil for independence. Together they went a long way toward solving the political problems of transfer and exercise of power and maintaining geographical unity. They constituted a major step toward nationhood, greatly facilitated by the goodwill of João VI.

João showed himself well disposed toward his new home by elevating its political status. True, pressures from Europe helped him to resolve the matter. The delegates to the Congress of Vienna did not disguise their annoyance with a monarch who elected to live in a distant colony rather than speed back to his European capital. Talleyrand suggested that if he chose to linger in his tropical paradise the least he could do would be to make his viceroyalty a kingdom. João concurred. On December 16, 1815, he raised Brazil to the status of a kingdom, the equal, at least in judicial theory, of Portugal. The promotion delighted the Brazilians, whose nativistic pride swelled over the new royal status. The following year the ill and aged Maria I died and the prince regent ascended the throne in his own right as João VI, "King of the United Kingdoms of Portugal, Brazil, and the Algarves." The clamor in Portugal for his return mounted. Yet he tarried.

Political Independence

Brazil's proclamation of independence followed and in a certain sense reacted to political turmoil in Portugal. Liberal thought disturbed the placidity of the entire Iberian peninsula as the second decade of the nineteenth century matured. The Portuguese liberals hoped to convoke a Côrtes, adjourned nearly a century and a quarter before, in order to write a constitution for the empire. While they debated the best method of procedure, a revolt in Spain forced King Fer-

nando VII to reinstitute the enlightened Constitution of 1812. The temporary success of the revolt encouraged the Portuguese liberals, and under their leadership rebellion swept southward from Oporto engulfing the nation. They convoked the long defunct Côrtes to which Brazil was to be allowed sixty-nine representatives while one hundred would represent Portugal. The revolutionary junta demanded that João return to Lisbon forthwith. Reluctantly the king realized that if he was to continue wearing the Portuguese crown he must sail to Lisbon. On April 26, 1821, he bid a melancholy farewell to the city he had transformed from a small, quiet viceregal capital into a larger, more cosmopolitan imperial capital. In reality the transformation of Rio de Janeiro symbolized a larger, more fundamental psychological change among the Brazilians themselves. Because of their experience as the seat of a world-wide empire, they could never quite be provincials again. João seems to have sensed that change. Tradition has it that as he bid farewell to his son Pedro, left behind as the regent, he advised, "Pedro, I fear Brazil might separate itself from Portugal; if so, place the crown on your own head rather than allow it to fall into the hands of an adventurer."

The twenty-three-year-old Prince Pedro, heir to the Portuguese throne, enthusiastically took up his duties as regent with authority over internal affairs. He was a talented and complex young man. Unfortunately his education had been neglected during his rather undisciplined childhood. Nonetheless, he exhibited a large measure of common sense and sagacity. His energy was great and not a little of it invested in amorous escapades. For many years, he lived openly with his mistress, the beautiful Domitila de Castro, who bore him five children and on whom he conferred the title of "Marquesa de Santos." Severely criticized by the court—and for that matter in Europe as well—their passionate relationship stands as one of the great love affairs of the Americas. To overemphasize his bedroom behavior, however famous it might be, would be unfair. He engaged in a host of other activities as well. He could be a dashing horseman one hour and a serious composer of music the next. As a matter of fact, he became a friend of Rossini's and at least one of his symphonies was

performed in Paris. Impetuous, sensuous, romantic in every sense of the word, he alternated between authoritarian and democratic behavior. Pedro thought of himself as a confirmed liberal; perhaps, considering the time and place, he was.

Aided by a bevy of Portuguese officials, the prince set about to rule Brazil. The challenge was formidable. In the first place, the vaults of the Bank of Brazil were empty; the departing court had withdrawn all the funds. Government income met only half of its expenses, a situation which would not be unusual in the decades ahead. The weak economy depended on the demand, or lack of it, in the markets of a few leader nations. Brazil bought more abroad than it sold, and consequently an already high debt mounted. During the decade of the twenties sugar outsold coffee, the former accounting for a third of the exports and the latter for a quarter. In the following decade that ratio altered and coffee became the principal export and hope for future prosperity. Besides relying on a few foreign markets to buy its raw products, Brazil, because of limited capital accumulation, sought foreign investments to initiate new enterprises, thus making the economy doubly dependent on the exterior. Not the least of the prince's problems as he assumed his new responsibilities was the Côrtes. The negative behavior of that cantakerous parliamentary body intensified and in the process solidified sentiment within Brazil for independence.

The Côrtes, which opened its sessions in Lisbon in January of 1821, quickly displayed its inexperience and amply demonstrated its lack of preparation to lead the empire. Belying the liberal sentiments that had animated them, the Portuguese representatives generally manifested a hostile attitude toward Brazil and verbally abused the forty-six Brazilian delegates who began arriving in August to take their seats. Failing to understand the alteration of Brazil's position vis-à-vis the metropolis, they dissipated much energy in an effort to put Brazil in its place, in other words to relegate the kingdom of Brazil to its former colonial status. Among other vexing restrictions, they refused to permit the establishment of a university there, tried to limit its commerce and trade, and

replaced the few Brazilians holding office with Portuguese. In order to break Brazilian unity the Côrtes authorized the establishment of provincial governing juntas dependent directly on Lisbon. Military commanders were ordered to report directly to the metropolis and many governmental agencies established overseas were abolished. The Brazilian press criticized the actions of the Côrtes and inflammatory pamphlets carried the local case to the small but powerful literate segment of the population. Clearly the Brazilians had no intention of acquiescing to the authoritarian, humiliating, and damaging rule of the Côrtes.

The first direct confrontation between the orders of the Côrtes and the desires of the Brazilians occurred in late 1821 and early 1822. The Côrtes ordered Pedro to return. Reaction in the Brazilian capital was instant and negative. Officials and inhabitants sought to counter the order. Couriers sped from Rio de Janeiro to São Paulo and to Minas Gerais to enlist the aid of those captaincies, important because of their proximity to the center of political power, their growing populations, and their prosperous economies based on sugar, coffee, cattle raising, and mining. Thereafter those three captaincies would form a vital political trinity, the core of political power in Brazil. They would provide leadership for the others and as a consequence national Brazilian history would revolve around that heartland. In this case, sentiment within the trio opposed Pedro's departure. A special committee requested an audience with the prince and on January 9, 1822, presented a petition informing him that the consensus favored his remaining. Pedro replied, "As it is for the good of all and the general happiness of the Nation, I am ready. Tell the people that I will stay." The response pleased the people and the words, "I will stay" (the famous "Fico," in the Portuguese) openly challenged the Côrtes.

The rapid pace of events required Pedro to reorganize his government. In the new cabinet, the well-educated, vocal, and nationalistic José Bonifácio de Andrada e Silva received the key post of "Minister of the Kingdom," the first Brazilian to hold such a high office. Otherwise Pedro continued to be surrounded by Portuguese who were personally

loyal to him and who also had adopted Brazil as their new homeland. But Bonifácio stood out as the most powerful figure in the newly reorganized government and, unlike either the prince or the other functionaries, he possessed a clear vision of what lay ahead. He guided the prince and Brazil toward independence.

A stellar example of the Brazilian intellectual of the period, Bonifácio was graduated from Coimbra in 1787 and went on to continue his studies in Italy and Germany. Traveling extensively in Europe, he met some of the Continent's outstanding intellectuals. Scholarly institutions in France, Germany, and England elected him to membership. He observed the French Revolution at firsthand. An avid reader of the *philosophes,* he particularly admired Rousseau, all of whose works he owned. In short, he immersed himself totally in the European Enlightenment. He returned to Brazil in 1819, intent upon applying the knowledge gained from his studies, travels, and experience. Few Brazilians could exhibit such a distinguished and extensive education, but if we examine the biographies of the leaders of the independence movement, one salient characteristic emerges: a majority of them studied abroad.

For that period, Bonifácio enunciated a very liberal ideology. First and foremost, he sought to retain the unity of Brazil and believed that could be accomplished only with a Braganza in Rio de Janeiro. Genetic governance best complemented the political evolution of Brazil. He favored the incorporation of liberal and democratic ideas into a traditional but constitutional monarchy. Bonifácio subscribed to Physiocrat philosophy. Only a stable monarchy could insure that the state encouraged agriculture, industry, and commerce, a necessity in the minister's opinion. Although supportive of individual liberties, he felt that in the last analysis they had to be subordinated to social order. In fact, he fretted a great deal about order and the need to defend property. Doubtless in reaction to the French Revolution and perhaps to certain events then taking place in Spanish America, he felt a strong monarch could defend both and thus prevent excesses of liberty. The ideal state would be achieved through broad

education, moral as well as scientific, which would insure progress and social integration. The moderate Bonifácio advocated no major change, despite his preference for independence. He favored continuity within existing institutions.

As minister of the kingdom, Bonifácio declared all the provinces under the control of Rio de Janeiro and moved to convoke a consultative council composed of delegates from them, thereby negating the vain effort of the Côrtes to decentralize Brazil. His attempt was not immediately successful. Only São Paulo, Minas Gerais, and Rio de Janeiro followed his leadership, and here once again that trio set the course for the rest. Strong Portuguese garrisons in the South and North tempered the reactions there. Pernambuco and Ceará vacillated. The Cisplatine Province, Bahia, Maranhão, and Pará remained loyal for the time being to the Côrtes. A small, radical press began to call for independence. In April, the *Reverbero Constitucional Fluminense* suggested that Pedro make himself "the founder of a new Empire." In May, the prince decreed that no act of the Côrtes would have force in Brazil without his approval and took the title "Perpetual Defender of Brazil." By that time talk of independence could be heard everywhere. Indeed, José Bonifácio was composing a letter to "friendly nations" in which he harshly criticized the colonial administration of the metropolis and asked them to establish direct relations with Brazil.

Having gone that far, it was but a short step to formal independence. Even so, it came at an unexpected moment. A messenger overtook Pedro on a journey from Santos to São Paulo on September 7, 1822, and delivered to him letters from, among others, the Côrtes, José Bonifácio, and Pedro's wife, Princess Leopoldina. The Côrtes informed Pedro that it had reduced his powers. Other letters told how the Côrtes had criticized the young prince. Bonifácio urged him to defy the humiliating orders and to heed *mazombo* opinion, which refused to allow Lisbon to dictate policies for Brazil. Princess Leopoldina, although Austrian by birth, had dedicated her energies and devotion to Brazil after she arrived in Rio de Janeiro in 1817 to marry Pedro. She too urged him to defy Portugal. Her letter stated, "Brazil under your guidance will

be a great country. Brazil wants you as its monarch. . . . Pedro, this is the most important moment of your life. . . . You have the support of all Brazil." Angered by the news from Lisbon and encouraged by the advice of Bonifácio and Princess Leopoldina, Pedro unsheathed his sword right there on the bank of the Ipiranga River and gave the cry "Independence or Death!" One man, then, without the backing of a congress or junta, far from the noise of a crowd, declared the independence of Latin America's largest nation. He left no formal, written document of his accomplishment. His declaration was solely verbal. In that solitary act, the personable prince accurately reflected public sentiment. He apparently expressed the will of the majority, or perhaps it is more exact to say the will of the majority of the elite, since the masses had little to do at any time with political decisions. On December 1, 1822, amid a splendiferous ceremony, Pedro was crowned "Constitutional Emperor and Perpetual Defender of Brazil."

The roots of independence burrowed deeply into the past. Imperial reforms in the eighteenth century had tightened Portuguese control to the alarm of the Brazilians who felt that greater bureaucratic authority and efficiency threatened their economic interests. The Enlightenment encouraged the Brazilians to know their land and to investigate its potential. Thus awakened, the Brazilians began to protest what they considered to be unjust restrictions on their development. Economic complaints became more audible. Concurrently the literature took on pronounced nativistic characteristics. The rapid changes during the period of João's residency in the New World swelled Brazilian pride. The old hostility between the *mazombos* and the *renóis* had not diminished. If anything, the enforced close contact of the Brazilians with the Portuguese in the preceding decade and a half intensified it. The highhanded action of the Côrtes further inflamed passions. Transformed from bucolic nativists into ardent nationalists, the Brazilian elite determined to create and defend a sovereign nation. That national consciousness triumphed in the "Cry of Ipiranga" in 1822. To fully understand the birth of Brazil, one must also realize that pro-

independence sentiment hung heavily in the hemispheric air. The United States and most of Spanish America had gained their freedom from Europe. The kingdom of Brazil lay in the midst of a community of newly independent states; inevitably the hemispheric disposition toward independence affected Brazilian opinions and actions.

Then, too, there converged in the early 1820s three interest groups whose combined impact hastened independence. Strongest of these was the *mazombo* planter aristocracy. Born and bred in Brazil, that landed gentry enjoyed considerable power and social prestige because of its great estates and control over the local *senado da câmara*. They identified fully with Brazil, Portugal being only a distant abstraction. They favored independence in order to expand their own power and to assure a greater freedom of access to international markets. Conservative by nature, they supported no structural reforms. The only change they sought was to substitute themselves for the Portuguese in power. Perhaps the foremost journalist of the period, Evaristo da Veiga, summed up their viewpoint when he pleaded, "Let us have no excesses. We want a constitution, not a revolution." This attitude encapsulated the reality that independence endorsed neither structural nor institutional innovation. The second group was the urban dwellers. So long as Brazil remained largely rural there was little possibility of revolt against Portugal. The growth of the cities in the eighteenth century provided the focal point for agitation: Ouro Prêto in 1789, Salvador in 1798, Recife in 1817, and Rio de Janeiro in 1822. Frequently the municipal council served as the forum of debate and the instrumentality for action furthering the cause of independence. On the one hand, the cities were a means of bringing together the planters; on the other, within the cities a small but vocal class of free persons appeared, neither plantation owners nor slaves, the latter an unstable class anxious to improve its status. Independence offered that amorphous middle group that possibility. Finally, the British, eager to expand their trade and to perfect their economic hegemony over Brazil, favored independence. Castlereagh for one, understood the advantage of a Brazil liberated from Portu-

guese rule but dependent on Britain, and Canning later acted to bring that to pass.

Obviously Pedro played a paramount role in the independence of Brazil. Until December of 1821, he submitted to the will of the Côrtes and of his father. Under the influence of some Brazilians who served him, the prince then began to perceive that the Côrtes really aimed to injure Brazil, the place where he grew up and which he loved. It became increasingly clear as well that his father was a prisoner of the Côrtes and an unwilling spokesman for it. In his powerful ministerial position, José Bonifácio impressed upon the prince the Brazilian point of view and, where possible, guided his decisions. The minister had the intelligence and ability to foresee the inevitability and desirability of independence. The prince had the flamboyance and dash to declare it. The turning point came in January, 1822, when Pedro resolved to remain and thereby ignored the wishes of the Côrtes. By May of that year, he was speaking and writing of "We Brazilians." He had identified his fortunes entirely with the Brazilian cause and served as the perfect instrument to effect national independence.

The fundamental problem confronting the new nation was not so much its need to assert its independence as to maintain its unity. A small navy under the command of Lord Cochrane, Earl of Dundonald, recently admiral of the victorious Chilean squadron, carried word of the declaration of independence to the principal cities along the coast from Montevideo to Belém. By bluster or force, the navy obtained the allegiance of all the littoral cities, although ports with strong garrisons like Montevideo and Salvador required siege and battle. Before the end of 1823 the navy had overcome all opposition to the declaration of independence, raised the imperial ensign over all the ports, established the authority of Pedro I, and incorporated such distant provinces as Pará and Maranhão into the new empire. The navy's role was an important one, but of course national unity was based on much more than military force.

That so diverse and so immense an area as Brazil retained its unity has intrigued students of the nation's evolu-

tion. The unity is all the more miraculous when one compares monolithic Brazil with the fragmented remnants of Spain's American empire. The three viceroyalties of Spanish South America disintegrated into ten republics, the viceroyalty of New Spain into an archipelago of states. The examples of Spanish America demonstrate that language, religion, tradition, geographic continuity, and common history do not always guarantee unity. They may help to solidify a state but they alone are insufficient to weld a nation together. In the case of Brazil, it is obvious that the vast majority of the inhabitants spoke Portuguese, professed Roman Catholicism, enjoyed the same combination of Afro-Indo-Iberian traditions, and shared three hundred years of history. They inhabited contiguous territories. Those similarities provided the basis for a superficial cohesion, but Brazil had something more that, taken with these factors, explains its phenomenal unity in the face of diversity and regionalism.

The fact that Portugal was far less well organized or structured than Spain permitted Brazil to develop at a more natural pace. After all, it was not until Pombal applied his heavy hand that all of Portuguese America was unified—at least in theory—into one colony. It seems that the colony acquired or altered institutions as needed, and that Lisbon from time to time reformed some of its organs of government. In contrast, the rigid hierarchical administration imposed almost at once on Spain's America minimized flexibility. The only method of change it allowed was destruction. During the passage of three centuries, the government of Brazil gradually became more uniform as it also became more centralized. Power first focused in Lisbon, but after 1808 its focal point was Rio de Janeiro.

The presence of the Braganzas in Rio de Janeiro for thirteen years forged a formidable link of unity. During this period the Brazilians acquired the habit of looking to Rio as the seat of government, the source of power, and the font of authority. Further, there was a Braganza on hand to lend legitimacy to each peaceful transition from viceroyalty to kingdom to empire.

The educated Brazilians and the rest of the elite seemed

disposed to accept the monarchy with which they identified. Like José Bonifácio, they saw in the monarch a guarantee of national unity, the accustomed patriarchy, the preservation of public order and the desired continuity. Consequently no acrimonious debates between Republicans and Monarchists rent the tranquillity of the new nation as in Spanish America. The presence of a sympathetic prince made monarchy the logical choice, and thus the transition from colony to nationhood flowed as smoothly as anyone could hope for. Pedro's power was at once legitimate. Thus the problem of legitimacy of power, so troublesome in the Spanish-speaking republics, did not beset Brazil. Heir to the long tradition of the house of Braganza, Pedro inherited his authority. He possessed and was surrounded by all the symbols of authority. Historical precedent strengthened his position. In that way, the throne occupied by the Braganza dynasty proved to be the perfect unifier of the new empire. A consensus, certainly among the elite, favored unification.

The Brazilians demonstrated a mobility that broke down regional barriers. The interior had for several centuries scattered and mixed people with no distinction as to their place of origin. In the *sertão*, a single "Brazilian" society formed. The resultant fusion provided a national nucleus which counterbalanced the regionalism more characteristic of the coast. Foreign threats, real or imagined, strengthened unity during the nineteenth century. From time to time waves of anti-Portuguese, anti-British, and anti-Spanish American sentiment inundated Brazil, and at those times a strong feeling of nationalism surged. Nothing served better to close regional divisions than an external threat. Ill-defined as nineteenth-century nationalism was, it contributed significantly to strengthening unity.

On several occasions, the young emperor had signified his willingness to rule under a constitution. Consequently the single most important political problem confronting the new empire was the writing and implementation of such a constitution. Elections were held for an Assembly that would have both constituent and legislative powers. On May 3, 1823, the Assembly opened.

By and large the deputies formed a liberal group; some of them had served as leaders of the Inconfidência of 1789 and the Revolt of 1817. The Assembly would furnish many of the future leaders of the nation.

Once again in terms of the times, liberal ideology seemed dominant among the elite, particularly those segments associated with the cities and with exports. Not surprisingly, then, they put forth, advocated, and adopted some of the major tenets of early nineteenth-century liberalism, a liberalism strongly influenced by the Enlightenment in general, but by English ideas and models in particular. They favored free trade; they looked to capitalistic models as guides; they stressed the value and sanctity of private property; they prized education; they argued the advantages of free navigation of rivers. Their loyalty to that type of liberalism revealed their aspirations to duplicate the material successes of those nations from which they drew their ideology. However, removed from its original context, that liberalism had the unfortunate effect of further subordinating the Brazilian economy to the needs of the capitalist markets of the North Atlantic. Free trade and competition, as we shall see, proved disasterous for a majority of the Brazilians. In short, the liberalism of the Brazilian elite had the ultimate effect of deepening Brazil's dependency.

From the start, the legislature and the emperor clashed. Passionately debated was the question whether the laws passed by the Assembly needed imperial sanction before they could take effect. After a close vote, the Assembly decided negatively. The emperor disapproved but upon reflection resolved to say nothing. In its brief history, the Assembly passed only six laws, all of which have been regarded as salutary. But the difference between the legislature and the executive was far more fundamental than that power struggle indicated. The legislators were Brazilian, sons of the old landed aristocracy or of the new urban society. The emperor—despite all his generously manifested devotion and dedication to the cause of Brazilian independence and commonweal—was Portuguese. He had been born in Portugal and he surrounded himself with Portuguese-born advisers. The ensuing struggle

between the legislature and the executive represented the continuing effort of the Brazilians to rid themselves of lingering Portuguese influence. The legislative debate showed that the legislators were almost pathologically anti-Portuguese and by implication hostile to the emperor. The sensitive and headstrong Pedro resented their attitude and disapproved of their encroachment on what he considered to be his prerogatives and power. As the lack of understanding and good will between the two grew, a rivalry developed in which each sought to curtail the powers of the other. Persuaded that the Assembly not only lacked discipline but scattered the seeds of revolution, Pedro decided to dissolve it. Troops arrived at the Assembly hall on November 11, 1823, to prohibit further sessions. The legislative leaders were sent into exile.

Pedro had promised the Brazilians a constitution, and despite the dissolution of the Assembly he meant to keep his word. He immediately convoked a committee of ten Brazilians who at his behest completed the basis for a constitution by early December. The emperor submitted the projected constitution to the municipal councils for approval. As they had during the days of agitation for independence, they played another significant role in national formation. Most of the municipalities approved. Stating that the voice of the Brazilian people had spoken through their local governments, Pedro promulgated the constitution on March 25, 1824.

Above all else, the new constitution provided for a highly centralized government with a vigorous executive. Although power was divided among four branches—executive, legislative, judiciary, and moderating—the lion's share rested in the hands of the emperor. Assisted by a council of state and a ministry, he exercised the functions of the chief executive, as well as wielding the moderating power, which made him responsible for the maintenance of the independence of the nation as well as the equilibrium and harmony of the other powers and the twenty provinces. He enjoyed a veto over all legislation as well as the right to convoke or dissolve the General Assembly. He selected the presidents of the provinces, the ministers, the bishops (for he claimed the old royal patronage the pope had conferred on Portuguese kings), and

the senators. He could pardon criminals and review judicial decisions. His powers were many—but then so were his responsibilities. In short, the emperor was expected to utilize his office as an omniscient harmonizer in a far-flung empire whose incredible geographic and human diversity challenged the existence of the state. In the final analysis the Crown was the one national institution, pervasive and genetic that could claim to represent all Brazilians. The General Assembly was divided into a Senate, whose members were appointed for life from lists presented by the provinces, and a Chamber of Deputies elected periodically and indirectly by a highly restricted suffrage. Considering the time, the place, and the circumstances, it is safe to conclude that the constitution was a liberal document. It was also flexible, generously allowing amendments and reforms without the necessity of adopting a new constitution. Proof of the viability of the document lay in its durability: it lasted sixty-five years until the monarchy fell in 1889.

With independence, unity, and the form of government established, the recognition of the empire by other nations demanded attention. On August 6, 1822, Pedro had signed José Bonifácio's "Manifestation to Friendly Governments and Nations" and had dispatched diplomatic agents to London, Vienna, and Rome. Serious difficulties complicated Brazil's acceptance into the community of nations. Foremost was the attitude of Portugal. The European states were reluctant to recognize Brazil before its former mother country did. Great Britain, for example, was eager to accord recognition but reluctant to weaken its influence in Portugal or alienate its profitable Portuguese market. Furthermore, the attitude of the Holy Alliance dissuaded the European states from welcoming Brazil. These European policies did not influence the course of the United States, which had begun to embrace the new Latin American nations in 1822. The United States extended the international hand of friendship to Brazil in May of 1824, when President James Monroe received José Silvestre Rebelo as chargé d'affaires.

Commercial pressures in England pushed the Court of St. James's to extend recognition. Britain wanted to protect

its valuable Brazilian market. English exports to Brazil in 1825 equaled those sold to the rest of South America and Mexico combined and totaled half those to the United States. The English hoped to renew the Treaty of 1810 before its expiration, scheduled for 1825, would elevate the tariff on British imports from 15 to 24 percent. Such a renewal required a prior establishment of diplomatic relations. No stranger to interference in Portuguese affairs, London sent Sir Charles Stuart first to Lisbon to confer with João VI and apply the necessary pressure on him to accord recognition, then to Rio de Janeiro to complete the necessary mediation. Sir Charles executed his mission brilliantly. By the end of 1825 Portugal had acknowledged the independence of Brazil in return for two million pounds sterling—in part a payment of Brazil's share of Portugal's debts and in part a payment to João for his property and palace in Brazil. As a sign of respect and love, Pedro permitted his father to use the honorary title "Emperor of Brazil." Both concessions infuriated the Brazilians and further inflamed their anti-Lusitanian passions. Further, the agreement with Portugal ended the possibility of a union between Brazil and Angola, encouraged by their intimate relations over the centuries. Pedro had to promise "not to accept the proposals of any Portuguese colonies to join the Empire of Brazil."

There was still more to be extracted from the Brazilians. British services and favors were not gratuities. In return for Sir Charles's efforts in his behalf and for promised British recognition, Pedro had to agree to a series of treaties with Great Britain, none of which offered a promising prospect to the new nation. First, he consented to a new commercial treaty, a reenactment of the one with Portugal in 1810, to continue the favorable import duty of 15 percent on British goods. In a second treaty, Brazil consented to abolish its slave trade within three years. The recognition by Portugal and then Great Britain broke the diplomatic impasse. Within a year, Austria, the Vatican, Sweden, France, Switzerland, the Low Countries, and Prussia welcomed the new empire into the community of nations.

From several points of view, Pedro met his downfall be-

cause of his inept handling of foreign affairs. First, the unpopular concessions to Portugal and Great Britain in exchange for their recognition aroused public ire. Second, Pedro fell into a diastrous war with Argentina over the east bank of the Plata, the final chapter of that century and a half of territorial struggle. João, taking advantage of the unrest caused by the struggle against Spain for independence in the Plata region, had dispatched troops into the Banda Oriental del Uruguay in 1811. He withdrew them the following year under British pressure, but sent them again in 1816 to reoccupy the coveted territory. In 1821, he annexed the area as "the Cisplatine Province," which was allowed to keep its own laws, language, and some local autonomy. The annexation to the kingdom of Brazil did not suit most of the inhabitants of the area and elicited cries of protest from the Argentines who were no happier to see the Brazilians in partial control of their strategic Río de la Plata than the Spaniards had been to see the Portuguese there. In 1825 war broke out between Argentina and Brazil over the future of the Cisplatine Province. Neither side distinguished itself on the battlefield. Both exhausted themselves financially and, when neither perceived a clear victory, they agreed on a compromise in 1828: the disputed province would become an independent buffer state. Thus was born the República Oriental del Uruguay. The loss of money, men, and a province embittered the Brazilians, who blamed the emperor for their reverses.

Pedro's third foreign involvement irreparably alienated the Brazilians. When the death of João VI in 1826 left the Portuguese throne empty, a temptation crossed the emperor's path. As the legitimate heir to that throne he could have worn two crowns, but the Brazilians refused to hear of the matter. Reluctantly he renounced the Portuguese crown in favor of his daughter, Maria II, who was to marry his younger brother, her Uncle Miguel. To further complicate matters, Miguel seized the throne in 1828 in defiance of Maria's rights. Civil war resulted, and Pedro devoted more and more of his time to the complexities of that struggle. The Brazilians deeply resented his absorption in those European matters. Anti-Portuguese sentiment, long simmering, began

to boil. To the degree that that anti-Portuguese feeling increased, Pedro's popularity decreased.

Internal affairs did not favor the emperor either. The financial situation deteriorated under the pressure of war; the foreign debt rose; the exchange rate declined. The Bank of Brazil resorted to the wholesale emission of paper money to meet budgetary deficits. All too quickly inconvertible, the paper drove gold and silver out of circulation. The unhealthy condition of the Bank forced the government to liquidate it. Its demise did not stem the flow of newly printed paper money, because the national treasury continued to issue it. Nor was the tariff policy calculated to relieve the financial strain. In a mood of impractical liberality, the government extended the 15 percent maximum tariff to Portugal, France, and others in 1826 and 1827. The Vasconcelos Tariff of 1828 uniformly fixed the tariff at 15 percent on all foreign merchandise.

Pedro's talents did not include the ability to deal with the legislature, whose first session opened in 1827. Ignoring the Chamber of Deputies as much as possible, he drew all his ministers from the Senate. It became apparent that there existed no mutual confidence and even less cordiality between the emperor and the Assembly. Pedro tersely and bitterly confined his speech from the throne closing the First Assembly in 1829 to "This session is closed." Indeed, he had quarreled with most of the prominent liberal leaders.

Several revolts disturbed internal peace. The most serious occurred in Pernambuco in 1824, where the emperor's selection of the provincial president met opposition. Furthermore, the rebels refused to accept the new constitution and swore their loyalty to the recently dissolved Assembly. Reaction from Rio de Janeiro was immediate. As in 1817, both land and sea forces surrounded Recife and swiftly crushed the rebellion. The so-called Confederation of the Equator represented a vigorous regionalism that was always a potential threat to national unity. In 1828 two battalions of German and Irish mercenary troops revolted in Rio de Janeiro in protest against inhumane treatment. Their lawlessness shook the capital before they were disarmed and, in many cases, de-

ported. In 1829 there was yet another rebellion in Pernambuco, this one brief and confined to the interior.

All these events, foreign and domestic, tended to diminish the popularity of the young ruler. The dissatisfaction coalesced into an active opposition to him. The small but outspoken newspapers gave voice to that opposition. Its criticisms stung, and Pedro requested legal means to deal with a press he asserted abused its freedoms under the pretext of liberty. Instead, new journals appeared so that by 1830 the empire counted forty-two of them. Those newspapers devoted full coverage to the overthrow of Charles X of France in 1830, noting pointedly that any monarch who sought to subvert the free institutions of his country deserved to see his reign end. It was a warning the emperor failed to heed. He boosted his popularity in mid-March of 1831 by appointing a popular, all-Brazilian cabinet, but in early April he replaced it with an unpopular one composed of senators and nobles. The opposition seized that cabinet change as the opportunity to bring pressure to bear on Pedro. They demanded the return of the March cabinet. The emperor retorted that it was his constitutional right to change ministries at will—and legally he was right. However, the legal technicality did not prevent the populace and the military in Rio de Janeiro from demonstrating in the streets. A delegation visited Pedro to demand the reappointment of the dismissed cabinet. He answered with his abdication.

As his father had before him, Pedro set sail for Europe, leaving a son behind to rule Brazil, in this case the five-year-old Pedro de Alcântara. Back in Europe, he entered fully into the struggle over the Portuguese succession and placed his daughter on the throne as Maria II in 1834. He died shortly thereafter, ending an eventful life of thirty-six years.

Pedro's reign in Brazil, from 1822 to 1831, the period called the First Empire, is not easy to evaluate. The loss of the Cisplatine Province rankled Brazilians, and it remains the only major territorial loss the nation ever suffered. The consequent failure to maintain at least partial control of the Plata would lead to endless diplomatic maneuvering, military intervention, and the major Latin American war. In general, Ped-

ro's diplomacy failed. Likewise, it is difficult to find much progress in national development during his reign. On the other hand, he gave Brazil independence bloodlessly and obtained prompt international recognition for the new empire (whatever the cost); both were considerable achievements, particularly compared to the long and costly wars the Spanish Americans waged for their freedom and the difficulty they had in getting Spain's recognition of their new republics. Pedro's rule maintained order and strengthened unity. And the Constitution of 1824 proved to be a useful and practical document that guided Brazil through its first sixty-five years. The balance of evaluation, then, seems to tip in favor of Pedro I.

Chaos Into Order

The years immediately following the abdication constitute a period of reaction against many events of the preceding decade. Of primary importance, is the fact that the Brazilians themselves, for the first time, took control of their own government. Members of the patriarchal elite, with their roots firmly in the plantation economy, replaced the Portuguese-born who, under Pedro, in a fashion reminiscent of the colonial era, had continued to monopolize the highest offices in the empire. A majority of the new, nationalistic leaders reacted violently against the highly centralized government of Pedro I. They favored federalism. That principle, widely debated and experimented with throughout Latin America in the nineteenth century, offered obvious appeal to a large and varied country such as Brazil. In addition, many Brazilians desired to increase the powers and participation of the elected representatives in the government. For the first time masters of their own ship of state, the Brazilian elite were eager to chart their own course. Few thought, however, in terms of a republic. The overwhelming majority gave their allegiance to the child Pedro II, but there was in the air a willingness—even at this stage a necessity—to experiment in government.

The constitution stipulated that until Pedro reached the

age of eighteen, and in the event that there was no one else in the family old enough to rule in his name, the General Assembly would elect a regency composed of three men, presided over by the eldest. The Assembly elected such a triumvirate but withheld from it some of the imperial powers. For example, the regents could not dissolve the Chamber, nor could they confer royal titles. In the intense political maneuverings initiated by the Assembly's exercise of its expanded power the first glimmerings of future party structure emerged. On the one side stood those of liberal or moderate persuasions. While swearing absolute loyalty to the monarch, they believed that the emperor should reign and not rule. They advocated the biennial election of the popular chamber, an elected senate, suppression of the Council of State, and a federal structure with elected bicameral provincial assemblies. On the opposing side, those of conservative persuasion supported a strong, centralized monarchy, the core of their political ideology. They felt comfortable with genetic governance and the traditional patriarchy. Liberals exercised considerable influence and power during the early years of the regency. After all, their ideology, with its emphasis on contractual rather than genetic governance, offered the most marked reaction to the immediate past.

The Liberals won their major victory with the passage of the Additional Act of 1834, a constitutional amendment. To increase governmental efficiency, the number of regents was reduced from three to one; the one would be elected by restricted suffrage and hold office for four years. The Act abolished the Council of State, regarded by Liberals as the bastion of conservatism. It also outlawed the entailing of estates. In an agricultural empire such as Brazil, that prohibition provided, at least in theory, for some fundamental future economic changes. To encourage federalism in the provinces, legislative assemblies with power over local affairs replaced the general councils whose duties had been primarily consultative. This last provision was a major concession to those who favored decentralization. Its passage coincided with a series of disastrous provincial rebellions whose cumulative effect threatened the very existence of the empire.

The experiments in government occurred during a period of economic difficulties. Tariffs and taxes provided a meager income for the central government. Sugar prices dropped steadily; the return on cotton was even less. Gold mining had fallen to a small fraction of its previous output and as one result the internal demand for cattle declined. A general impoverishment beset the nation. The obvious consequence of the economic distress was an unrest that a political structure weakened by uncertain experimentation and the instability of the regency only exacerbated.

The period between 1831 and 1835 saw frequent, short-lived, and tumultuous rebellions. In Pernambuco, Bahia, and Mato Grosso the trouble stemmed primarily from anti-Portuguese sentiments. Those disturbances, however, were but preludes to what was to follow.

Five major provincial revolts erupted between 1832 and 1838 in diverse parts of the empire ranging from the far North to the far South, but all occurred outside the controlling core of the empire, Rio de Janeiro, Minas Gerais, and São Paulo which might partially explain their eventual failure. The five were: the War of the Cabanos in the interior of Pernambuco and Alagoas, 1832–1836; the related Cabanagem Rebellion in Pará, 1835–1840; the Sabinada Rebellion in Bahia, 1837–1838; the Balaiada Rebellion in Maranhão, 1838–1841; and the Farroupilha Rebellion in Rio Grande do Sul, 1835–1845. These revolts had complex origins, in each case largely regional, but it is possible to find some common denominators. A varied combination of economic, social, and political dissatisfactions gave rise to all. Each of the areas suffered from economic reverses. In at least two and possibly three of the revolts, the antipathy felt by the Brazilians toward resident Portuguese merchants and landlords played a role. Resentment toward the provincial presidents appointed from Rio de Janeiro figured in three of them. Confusion in the capital, accompanied by relaxed centralism, contributed to the causes of all.

At least some of the tumult and revolt resulted from genuine expressions of popular discontent or frustrations; the restive humble worried about the effects of political and

economic changes. Many perceived threats to their folk cultures.

In fact, the first half of the nineteenth century may well be the period of Brazilian history during which the masses protested most and played their most active political role. Large numbers of the popular classes throughout the provinces resented their status and feared the changes imposed on them. Bahia, in particular, during the years from 1824 to 1840 seethed with social protest. In general terms, it is safe to conclude that the Bahian dissidents were people of color who opposed or fought against "European types." Their ideology was vague and often contradictory. They frequently sacked shops and warehouses in a quest for food and killed military officers and landowners in a challenge to authority.

Three major popular rebellions of the 1830s, the Cabanos, Cabanagem, and Balaiada revolts, further revealed the unrest of the masses. Those rebellions appear to have expressed the frustrations of poor whites, mestizos, mulattoes, black slaves, and Indians. The rebels hoped to improve their standards of living, although their programs were vague, and to share in the exercise of power. The War of the Cabanos was particularly significant because it was entirely agrarian. Vicente Ferreira da Paula commanded the rural masses and can be considered a genuine populist *caudilho*. The leaders of all three rebellions were revered by their followers, who considered them to be one of themselves; however, to the governments they were "criminals," "bandits," and "outlaws," and are still so termed whenever mentioned in official histories.

The regents had neither the prestige nor the authority to hold together a vast empire convulsed by revolt. The first single regent, Diogo Antônio Feijó, a radical liberal, was elected in 1835. He had served in the Côrtes, been an early advocate of independence, held the portfolio of Minister of Justice, and sat in both the Assembly and the Senate. He failed to calm the provincial storms and resigned under heavy criticism in 1837. The second regent, Pedro de Araújo Lima, a conservative, was no less qualified: he too had represented Brazil in the Côrtes and served as a senator and minister. Some

notable cultural advancements took place during his regency: the founding of an elite secondary school, the Imperial College of Pedro II; the creation of the National Archives; and the organization of the Brazilian Geographical and Historical Institute. But the provincial rebellions raged on, if anything increasing in scope. A strong reaction against the mounting chaos prompted the elite, concerned for the very unity of the empire, to turn to the throne as the instrument and symbol of national unity, to duplicate the miracle it had wrought in 1822. Events thus suggested, at least at that time and under those circumstances, the superiority of the genetic principles of monarchy over the contractual government of elected executives.

Experience indicated that too much autonomy had been given to the provinces under the Additional Act, a degree of autonomy they were unprepared to exercise responsibly. In the name of unity, to say nothing of efficiency, it proved necessary to check the centrifugal tendencies. The General Assembly passed the Interpretive Law in 1840 to end the federal experiment and return to centralism. At the same time, a clamor to coronate the young prince rose. The constitution barred Pedro from ascending the throne until he reached eighteen. Since he was born on December 2, 1825, the nation theoretically would have to wait until that date in 1843. Most feared that the spiraling chaos and crises would shatter the nation before then. A movement was organized to declare Pedro of age at once and to crown him. Newspapers and public opinion seemed increasingly favorable to the idea. When the legislature failed to come to an agreement on the plan, the Liberals took matters into their own hands. They sent a mission to Pedro on July 22, 1840, to ask if he was willing to accept the crown at once. He replied affirmatively. The following day he appeared before the General Assembly to take the oath to uphold the constitution. The appearance of the handsome and dignified adolescent, blond and blue-eyed, sparked delirium and cheering among the crowds filling the assembly hall and packing the square and streets around it. The cry "Viva Senhor Dom Pedro II, constitutional emperor and perpetual defender of Brazil!" rang out repeat-

edly. Later, there was an expectant hush in the chamber of the General Assembly as he took his oath. The formal coronation took place one year later. As is evident, the premature proclamation of his majority was devoid of any legality. Rather it was a kind of coup d'etat sanctioned by the anxieties of the nation. It calmed turbulent political waters. The presence of the young emperor on the throne provided the authority figure that reunified the sprawling empire. Hierarchy reigned; order slowly returned. His early coronation reaffirmed the patriarchal principle that had dominated Brazil for centuries. The escape from national disintegration also slowed the impact of political innovation for at least another generation. Those who lived through the centrifugal dangers of the regency period deeply venerated the monarchy thereafter, because it had preserved Brazilian unity during the moment of its greatest stress. As long as that generation lived, the monarchy remained an unquestioned institution. Strong centralization was regarded, at least for the time being, as the remedy for the evils of the past. If the abdication of Pedro I had opened the posts of government to the Brazilians, the coronation of Pedro II gave them a genuine national emperor, for the young Pedro had been born and reared in Brazil and was entirely identified with his native land. His coronation logically concluded the Brazilianization of the government that had begun in 1808 and accelerated in 1831.

The decade beginning in 1840 with the Proclamation of the Majority was a significant period of political transition. The pace of creating a nation-state quickened.

The emperor first focused his attention on the problem of reestablishing peace in his domains. The Balaiada and Farroupilha revolts raged on, and in 1842 the Liberals in São Paulo and Minas Gerais took up arms to protest the selection of a Conservative cabinet and the rapid return to centralization. Fortunately for the emperor there appeared at that time an extraordinarily capable military leader, Luís Alves de Lima e Silva, Baron and later Count, Marquis, and Duke of Caxias. Ably and firmly he suppressed the uprisings in Maranhão, Minas Gerais, and São Paulo before going on to quell the rebellion festering in Rio Grande do Sul. Peace returned to

the shaken empire, and the entire Brazilian nation gathered around the throne to pay homage to Pedro II.

The empire matured politically during that decade. The emperor did not hesitate to use his moderating powers to seat and unseat ministries and thus to alternate the two political parties, the Liberals and the Conservatives, in power. He would select ministers from one party. If that party held a majority in the popular chamber, the ministry governed without difficulty. If that party did not hold a majority, he dissolved the Chamber and called for new elections. Since the new ministry controlled the electoral machinery, its party inevitably won the majority needed in the new Chamber to enable it to govern. Such an arrangement demanded astuteness on the part of the emperor to correctly assess public opinion so that he knew when the nation favored a shift of political parties. In 1840, the emperor nodded to the Liberals, but the following year he reversed himself and brought the Conservatives to power. At once they initiated a concentrated campaign to recentralize the government. They restored the Council of State, whose primary duty was to advise the emperor on the use of his moderating power, and curtailed the powers of the provincial legislatures. The central government assumed direction of all police forces throughout the realm. The Liberals loudly protested these measures—even resorting to violence in Minas Gerais and São Paulo—but, upon returning to power for four years in 1844, they did nothing to negate that recentralization. Sobered by the responsibilities of power, they accepted it as inevitable and necessary.

In 1847, Pedro decided that he would no longer select the entire ministry, but just name a president of the Council of Ministers who, in turn, would pick his own subordinates after due consultation, of course, with the emperor. The creation of the post of prime minister facilitated the adoption of a parliamentary system—quite sui generis. Under the firm tutorial guidance of their ruler, the politicians learned the give and take of politics and, because they trusted his sagacity, they accepted his decisions with a minimum of complaint. On his part, Pedro exhibited unusual skill in balancing the two parties. During his forty-nine-year reign, he appointed or

approved thirty-six different cabinets, most of which received and merited public support.

The decline in the use of rebellion as a political weapon in the late 1840s and thereafter reflected the acceptance of the legitimacy and authority of Pedro II. Still, the policies of the new emperor did not go unchallenged, as indicated by the Liberals' revolts in 1842 and in 1848. Mention has been made of the former; the latter occurred in Pernambuco. In part it protested the recall of the Conservatives to power and in part it demonstrated local antipathy toward the Portuguese merchants residing in the province. The two causes were not divorced in the minds of the disgruntled Pernambucan Liberals who, in heated emotion, frequently equated the Conservatives and the Portuguese merchants. As a matter of fact, the Portuguese did control a considerable share of Brazilian business. It has been estimated that they owned approximately one-third of all commercial houses, and they tended to favor the conservative cause. The Liberals resented their presence and influence. In one sense at least, the War of the Mascates was still being fought. Some participants in the Praieira Revolt of 1848 favored a land reform. The articulate mulatto Antônio Pedro de Figueiredo wrote against the abuses of the *latifundia* class and advocated measures, such as a heavy tax on unused land, to reduce the size of the huge estates and to encourage a rural middle class. Such sentiments found friendly acceptance elsewhere in Brazil but no practical remedies were forthcoming. In 1850, the Crown abolished the centuries-old *sesmaria* system and prohibited further free distribution of the land. It hoped to check thereby some of the abuses of the past, but failed to end the abuses of the *latifundia* or to aid the rural poor. The Praieira Revolt itself was suppressed in 1850.

Economic changes during the period were impressive. Already coffee had surpassed sugar as the major export, accounting for about one-half the exports compared to one-quarter thereof for sugar. But imports still exceeded exports. As a result of a bare treasury, the minister of finance resorted to the frequent issuance of paper money. The statesmen regretted their earlier economic liberality and determined that,

as soon as the commercial treaties ran out, they would raise the tariff with the dual purpose of increasing revenue and encouraging national industry. In the face of powerful English pressure to renew their expiring commercial treaty, the Brazilians stood firm and, in 1844, enacted the Alves Branco Tariff, which more than doubled duties. The tariffs thereafter accounted for approximately half the government's income. Throughout the remainder of the century the government adamantly refused to negotiate any commercial treaties and thereby gained a shade of economic independence from Great Britain. The tariff was not really high enough, however, to promote domestic industrialization. In 1846 the government gave a stronger impetus to potential industrialists by permitting the free importation of machinery. Despite the establishment of a few fragile industries and the slow but steady growth of the coastal cities, Brazil remained overwhelmingly rural. Large and generally inefficiently run plantations continued to dominate the countryside. As always, they catered to the caprices of the international market, now smiling, now frowning. To all appearances, the *fazenda* remained the same in structure and operation as it had been for hundreds of years. One observant traveler, Daniel F. Kidder, visited a *fazenda* at Jaraguá in the interior of São Paulo during the early years of the Second Empire. The estate belonged to an enterprising woman who resided most of the year in the city of São Paulo. The variety of crops impressed Kidder: sugar-cane, manioca, cotton, rice, and coffee. He left this description:

> Around the farm-house as a centre, were situated numerous out-houses, such as quarters for negroes, store-houses for the staple vegetables, and fixtures for reducing them to a marketable form.
> The engenho de cachassa was an establishment where the juices of the sugar-cane were expressed for distillation. On most of the sugar estates there exist distilleries, which convert the treacle drained from the sugar into a species of alcohol called cachassa. . . . The apparatus for grinding the cane was rude and clumsy in its construction, and not dissimilar to the corresponding portion of a cider-mill in the United States. It was turned by four oxen.

He went on to describe the customs of the plantation house and of his hosts:

> Our social entertainments at Jaraguá were of no ordinary grade. Any person looking in upon the throng of human beings that filled the house when we were all gathered together, would have been at a loss to appreciate the force of a common remark of Brazilians respecting their country, viz: that its greatest misfortune is a want of population. Leaving travelers and naturalists out of the question, and also the swarm of servants, waiters, and children—each of whom, whether white, black, or mulatto, seemed emulous of making a due share of noise—there were present half a dozen ladies, relatives of the Donna, who had come up from the city to enjoy the occasion. Among the gentlemen were three sons of the Donna, her son-in-law, a doctor of laws, and her chaplain, who was also a professor in the law university, and a doctor in theology. With such an interesting company, the time allotted to out stay could hardly fail to be agreeably spent. . . . It is a pleasure to say, that I observed none of that seclusion and excessive restraint which some writers have set down as characteristic of Brazilian females. True, the younger members of the company seldom ventured beyond the utterance of Sim Senhor, Não Senhor, and the like; but ample amends for their bashfulness were made by the extreme sociability of Donna Gertrudes. She voluntarily detailed to me an account of her vast business concerns, showed me in person her agricultural and mineral treasures, and seemed to take the greatest satisfaction in imparting the results of her experience on all subjects.

Kidder spoke favorably of the food. The national diet revolved around the basic staples of rice, beans, manioc flour, sugar, coffee, corn, and dried meat. Apparently the *fazenda* offered its guests considerably more. Our traveler noted:

> There was a princely profusion in the provisions for the table, but an amount of disorder in the service performed by near a dozen waiters, which might have been amply remedied by two that understood well their business. The plate was of the most massive and costly kind. The chairs and tables were equally miserable. The sheets, pillow-cases and towels, of the sleeping apartments, were of cotton, but at the same time ornamented with wide fringes of wrought

cambric. Thus the law of contrast seemed to prevail throughout. Dinner was served at six P.M.; supper at about nine.

Life on the large plantation appeared genteel enough, for the owners that is. As limitless as Brazil seemed, there was a scarcity of tillable, accessible land for the small farmer. Long before the "Cry of Ipiranga," that land had been distributed in *sesmarias,* and the tendency had been more toward the consolidation of land holdings than otherwise. The *Diário de Pernambuco* in the mid-nineteenth century summarized and decried the situation as follows:

> Now, agriculture is closed by an insurmountable barrier to the less favored man, to anyone who does not have a certain amount of money. Agriculture is the chief source of production, the chief hope of our country. But since agriculture is closed by a barrier it is necessary that that barrier fall, cost whatever it may. . . . And what is that barrier? Large landholdings. It is the terrible curse which has ruined and depopulated many other nations.

If the land-holding system had altered not a whit since the colonial period, now two generations in the past, neither had the labor system. The black slave performed all the menial tasks.

In the 1840s increasing internal objections to the nefarious slave trade arose. Foreign objections were not lacking either, but then they had been in evidence for many decades. From the beginning of the century the English, for a mixture of humanitarian and commercial reasons, had applied pressure, first to limit it and then to abolish it. Many Brazilians accused the British of seeking to eliminate slavery in order to raise the prices of Brazilian products on the world market, thereby permitting similar products from English colonies to undersell them.

London coerced Portugal into accepting by treaty a series of restrictions on the traffic: in 1810 the slave trade was limited to the Portuguese colonies in Africa; in 1815 all trade was limited to the Portuguese colonies south of the equator, all of which were required to observe a number of ameliora-

tive conditions; and in 1817 the British navy received permission to stop and search Portuguese vessels believed to be violating the conditions imposed upon the trade. In return for British recognition, the Brazilians reluctantly signed a treaty in 1826 agreeing to terminate the traffic within three years after ratification. Furthermore, British ships were to be permitted to search vessels suspected of engaging in the trade, and mixed British-Brazilian commissions would judge all violations. The landowners greeted the treaty with cries of protest. They predicted the shaky agricultural economy would collapse without the continued importation of slaves. Under duress, the Brazilians grudgingly passed a law to implement their treaty obligations. All slaves imported after 1830 were to be immediately freed, and the importers punished and forced to repatriate them. Shortly thereafter chaos enveloped the empire and even if there had been the will—which there emphatically was not—there was not the power to enforce that law, although Great Britain quixotically tried. In 1845, the convention permitting British search and establishing the mixed commission to judge cases expired, and the imperial government stubbornly refused to renew it. England reacted with the Aberdeen Bill, which unilaterally provided for continued search and seizure of suspected slave ships and appropriate trials in Admiralty courts. That high-handed Act offended Brazilian sensitivity. By all estimates, the number of slaves imported yearly doubled after the British announcement. Part of the explanation can be found in Brazilian defiance but, more important, most Brazilians realized that the inhuman traffic would halt soon. As a more enlightened attitude came to prevail, public opinion increasingly opposed the continued importation. Also the Brazilians resented the fact that they bore the blame and shame for the trade while most of the slave ships were foreign-owned, particularly by Portuguese, and their owners exacted handsome profits from the impecunious planters. Finally the Brazilians indicated their readiness to suppress the trade, which was effectively accomplished by the Queiróz Law, passed in 1850.

In the nineteenth century, the area around Rio de Janiero was the undisputed depot of the slave trade. The termi-

nation of the slave trade brought to a close a long phase
(more than three hundred years) in Brazilian history. It heralded many changes. For one thing, money tied up in the
slave trade—and it was a staggering sum—was freed for other
investments. For another, the continuing need for labor dictated a greater encouragement and welcoming of European
immigration.

A more rapid pace of urbanization began to alter Rio de
Janeiro. By the end of the first decade of Pedro II's reign it
was the largest city in South America, with a population exceeding a quarter of a million. Pressed between sea and
mountains, the city wound its way along beaches and into
mountain valleys. Where the land was flat, streets intersect-
ing at right angles defined the city, but frequently the terrain
admitted only single, crooked streets. Some imposing buildings dominated the city: the National Assembly, Senate, Palace of the Municipal Government, the naval and military ar-
senals and academies, the customs houses, the former Viceregal Palace that had been coverted into government offices,
the National Library, National Museum, and Academy of Fine
Arts. Magnificent religious structures were in full evidence as
well. The houses rose three or four stories, with the ground
floor commonly given over to business or commerce and the
family residing above. Already, however, a migration to the
picturesque suburbs of Botafogo and Engenho Velho was
under way.

Urban society enticed ever larger numbers of the planter
aristocrats to spend less time on their estates and more amid
the conviviality of the cities with their noisy, friendly streets
and their sedate salons. The attractions, social or political, of
the court in Rio de Janeiro tempted the landed gentry from
all corners of the empire to visit the capital, if not to reside
there. That same class began to send some of its sons to
study law in São Paulo or Olinda (later to Recife where the
law school was transferred in 1854) or to study medicine in
Rio de Janeiro and Bahia. Adapted to the ways of the city,
those university graduates abandoned the plantations for-
ever.

In the invigorated urban environment literature flow-

ered. Educated Brazilians always had been given to poetry, but in the decade of the 1840s prose assumed a new importance with the appearance of the novel. Antônio Gonçalves Teixeira e Sousa introduced the first with the publication in 1843 of his brief *O Filho do Pescador* (The Fisherman's Son). Five more novels, all of them undistinguished, issued from his pen. The prolific Joaquim Manuel de Macedo (twenty-one novels to his credit) published his first and most successful novel, *A Moreninha* (The Little Brunette) the following year. An instant success, it has gone through more editions than any other Brazilian novel. Sentimental and romantic, it is a classic of middle-class literature in both origin and appeal. Offering valuable insights into an invigorated urban, bourgeois society emerging during the early Second Empire, Macedo used the romantic novel as a means to make subtle political statements on social change. Through the character of Carolina, the novel presents a very early statement favoring an impressive array of women's rights. The third novelist was Manuel Antônio de Almeida, whose only book, *Memórias de um Sargento de Milícias* (Memories of a Militia Sergeant) appeared first in serialized form in the newspapers and then in 1854–1855 as a book. He depicted the picaresque *carioca* life of the first quarter of the nineteenth century.

The theater also flourished at this time and no one contributed more to its vitality than Luís Carlos Martins Pena, witty satirist of manners and morals. His comedies amused but they also contained telling observations of Brazilian foibles. The *Correio Mercantil,* which began publication in 1843, regularly contained a literary section, which more often than not printed translations of French works, but occasionally Brazilian works too. *The Correio,* and with it the *Jornal do Commércio,* first issued in 1827, were for many years the leading newspapers of the realm. They attempted to give full coverage of the news—local, national, and international—and ran pithy and influential editorials. Both the quality and quantity of the intellectual life of the empire were increasing.

Brazil already had proved its political viability by triumphing over the threats of disunity, consolidating its territorial integrity, challenging British hegemony, and imple-

menting an effective two-party parliamentary government under the guidance of a benevolent emperor. Indeed, by mid-century the nation-state had emerged. In the course of a half-century the Brazilians had completely taken over their own government. Starting from their traditional base in the municipal councils, they had slowly moved upward until, after 1840, a Brazilian even sat on the imperial throne. The transfer of political power from the Portuguese to the Brazilians marked a significant political change. The psychological implications were momentous, and not the least in consequence was the growth of nationalism. The prohibition of the slave trade constituted the first effort to challenge the rigid economic structure of the colonial past and opened the door to socio-economic change. For the first time the prospects of the empire looked bright. An American visitor, Thomas Ewbank, predicted a glorious future: "As for the material elements of greatness, no people under the sun are more highly favored, and have a higher destiny opened before them."

Chapter Four

Modernization and Continuity

Undergoing a major political change during the first half of the nineteenth century, Brazil evolved from colony to nation. By stages the elite took control of the government. The coronation of Brazilian-born Pedro II climaxed that process, and he brought tranquillity, order, and stability to the empire. The succeeding decades witnessed economic growth wrought by the expansion of the lucrative coffee industry. The combination of political stability and economic prosperity facilitated the introduction and consideration of new ideas. Those ideas emanating from the capitalist nations admired by the elite helped initiate and propel modernization, a process by which limited groups within the population, particularly the urban middle and upper classes adopted the life-styles and attitudes prevalent in the "modern" North Atlantic nations. Gilberto Freyre, labeling this significant trend "the re-Europeanization of Brazil," judged it the major characteristic of the nineteenth century.

Coffee as a Motor of Change

A coffee export boom contributed significantly to shaping a remarkable period from 1830 to 1930, in Brazilian history. It

made possible the transition from neo-capitalism to capital-ism. It did so, curiously, while strengthening some of the basic characteristics implanted by the sugar industry during the 1530 to 1560 period: the _latifundia, monoculture_, export orientation, and dependency. Although obviously rooted in the countryside, the coffee boom facilitated modernization, urbanization, and industrialization. It fueled change.

In the course of the century—particularly after 1850—the coffee industry attracted foreign capital; created domestic capital for investment, often, most important, in industriali-zation; facilitated the introduction of new technologies; en-couraged railroad construction; opened up and populated Western Brazil; and pioneered the transition from slave to salaried labor. A combination of the decline of slavery, the need for salaried workers, and coffee prosperity attracted ever larger numbers of European immigrants to Brazil. Coffee production created a new, more dynamic, more modern bourgeoisie, thoroughly international in character. Respond-ing to the coffee markets, Brazil integrated itself ever more tightly into the capitalist marketplace of the North Atlantic. Rising coffee sales to the United States set Brazilian foreign policy on a new course, making it all but inevitable that Wash-ington would emerge as the new metropolis in the twentieth century. Coffee provided the economic prosperity to accom-pany and to reinforce the political order of the Second Empire and to create a new political order under the Old Republic (1889–1930).

The age of sugar, the dominant export of the colonial economy, faded rapidly in the nineteenth century. In the first decade of independence, sugar still ranked as the single most important crop, accounting for over 30 percent of the ex-ports. The following decade it fell to second place behind coffee and never again recovered its preeminence, so that by the last decade of the century it furnished but 6 percent of the nation's exports, although it remained an important crop of internal consumption. At mid-century Brazil possessed ap-proximately 1,651 sugar mills of which 144 operated by steam, 253 by water power, and 1,275 by animal power. A decade and a half later there were only 511 sugar mills, the reduced

figure brought about both by the decline in the industry and a consolidation of the mills. Aggressive and efficient foreign competition challenged the empire's shaky position in the world's markets. The new mills in the West Indies were mechanized rapidly, and radiating railroad lines increased the size and efficiency of the plantations. These mills produced sugar so economically that they drove the more highly priced (because inefficiently produced) Brazilian sugar off the international market. Also, countries that once had imported sugar freely began to experiment with the sugar beet. In some regions of Brazil, deforestation and impoverishment of the soil further contributed to the decline of the sugar industry. Although the total quantity of sugar exports rose 33 percent in the last half of the nineteenth century, prices for that sugar fell by 11 percent. The sugar statistics seem gloomy when compared to other exports. During that same period, total exports rose by 214 percent and the average price 46 percent. Between 1833 and 1889, the value of foreign trade increased by six to seven times. Coffee made that remarkable record possible.

Although a new and welcome impetus to the national economy, the coffee industry on closer examination proved in fact to repeat many old economic characteristics: the prevalence of large plantations, an emphasis on a single crop raised mostly for export, and a consequent dependency on foreign markets for prosperity. Moreover, in the beginning it was slave labor that worked the plantations. Also coffee preserved a patriarchal social system reminiscent of its agricultural predecessor, the sugar plantation. The size and operation of the coffee *fazenda*, as well, gave it certain other similarities to the sugar plantation. Both centered on the big house with its chapel, slave quarters, storehouses, stables, sheds, and machinery. However, coffee growing and processing required larger investments and consequently was more prohibitive for the small or medium-sized farm.

On the other hand, some basic differences in outlook distinguished the sugar and coffee producer. The sugar planters, who were spokesmen for conservative doctrines and intimately allied with the imperial government depended on

protective tariffs. Less prone to change than the coffee producers, they made too little effort to increase productivity or efficiency. They acted on the assumptions that slavery would always exist, that the sugar aristocracy would always be important to the government, and that the government would always support the sugar industry. Less wedded to the past, the coffee planters tended to hold more adaptable economic and social views. Their increasingly heavy dependence on an expanding foreign trade made them receptive, for example, to liberal trade-doctrines. They seemed readier to experiment with new techniques, machinery, and labor practices. Since most of the coffee industry began after the cessation of the slave trade, it depended less on slavery than the sugar industry had. In fact, the *fazendas* relied ever more heavily on immigrant workmen hired at modest salaries. Many representatives of the coffee class favored accelerated immigration, an attitude seldom expressed and rarely acted upon by the sugar class.

Coffee appeared late in Brazil and its cycle in the economy began modestly. The seeds were introduced into Pará from French Guiana around 1727. The cultivation of coffee trees penetrated the Amazon region, but more importantly it spread southward, passing through Bahia and reaching Rio de Janeiro around 1770. At approximately the same time it appeared in Minas Gerais. The coffee industry at first centered on the high terraces and lower mountain slopes on the southern side of the valley of the Paraíba River. There climatic and topological conditions were nearly perfect for the temperamental trees. The Paraíba originates just northeast of the city of São Paulo, meanders across the entire length of the state of Rio de Janeiro, and flows into the Atlantic some twenty miles south of Espírito Santo. Along that course, coffee production reached its peak in the mid-nineteenth century. Careless and wasteful agricultural practices soon diminished the harvests in the once-fertile valley, pushing production westward. The green waves of coffee trees soon inundated Minas Gerais and São Paulo.

At the same time, coffee cultivation had spread through the Caribbean region. By the second decade of the nine-

teenth century, Haiti, Jamaica, Cuba, and Venezuela were exporting the bean. Colombia and Costa Rica began producing coffee for export before mid-century, and Guatemala and El Salvador marketed the beans during the last half of the century. Together they grew far less coffee than Brazil.

To cultivate coffee, whether in the Paraíba Valley or to the west, the first step was to clear the land. The proprietors employed the traditional slash-and-burn method adopted from the Indians. The workers chopped down all the underbrush and trees and hauled away the usable timber for building purposes. After providing a suitable firebreak for the area, they ignited the dried wood and brush prior to the September rains. A simple hoe prepared the land. Seedlings planted in even vertically oriented rows climbed the hills or mountain slopes. The laborers weeded those fields semiannually. By the end of the third year the young trees, then nearly six feet high, began to produce, reaching full production—between three and four pounds of berries per tree—by the end of the sixth year. They could bear fruit for fifteen to thirty years depending on the soil and climate.

Harvesting began in May when the reddish brown berries, a little larger than cranberries, weighed down the tree branches. The harvester encircled each branch with thumb and index finger, pulling toward him to strip the branch of its berries. They, along with twigs and leaves, fell into the screen of woven bamboo each worker carried. Tossed into the air, the berries fell to the bottom of the bamboo strainer and the leaves and twigs remaining on the top were brushed off. The workers then dumped the berries into bags to be carried to a field shed from which they were transported to a drying terrace. On an average, the worker gathered three bushels of coffee berries a day, enough to produce approximately fifty pounds of dried coffee. An acre of trees yielded on the average between four and five hundred pounds of berries.

Each berry, coated with pulp and a tough shell (*casco*), contained two seeds, the coffee beans. Each coffee bean was enclosed in a thick covering (*casquinho*) and a delicate adherent membrane (*pergaminho*). The task of processing was to remove all the covering from the tiny beans. A vigorous wash-

ing removed the pulp and shell. The beans were then dried for approximately sixty days on an open expanse of beaten earth or concrete called the *terreiro*. (A few progressive planters used steam sheds to complete the drying in a few hours.) When the skins became shriveled, hard, and nearly black, the beans were pounded in wooden mortars, either by hand or by water-driven or steam-driven machines. The blows burst open the covering skins without injuring the tough bean. Sifting then separated the skins from the beans. Finally, the workers sorted them according to size and quality and sacked them. During the harvesting season, the plantation worked long and hard hours.

Mules and railroads carried the sacks of coffee beans to the nearest ports for export. During the heyday of the Paraíba Valley, the port of Rio de Janeiro handled 88 percent of Brazil's coffee exports as compared to 10 percent for Santos, 1 percent for Bahia, and 1 percent for the remaining Brazilian ports. For about a half-century the bulk of the coffee traffic headed for Rio de Janeiro. The mules, each with a pair of coffee sacks slung from a rough pack frame, paraded single-file along the paths and good hard roads of the valley to the railroads, which began to penetrate the state of Rio de Janeiro in the 1860s and 1870s. At the railroad stations the mules discharged their cargo, and the coffee bags were piled high on the platform and in nearby warehouses to await shipment. The *comissários*, or planters' agents, in Rio de Janeiro received the coffee and sold it for a small commission to the packers; the packers then transferred it by horse carts from the railroad to the huge warehouses in the northern and eastern parts of the capital. In the caverns of those warehouses the coffee was resacked, each bag being carefully weighed at 130 pounds (60 kilograms). From the packer the coffee went to the exporter, usually an Englishman, to be sent abroad when the market was favorable. Long was the odyssey of the coffee bean from the tree to the cup, and complex was the business managing that journey. Many made their fortunes on those beans. The government, too, profited handsomely, thanks to taxes it levied on the business.

Coffee exports mounted annually. The first coffee ex-

ported left Maranhão in 1731 for Lisbon. Maranhão and Pará continued to ship coffee to the metropolis throughout the rest of the eighteenth century. In 1779, Rio de Janeiro sent its first shipment of coffee to Lisbon, a modest ton and a quarter. By the period of independence, coffee accounted for about one-fifth of the exports, a figure which rose to two-thirds by the time of the fall of the monarchy in 1889. Those figures indicated an increase from 190,060 to 5,586,000 in the number of sacks of coffee beans shipped yearly to the world markets in a sixty-seven-year period. The value of the coffee sold during those years equaled that of all the exports during the entire colonial period. Of all the major Brazilian exports of the nineteenth century, only coffee met no intense international competition. By the 1858–1860 period, coffee provided half the income from exports. As one result of the rising coffee exports, the country after 1860, for the first time in its independent history, exported more than it imported. Accordingly the balance of trade tipped in favor of Brazil, a novelty that became commonplace over the succeeding decades. The favorable balance was all the more notable because the amount of imports continually rose.

The emperor paid tribute to the producers of the new wealth. In 1841, he first elevated a coffee planter to the nobility: José Gonçalves de Morais became the Barão de Piraí. With each passing decade thereafter, the coffee class figured ever more prominently among the new nobility. Indeed, some of the coffee planters were the wealthiest men of the realm. Joaquim José de Sousa Breves alone harvested 1.5 percent of the empire's total crop in 1860 on his extensive and fertile *fazendas* and lived in a fashion commensurate with his economic power. Antônio Clemente Pinto, Barão de Nova Friburgo, who could trace his riches directly to coffee exports, enjoyed a home in the capital more luxurious than the royal palace. In fact, his *palácio* became the residence of the president after the proclamation of the republic. Visitors to the coffee regions commented favorably on the vast plantations and the solid, often sumptuous residences that, like those in the sugar areas, embodied an entire way of life.

The impressive coffee *fazenda* of Commendador Silva

Table 4.1 Brazilian Exports in the Nineteenth Century

(Percent of Total Exports)

Decade	Total	Coffee	Sugar	Cocoa	Maté	Tobacco	Cotton	Rubber	Skins & Hides
1821–1830	85.8	18.4	30.1	.5	—	2.5	20.6	.1	13.6
1831–1840	89.8	43.8	24.0	.6	.5	1.9	10.8	.3	7.9
1841–1850	88.2	41.4	26.7	1.0	.9	1.8	7.5	.4	8.5
1851–1860	90.9	48.8	21.2	1.0	1.6	2.6	6.2	2.3	7.2
1861–1870	90.3	45.5	12.3	.9	1.2	3.0	18.3	3.1	6.0
1871–1880	95.1	56.6	11.8	1.2	1.5	3.4	9.5	5.5	5.6
1881–1890	92.3	61.5	9.9	1.6	1.2	2.7	4.2	8.0	3.2
1891–1900	95.6	64.5	6.0	1.5	1.3	2.2	2.7	15.0	2.4

SOURCE: Hélio S. Silva, "Tendências e Características do Comércio Exterior no Século XIX," *Revista de História da Economia Brasileira* (June 1953), p. 8.

Pinto in Minas Gerais encompassed an area of sixty-four square miles. On it grew cotton, sugar, corn, mandioca, and a variety of fruits; in its ample pastures herds of livestock grazed. None of these items found their way into the marketplace. They were used to feed and clothe the household and slaves, who at one time numbered seven hundred. The commercial crop was coffee, a source of considerable wealth which enabled the Silva Pinto family to live in grand style.

The decade of the 1860s owed its remarkable prosperity to factors other than mounting coffee sales, important as those were. The Civil War in the United States reduced the world's cotton supply and impelled Europe's textile manufacturers to seek other sources. Brazil increased cotton production to meet the new demands. Cotton during the 1860s accounted for 18.3 percent of the total exports, a threefold increase over the preceding decade. Furthermore, burgeoning European and North American industries demanded more raw products. For one thing, Brazil sold rubber, whose export accounted for less than .5 percent of the total in the 1840s and a full 15 percent in the 1890s. The general trend during the last half of the century, as table 4.1 indicates, was for coffee, rubber, cocoa, and erva-maté exports to increase, while sugar, skins and hides, and cotton (with the exception of the 1860s) decreased. Tobacco remained about the same, consisting of between 2 percent and 3 percent of the exports.

Great Britain maintained its dominant position in Brazilian foreign commerce. The British supplied the lion's share of the imports—the most important of which were textiles, manufactured items for wear, and prepared foods—and controlled and handled most of the empire's export trade. Furthermore, they supplied the loans and foreign investment the empire needed. After 1870 the United States emerged as the major customer for Brazil's exports, buying more than 50 percent of the coffee and rubber exported, as well as much of the cocoa crop. It was at this time that those two giant countries of this hemisphere began to discover each other. Economic approximation was under way when Pedro II made a visit to the United States in 1876 to see the country and to contribute to the centennial celebrations in Philadelphia. Curious Americans welcomed the philosopher-emperor from the tropics. An equally curious emperor examined the booming North American colossus. Both liked what they saw and Dom Pedro's visit was a great success. The trip marked the opening of a political rapprochement.

The prosperity brought about by mounting coffee sales not only influenced Brazil's relations with the outside world but helped to transform the country internally. A variety of material changes resulted.

Material Transformation

The modest Alves Branco Tariff of 1844, permission to import machinery duty-free in 1846, the first laws for the incorporation of commercial companies in 1849, the promulgation of the Commercial Code in 1850, the end of the slave trade in the same year with the consequent liberation of capital for investment, and the establishment of the second Bank of Brazil in 1851 were powerful economic inventives for material expansion. The suppression of the Praieira Revolt in 1850, the long and tranquil government of the Conservatives that began in 1848, and the strength and assurance which the able young emperor brought to his realm were political stimuli to

the same end. Good and strong government, public order, favorable economic laws, and prosperity gave an impetus to the material transformation of the empire.

The decade of the 1850s was one of unprecedented activity. João Capistrano de Abreu characterized the decade as "the most brilliant of the empire." The organization of credit, the better circulation and wiser investment of capital, and the increased emission of money, all made possible by the establishment of banks, contributed to that change. In 1845, there existed only one bank in the empire, the Commercial Bank of Rio de Janeiro. That year, with the foundation of the Commercial Bank of Bahia, initiated the beginning of the rapid expansion of the banking network.

Irineu Evangelista de Sousa, Visconde de Mauá (1813–1889), established the Bank of Brazil in 1851. His bank and the Commercial Bank of Rio de Janeiro merged in 1853 and continued to bear the name Bank of Brazil, the first large-scale institution of its type. For a few years it monopolized the emission of bank notes for the government. A world financial crisis in 1857 briefly shook Brazil, but after calm returned the confident government extended to other banks the privilege of emitting money. Abuse of the new privilege flooded the empire with currency, a scandal in which the Bank of Brazil was deeply implicated. As a result, in 1866, the government assumed the responsibility for all issuance of money, a monopoly it exercised until 1888. Foreign banks made their appearance in Brazil for the first time with the inauguration of the London and Brazil Bank in the capital in 1862. During the next two years, it opened five branches. The Brazilian and Portuguese Bank was chartered in 1863. The banks ended most of the personal financial transactions characteristic of the early decades of the empire. Impersonal institutions of growing resources, they multiplied the power and importance of the city and, conversely, diminished the prestige of the landowners, particularly the sugar planters, whose debts to the urban banks increased.

The telegraph initiated a communications revolution in Brazil in 1852. The first line connected the imperial palace at São Cristóvão, on the outskirts of the capital, to the military

headquarters at Campo Santa Ana in the capital. By 1857, Petropolis, the cool summer capital in the mountains behind Rio de Janeiro, communicated telegraphically with Rio de Janeiro. The outbreak of the Paraguayan war initiated a flurry of activity to string lines southward to the theater of action. In a record time of six months a telegraph line connected the southern provinces to the court. In the opposite direction, the lines reached Belém in 1886 and thereafter penetrated into the interior. The number of stations increased. In 1861 there were 10 stations with 40 miles of lines transmitting 233 messages. By 1885 there were 171 stations with 6,560 miles of lines handling over 600,000 messages. The progressive Visconde de Mauá formed a company with an English partner to lay a submarine cable from Europe to Brazil. The idea of not only direct but instantaneous communication with Europe titillated the Brazilian imagination. A grand festival inaugurated that line. Seated before a special machine in the National Library on June 23, 1874, Pedro II dictated the first message to be cabled to Europe, as, very significantly, Rio de Janeiro was linked to Europe by telegraph long before it could similarly communicate with other parts of its own empire. The next stage in international communications was to establish telegraph contact with the Plata neighbors. The lines reached Montevideo in 1879 and Buenos Aires in 1883.

A revolution in transportation accompanied that in communications. Historically the water routes had been the most important means of transportation and so they continued to be throughout most of the nineteenth century. The steamship first appeared in Bahia de Todos os Santos in 1819 to serve Salvador and neighboring towns. Gradually the shipping companies adopted steam power for coastal trade. By 1839, a steamship line plied between the capital and the northern provinces. The navy also purchased steam vessels. The nation understood the dramatic significance of the steamship in 1843, when the puffing and chugging *Guapiassu* churned the waters of the Amazon for the first time. That steamship journeyed from Belém to Manaus, nine hundred miles upstream, in nine days and returned in half the time, a remarkable record considering that hitherto the sailing ves-

sels required two to three months to ascend and a month to descend. In 1852, Mauá formed the Amazon Steam Navigation Company to exploit the entire Amazon basin with the benefit of the steam engine. In the previous year, the Royal English Mail Line had established regular steamship service between European and South American ports. Steam navigation proceeded at a modest pace. By 1875, some 29 percent of the vessels entering Brazilian harbors were steam-propelled; the rest were sailing ships.

For many years the government eagerly had hoped that some entrepreneur would undertake to construct a railroad. A new law in 1852 provided favorable conditions for anyone who would do so. Mauá accepted the challenge. Completed in 1854, the first line ran ten miles from the head of Guanabara Bay to the foot of the mountains in which Petropolis nestled. It was a modest start and came less than two years after the first rail line in South America was inaugurated in Chile. In 1858 Brazil's second and third railroad lines commenced operation. One, in the province of Pernambuco running from Recife to Cabo, a distance of twenty miles, the first stage of a line which would link Recife with the São Francisco River and its commerce, crossed rich sugar lands. The other connected Rio de Janeiro with Quemados, a distance of thirty miles, the first stretch of the Dom Pedro II railroad, which reached São Paulo in 1877. By 1874, there were approximately eight hundred miles of tracks, which meant that in the twenty years since Mauá inaugurated the first line only about forty miles of track had been laid each year.

After 1875, construction increased rapidly: from 1875–1879, 1,023 miles of track were laid; from 1880 to 1884, 2,200; from 1885 to 1889, 2,500. In 1889, then, trackage totaled approximately 6,000 miles. Fourteen of the twenty provinces had at least some rail service, although most of the trackage was concentrated in the southeast. There, as the plantations moved rapidly inland to exploit virgin soil, the coffee interests needed fast and efficient transportation to get the coffee beans to the ports. The governments, both provincial and national, catered to their needs. One emerging characteristic of rail construction was that the new lines generally ran be-

tween plantation and port. Thus, they helped to speed exports to market rather than to unify the empire or to create an internal economic infrastructure. Whatever the residual benefits for Brazil, the railroads further linked Brazil to world markets and thereby deepened dependency.

The railroad brought changes in its wake. Along the new tracks and at rail junctures and heads, new villages and towns sprang up and older ones took on a new life. Inevitably the railroad raised the value of land, more often than not causing squatters and peasants alike to lose their land to speculators and large landowners.

Other means of transportation developed slowly. The *bandeirante* tracks provided the most widespread network for travel. The more densely populated areas had narrow dirt roads, more often than not rough and unusable after heavy rains. Over those, horses, carts, coaches, and mule trains passed. A singular experiment in road construction was the Union and Industry Highway built to connect Petropolis and Juiz de Fora, the gateway to the province of Minas Gerais. In 1861 the Government completed the ninety-mile road begun in 1856. Eighteen feet across, it rested on a roadbed of crushed rock with roadside ditches of brick. Its builders had employed the latest principles of road engineering. Coaches sped along the road at an average of twelve miles per hour. With time out to rest, they could cover the distance between the two towns in a record nine hours. In the decade of the 1860s two other highways were built, both connecting the lowlands with the highland interior, one in Paraná and the other in Santa Catarina. In the immensity of Brazil, those short roads were significant only because they were built in areas of accelerating economic growth.

Once the process of growth had begun the effects were cumulative. The expanding transportation system opened new markets and tapped new resources. Coffee sales and profits from other agricultural sales, such as the high prices received for cotton in the 1860s, introduced new wealth into the economy, which in turn increased demands and provided capital for investment. After 1860, the favorable balance of trade infused greater sums into the economy. The new banking

system provided the instrument for both investment and credit. The lengthy struggle against Paraguay, 1865–1870, revealed many inherent weaknesses in the Brazilian economy, not least of which was the need for industries that could support an active army. The world financial crisis of 1875, the repercussions of which sent the Brazilian economy reeling, and a decline in coffee prices between 1880 and 1886 caused the most thoughtful Brazilians to reassess their vulnerable economy and intensified their first aspirations toward an economy diversified and strengthened through industrialization. Thanks to steamships, railroads, telegraphs, banks, an enlightened and stable government, and the capital provided by coffee, industrialization was for the first time within the realm of possibility.

In the 1850s it was already possible to discern the first faint glimmerings of industrialization and to observe a hitherto unprecedented growth of business. In that decade some 62 industrial firms were founded as well as 14 banks, 20 steamship companies, 23 insurance companies, 4 colonization companies, 8 mining companies, 3 urban transportation companies, 2 gas companies, and 8 railroad lines. Many of those enterprises represented pure speculation that led to financial crises in 1857 and 1864. Discounting such paper activity, a tiny but expanding industrial base was laid. In 1850, there were approximately 50 factories in Brazil; in 1889, there were 636. The textile industry was the most important. The 9 cotton mills in 1865 became 100 before the end of the empire. Other important industries were food processing, clothing manufacturing, and woodworking, as well as chemical and metallurgical industries. Even the sugar barons stirred themselves in an attempt to revive their moribund industry by introducing steam power into their operations. By 1878 many of the inefficient if picturesque sugar mills had been replaced by the *usinas*, mechanized refineries. Some limited industrialization began in the traditionally sugar-oriented Northeast after the ports were closed to the slave trade. In the quarter century thereafter, Recife acquired nine textile mills, a candle factory, a tobacco factory, a soap factory, and a biscuit factory along with some other industries. The Conservatives enacted

a frankly protectionist tariff in 1885 with the aim of encouraging national industry. On the one hand it reduced duties on primary materials needed by Brazilian manufacturers, while on the other it raised the tariff to an average of 48 percent on goods competing with those made locally.

In the vanguard of those concerned with encouraging business and industry stood the Visconde de Mauá, whose biography follows the classic Horatio Alger format. Born of humble parents in Rio Grande do Sul, he worked his way up from clerk to manager of a British commercial house in Rio de Janeiro. His name was connected with almost every phase of the progress and transformation of Brazil during his lifetime. In the mid-1840s, he began to lay the foundations for a vast economic empire which included shipyards, steamship companies, banks, and railroads. In Rio de Janeiro alone he built floating docks, increased the city's water supply, installed gas lighting in the public streets, and initiated a streetcar system. "The spirit of association," he told one group of stockholders, "is one of the strongest elements of the prosperity of any country. It is, so to speak, the soul of progress." His enthusiasm, as well as his efficiency, brought new foreign capital into Brazil. "Credit is the basis of capital and the source of new wealth," he proclaimed. Elsewhere the idea might have been conventional, but the Brazilians remained somewhat wary of his capitalistic ideas. Unfortunately he overextended himself and the government refused to come to his aid during the financial crisis of 1875. His economic empire came tumbling down around him. No doubt Mauá would have felt much more at ease among the captains of industry who were then at the helm of the United States economy—Fisk, Frick, Vanderbilt, Gould, et al.—than he did in the neocapitalist economy of Brazil where few appreciated his efforts and many suspected him of questionable practices. Yet in his very active lifetime, this one man did more than any other individual, or group for that matter, to orient the empire's steps along the path of industrialization. Furthermore, his railroads, steamship lines, and banks contributed to national unity.

The capital faithfully reflected the changes affecting the

coastal belt of Brazil. In the 1850s and early 1860s, Rio de Janeiro became a bustling metropolis. By 1868, it boasted of a population over 600,000. All the principal streets had been paved and an efficient drainage system installed. The new streets were wide and lined with buildings of architectural beauty. New public markets and an increased number of shops provided a greater variety of wares than ever. Omnibuses drawn by mule teams, carriages, and Tilbury coaches crowded the main streets which, along with principal buildings and comfortable homes, were illuminated with gas. At night both city and suburb appeared well lighted.

Undeniably the decade of the 1850s stands out as a period of innovation. It was a propitious start heralding other changes which, as we shall see, continued to transform the empire. Much of the financial burden to underwrite the changes fell on the government, which levied a wide array of taxes to meet its expenses. Taxes were placed on official stamps, the salaries of government employees, water service, stores, buildings, professions, lotteries, vehicles of transportation, stock transfers, promissory notes, exports, imports, slaves, cattle, transfer of property, mining, storage, docks, anchorage, transportation, alcoholic beverages, and the mail and telegraphs. National income rose rapidly. In 1838, it had totaled 20,000 contos; in 1858 it exceeded 100,000. During that same period, the income from import duties tripled. Periodically the government found it necessary to borrow money for extraordinary purposes, and customarily these loans came from British bankers. Prior to 1858 the government contracted loans to finance the indemnization to Portugal, to cover budget deficits, or to pay the service on previous loans. The loan of 1858 marked a turning point and demonstrated once again the progress being made: it was the first loan secured for a productive purpose, railroad building, and the first liquidated strictly according to the terms of the contract.

The monarchy continued to do whatever it could to encourage the growth. In 1860, the government authorized its seventh ministerial post, for Agriculture, Commerce, and Public Works. The Central School opened its doors in Rio de Janeiro in 1858 to train engineers, an education hitherto available

only in the military academies. In 1874, it was reorganized and became the Polytechnical Institute. The School of Mines was established in Minas Gerais that same year. São Bento das Lages, the first agricultural school, began to offer classes in 1877. Agricultural societies were formed throughout the empire, and national and regional fairs and exhibits increased in number. These accomplishments attested to the official policy favoring modernization by which the elites hoped to reshape their country.

Progress and Dependency

The Brazilian elite boasted of their European heritage and even those who had Indian and/or African ancestors dwelt more on their European ties than otherwise. They readily understood what was happening in Europe and ably discussed the latest ideas radiating from the Old World, which they welcomed to their shores. But European thought was less an intellectual spring and more an ideological flood that swept before it most Brazilian originality. Generally speaking, three major European philosophies shaped the ideology of the elites during the nineteenth century: the Enlightenment, the ideas of evolution put forth by Charles Darwin and Herbert Spencer, and Positivism. The concept of "progress," perhaps the key word for the understanding of nineteenth-century Brazilian history, linked the three.

Stressing the vincibility of ignorance, the Enlightenment philosophers concluded that if people had the opportunity to know the truth, they would select "civilization" over "barbarism." Adherents to the Enlightenment believed in a universally valid standard to judge "civilization," and the criteria for such a judgment rested on European concepts of progress. Civilization and the progress which led to it became identified with Europe, or more specifically with England, France, and Germany. Moreover, a burgeoning faith in science directed judgments on progress as well as progress itself away from philosophical and moral matters toward material change. The popularized ideas of Darwin that organic forms devel-

oped over the course of time and represented successive stages in a single evolutionary process toward perfection further heightened the interest in progress, giving it in fact a scientific veneer. Very propitiously, Spencer, who commanded considerable attention in Brazil, applied the same principle of evolution to society. To Spencer progress signified a march toward "the establishment of the greatest perfection and most complete happiness." However, that march subsumed a great many economic changes and adaptations. As one example, Spencer advocated railroads as a vital part of the infrastructure of a modern society. As another, he regarded industrialization as a certain manifestation of progress. Many Brazilians drew from Spencer the notion of the interrelationship of science, industry, and progress, a combination pointing to future glory through societal evolution. Like most European thinkers, Spencer said much that damned Brazil, his racist statements for example. But the Brazilian elites proved to be selective readers, choosing to ignore what displeased—or frightened—them.

Many of the ideas on progress gleaned from the Enlightenment, Darwin, Spencer, as well as from other sources, seemed to converge in the form Auguste Comte's Positivism assumed in Brazil during the last quarter of the century. Positivism affirmed the inevitability of social evolution and progress. To Comte that progress was attainable through the acceptance of scientific laws codified by Positivism. Outward manifestations of progress—again railroads and industrialization—assumed great importance in Positivism, emphatically so among the Brazilians, whether they acknowledged Comte or not.

Clearly those distant intellectual mentors provided powerful arguments for those elites desiring to replicate European civilization in Brazil, which to their thinking evinced all too many "barbaric" Indian and African traits. In the first issue of the literary and scientific magazine *Minerva Brasiliense* (November 1843), Sales Tôrres Homem saluted the progress of the nineteenth century. The breathtaking advances in science as well as the achievements of "political and moral sciences" excited him. He believed Brazil would

participate in the progress emanating from Europe. He expressed tremendous faith in the future, a faith shared by many of the elites who constructed a philosophic overview echoing the European concept of "progress." Politically, they required order to implement it. Economically, they adopted capitalism, which seemed to have transformed the North Atlantic states into modern nations, to finance it. The enthusiastic embrace of foreign ideas tightened the grip of dependency.

In the last half of the century, the elite sharpened their awareness of the material progress being made on the continent. Many of them had mastered French, the second language of the Brazilian elite, and some had a knowledge of English or German, so that they had direct access to the information and literature of the nations whose progress impressed them. The newspapers carried accounts of what was happening in the leading nations of the Western world, and the programs of the learned societies featured discussions of the technical advances of the industrializing nations. Many members of the elite traveled abroad, thereby exposing themselves first hand to the innovations. They returned to Brazil with a nostalgia for Europe, particularly Paris, and the irrepressible desire to copy everything they saw there. Of course, the imports bore testimony to larger segments of the population of the manufacturing skill and ingenuity of those technologically advanced societies.

As the century matured, many Brazilians interpreted the experience of the United States as a verification of the wisdom of implementing European ideas in the New World. After all, the United States once had been a colony too, and yet by mid-century, not even three-quarters of a century after achieving independence, it seemed to exemplify Progress itself, certainly the material manifestations of it. Progress seemed ever more obvious in the post–Civil War period, which boasted of the transcontinental expansion of the railroads and the triumph of industrialization. The Brazilian elites attributed the success of the United States to two factors: the preponderance of Europeans in the racial composition and the adoption of European ideology, political as well as economic. In short,

the United States represented in their eyes the triumph of progress in the New World and further demonstrated the means of achieving it.

The elite's perception of progress is perhaps more correctly and easily defined by example rather than by more complex social science terminology. Later generations of scholars substituted the word *modernization* but such a replacement did little to clarify events in nineteenth-century Brazil. Both words, used interchangeably hereafter, implied a questioning and rejection of habits, patterns, and values associated with the Luso-Brazilian past and an admiration for the ideas, modes, technology, and styles of Europe and the United States and a desire to adopt—rarely to adapt—them. Consequently, "progress" meant a recreation of the nation as closely as possible to the European and North American model. So, the elite set out to spread education, to raise the level of technology, to industrialize, and to urbanize. They felt certain they would benefit from such a program, and by extension they assumed that their nation would benefit as well. They tended to identify (and to confuse) class well-being with national welfare.

As it turned out, the "progress" pursued by the Brazilians was superficial. They preferred a façade of change to the risk of tampering with basic neocolonial institutions—the land structures, for example—whose transformation might have instituted a more meaningful form of progress, but might also have threatened the privileges of the elite. They relied, for example, on monoculture and the export of coffee to finance most of the progress they sought, and thereby they tied their modernization to neocolonial practices that previously had neither benefited the majority of the Brazilians nor induced economic development. "Progress" in nineteenth-century Brazil was measured largely in quantitative terms. It could be measured—at least according to the elite, the politicians, and the scholars—by the number of miles of railroad tracks or telegraph lines, no matter where they went or what ends they served. The expansion and renovation of port facilities have been equated ipso facto with progress, even though in the

final analysis those ports more tightly linked Brazil with foreign markets, strengthening the monoexport sector of the economy and further contributing to Brazil's dependency. The large cities sought to transform themselves into copies of admired European cities, using Paris as the primary model. To the extent that Brazil aped Europe, the elite classified themselves, their cities or regions, and Brazil as "cultured," "civilized," or "progressive." The arrival of increasing numbers of European immigrants in the last quarter of the century signified the acceleration of the progress cherished by the elites since the newcomers brought with them much admired tastes and skills.

The establishment of peace and stability after 1850, and the prosperity infused by coffee exports permitted the acceleration of the process of modernization. Brazilian progress paralleled similar advances in the other major Latin American nations. Chile after the promulgation of the conservative constitution of 1833, Argentina after the unification of Buenos Aires with the other provinces in 1862, and Mexico after the execution of Emperor Maximilian in 1867 followed similar courses.

In speaking of "progress" a serious confusion can and does often arise, since progress signified to many some form of development. Here a semantic confusion intrudes that confuses development and growth. They are quite distinct and must be separated to understand better the economic fate of Brazil. Growth indicates simply and exclusively numerical accumulation and in no way indicates how it occurred, or what grew, or who benefited. The part of Brazil associated with coffee exports grew wealthier in the last half of the nineteenth century, but that wealth concentrated largely in one region, the Southeast, and in the hands of relatively few. One could argue that such growth through monoexportation undermined the well-being of Brazil. Development, on the other hand, signifies the maximum use of a nation's potential for the greatest benefit of the largest number of the inhabitants. Development can imply or include growth, although it is conceivable that a nation can develop without growing.

Nor does modernization or "progress" necessarily denote development.

The study of the efforts to modernize the moribund sugar industry by Peter L. Eisenberg, *The Sugar Industry in Pernambuco, 1840–1910: Modernization without Change,* illustrated perfectly the insidious aspect of modernization without basic institutional change. Modernization in the sugar industry meant the use of the latest technological advances and the abolition of forced labor. Governmental subsidies facilitated the planters and mill owners' conversion to modernization. They managed to survive and prosper to a certain extent, but they transferred losses suffered in the export market to the workers in the forms of low wages and dismal working conditions. Eisenberg found that after 1870 the daily wage for unskilled rural labor fell, while the cost of living continued to rise. He concluded, "One cannot escape the conclusion that the free rural laborer in the later nineteenth century enjoyed little material advantage over the slave." The declining standard of living for the rural worker in the Northeast was reflected in the growing number of deaths per one-thousand inhabitants in the later years of the century. Apparently urban workers in Rio de Janeiro, to cite another example, suffered a similar restriction in their quality of life. Professor Eulalia M. L. Lobo, who has conducted lengthy investigations of salaries and prices in the capital during the nineteenth century, emphasized the general trend toward the lowering of the real buying power of the workers' salaries in the last half of the century.

Scant evidence exists that Brazil *developed* in the nineteenth century. The type of progress selected or imposed complemented the export sector and benefited the elite associated with it. By spending accumulated capital on luxuries and "show pieces" of progress, by draining away potential capital in the form of interest payments on foreign loans, deposits of funds in foreign banks, or profits on foreign investments, the elite seem to have further impoverished the majority of the Brazilians. Brazil testified to the harsh reality that when growth occurs in an agrarian economy through the expansion of a narrow modern sector linked to exports, in-

equality in the distribution of income multiplies. Progress helped to perpetuate the glaring social inequalities which already had characterized Brazil because it took place within the framework of old institutions which previously had given ample evidence of their inability to provide socio-economic justice to the majority. "Progress," thus, should be understood as a most subjective concept, which in the nineteenth-century Brazilian experience contributed to retarding development, impoverishing the masses, and increasing dependency.

Statesmen and Diplomats

The empire matured politically under the skillful guidance of Emperor Pedro II. He personified the success of genetic governance. In nearly every way he contrasted with his dashing and romantic father. Pedro II was calm, deliberate, and serious. He eschewed military uniforms for somber black suits and preferred books and study to the active life of the outdoors. He practiced a morality in both private and public life which few could equal. The empress, Tereza Cristina Maria de Bourbon (1822–1889) of the Kingdom of the Two Sicilies, whom Pedro married in 1843, was the model of domesticity. By their example, the two monarchs impressed a Victorian morality on the court and government in an otherwise relaxed nation.

By all accounts—and his portraits and photographs do not contradict it—the emperor was an imposing and handsome man, simple in manners and unaffected in appearance. He seldom failed to win the sympathy of those who met him. Certainly all the foreign visitors exuded praise.

When Pedro had agreed to mount the throne at the age of fourteen, he was a puppet in the hands of the courtiers. He achieved political maturity within a few years. By 1847, he had consolidated his position and was virtually independent of political forces and influences. Thereafter he tightly controlled the reigns of government. As the constitution pre-

scribed, he functioned on a plane above political factions, the grand manipulator of all the instruments of government. Those responsibilities, as well as all his duties, the emperor took very earnestly. Perhaps one of the tersest and surest guides to his conception of his role as emperor can be found in this poem he penned in 1852:

> If I am pious, clement, just,
>   I'm only what I ought to be:
> The sceptre is a weighty trust,
>   A great responsibility;
> And he who rules with faithful hand,
>   With depth of thought and breadth of range,
> The sacred laws should understand,
>   But must not, at his pleasure, change.
>
> The chair of justice is the throne:
>   Who takes it bows to higher laws;
> The public good, and not his own,
>   Demands his care in every cause.
> Neglect of duty,—always wrong,—
>   Detestable in young or old,—
> By him whose place is high and strong,
>   Is magnified a thousandfold.
>
> When in the east the glorious sun
>   Spreads o'er the earth the light of day,
> All know the course that he will run,
>   Nor wonder at his light or way:
> But if perchance the light that blazed
>   Is dimm'd by shadows lying near,
> The startled world looks on amazed,
>   And each one watches it with fear.
>
> I likewise, if I always give
>   To vice and virtue their rewards,
> But do my duty thus to live;
>   No one his thanks to me accords.
> But should I fail to act my part,
>   Or wrongly do, or leave undone,
> Surprised, the people then would start
>   With fear, as at the shadow'd sun.

Fortunately he ruled better than he rhapsodized. The poem would scarcely last as a piece of literature, but as an indication of the emperor's own perception of his role it has considerable political value. Pedro ruled benevolently but firmly. As the years of his long reign waxed, he preferred to exercise power more indirectly but nonetheless his presence was always felt. The emperor believed that if power was shared by too many no one effectively exercised it. An immigrant leader of the German colony in Rio Grande do Sul observed in 1885 that the emperor "reigns, governs, and administers," exercising more power than most other sovereigns of the epoch.

As Brazil moved from its ambivalent neofeudalistic/neo-capitalistic stage toward a more fully developed capitalism, the emperor served as both a symbolic and effective guarantee of order and prosperity for the varied regional, rural groups. He watched over the interests of the sugar, cacao, and coffee classes in return for their loyalty. Rarely did he restrict their local autonomy or threaten their patrimonial domination. After all, Brazil was overwhelmingly rural, and Pedro calculated correctly that he needed the loyalty and support of those who exercised authority in the countryside if he was to reign peacefully.

Historians praise the honesty, integrity, and moderation of Pedro II. His rule probably benefited Brazil. Some critics, then as well as later, have considered him a man of mediocre intelligence who hesitated to propel the empire into the modern world. Arguments can and have been made that such caution was salutary. Pedro tried to rely on national opinion, which he distinguished from public opinion, as his guide. He seemed to equate national opinion with national well-being and thus divorced it in his mind from public opinion, which was according to his thought, often misguided, erroneous, and emotional, and therefore not always in accord with the best interests of the realm. In short, he relied on elitist views to guide him. He pointed out to his daughter, Princess-Regent Isabel (1846–1921), who on three occasions served as regent, that the surest way to ascertain national opinion was "to hear honest and intelligent men of all political views, to read fully everything the press throughout Brazil has to say,

and to listen to what is said in the legislative chambers both on the national and provincial levels." More often than not, the emperor sought his advice in the Council of State, in theory—and probably in practice as well—an august body of wise men.

The Liberals regarded the Council with suspicion as a bastion of conservative, if not reactionary, thought and the bulwark of centralized authority. It had been abolished during the radical heyday of 1834 only to be reestablished again in 1841 during the Conservatives' ascendancy. Twelve regular members and twelve extraordinary members composed the Council. They met in plenary session to discuss matters of the greatest importance but otherwise they sat in committees to handle routine work. Their primary duty was to advise the emperor on the use of the extensive moderating power which he wielded. From 1842 to 1889, Pedro appointed seventy-two councilors. The largest number, seventeen, came from the province of Rio de Janeiro; Bahia furnished fourteen and Minas Gerais thirteen. Indeed, the preeminence of the triumvirate of Rio de Janeiro, Minas Gerais, and São Paulo stood out. Together they provided thirty-three of the councilors, considerably outweighing the Pernambuco-Bahia axis and their satellite provinces from which came twenty-four councilors. Effective power, economic as well as political, gradually shifted to the Southeast. The preferential treatment of the Southeast elicited complaints from a jealous Northeast.

During the first decades of his reign, Pedro tended to rely on a handful of politicians whose honesty, skill, and long service to the nation impressed him. Principal among them were Honório Hermeto Carneiro Leão, Marquês de Paraná (Minas Gerais, 1801–1856); Pedro de Araújo Lima, Marquês de Olinda (Pernambuco, 1793–1870); José da Costa Carvalho, Marquês de Mont'Alegre (Bahia, 1796–1860); and Joaquim José Rodrigues Tôrres, Visconde de Itaboraí (Rio de Janeiro, 1802–1872). All four were Conservatives, representatives of the old landed class, whom Pedro elevated to the nobility. Their political experience reached far back into the nation's history: Olinda had been a deputy to the Côrtes; all four served in the legislature of the First Empire and played active

roles during the Regency, Mont'Alegre serving as one of the triumvirate of regents and Olinda as the single regent from 1837 to 1840. All four served on the Council of State and organized at least one cabinet. Olinda organized four cabinets and held portfolios in ten others; Itboraí served as president of the Council of Ministers twice and as a minister ten times. Three of them died before the end of the Paraguayan war, and the fourth, Itaboraí, left office in 1870. One Liberal provided perhaps the most perfect political and historical continuity. Antônio Paulino Limpo de Abreu, Visconde de Abaeté, was born in Portugal in 1798, came to Brazil with the royal court in 1808, began to serve as a minister during the Regency, held twelve portfolios during his political career, presided over the Council of Ministers from 1858 to 1860, became a councilor of state, and was elected president of the Senate in 1860, a post he held with distinction until his death in 1883. Statesmen such as these provided the perfect continuity with the past and gave a solid cohesion to the first decades of Pedro's reign. The death of the Visconde de Abaeté symbolically marked a significant break in human continuity with the pre–Second Empire past. New political generations came of age. Politicians whose memories recalled only the order, prosperity, and progress of the 1850s and thereafter filled the vacant offices. Understandably they possessed a different perception of the present and advocated new agendas for the future.

Using his moderating power and relying on the consensus of national opinion, the emperor alternated the Conservative and Liberal parties in power during the Second Empire. That alternation produced the following political pattern: 1840–1841, Liberals; 1841–1844, Conservatives; 1844–1848, Liberals; 1848–1853, Conservatives; 1853–1857, the Period of Conciliation in which both parties shared power; 1857–1862, Conservatives; 1862–1868, Liberals; 1868–1878, Conservatives; 1878–1885, Liberals; 1885–1889, Conservatives; and the Liberals had taken power again just prior to the overthrow of the monarchy. Cabinet approval rested with the Assembly. Until 1881, deputies to the Assembly were elected indirectly by electoral colleges. Reforms in that year mandated direct

elections of deputies for three-year terms by all males who met the income requirements. Pedro used his power to dissolve the Assembly and thereby obtain support for a newly appointed cabinet eleven times during his reign. During those forty-nine years, the two parties formed thirty-six different ministries. The longest-lived was that of José Maria da Silva Paranhos, Visconde do Rio-Branco, from early 1871 to mid-1875. The briefest lasted but six days in May of 1862, the first cabinet organized by Zacarias de Góes e Vasconcelos. After the creation of the post of president of the Council of Ministers in 1847, the Liberal party formed the government sixteen times, to hold power for more than seventeen years; the Conservatives, twelve times, for more than twenty years. Omitted here is the Period of Conciliation, 1853–1857, when Paraná organized a nonpartisan government. That period witnessed such genuine cooperation among the leading men of both parties that it can be considered apolitical. Eleven of the thirty *presidentes do Conselho de Ministros* (prime ministers) came from Bahia, a monopoly unapproached by any other province. Second place fell to Pernambuco, natal province of five. Four originated in Rio de Janeiro, and São Paulo contributed only two.

With the notable exception of the Period of Conciliation, the party out of power engaged in unrestricted criticism of the party in power. Freedom of expression in all forms was fully guaranteed, respected, and exercised. After 1850 the opposition no longer resorted to violence (at least not for thirty-nine years), but relied on constituted and orderly channels to voice disagreement. In short, discussion replaced violence.

The clientele of the two dominant political parties, the Liberals and the Conservatives, by no means espoused unanimous opinions. In fact, there might have been more differences of opinion within each party than between them. The powerful rural elite split between the two parties, just as the urban elite did. In general the Conservatives attracted landowners largely from areas of economic decline, the Northeast, Bahia, and Rio de Janeiro, as well as most bureaucrats in the cities. On the other hand, the Liberals seemed to draw landowners from areas of economic expansion such as Minas

Gerais, São Paulo, and Rio Grande do Sul, and urban professionals. The major issue clearly dividing those two parties
focused on questions of centralization of power. The Liberals
sought to diffuse power, giving greater strength to the provinces, an attitude firmly opposed by the Conservatives. Little
was done to diminish central authority during the Second
Empire. The crown exercised tight control over the provinces
through appointments. The monarch named the provincial
senators and presidents, for example. Local electors selected
provincial legislatures as well as national deputies. In the
course of the long reign of Pedro II, the Conservatives found
their most steadfast support in the province of Rio de Janeiro;
the Liberals in Minas Gerais, São Paulo, and Rio Grande do
Sul. Bahia and Pernambuco divided almost equally between
the two parties.

Since similarities rather than differences characterized
the two parties, a change of party in power did not signal a
great change of policy. The Liberals seldom advocated anything so drastic that it could not eventually be enacted by the
Conservatives, a procedure frequently followed. For example, the Conservatives terminated the slave trade in 1850,
passed the Law of the Free Womb in 1871, and finally abolished slavery in 1888—all goals originally suggested by the
Liberals. Such continuity prompted the observation by Visconde de Albuquerque that there was nothing so like a Conservative as a Liberal in power. The playwright Joaquim José
de França Junior joked knowingly about the political similarities of the parties in his humorous play *Como Se Fazia Um
Diputado* (How a Deputy Was Created, 1887). One of the
characters in the play when accused of changing his party
affiliations replies, "I changed my opinions for the soundest
reasons of social order. Look here, my friend, if changing
party labels were a crime, our jails wouldn't be big enough to
hold all the criminals now on the loose." The same character
later confessed, "My friend, I don't know of two beings more
similar than a Liberal and a Conservative. They are both the
offspring of the same mother, Lady Convenience, who rules
everything and everyone in this world. Anybody who thinks
otherwise had best leave politics to become a cobbler." The
men who belonged to the parties were far more important

then the platforms. Clashes between parties were, more likely than not, conflicts of personalities.

In the final analysis both parties were deeply rooted in the landowning oligarchy. After all, Brazil remained throughout the nineteenth century an overwhelmingly agrarian nation. Because of the basic similarity of their clientele, neither party ventured beyond well-circumscribed political boundaries, never desiring to deal with certain basic socio-economic issues. Land reform, for example, was taboo. Yet, a basic political complexity was emerging in the final decades of the Second Empire, which sooner or later would challenge traditional political patterns and behavior. Within an agrarian nation with strong patriarchal and folk customs, the government became increasingly Europeanized in form and mentality. While sympathetic to the interests of the rural elite, the government became increasingly molded by urban interests that strengthened greatly in the last years of the empire. Those urban interests were more congenial to the dynamic sector of the economy—coffee exporters—and became more alienated from the older and declining economic center, the Northeast. As the Northeast and Southeast competed for the favors of the government, the urban interests tended to support the coffee class. The potential for a more fundamental political conflict increased.

The weaknesses of the parliamentary system were many: among them were its limited representation, its reluctance to come to grips with some of the nation's major problems, its ritualized, stilted behavior, and its exclusivity. Still, it did implant in the politicians a respect for their adversaries, a willingness to accept electoral defeat, and in general an attitude of fair play and sportsmanship in politics. Furthermore, since the parties prepared younger men for responsibility, the system provided political continuity. It seemed a practical step toward self-government after three centuries of authoritative colonial rule in which the Brazilians gained a minimum of experience. The advantages of the imperial political system are more visible when one compares it to its counterparts in the Spanish-speaking republics. Under the parliamentary system guided by Pedro II there was a peaceful rotation of par-

ties and personalities in office. At least on the surface, the Brazilians' genetic solution for political leadership, more attuned to earlier Iberian and Latin American experiences, seemed better able to provide political order than did the contractual theories the Spanish-speaking Americans struggled to impose.

The fall of the Liberal ministry of Zacarias de Góes e Vasconcelos in 1868 marked a dividing point in the political history of the Second Empire. He thoroughly controlled the Assembly, and when a vacancy in the Senate occurred he informed the emperor that he would like the Liberal party chief of the province of Rio Grande do Norte appointed from the customary triple list. The emperor, of course, had the final voice in those nominations; he preferred Sales Tôrres Homen, a well-known orator, writer, and intellectual. When Pedro insisted on making his choice, Zacarias resigned. As was customary when the prime minister left office, the entire ministry followed. Pedro invited Itboraí, a Conservative, to form a new cabinet. Because the Conservatives did not have a majority, the emperor dissolved the Assembly and ordered new elections. Predictably, the Conservatives, in charge of the electoral machinery after the appointment of Itaboraí, won those elections. The loss of power infuriated the Liberals. They regarded the events as nothing short of a coup d'état manipulated by the emperor himself. Their anger strongly united the liberals, impelling them to reconsider their program. As a result, in 1869 they issued a reform manifesto calling for the abolition of the moderating power, the Council of State, the National Guard (they disliked its privileged officers), and slavery. The manifesto favored the establishment of direct elections, expanded suffrage, periodic elections of senators for a limited term of office, popular election of provincial presidents, an independent judiciary, more educational institutions, and other reforms. If enacted, their program would have weakened the government in Rio de Janeiro because, in effect, what they envisaged was federalization with subsequent decentralization. Consequently, it would diminish the role of the emperor. The new liberal program harkened back to the early years of the 1830s. Indeed, the

generation that had lived through the chaos, anarchy, and threatened disintegration of that critical period in Brazilian history had passed, or was passing rapidly, from the political scene. In the 1860s and early 1870s a number of politicians appeared who were perfectly loyal to the monarchy but who had not experienced the rebellions of the Regency period.

Although impossible to pick out a politician typical of that new group, it nonetheless would be instructive to review the ideology of at least one. Aureliano Cândido Tavares Bastos (1839–1875), an articulate national deputy from Alagoas, wrote and spoke passionately of his beliefs and fought for them in the Assembly. His background placed him well within the emerging middle sectors. First as a conservative and later as a liberal, that young intellectual advocated a "progress"— he often referred to it as "unlimited progress"—derived from British and North American experiences from which he insisted Brazil could benefit: "I am an enthusiastic fanatic of England, but I understand the greatness of that people only when I contemplate the republic the English founded in North America. It is not enough for us to study England; it is necessary to know the United States. It is from this second country that we can derive practical lessons to improve our agriculture and our economy." He called for closer relations with the United States.

Tersely he summed up the three urgent necessities of Brazil as "education, emancipation, and transportation," but he elaborated complex plans to engineer Brazil's progress. Agriculture was to be the business of Brazil, and in his campaign to develop agriculture he linked himself closely with the coffee planters. He adhered to the idea of Adam Smith that each nation should engage in what it did best, and therefore he believed others should supply Brazil with the manufactured goods it needed and even provide the ships to carry on the trade. Tavares Bastos defended private initiative and property, yet believed the government should undertake public works projects so long as they contributed to expanding exports. Progress could be measured, in fact, by foreign commerce, and to him mounting coffee exports signified such progress. However, inefficient and retrograde slavery doomed

Brazil's agricultural development, he felt; Tavares Bastos accordingly urged gradual emancipation and the incorporation of former slaves into the nation through education. Free coastal navigation and the opening of the Amazon to international trade—first advocated by him in 1862 and enacted by the government five years later—were other methods he lauded as necessary for increased commerce and thus certain progress.

Tavares Bastos worried a great deal about unbalanced budgets; he advocated strengthening the currency and reducing debts. Education should be practical, useful, and widespread. Immigration should be encouraged, particularly from the United States and northern Europe. He advised, "Without the immigrants of Germany and Great Britain, Brazil will never progress. It is necessary that the pure blood of the Northern races come to develop and renovate our degenerate race." The Brazil the Alagoan envisioned was largely agrarian; it engaged in a lively international commerce; it was strengthened and refined by emancipation, education, and immigration. Other younger politicians might adhere to parts of this program, but one certain variation would be the encouragement of industrialization.

Reflecting the temper of their times, the new generation of statesmen showed themselves to be reformist in outlook and, regardless of their political party differences, instrumental in implementing many of the reforms called for by the Liberal Manifesto. The emperor stepped into the political background to allow his ministers more prominence. The Council of State became more administrative and less political in its operation. Slavery was abolished gradually and finally eliminated in 1888. Judiciary reforms made that branch of government increasingly independent. The Saraiva Law of 1881 provided for direct elections. Although it did not remove property ownership qualifications for voting, it did lower them. However, with the possible exception of the elections immediately following the reform—and despite the best intentions of the law—the elections continued to be manipulated by the party holding power to ensure the victory of its candidates for the legislature. The electorate continued to be but a frac-

tion of the total population. In 1881 it numbered only 142,000 out of a population of approximately 15 million. The enactment of these reforms by both the Liberals and Conservatives again blurred the distinctions between the two parties.

The crisis in 1868 reawakened republican sentiment that had manifested itself periodically, if weakly, in the past, particularly in the *inconfidências* of 1789 and 1798, the revolts of 1817 and 1824, and throughout the Regency period. A Republican Club organized in Rio de Janeiro in 1870 published a manifesto calling for the abolition of the monarchy and the establishment of a federal republic. In other respects, its program resembled that advocated by the Liberals except that the Republicans tended to be vaguer on the question of slavery. The early Republicans inherited much of their thinking from the Enlightenment and were strongly influenced by federalism as practiced in the United States. A later breed of Republicans, however, adhered more to Comte's Positivist concept of an authoritarian republic ruled by an elite. Naturally they regarded themselves as that elite. Republican leaders—men like Antônio da Silva Jardim, Quintino Bocaiúva, Lafayette Rodrigues Pereira, Aristides Lobo, Salvador de Mendonça, Rangel Pestana, Manuel Ferraz de Campos Sales, and Américo Braziliense—were talented and enthusiastic, but they failed to attract a popular following. Almost exclusively urban in orientation, the party's strength was centered in the cities of Rio de Janeiro, Minas Gerais, São Paulo, and Rio Grande do Sul. Of those provinces, São Paulo boasted the strongest and best organized branches of the Republican party. In 1884, São Paulo elected three Republican deputies to the national legislature, among them Campos Sales and Prudente José de Morais e Barros, both of whom were destined to become presidents of the republic. They were the first Republicans to sit in Parliament. The Republicans abjured the use of force to implement their program; instead, they hoped that, if educated on the issues, the public would accept it. In their program they considered federalism paramount, the panacea for the ills besetting their country. They, too, were of a generation that had not known the turbulence of the Regency period.

One of the major issues to disturb the political tranquillity of the Second Empire had little to do with the political parties. Nascent ultramontanism among the clergy challenged the regalist doctrines of the state. An acrimonious struggle jolted the customarily amiable relations between church and state—unusually harmonious in Brazil, especially when compared to the habitual strife between the two that characterized nineteenth-century Spanish America. Most of the clergy in Brazil had supported independence, and all had sworn allegiance to the new emperor. Although permitting religious liberty, the Constitution of 1824 established Roman Catholicism as the state religion, and the emperor continued to exercise royal patronage over the Church within his domains, as his Portuguese ancestors had done for centuries. The Vatican remained silent on the question of patronage, accepting Pedro's interpretation without overtly conceding to him the privileges and responsibilities of the patronage. The first major dispute between Rome and Rio de Janeiro erupted in 1834 over the nomination of Antônio Maria de Moura as bishop of Rio de Janeiro. Moura advocated the abolition of clerical celibacy and held other ideas the Church fathers regarded as radical. The government, encouraged by the radical priest-politician Diogo Antônio Feijó, supported his candidacy; Rome refused to install him. The question was resolved in 1835 when Moura himself withdrew his candidacy. Relations between the Vatican and Rio de Janeiro returned to normal.

Pedro II was an uncompromising regalist, and the ecclesiastical hierarchy acquiesced timidly. In truth the state was far stronger than the Church, whose lamentable physical and moral condition within Brazil weakened its position. Its buildings were in a sad state of disrepair and deterioration, the morals of the clergy were embarrassingly loose, and there was a dire shortage of priests. The puritanical emperor appreciated the subservience of the clergy to the throne but deprecated their morality. He resolved to purify the Church by sending promising candidates for the priesthood to Europe for study. They returned morally stronger, much to his gratification, but they had drunk heavily from ultramontane ide-

ology as well, a consequence of their European sojourn that Pedro had not considered. The inevitable contest of strength between the regalist monarch and a new ultramontane Church hierarchy occurred in the 1870s as a result of conflicting views on Freemasonry.

An encyclical of Pope Pius IX denounced the Masonic Order in 1864. The emperor never sanctioned its publication, realizing that the rabidly anticlerical Masons of Europe had little in common with the fraternal Masons of Brazil—most of whom were devoted servants of the Church and many of whom were clergymen—and that, therefore, the encyclical should not be circulated in Brazil. But the new ultramontane bishops thought otherwise. In 1872 a priest in Rio de Janeiro, after speaking enthusiastically in a Masonic lodge to commemorate the Law of the Free Womb promulgated a year earlier, received an ultimatum from his bishop either to sever his Masonic relationships or be suspended from the Church. The priest refused to renounce his Masonic ties and thereby challenged the Church. Bishop Vital Maria Gonçalves de Oliveira of Pernambuco, educated in France in ultramontane doctrines, took up the challenge. He ordered the religious brotherhoods—significant religious and social institutions composed of laymen—to expel their Masonic members, who, more often than not, happened to be some of their most prominent members. When the brotherhoods refused, the bishop suspended the religious functions of the Brotherhood of the Santíssimo Sacramento. Here now was a direct challenge to the Crown since the bishop resolved to enforce an encyclical that the emperor had not allowed circulated in the country. The brotherhood appealed to the throne in June of 1873, and the emperor ordered the bishop to remove the interdict forthwith. Bishop Vital defied the emperor's order, and the government was left with no alternative but to institute legal action against the recalcitrant churchman, charging him with violating the criminal code and the constitution. He stood trial in Rio de Janeiro in 1874 amid byzantine diplomatic maneuverings by the pope and the emperor. The court found the bishop guilty and sentenced him to four years of hard labor, a sentence commuted by the throne to simple impris-

onment. A similar case involved Bishop Antônio de Macedo Costa of Pará, educated in France, like Bishop Vital. Eventually the Vatican and Rio de Janeiro came to an agreement. The emperor issued a decree of amnesty in 1875, and the pope ordered the interdicts against the Masons lifted and the brotherhoods restored to their positions prior to 1873. In that overt challenge of the state, the Church lost; regalism triumphed. Many in the Church hierarchy brooded over the defeat. Their enthusiasm for the regalist monarch waned, and thereafter they regarded him as unfriendly. Politically the struggle between church and state was nonpartisan. Politicians of all hues and beliefs supported the emperor.

Foreign relations were another nonpartisan matter. After obtaining recognition with relative ease, the empire turned its attention to establishing friendly relations with its neighbors, and, above all else, to demarcating favorably its extensive frontiers, believed to border all the republics and colonies of the South American continent save Chile. Attention focused on the headwaters of the Amazon and on the Plata River network. Brazil possessed the course of the Amazon and its tributaries but not their headwaters. Vague geographical knowledge about the trackless Amazonian hinterland complicated efforts to settle frontiers there. Brazil guarded its South American heartland jealously, preoccupied with the thought that a neighbor might expand and fearful that some stronger, extracontinental power might trespass. For many decades Brazil kept the Amazon River closed to international traffic and used the promise of opening it to coax the other riparian nations to agree to a boundary settlement. When that tactic proved unsuccessful, Brazil bowed before international pressure and in 1867 permitted the vessels of all nations to ply that river's waters.

Unlike the vast, unoccupied Amazon region, along the banks of the Plata, an area historically disputed by Spain and Portugal, sizable population concentrations with differing loyalties confronted one another. In the national period, Argentina and Brazil, both potential powers, vied there for dominance. Geopolitically, Brazil needed to have the Plata open to commerce and communication so as not to isolate

the immense province of Mato Grosso, which was under-populated, weakly held, and tenuously tied to the effective national territory. As long as the Cisplatine Province (the Banda Oriental del Uruguay) remained within the empire, Brazil exerted control over the left bank of the mouth of the Plata and could ensure that the river network was kept open to its vessels. The loss of the Cisplatine Province as a result of the war with Argentina complicated the situation. Brazil found itself owner of the headwaters but without control over the main courses and mouth of the Plata waterway, the reverse of the situation in the Amazon. Brazil's use of the Plata remained at the mercy of Argentina, Uruguay, and Paraguay. The confrontation with those Spanish-speaking republics over the use of the river and over unresolved boundaries required Brazil to concentrate most of its nineteenth-century diplomacy on the Plata basin where an intensely dramatic and complex power struggle took place.

At stake for Argentina and Brazil in that struggle were control of the Plata and domination of Paraguay, Uruguay, and, to a lesser extent, Bolivia. Argentina remembered only too well that Brazil had once annexed the left bank of the Plata and suspected that the empire would be eager to reabsorb that strategic area. Brazil likewise believed that Argentina entertained expansionistic designs in the region. The authorization that the legislature of Buenos Aires in 1850 gave Juan Manuel de Rosas, the Argentine caudillo, to incorporate the "province" of Paraguay into the Argentine Confederation by any means possible only heightened Brazilian anxieties. For that matter, during his long administration, 1829–1852, Rosas spoke often of a "Greater Argentina" that would encompass the territory of the former vice-royalty of La Plata, that is, Argentina, Uruguay, Paraguay, and part of Bolivia. Brazil did not desire such an overwhelming neighbor. Furthermore, Brazil feared that Argentina might like to annex the province of Rio Grande do Sul, over part of which Spain and Portugal had contended. Brazilian concerns mounted when French and British blockades of Buenos Aires not only failed to humble Rosas but, if anything, strengthened the internal position of the Argentine leader.

The empire's first move to counter Argentine ambitions in the Plata was to recognize Paraguay's independence in 1844, a move that infuriated Rosas. Brazil maneuvered thereafter to exert a maximum amount of influence in that landlocked nation in order to check any Argentine designs. As one Brazilian diplomat explained in 1846, "The annexation of Paraguay to the [Argentine] Confederation would give to the latter, in addition to the pride of conquest, an increase of territory and forces such that the equilibrium would cease to exist, and all of the sacrifices made by Brazil when it adhered to the independence of Montevideo would be entirely fruitless." The second move of the empire to counter Argentine pretensions in the Plata was the extension of Brazilian influence into Uruguay, a move complicated by the chaos perennially engulfing that country. Civil war between the Blancos (Conservatives) and the Colorados (Liberals) raged. In 1842, approximately twenty thousand Brazilians lived in and around Montevideo, and by 1864 fully a fifth of the population of the nation was Brazilian. As was inevitable in those endless civil wars, some estates owned by Brazilians in Uruguay were invaded, sacked, and at times confiscated. To further complicate the matter, Uruguayan bandits frequently crossed the frontier into Rio Grande do Sul to carry out their crimes. The large cattle ranches particularly attracted them. The imperial government claimed that such border raids had cost the ranchers some 800,000 head of cattle.

Rosas kept a sharp eye on Uruguay, not only because it had once formed a part of the viceroyalty of La Plata but also because Argentine exiles had settled in Montevideo, where they ceaselessly plotted his overthrow. In the internal political struggle, the Argentine caudillo threw his support behind the leading Conservative politician, Manuel Oribe. In its turn, Brazil aided the leading Liberal politician, Fructuoso Rivera. The intricate political dance reached a climax in 1851 when Brazilian military forces marched into Uruguay to strengthen Rivera. Once military intervention in the Plata had begun, the Brazilians resolutely carried it to its ultimate conclusion. They allied with the new government of Uruguay and the dissident Argentine provinces of Entre Ríos and Corrientes to attack

Rosas. The Argentine regional caudillo, Justo José de Urquiza, led the combined forces to victory at the battle of Monte Caseros in 1852. To the relief of the Brazilians, the defeated Rosas fled his homeland for a European exile. Diplomatic relations between the two Plata powers were reestablished in 1856, when they signed a treaty of friendship, commerce, and navigation. But ingrained suspicion, distrust, and rivalry could not be disguised under the cloak of momentary cooperation. Argentina and Brazil eyed each other warily through the chaos that continued in Uruguay and over the fortress Paraguay had made of itself.

In the early 1860s, a new complication threatened the delicate Platine balance of power. As a small country whose boundaries had not been recognized by its neighbors, Paraguay had historically lived in a state of anxiety, if not impending danger. Repeated Argentine threats, even efforts, to annex their country did little to allay Paraguayan fears. Brazilian meddling in the other small Platine republic, Uruguay, only served to augment Paraguayan distress and concern. Being buffeted about by its two immense neighbors, Paraguay naturally felt insecure. Such insecurity had prompted the first chief of state, José Gaspar Rodríguez de Francia, to isolate his country from most foreign contacts for a generation. Although he opened the frontiers, the second chief of state, Carlos Antonio López, was hardly less suspicious of his neighbors. He feared Brazilian imperialism. To become master rather than victim of the situation, Paraguay resolved to take greater control of its own destiny. The nation methodically armed itself and trained the largest army in South America.

In the meantime, Brazil seemed to have defined more sharply its Platine policy: Paraguay and Uruguay must be kept as independent buffer states friendly to the empire, and the Plata River must be kept open to Brazilian traffic. Careful and generally able Brazilian diplomacy seemed for a time successful in its labyrinthine maneuverings in that volatile region. The same imperial hand which on one occasion proffered aid could, on another, administer a slap. The methods varied, but the aims were uniform. The always delicate situation on the Uruguayan-Brazilian frontier deteriorated in late 1863. Re-

newed border incursions into Rio Grande do Sul on the part of the Uruguayan bandits annoyed the government in Rio de Janeiro. To emphasize the exhaustion of Brazilian patience, the emperor dispatched José Antônio Saraiva to Montevideo in April 1864 to present Blanco President Atanasio Cruz Aguirre with an ultimatum: either Uruguay would pay for the damages suffered by the Brazilians and punish the guilty, or the Brazilian army would be dispatched to Uruguay to seek satisfaction. Aguirre refused to bow to Brazilian demands. As an alternative he turned to Francisco Solano López, chief of state of Paraguay since 1862.

The idea of serving as a mediator and of maintaining an equilibrium of power in the Plata obsessed López. He believed that peace and Paraguay's well-being in the Plata required a balance of power between Argentina and Brazil, an equilibrium that Paraguay had the obligation to force if necessary. López felt that Brazil's threat to Uruguay, if carried out, would upset the Platine balance. The strange concurrence of Brazilian and Argentine policy, both seeking to overthrow the Blancos, further aroused his suspicions. Indeed, rumors circulated that Brazil and Argentina had reached an agreement whereby the former would absorb Uruguay and the latter would absorb Paraguay. With such fears in mind, López let Aguirre understand that Paraguay would support Uruguay's defiance of Brazil. Receiving no satisfaction from Aguirre, Saraiva then returned to Rio de Janeiro. Clearly the Brazilian foreign minister had expected the Uruguayan to meet his demands, and, when he did not, Brazil found itself in an inflexible position. It seemed necessary to make good the threat. Obviously at that point the usually perceptive Brazilian diplomacy had failed, and not the least of its failures was an inability to link events in Uruguay with those in Paraguay.

Brazil rendered support to Aguirre's rival, Venancio Flores, who had declared himself favorable to the Brazilian cause. The Imperial Navy blockaded Uruguayan ports and the Imperial Army invaded without a formal declaration of war, an act openly violative of international law. Before such a use of force, Aguirre quickly fell. Flores assumed the presidency

and promptly agreed to restore confiscated Brazilian property and to recognize Brazilian claims.

López watched the drama with mounting concern. He saw in Aguirre's fall the first act of a tragedy which would end with the disappearance of the two smaller Platine states. To his mind, the precarious balance of power had been tipped to favor Brazil and it was essential for him to right it. In the words of his official newspaper, *El Semanario*, the Brazilian occupation of Uruguay was "a threat to the liberty, independence, sovereignty and territorial integrity of the Republic of Paraguay, and of the other states in this part of America." With the determination to challenge his large neighbor, he selected Brazil's most vulnerable point to display his strength. On November 11, 1864, he closed the Paraguay River, a vital branch of the Plata network, to Brazilian traffic. Furthermore, he ordered one of his gunboats to capture the *Marquês de Olinda*, an Imperial river steamer then transporting the provincial president to Mato Grosso. López then informed the emperor's minister in Asunción that Paraguay was breaking diplomatic relations with Brazil because of the intervention in Uruguay.

A Paraguayan army unit at once invaded Mato Grosso, but the real objective of López was to unite his main forces with those of Aguirre in Uruguay. To do so required crossing Argentine territory. He requested such permission from Buenos Aires. Argentina had everything to gain from the struggle among the three neighbors and common sense dictated that the nation should impartially observe and, emphatically, not participate. Following the dictates of such a policy of neutrality, President Bartolomé Mitre refused to concede the permission López sought. Just as Brazil had misjudged the situation earlier, Argentina did so now. To the amazement of the Argentines, López boldly captured their vessels on the inland waters and invaded the province of Corrientes. Argentine hopes of neutrality evaporated and, quite unexpectedly, the government in Buenos Aires, on May 1, 1865, found itself, along with the puppet government of Uruguay, signing a treaty of alliance with Brazil. Those allies accused López of wanting to create a Platine empire made up of Paraguay,

Uruguay, and the Argentine provinces of Entre Rios and Corrientes.

No adherent to this Triple Alliance was prepared for war. Brazilian troops were scattered throughout the length and breadth of a vast empire; it was necessary first to collect and transport them south, and the problem of supplying them was never satisfactorily resolved. Still, the sheer weight of the Allies pressed down on small, landlocked Paraguay. In the naval engagement of Riachuelo on June 11, 1865, the Allied fleet destroyed the Paraguayan squadron and took command of the inland waterways. It was not, however, until April 1866 that the Allies first invaded Paraguayan territory. The key to the defense of Paraguay was the solid fortress of Humaitá that guarded the ascent of the Paraguay River and stood as a formidable roadblock on the way to Asunción. The siege of Humaitá began in July 1867, when the Allies brought all their strength to bear upon that fortress. Yet it stood in heroic defiance of the impressive forces arrayed against it. The war lengthened beyond what even the most pessimistic among the Allies dreamed possible. Convinced that they were defending the very existence of their homeland, the Paraguayans demonstrated uncommon courage. Their pluck was well-illustrated by Commander Estigarribia, trapped in Uruguaiana, Rio Grande do Sul, by an overwhelming Allied army. The Allied commander requested his surrender, stating that the Allies had no quarrel with the Paraguayan people but rather sought to overthrow the tyrant López who commanded them and treated them as slaves; he said the Allies would give them liberty and the right to a government of their own free election. Estigarribia pointedly replied, "If Your Excellencies are so anxious to grant freedom to Paraguay's peoples, why haven't you commenced by liberating the unhappy Negroes of Brazil who compose the majority of the population and who exist under the hardest and most frightful slavery in order to enrich and provide idle time to some hundreds of the empire's principal figures." Such was the spirit that made the Paraguayans a formidable foe.

As the war stretched on, opposition to it within Brazil mounted. The empire bore the chief responsibilities for the

conduct of the war, furnishing most of the money, matériel, and men for the Allied cause. The rapid material development of the realm was hindered by the military sacrifice. The mounting costs—in total over $300 million—weakened the national currency and required the government to contract debts abroad. The casualty lists, which numbered between 33,000 and 50,000 men, sobered the enthusiasm of the populace. Despite much complaint at home, the Allied governments determined to press on and refused anything except an unconditional surrender.

The fall of Humaitá in August 1868, after a prolonged siege, opened up all of Paraguay to the Allied armies. They descended on Asunción and took the capital on January 5, 1869. In the process they destroyed most of the remaining Paraguayan army. However, López miraculously escaped to the mountains far to the northeast of the capital. There his fragmented forces continued to display the courage that characterized the Paraguayan soldiers throughout the long war. A pursuing Brazilian army defeated the Paraguayans again at Cerro Corá on March 1, 1870. Among those killed in that battle was Marshal Francisco Solano López.

The war was over. To the Paraguayan people, López still remains their national hero. He is the leader who saved the republic from extinction. Outside of Paraguayan histories, he has been accorded quite a different treatment. Brazilian historians traditionally and uniformly regard him as a mad and insane despot, if not worse.

Paraguay's defeat—its near destruction—removed all pretensions that nation might have had as a Platine power and relegated it once again to its position as a buffer state. The war reduced the population to about half its former size, with a shocking loss of adult males. Nonetheless, López seems to have achieved one of his major objectives: the war ended the direct interventions of Argentina and Brazil in Uruguay. Moreover, the two major powers seem to have understood more clearly thereafter the useful purpose served by the independence of the two buffer states. Argentine and Brazilian imperialist ambitions to absorb one or both of them disappeared. One of the major causes for Brazilian intervention in Platine affairs was removed with the definitive opening of the

Plata River network to world commerce. Contrary to the pledges of the Triple Alliance, in 1872 Brazil signed a separate treaty of peace with Paraguay that, among other things, delineated their common frontiers to Brazil's advantage. By conceding a small amount of territory to Brazil, Paraguay enlisted the empire's support against exaggerated Argentine claims. Argentina reacted adversely to the treaty, accusing Brazil of violating Article Six of the Treaty of the Triple Alliance, which forbade separate peace treaties with Paraguay. In the disagreement that ensued the Paraguayans cleverly played off one power against the other and, in the process, saved some of their territory coveted by Argentina.

An exhausted Brazil turned its attention inward again after the successful conclusion of the war. The traumatic international involvement caused severe internal reactions that, in the long run, would modify the course of national evolution. Those effects would be most noticeable in the 1880–1890 period. Of major significance for the future, a new national institution emerged as a consequence of the war: the military. With no war for independence to fight comparable to the protracted and bitter wars that ravaged much of Spanish America, the Brazilian military had been weak and inconsequential. Pedro I even had to rely on mercenaries to fight against Argentina in the 1825–1828 war over Uruguay. In fact, not until a decree of 1839 was the army even systematically organized. Five years of long struggle with Paraguay necessarily changed all that. A large, well-organized, powerful, and, above all else, professional military emerged from that war. Of further significance, that new institution did not represent the rural aristocracy who, from the beginning, had controlled Brazil. The officer class instead originated in the newly formed urban middle groups. Their loyalties, values, and ambitions were markedly different from those of the landed oligarchy. As long as war absorbed their attention, the officers exerted no influence on the structure and functions of the state, but the long years of peace after 1870 made the army restless, ambitious for political participation, and consequently vulnerable to Republican and Positivist propaganda.

To arouse public support for the long war, it was necessary to engender among the civilians a respect for the military

they never before had demonstrated. Considerable propaganda lauded the soldier as the true patriot fighting in defense of the fatherland. It is interesting to observe the changing attitude of the august Brazilian Historical and Geographical Institute, an elitist club influential in forming the opinion of the educated public. Prior to the war, the members of the institute in their meetings and in the pages of their prestigious *Revista* spent most of their energy glorifying the Indian past of Brazil. The war worked a sudden change. They turned their attention to the military hero. Military biographies filled the pages of their journal. A once neglected institution became the worthy topic for their discourses. The government enlisted artists to depict the military victories in Paraguay. The two major painters of the period responded, Vitor Meirelles (1832–1903) with huge canvases exalting naval victories and Pedro Américo (1843–1903) with gigantic scenes of major land battles. Art served the state in its encouragement of both patriotism and nationalism. In this case, it also exalted militarism. From the war, then, emerged not only a well-established military institution but also a new respect for the military.

It had been the use of force that permitted Brazil to advantageously mark its frontiers with Paraguay in 1872, just as it had been the judicious use of the presence of force that accomplished the same end with Uruguay in 1851. Those boundaries with the two Platine states were the only ones delineated during the Empire despite the tireless efforts the diplomats dedicated to fixing the distant limits of their nation. One of the ablest of the foreign ministers was Paulino José Soares de Souza, Visconde do Uruguai, who held the portfolio from 1849 to 1853, years of an intensive diplomatic offensive in both the Amazon and Plata. Uruguai made aggressive efforts to settle all Brazilian territorial claims on the basis of *uti possidetis,* the concept, introduced onto the continent by the Treaty of Madrid of 1750, which dominated all Brazilian border diplomacy. The imperial diplomats did succeed in laying the groundwork upon which future favorable settlement could be made.

Throughout the imperial period Great Britain continued

to be the paramount foreign power exercising influence over Brazil. Elsewhere we have noted the intimate commercial and financial ties between the two nations. The Brazilians were not entirely happy with that British presence, but in the nineteenth century they had little alternative but to accept it. Twice, however, the Brazilians challenged the British and on both occasions triumphed—at least temporarily. The first encounter was over the renewal of the commercial preference, and Brazil not only refused to renew it in 1844 but instead enacted a modest tariff increase. The second, the so-called Christie question, involved several complicated but usually mundane matters. In 1861, the cargo of a British ship wrecked on the coast of Rio Grande do Sul was pillaged. The following year three drunken British sailors out of uniform insulted a Brazilian official and were arrested. Upon learning their identity, the Brazilians released them. The highhanded British minister, William D. Christie, demanded indemnification for the pillaging and full satisfaction, including the punishment of those responsible, for the arrests. To enforce his demands, Christie ordered British warships then in Brazilian waters to blockade the port of Rio de Janeiro, which they did for six days. Under protest, the government reluctantly paid the indemnification but refused to accede to the British demands for satisfaction. Furthermore, the government requested an apology and compensation for the Brazilian ships seized during the blockade. Britain declined both. The Brazilians asked that Christie be recalled and then broke diplomatic relations with the Court of St. James's. Meanwhile, the question of the three sailors was submitted to the king of Belgium for arbitration. His decision favored Brazil. Britain presented its apologies to Brazil and asked to renew relations. The events gave Brazil some moral satisfaction but Great Britain continued to exercise its commercial and financial hegemony as the metropolis.

Although challenging Britain's position in the Caribbean, the United States was unable to do so with much authority in South America during the nineteenth century. In mutual recognition of each other's growing importance, in 1842 Brazil and the United States elevated their diplomatic representa-

tives in Rio de Janeiro and Washington from chargés d'affaires to envoys extraordinary and ministers plenipotentiary. Both nations, however, were too engrossed in continental matters to pay much heed to distant hemispheric neighbors. The decade of the 1860s proved to be an unusually trying one in the relations of the two. Brazil recognized the belligerency of the Confederacy in the Civil War, and, with that status, Confederate ships were able to use Brazilian harbors, which they occasionally did, much to the chagrin of the government in Washington. Eventually the presence of a Confederate war vessel in a Brazilian harbor led to the violation of Brazilian sovereignty by the United States. The *Florida* put into Salvador da Bahia for supplies and repairs. A Union warship then entered the harbor and captured her. That bravado angered Brazilians sensitive to the insult it implied. Eventually the United States offered its apologies, but only long after the triumph of the Union did it salute the Brazilian flag in the port of Bahia as the imperial government had required.

The War of the Triple Alliance brought new diplomatic complications to the relations between the two nations. In 1867, during the siege of Humaitá, the Brazilians refused to permit the United States minister to Paraguay, Elihu Washburn, to pass upriver to Asunción. That refusal ruffled diplomatic feathers for some time. Nor could the behavior of the United States minister (1861–1869) to the imperial court, General James Watson Webb, be considered the model of diplomatic propriety. It came to light soon enough that he had grossly abused his official position by extorting some $50,000 from the Brazilian government, a sum promptly returned with interest when the Department of State uncovered the irregularity. In the 1870s relations between the two nations improved. By then the United States had emerged as the principal market for Brazilian coffee and other products. Closer commercial relations called forth better diplomatic harmony, which began with the visit to the United States of Pedro II in 1876.

Chapter Five

Change and Continuity, 1888-1897

In 1888, a decade of significant changes exploded. The abolition of slavery marked the opening of that decade; the cataclysmic destruction of the folk society at Canudos closed it.
The years between witnessed the overthrow of the monarchy,
the establishment of a federal republic, the separation of
church and state, the entry of the cities and the middle class
into politics, the embrace of industrialization as an economic
panacea, and an official shift of economic and political power
to the southeastern states, in particular the recognition of the
importance of São Paulo within that triumivirate. Although
these changes occurred historically at nearly the same moment, the beginnings of each can be traced deep into the
nineteenth century. On the one hand some observers might
consider these changes a challenge to those basic social,
economic, and political institutions established during the
formative decades from 1530 to 1560; yet, on the other hand,
others could also argue that they perfected, while they up-
dated, those very institutions.

The changes between 1888 and 1897 shared a common
denominator: modernization. Their conglomerate recognized the end to the centuries ambiguously combining neo-
capitalism and neo-feudalism. That conglomerate celebrated

the triumph of capitalism and modernity. As events have now amply demonstrated, it also set the direction and the goals for the twentieth century. In some ways concluding three and one-half centuries of history and in other ways initiating trends that would characterize the twentieth century, this single ten-year period of change stands out as unusually significant for any interpretation of the history of Brazil.

New Social Groups and New Ideas

After 1865 the Brazilian intellectuals, under the influence of European realism, indoctrinated—at least informally—by Positivism, and awed by the century's scientific advances, began to reflect a new concern with their own national reality. That concern drew them into to those national crises disturbing the tranquility of the empire. The expensive and long war with Paraguay, the rise of republican sentiment, the church-state conflicts, and the abolitionist campaigns that attacked the hoary institution of slavery excited debate and prompted the rise and fall of several governments. Those crises stimulated literary production and were in turn aggravated by social criticism from the intellectuals who increasingly occupied themselves with national self-examination. In the broadest sense, then, the city challenged the countryside; the Southeast, the Northeast; the middle sectors—with their distinctive Europeanized outlook—opposed the folk societies, with their distinctive Indo-Afro-Iberian cultures; and the proclivity toward greater capitalist inclinations clashed with the more relaxed and more traditional neocapitalism.

The surge of new ideas resulted to a large extent from the emergence of a new element in society, the urban middle groups, sizable enough for the first time to exert influence, flexible enough to welcome innovations, and strong enough to challenge the traditional powers of the rural aristocracy. To the merchants, commercial agents, exporters, artisans, government bureaucrats, lawyers, doctors, priests, teachers, bankers, and military officers who made up the core of the urban middle, groups were added in large numbers during

the last third of the century: the salaried labor force of stevedores, mechanics, factory workers, and shop clerks. In short,
in the last half of the nineteenth century it was possible to
talk unmistakably in terms of a middle segment of the population, never cohesive—many times interrelated with the
planter class—but increasingly vocal and influential. The intellectual and professional components of the middle groups
were the most articulate and effective, if not the most representative, spokespeople. Much separated the various layers
of those middle groups, but they more or less shared a perspective incorporating the values, attitudes, and behavior of
their European counterparts who exerted increasing influence over them. They participated in sundry ways in a modern life characteristic of the city and different from the more
traditional rural ways. They complained of their difficult position, wedged between the landowners above and the slaves
below. They evinced ambitions to improve their status and
favored whatever reasonable means would widen their future
social horizons and strengthen their present base. Education,
they quickly realized, facilitated upward mobility. Yet, despite
these random similarities, they were still not cohesive enough
or sufficiently defined to compose a "class," and for that
reason the purposely chosen, more nebulous term *middle
groups* is applied to them for this period, the last half of the
nineteenth century.

Even in the quainter backland towns, the middle groups
had their representatives. The merchants together with the
local telegraph operator, teacher, priest, and the municipal
clerks and tradesmen constituted a small buffer society between peasants and planters. Tobias Barreto estimated that in
Escada, an inland city of Pernambuco with a population of
twenty thousand in 1877, approximately 10 percent of the
inhabitants lived adequately or better, an indication of the
size of the middle groups in one provincial *cidade*. Those
provincial middle groups were not ignorant. They too shared
the belief in progress, even though their opportunities to
learn about the modern world might have been more limited.
Nonetheless, they demonstrated their desire to change.

The cities, larger, more important, "progressive," and

Table 5.1 Rio de Janeiro: Population Growth and Presence of Foreign Born

	Population		Percentage of Foreign-Born
1799	43,376	1836	7%
1807	50,000	1856	35%
1815	100,000	1870	34%
1821	112,695	1890	30%
1838	137,078		
1849	226,466		
1856	181,158		
1870	235,381		
1890	552,651		
1895	650,000		

receptive to change, steadily eroded the influence of the rural aristocracy. Indeed, when the landowners themselves began to maintain residences in the city and to spend more time in them, they lent prestige and authority to the city, enhancing its position. The government bureaus, export agencies, and banks, rooted in the cities, reached out to exert economic control over the rural areas, a trend that accelerated throughout the nineteenth century. Landowners could make fewer decisions in the confines of their *fazendas*. They had to go to the city to consult their bankers or agent; they had to petition a government official for a favor. If their children were to receive a higher education, they had to be sent to the cities. There the sons of the rising bourgeoisie as well as of the plantation aristocracy enrolled in ever larger numbers in the law, medical, engineering, and military schools. Upon graduation, they pursued urban careers, adding their numbers and abilities to the strength of the city. After 1870, greater currents of immigration flowed into Brazil. A high percentage of those foreigners chose to settle in the cities, where their differing customs and thoughts contributed to the changing milieu. Table 5.1 shows both the growth of Brazil's major city, Rio de Janeiro, and the very high percentage of foreign-born who came to make up the population. A prosperous economy afforded the new generation more time for thought and reflection than their ancestors had enjoyed. For the urban dwellers there was not only more time to read but a wider

selection of material to choose from, and they showed a strong preference for European authors.

Always susceptible to the influence of European thought, the Brazilian elite, particularly in the cities, was brought into closer contact with it by the more frequent and rapid steamship service and by the submarine cable. The expanding middle groups also succumbed to European influence. France continued to shape Brazil's intellectual and cultural life. Three French cultural missions—the first in 1816 and the last in 1840—succeeded in strengthening a preference for Parisian values. French became the second language of the educated classes, who read French literature avidly and knew it better than their own. Polite society as well as the intellectuals animatedly discussed the novels of Gustave Flaubert, Honoré de Balzac, and Emile Zola. Their works dominated the bookshops. In the stores of the major cities, every Parisian luxury could be found. Shops on one of the principal streets in the capital, Ouvidor Street, almost exclusively displayed French wares. The ladies vied with one another in copying the latest Parisian styles.

On a more mundane level—commerce, banking, and politics—the influence of Great Britain held sway. Although Brazil's parliamentary monarchy was sui generis, it found a vague model in the British system whose order and stability appealed to the aristocrats. Regarding anything foreign as superior, the elite aped Europe to the fullest extent possible and the middle groups followed suit. Consequently they deprecated national products and culture and averted their eyes from the local scene.

Hypersensitivity to foreign criticism further prompted the elite and middle class to adopt unquestioningly in the tropics all the trappings of a temperate-climate civilization. Beset with a feeling of inferiority, they sought to be more European than the Europeans. In the process, of course, they imported many new ideas—Positivism, for example—whose influence modified traditional society.

A few voices protested the slavish imitation of foreign cultures. The literary critic Sílvio Romero (1851–1914) and the

historian João Capistrano de Abreu (1853–1927) began in the decade of the 1870s to advise their compatriots that much could be gained from introspection. They suggested that more harm than good resulted from the unrestricted and unselective importation of ideas and encouraged their countrymen to demonstrate some intellectual originality. Their admonitions formed the headwaters of a stream of cultural nationalism that, within two generations, would become a turbulent river.

Although he was also under the influence of European ideologies of his day, Romero attempted to free himself so that he could see his own country through Brazilian eyes. He condemned blind imitation and called for intellectual—and literary—independence. He aimed his critical barbs at "the figure of the imitator, of the slavish and witless copier of each and every trifle that the ships from Portugal or France or any other place bring us." Advocating national introspection, he crusaded for a Brazilian literature with its roots in the people, one that would interpret the national environment, traditions, and sentiments.

Romero wrote prolifically but no work exceeds in importance his monumental *História da Literatura Brasileira* (1888). Of lasting value, it is as essential today for an understanding of Brazil as it was when first published. Romero considered literature a national expression, an integral part of society, an inescapable conclusion in Brazil where the literati played multiple roles in society. Romero lamented that Brazilian literature had placed excessive emphasis on the elite to the neglect of the people, whom he considered the basic force of society. In one effort to bring the masses and literature together, he published two anthologies of folk poems and songs. He had to deal with European racist doctrine that influenced and would continue to influence so many Brazilian intellectuals. Still, he repeatedly affirmed that Brazil was not the exclusive product of Europe but the joint effort of Indians, Europeans, and Africans—a truly revolutionary thought at that time. Romero had a vision of the future as well as of the past. He understood a reality that still eludes most: before Brazil could develop, it would be necessary to reform

basic agrarian institutions by abolishing slavery and redistributing the land. Such a realistic blueprint for the future required fundamental changes that the elite stubbornly resisted.

Brazil's foremost historian, João Capistrano de Abreu, /$\cancel{1853-1927}$/ emerged at the same time as Romero with a similar message: Brazilian culture in its imitation of Europe modes was not expressive of the national soul. Isolated from its own environment, the culture did not represent the "conscious expression of the people." He revolutionized historical studies in Brazil by turning his attention away from the coastal band with its obvious link to Europe and toward the previously little-known interior. He presented his major thesis in 1889 in a short but brilliant essay, *Os Caminhos Antigos e o Povoamento do Brasil* (Old Roads and the Peopling of Brazil), the single most important statement on Brazilian history to that date. Neglecting the archbishops, generals, and viceroys who had previously populated the histories of Brazil—even refusing to treat the official national hero, Tiradentes, whom he considered more the creation of the elite than representative of the Brazilian people—he concentrated on the contributions of the masses, meaningful periodization of the past, and significant themes.

If the masses made history, the vast interior constituted the true Brazil, the valid national reality. Only when the coastal inhabitants turned their backs on the sea and penetrated the interior did they shed their European ways and become Brazilianized. Abreu's *Caminhos Antigos* contained a remarkable global vision of the Brazilian past that emphasized the themes of exploration and settlement of the interior, the creation of overland and fluvial transportation networks to weld the vast nation together, the significance of cattle raising and gold mining growth, of unity and change, and the psychological impact those events exerted on the Brazilian people. Capistrano de Abreu focused attention on the national heartland and the people who opened and settled it. In doing so, he Brazilianized the study of Brazilian history.

José de Alencar (1829–1877), a master exponent of Romanticism, cast his influential novels in a national mold. In

three of them, *O Guaraní*, *Iracema*, and *Ubirajara*, the Indian figured predominantly. The handsome, brave, noble savages of Alencar shared much in common with those of Chateaubriand and James Fenimore Cooper. Alencar's masterpiece of Indianist literature, *O Guaraní*, appeared in 1857. It mattered little to his readers that the novel's Indians spoke and acted like Europeans garbed in feathers. They conformed to the stereotype of how the elite thought the native should be. Amid splendid descriptions of the natural beauty of Brazil, Alencar treated the relationship between the Indians and Portuguese in the sixteenth century, in particular between Peri, an Indian chief, and Cecília, the daughter of a Portuguese nobleman. An affection between the golden-haired European and the bronze savage flowered into an exemplary love before the end of the novel. To Peri the author ascribed a catalog of desirable virtues—honesty, trustworthiness, courage, strength, bravery, et al.—while most of the Portuguese in the novel (Cecília, of course, excepted) displayed serious personality defects. Beneath the heavy romanticism of *O Guaraní* lies a profound nationalist message: Brazil is the product of the union of the New and Old Worlds. But the domination of the values of the Old World was explicit.

The foremost composer of the imperial period, Carlos Gomes (1836–1896), picked up the themes of *O Guaraní* and composed a melodic opera of the same name whose rousing overture awakens the same patriotic response among Brazilians as their national anthem. While the music sounded Italian (Gomes studied in Verdi's Italy), the plot remained firmly rooted in Brazil. His *Lo Schiavo* (The Slave) contained the same combination: a Brazilian theme dressed up in Italian form. At the same time, Brazilians began to compose, play, and dance to a distinctive local music. Around 1870, the *maxixe* appeared. A mix of the European polka with the African *lundu*, it was the first truly national dance in both movement and music. Francisca H. "Chiquinha" Gonzaga (1847–1935) composed the first registered *marcha*, indeed the first song composed specifically for the Carnival, in 1899. Drawing on lively Afro-Brazilian rhythms, her "Ô Abre Alas" (Hey, Make

Way) enjoyed popularity as a Carnival "classic" throughout the twentieth century.

Literature felt the effect of intensified intellectual probing. Romanticism eventually passed out of vogue in a society struggling with new ideas. Realists and naturalists rushed in to fill the literary void. In the process, the novel of manners gave way to works of social implication, "slices of life" depicting people's struggles. The first exponent of the naturalist novel was Aluísio Azevedo (1857–1913), whose *O Mulato* (The Mulatto), published in 1881, explored the always intriguing question of racial relations in Brazil. The plot concerned the love of a mulatto for a white girl, and, of course, the bigoted views of the girl's family toward the handsome and talented young man of mixed blood thwarted their pristine love. Azevedo poignantly conveyed the feelings of Raimundo, the light-skinned, blue-eyed mulatto, in an exposé of the subtleties of racial prejudice. Eventually Raimundo is assassinated, a vengeance society wreaked upon him because he dared to be the equal of the "white" Brazilians. The plot exposed the violence that characterized one aspect of Brazilian life. In a second novel, *O Cortiço* (The Tenement), Azevedo treated life in a Rio de Janeiro slum naturalistically. Significantly, urbanization had then reached a point—as Azevedo's work indicated—where it was creating new social problems unique in a hitherto rural nation.

The new trend in literature emboldened young writers to experiment with themes unexplored in Brazil in print before. The models were European. Raul de Avila Pompéia (1863–1895) satirized the private educational system in the capital in *O Ateneu* (The Athenaeum). Herculano Inglês de Sousa (1853–1918) depicted a Roman Catholic priest falling victim to his sensuous tropical environment in *O Missionário* (The Missionary). And *A Carne* (The Flesh) by Júlio César Ribeiro (1845–1890) analyzed an intellectual woman succumbing to all her carnal desires. And in his *Bom Crioulo* (The Good Blackman), Adolfo Caminha (1867–1897) forcefully introduced the homosexual theme by exploring the relationship between a black sailor and a white apprentice. At the same time, Brazil's most

gifted novelist, Joaquim Maria Machado de Assis (1839–1908) strode to the center of the literary stage. The son of a mulatto housepainter and a Portuguese woman, he was orphaned at the age of ten. Afflicted with epilepsy, and always sensitive about his racial mixture and his humble origin, he lived an introverted, conventional life, much devoted to his wife. His outward calm disguised a drive that drove him to write drama, criticism, poetry, short stories, and novels over a period of nearly half a century. Best known of his literary output are his last five novels: *Memórias Postumas de Bras Cubas* (translated into English under the title *Epitaph of a Small Winner*), *Quincas Borba* (bearing the English title *Philosopher or Dog*), *Dom Casmurro* (translated under the same name), *Esau e Jacob* (the English translation is *Esau and Jacob*), and *Memorial de Aires* (rendered into English as *The Memorial of Ayres*). Rio de Janeiro in the nineteenth century served as the setting for these novels of urban society. Their treatment of the individual's relations to society gave them an application to all people, everywhere, at all times. His superb style cleverly combined humor and pessimism. The Brazilian reading public enthusiastically greeted his novels of pessimism and realism, and critics and readers abroad have been slowly according them their merited place of honor.

Literature was the luxury of a small, privileged group, for few knew how to read, let alone write. The illiteracy rate during the imperial period never dropped below 85 percent among the free population, and it was considerably higher if one took into account the slaves. The few schools that existed tended to be concentrated in the cities. The provincial governments controlled primary and secondary education. Rio de Janeiro with its more affluent society, scholarly institutes, academies, printing presses, bookstores, and National Library was the principal educational center. Approximately 12,000 students attended the capital's primary schools in 1879. There was only one public secondary school, Dom Pedro II College, with an enrollment of 418, but 2,706 other students attended 62 private secondary schools. Such was the record for the cultural center of the empire. The conditions in the provinces were worse. In 1879 Mato Grosso, a province nearly twice the

size of the state of Texas, had only 30 primary schools attended by 1,375 pupils; there was no secondary school. In the 1880s, with a population in excess of 13 million, the total national enrollment in primary schools fell short of a quarter of a million. However alarming the record might seem, the facts testify that school attendance had multiplied during the Second Empire. In 1869, there were 3,516 schools with 115,735 students; three decades later the schools numbered 7,500 and enrollment 300,000. School population tripled, although national population did not quite double during that period. Still, the number privileged to attend school was tiny in comparison to the total population. The unschooled masses silently witnessed the events that surrounded and affected them, but in which they could play only the most limited role. A small minority, the emerging urban middle groups and the staid rural aristocracy, controlled the nation. They wrote and read the literature of the period.

Dutifully mirroring the intellectual modes of Europe, that minority warmly welcomed Positivism as a convincing formula for progress. Auguste Comte, the French founder of Positivism, held that human thought had evolved beyond its theological and metaphysical stages to reach its highest level, the scientific or positivistic stage. In that stage people eschewed purely speculative knowledge for that based on experience. By synthesizing the whole of human knowledge and reducing social facts and events to laws, Positivism promised to reconstruct society.

The Brazilian intelligentsia acclaimed the ideas of Comte with a degree of acceptance they had scarcely enjoyed in Europe. In particular the young bourgeois Brazilian intellectuals embraced the ideology. It is not surprising, therefore, that the focal points for the discussion and dissemination of Positivism were the schools—especially the engineering and military schools—where the sons of the commercial and bureaucratic middle groups studied in order to advance their social and economic positions.

Positivist ideas were manifest in Brazil as early as 1850 and, as might have been expected, they appeared first among the students and graduates of the technical and military schools

of Rio de Janeiro. The first important Brazilian sociological statement of Positivist ideas appeared in Francisco Brandão Júnior's *A Escravatura no Brasil* (Slavery in Brazil), printed in 1865. Nine years later a trenchant statement of Positivist thought appeared in *As Três Filosofias* (The Three Philosophies) by Luís Pereira Barreto. His introduction revealed the profound characteristic that Positivism already had assumed in Brazil: "Brazil already harbors in its midst a small group of Positivists recruited principally from the middle class and the profession of engineering. This group, far from diminishing in size, grows quickly and will continue to do so." In 1876, the young disciples of Comte founded the first Positivist Association of Brazil. Similar Positivist approaches to change and material progress characterized the intellectual development of most of Latin America in the last half of the nineteenth century.

Doubtless the most influential devotee of Comte among the Brazilians was Major Benjamin Constant de Magalhães (1836–1891), a popular professor of mathematics at the military academy. Energetically he advocated republican doctrines, to which many of the Positivists paid lip service only, and infused among the young cadets in his classes a similar enthusiasm for republicanism. His students, mostly sons of the bourgeoisie, saw in a republic their best hope for the future. Like their professor, they drew from only a part of Comte's philosophy and were often better republicans than Positivists.

During the last quarter of the nineteenth century, Positivism assumed an importance belying the size of its following because it appealed to and influenced members of key urban groups that exercised power far beyond their numbers, and because it codified a program sanctioned by the changing times and attitudes. Many favored parts of the Positivist doctrine without being practicing Positivists, or conceivably without even knowing that their preferences coincided with the Positivist doctrine.

For many Positivism summed up the longing for progress and provided a recognizable philosophical base. It provided for change within an acceptable and familiar framework. The essentially conservative middle groups found in Positivism a

way to incorporate themselves into the national institutions without destroying their elitist essence, that is, their projected reforms tended more toward conserving the social order rather than altering it radically. In general, Brazilian Positivism advocated governmental planning for progress and industrialization, restricting foreign economic influence and penetration, modernizing agriculture, expanding the communications and transportation infrastructures, encouraging education, controlling immigration, and enacting social legislation. Positivism hoped to insure social stability by incorporating the proletariat into society by means of education, higher wages, and regulation of wages, hours, and working conditions. The Positivists held conservative economic and monetary policies based on the defense of private property and yet they challenged some prevailing notions of laissez-faire policies. They felt the government should intervene in the economy to provide those essential services that the private sectors could not or would not provide. They denounced foreign economic domination, colonialism, and imperialism. Their ideas of racial equality were extremely enlightened. They regarded women as superior to men. They favored the abolition of slavery, the establishment of a republic, and the separation of church and state, changes which eventually occurred in Brazil. Very significantly for future political thought, the Positivists emphasized the role of the state in society rather than the democratic and laissez-faire capitalist ideals of the supremacy of the individual. Such an emphasis linked Brazilian political thought with traditional genetic governance—a tie to the patriarchal, paternalistic past—and propelled it toward an authoritarianism characteristic of the nation's twentieth-century political experience.

The principal contributions of the Positivists seem to have been to codify the diverse yearnings for progress expressed in many sectors of Brazilian society and to present an appealing program to implement them. Further, Positivism provided one insight into the mentality of the middle sector of society as it emerged into political prominence. Positivism unwittingly synthesized the ideas of a new class taking shape in urban Brazil. It profoundly influenced the ideas, actions,

events, and changes characteristic of the dynamic ten-year period from 1888 through 1897. It also left an unmistakable imprint on the twentieth century.

Abolition, Immigration, and Labor

The termination of the slave trade in 1850 aggravated one of Brazil's most serious problems, unsolved since the first years of colonization: the acute labor shortage. At that time, there were approximately three million slaves in a total population of seven million. The land was vast and nature was generous, but only labor could turn the land and its products into wealth. Africa had been Brazil's principal source of labor, and the planters counted almost exclusively on the strength and skill of the imported Africans to plant, harvest, and prepare their crops for export. The slaves worked as artisans and mechanics in the city as well as on the plantation. On many levels they constituted the most important part of the population. Slavery had existed in Spanish America as well, but only in a few places—Cuba would be the best example—did it become the warp and woof of the economy and society as it did in Portuguese America. In fact, some authorities claim Brazil imported about a half million to a million more slaves than did all of Spanish America.

The institution of slavery patterned the entire social-economic-political fabric of the nation. Numerically the slaves had predominated. At the opening of the nineteenth century, for example, slaves constituted a majority of the population. So dominant were the Africans and their descendants and their influence that a statesman like Bernardo Pereira de Vasconcelos could proclaim in the Chamber of Deputies during the early years of the Second Empire that Brazil owed its civilization to Africa. He reminded his startled listeners that the African provided the leisure for the aristocracy to pursue the arts and to govern. Consequently the civilization that had developed in Brazil rested squarely on the Afro-Brazilians' labor.

Slowly intellectuals began to point out the invaluable

contributions made by the Africans to Brazilian development. When the Brazilian Historical and Geographical Institute sponsored a contest to find out how the history of Brazil should be written, the German naturalist, Karl Friedrich Philipp von Martius, who had spent three years traveling extensively in Brazil, responded with the prize-winning essay. Published in the Institute's *Revista* in 1844, it called attention for the first time to the need to investigate the African-Brazilians' influence and contribution to Brazil. Later, the perceptive Sílvio Romero assigned them their just place in the formation of Brazilian civilization. He emphasized the adaptability of the Africans to the New World, their ability to learn quickly and their miscibility with the European. Concluded Romero, "We owe much more to the Negro than to the Indian; he entered fully into all aspects of our development." In the 1870s, Romero and Capistrano de Abreu carried on a discussion—not quite a debate—in the pages of the *carioca* newspaper *O Globo* on the extent of the African contribution to the formation of Brazilian civilization. They constantly contrasted and compared it with that of the Indian. Later, in his important history of the colonial period, *Capítulos de História Colonial*, Capistrano reaffirmed the economic and social importance of the African to Brazil.

The Brazilians closed off their principal source of labor in 1850 without finding another, just at the time when the increasing number of coffee plantations intensified the need for workers. Planters and deputies talked of plans to import Chinese coolies and to encourage European immigration. For the meantime, such plans remained theoretical. The government never sought the coolies, and the flow of European immigrants barely trickled into the immense and underpopulated empire. The slaves retained their vital importance in the economy. With the planter aristocracy in firm control of the government throughout the First Empire and the Regency, and for the first decades of the Second Empire, a propitious political atmosphere certainly did not exist for the discussion of abolition. An economy pinched by a labor shortage further discouraged such discussion. Nonetheless, a few distinguished liberals dared to speak out for abolition. Many of

Brazil's delegates to the Côrtes in 1822 damned the institution of slavery. Such eminent statesmen as José Bonifácio labeled it a "crime" and a "sin." In 1831 and 1852 projects to emancipate the slaves were presented to the Chamber of Deputies, which refused on both occasions to discuss the subject. Various writers denounced slavery in print.

No one seriously advocated an immediate end to slavery. The economy could not absorb the shock of so radical a move. All the abolitionists favored a gradual emancipation, to take place over a lengthy period. That moderate solution to the problem steadily gained supporters. Still, with considerable sums tied up in their slaves, the planters rallied to the defense of their investment. They pointed out that the shortage of laborers was already grave enough and indicated their apprehension that, once freed, the Afro-Brazilians would abandon the plantations in a mass exodus, with disastrous economic results for the nation. Hence, for a long time the planter aristocracy from both the traditional coastal sugar lands of the Northeast and the newer coffee lands of the Paraíba Valley refused even to consider the subject of abolition, no matter how gradual. Mass public opinion, still amorphous, had little to say on the subject.

The cause for emancipation had an effective ally, however, in the person of the emperor, who quietly opposed slavery. In 1840, he liberated all his own slaves. Nonetheless, he understood the importance of the institution to the economy and realized that for the time being nothing must be done to frighten the planters, and thus harm the newly invigorated economy, or to alienate his loyal rural supporters. He waited patiently for opinion in favor of gradual emancipation to solidify, a course he deemed inevitable after the termination of the nefarious slave traffic. In the early 1860s, he perceived that national opinion was ready to accept preparations for the first stage of emancipation. Accordingly, in January of 1864 he wrote to Prime Minister Zacarias de Góes e Vasconcelos to suggest that the first step be taken but cautiously counseled gradual emancipation to avoid disturbing the economy. After the close of the Civil War in the United States, new pressures for emancipation were exerted from the exte-

rior. In the Western Hemisphere only Cuba and Brazil still tolerated slavery, to the undisguised disgust of the rest of the Western world. Those pressures were persuasive in Brazil, sensitive to such mounting foreign criticism, and prompted the emperor to speak out, this time publicly, in favor of reforming the moribund institution. He signified his hope for change in a speech from the throne in 1867 opening the legislative session. Brief and certainly moderate in tone, his statement directed the nation's attention to the question of emancipation and made it the subject for general discussion. He thereby publicly committed his immense prestige to the cause of emancipation.

During the Paraguayan War the government considered it unwise to take any action on the question, but it began preparing public opinion. Slaves volunteering for military duty during the war received their liberty and some six thousand gained freedom in that manner. The army then and thereafter played a significant social role by absorbing emancipated slaves, training them for new tasks, thus facilitating their integration into a free society. As mentioned, the abrupt change of government in 1868 that brought the Conservatives back into power so angered the Liberals that they strengthened their flagging unity and issued a far-reaching reform program that, among other things, called for gradual emancipation.

After the defeat of Paraguay, the empire's attention once again focused fully on internal matters, among them the slavery question. Events in the Caribbean intensified foreign pressure on Brazil to free its slaves. In 1870, the Spanish government promulgated the Moret Law, which retroactively emancipated all children in Cuba born of slave mothers after September 1868, and all slaves upon their reaching sixty-five years of age (later amended to sixty years). In Brazil shortly thereafter, the Conservative government headed by Visconde do Rio-Branco resolved to carry out the suggestion made by the emperor in 1864. The legislature enacted the Law of the Free Womb in 1871 declaring free all children born to slaves. At the time this law was passed there were approximately 1.5 million slaves and a free population of 8.6 million. The law slowly doomed slavery. Africa as a source of slaves had long

been closed; after 1871, the other source, the womb, would bring forth no more slaves. At about the same time, several pieces of legislation were enacted to mitigate some of the harsher aspects of slavery. A law of 1869 prohibited the separate sale of husband, wife, and minor children. Another of 1871 compelled masters to accept the self-purchase of a slave at his market price. The promulgation of these laws quieted for the time being the agitation in favor of emancipation. The empire settled back to adjust to the new situation.

As the emperor's speech from the throne in 1867 indicated, considerations of emancipation were not made without giving thought to European immigration. The two were inextricably intertwined. With each step taken to end the institution of slavery, European immigration increased proportionately. Certainly as long as slavery remained a vigorous institution, the Europeans were not attracted to Brazil, where most of them in effect would be competing with the slaves. In addition to that major socio-economic handicap, Brazil had other disadvantages, at least in the minds of the Europeans, that tended to dissuade them from migrating there. Most Europeans believed that all of Brazil suffered an enervating tropical climate. The fact that the Roman Catholic church was the established state religion dissuaded Protestants. The restrictive political system with its limited vote and oligarchical domination discouraged many. Despite these negative factors some Europeans immigrated. Aided by the government of João VI, about two thousand Swiss settlers arrived in 1819 to establish a colony, the first non-Portuguese colony, at Nova Friburgo in the cool, mountainous region of the province of Rio de Janeiro. Four years later, German immigrants founded a colony at São Leopoldo in Rio Grande do Sul. In 1827, some Germans settled in Paraná. By 1830 approximately seven thousand Germans had entered Brazil. Then and thereafter the majority of the European immigrants settled in the South, where the climate most resembled that of Europe. In order to encourage immigration, the government prohibited the employment of a free man in the same job as a slave, set up an immigration center in Europe, and provided reception centers for the new arrivals.

The lack of ready access to land dissuaded some ambitious Europeans from relocating. The prime lands long before had been claimed—although claims to extensive tracts were vague, and the immense estates never developed a notable efficiency. In 1822 the state had stopped granting land in *sesmarias*, but those who wanted land thereafter simply squatted and/or declared their possession of it. They developed an impressive repertoire of means to show or prove they owned public lands. Under pressure from those who claimed such lands, the government in 1850 legitimized the claims. Whatever public land remained continued to be usurped by new encroachments. After 1854, the *Repartição Geral das Terras Públicas* (General Bureau of Public Lands) tried to exercise a monopoly over the sale and distribution of public lands that benefited, at least theoretically, new arrivals who sought farms for themselves. Unfortunately none of the procedures or laws worked satisfactorily. In the last analysis, the powerful—who, through force, could make good their claims and, through influence, protect them—took advantage of the situation to increase the size and number of their land holdings.

In the search for a substitute for slave labor on the coffee plantations, the progressive Nicolau de Pereira de Campos Vergueiro began to experiment with a system that combined features of indentured service and sharecropping. A Portuguese who arrived in Brazil before João VI, Vergueiro favored and promoted the independence of his adopted land. He served as deputy to the Côrtes and, after independence, served constantly as either a deputy or a senator and was a minister of the empire under Pedro I. He generally supported liberal policies and was highly praised for his enlightened ideas. In 1840, he began his planning to induce European laborers to migrate to his plantations.

Vergueiro's agent in Europe made contact with peasants willing to emigrate. The emigrant paid his own passage, or Vergueiro paid it for him under an agreement that the emigrant would repay the loan over a long period at a small rate of interest. To further decrease costs, the agent chartered a vessel to transport the emigrants. Vergueiro paid for trans-

portation from the coast to the plantations, furnished housing, and supplied at cost all the necessary provisions and clothing. The colonist then received a specified number of coffee trees proportional to the size of his family. He agreed to tend those trees and to share the profits from the coffee harvest with his employer. He was obliged to repay any debt and to give one year's notice before he could leave the plantation. The senator found his system, in which each man had a stake in the success of the coffee harvest, to be much more profitable than slave labor. He thought his plan also instilled in the European peasants a brighter hope for the future and an opportunity, hitherto missing, to raise their standard of living.

Others apparently thought so too. In the decade between 1847 and 1857 some seventy similar efforts were made, often with governmental financial aid, in the São Paulo area. Before the plan spread more widely some defects marred its further acceptance. Some agents in Europe recruited unscrupulously, deceiving both planter and emigrant so that the two scarcely knew what to expect of each other; consequently misunderstandings multiplied. Eventually the government took charge of the search in Europe for immigrants, soliciting them as well as paying their passage. By the mid-1870s a system that made use of salaried workers replaced the sharecrop system. The fixed salary earned by the immigrants guaranteed them a greater measure of security, although the low wages provided for little more than the basic existence of the workers and their families. Coffee workers never organized, but nonetheless some bitter strikes disturbed the countryside from time to time.

Table 5.2 indicates the flow of immigrants into the empire after the termination of the slave trade and until the abolition of slavery. Immigration increased rapidly after 1871. Only five times did immigration fall below 20,000 and even then it was far higher than the yearly average between 1850 and 1870. Not only was there a continual numerical increase but an ethnic change soon occurred as well. The Italian immigrants outnumbered the Portuguese for the first time in the 1870s, and throughout the remainder of the century Italy

Table 5.2 Annual Arrival of Immigrants in Brazil, 1850–1888

(*Prior to 1850 the annual number of immigrants rarely exceeded 1,000*)

1850	2,072	1863	7,642	1876	30,747
1851	4,425	1864	9,578	1877	29,468
1852	2,731	1865	6,452	1878	24,456
1853	10,935	1866	7,699	1879	22,788
1854	9,189	1867	10,902	1880	30,355
1855	11,798	1868	11,315	1881	11,548
1856	14,008	1869	11,527	1882	29,589
1857	14,244	1870	5,158	1883	34,015
1858	18,529	1871	12,431	1884	24,890
1859	20,114	1872	19,219	1885	35,440
1860	15,774	1873	14,742	1886	33,486
1861	13,003	1874	20,332	1887	55,965
1862	14,295	1875	14,590	1888	133,253

SOURCE: Instituto Histórico e Geográfico Brasileiro, *Diccionário Histórico, Geográphico, e Ethnográphico do Brasil* (Rio de Janeiro: Imprensa Nacional, 1922), 1, 295–96.

supplied the greatest share of the new arrivals. Portugal, Germany, and Spain also contributed heavily. Russians, French, English, Syrians, Austrians, and Swiss immigrated in smaller numbers. The inclusion of non-Iberians as well as non-Catholics among the immigrants introduced possibilities for social change in Brazil. Most of the immigrants went to the South or Southeast. Many remained in the cities. By the end of the century, practically all the industrial workers were foreigners. Although the *senhores de engenho* of the Northeast talked about attracting foreign immigrants, they had scant success. Disenchanted with what they found or unable to adjust to their new surroundings, many immigrants either returned to Europe or moved on to a Spanish American republic to try their luck again. Many went to Argentina, the Latin American nation that received the largest number of immigrants. In a population of 9,723,604 in 1872, Brazil counted 388,459 foreigners, about 3.9 percent of the population; in 1890, the population was 13,982,370 but the number of foreigners had dropped to 351,545, or 2.5 percent. The immigrants who remained scorned slavery and contributed to the opinion favoring its abolition.

Patience with the long-term results of Rio-Branco's Law of the Free Womb wore thin. After 1871, the question was not whether slavery should be abolished—all agreed that it should

be—but rather how quickly abolition should take place. The Conservatives hoped to make it as gradual a process as possible. The Liberals sought to speed it up. When the Liberals returned to power in 1878, they again pressed the slavery question on the nation. By then, the Positivists were attacking slavery as incompatible with scientific human progress. Under the prodding of the Liberals and Positivists, abolitionist sentiment welled up within the middle groups. The movement to abolish slavery was primarily urban, finding its greatest support among those least connected with the institution. In short, the urban middle groups overtly challenged the traditional rural oligarchy. The cities once again served as the bellwether of change.

The concern for the welfare of the remaining million and a quarter slaves called forth some mesmeric spokesmen. Joaquim Nabuco (1849–1910), lawyer, diplomat, and statesman, served in the Chamber of Deputies as a representative of his natal province, Pernambuco, on several occasions beginning in 1878, and eloquently supported the cause of emancipation. A graduate of the Law School of Recife in 1870, he exemplified the nineteenth-century university graduate who spurned his rural background to adopt the mentality of the city. Nabuco compiled his most cogent arguments against slavery in his fiery book *O Abolicionismo* (Abolitionism), in one paragraph of which, with telling mathematics, he ridiculed the Rio-Branco Law by pointing out that a black girl born on the eve of the proclamation of the law might give birth to a child in 1911 who would remain in provisional slavery until 1932. In 1880, he became president of the newly organized Brazilian Anti-Slavery Society, the most important of many such societies that sprang up throughout the empire in that decade. Several highly articulate Afro-Brazilians contributed to the leadership of the abolitionist campaign: José Carlos do Patrocínio (1854–1905), a persuasive journalist, wrote ceaselessly for the cause and became a symbol of the campaign; André Rebouças (1838–1898) organized abolitionist clubs and spoke and wrote profusely in support of abolition; and Luís Gonzaga de Pinto Gama (1830–1882) spent his youth as a slave and later became a distinguished lawyer who specialized in de-

fending slaves in court. He claimed credit for freeing five hundred slaves through the courts. A fiery advocate of immediate abolition, he declared, "Every slave who kills his master, no matter what the circumstances may be, kills in self-defense." He also preached "the right of insurrection." As a poet, he rhapsodized, "My loves are beautiful, the color of night."

Poets contributed significantly to the abolitionist cause. A mulatto, Castro Alves (1847–1871), wrote some of the most beautiful poetry produced in Brazil in the nineteenth century. Dedicating himself fervently to the cause of the slaves, he depicted their plight with such moving verses that he awoke the social conscience of his readers to the injustices inflicted on them. One of his best known poems, "Navio Negreiro" (The Slave Ship), evoked the inhuman suffering of the captives during the crossing from Africa to Brazil. Life on the slave ship recalled some of the scenes of Dante's *Inferno*.

The slavery question forced itself to the forefront of politics. The Liberals called for a second step toward the ultimate goal, if not the coup de grace itself. The Conservatives fought a delaying action. In 1884, the provinces of Ceará and Amazonas freed all their slaves. Voluntary manumissions became increasingly frequent. In the province of Rio de Janeiro, a slavery stronghold, approximately 15,100 slaves received their freedom from their masters between 1873 and 1885. In 1887, two of the province's largest landowners, the Condes de São Clemente and Nova Friburgo, manumitted 1,909 slaves. Furthermore, a sympathetic public extended every possible facility to aid and encourage runaway slaves. The Conservatives, in power in 1885, addressed the issue as they had in 1871 and enacted yet another measure to forestall the total abolition of slavery. The Saraiva-Cotegipe Law liberated all slaves once they reached the age of sixty. At the time of its passage this law affected some 120,000 slaves. Slavery was then cut off at both ends. Blacks who were not born into freedom could look forward to retiring into it.

Discredited as slavery was, the rural aristocracy continued to apologize for it. They argued that their slaves lived better than most European workers and accused the aboli-

tionists of painting far too gloomy a picture of the institution. They regarded the Brazilian brand of slavery as extremely mild. On this point of the severity or leniency of the institution arguments still rage. Certainly a large number of foreign visitors to Brazil described mitigating aspects of the Brazilian slave system, with its permissive and indolent masters. They emphasized the possibilities for the slaves to achieve their freedom as well as their acceptance into society once free. Kidder and Fletcher noted, "The comparative ease with which a slave may obtain his freedom, and, by the possession of property, the rights of citizenship, will probably in twenty years put an end to servitude in this South American Empire." Such foreign commentators and subsequent students who adopted similar points of view dwelt on the humanitarian customs surrounding the institution of slavery in Brazil.

The attitudes toward slavery taken by the more enlightened Brazilian patricians added weight to that point of view. At worst, they regarded slavery as a necessary evil—the sole source of labor—to be mitigated by compassionate treatment of the slaves. At best, they gradually manumitted their slaves. José Lino Coutinho, a well-to-do Bahian physician who served in both the Portuguese Côrtes and the Brazilian legislature, represented that group. Lamenting the necessity of slaves, he advised his daughter: "As I have said, dear Cora, be humane and charitable with them [the slaves]. When they are well, see that they are well fed and dressed; when they are ill, see that they receive treatment. Even though they are our slaves, they are also our fellow human beings. Whoever shows kindness and consideration to them will be rewarded with their gratefulness."

The slaves in Brazil were at least partially integrated into society and possessed rights, quite a legal contrast to the plight of the slaves in the United States. Hence their transition from slave to freedman was facilitated. One paramount privilege the slaves enjoyed was their ability to purchase their own freedom. Blacks, taking advantage of the many Catholic holidays to work on their own, saved money for that purpose. They occasionally formed their own mutual aid societies to facilitate their purchase of freedom. In general Brazilian his-

torians have concluded that the Brazilian brand of slavery was less rigorous than that practiced by the French, English, North Americans, and Dutch. Manuel de Oliveira Lima represented that position very well. He held that the patriarchal aspect of Brazilian slavery in which the slave was but an extension of the master's family, fondly looked after and cared for, eliminated much of the harshness and cruelty attendant upon the institution in other lands. To his thinking, humaneness characterized the Brazilian master.

The opposite school of thought, the revisionists, put its emphasis elsewhere. Those historians called attention to the immense gap between the beneficent theory of the law and the brutal practice of the masters. During the sugar harvest slaves in the Northeast worked fifteen to eighteen hours a day, seven days a week, eating on the job. The coffee harvest required the same exhausting effort. Little wonder the life span of a slave averaged only fifteen years (some authorities calculate only seven years)! Cruel punishments constituted another sad chapter in the history of slavery. Chains, iron collars, tin masks, wooden stocks, whippings and brandings were but a few of the better-known and widely used methods of punishment. Herbert H. Smith, one of the most intelligent foreign observers of the Brazilian scene in the late imperial period, damned slavery without reservation. He testified, "Around Rio and Bahia, where the vast majority of the slaves are now owned, there are masters who treat their servants with a severity that is nothing short of barbarism." His experiences convinced him that "all other evils with which this country [Brazil] is cursed, taken together, will not compare with this one [slavery]; I could almost say that all other evils have arisen from it, or been strengthened by it." In his opinion, slavery induced indolence, pride, sensuality, and selfishness among the owners and physically and mentally debilitated the African-Brazilians, making them unfit for civilization.

Slave revolts against inhuman treatment and the existence of the ubiquitous *quilombos* provided convincing arguments for the historical revisionists. The major slave revolt of the nineteenth century took place in 1835 in Bahia, scene

of nine revolts or attempted revolts since the opening of the century. Well organized and directed by Nagos slaves, the rebels sought to kill all whites and free all slaves. The revolt failed, but it sent shivers of fear throughout the white community that never abated until slavery was abolished.

Slaves sometimes murdered their overseers, masters, and their families. To take revenge on the brutal system that exploited them, the slaves frequently put the torch to their masters' houses, barns, warehouses, sugar mills, forests, and cane fields. Many turned their backs on the system, fleeing into the vast and underpopulated interior. Still others, unable to bear the burden of their slavery any longer, committed suicide. The blacks thus met violence with violence on such an intense level as to cast into doubt the bucolic legends of plantation harmony.

Brazilian society lived in a state of tension, fearful of slave revolts or reprisals. In his authoritative study, *A Escravidão no Brasil* (Slavery in Brazil), published in 1866, Agostinho Marquês Perdigão Malheiros described the slave as "a domestic enemy" and "a public enemy." He cautioned, "He is a volcano that constantly threatens society, a mine ready to explode at the least spark." Foreign travelers sensed the tension. Prince Adalbert visited one large and well-run plantation which he praised as a model. After noting the friendly relations between master and the slaves, he revealed, "The loaded guns and pistols hanging up in his [the owner's] bedroom however, showed that he had not entire confidence in them [the slaves] and indeed, he had more than once been obliged to face them with his loaded gun." The abolition movement increased rather than diminished that tension. Evidence indicates that the *fazendeiros* lived in fear of being attacked by their slaves as the day of deliverance approached. In June of 1887, the minister of agriculture confessed that the large number of escaped slaves in Santos constituted a "grave and imminent danger to public order and property." He reported that the government had dispatched troops to São Paulo not to recapture slaves but "to maintain public order and calm the frightened agricultural and commercial interests" of that province. In his official message the following year, the pres-

ident of São Paulo spoke with alarm of the increasing number of slaves who fled their plantations "armed." The picture that emerges is far from that of the docile slave faithfully and good-naturedly attending his master on the plantation. The revisionists—like the abolitionists—concluded that slavery at best was a despicable institution contrary to human reason and without defense.

With abolitionist sentiment aflame, the days of slavery in Brazil were clearly numbered. At the same time, the economic arguments against the institution began to carry the same weight as the emotional appeal. It became obvious to more and more concerned Brazilians that in the long run salaried labor was more economical than paying the rising price for slaves and their upkeep, to say nothing of the capital loss if a slave died young, proved to be recalcitrant or inefficient, or ran away. After 1850 many planters in the Northeast found it cheaper to pay wages than to keep slaves. Within two decades free workers outnumbered slaves on the sugar plantations. Efficient and well-organized exploitation of slaves in some new coffee regions made the system temporarily profitable for some *fazendeiros,* but other statistics appeared to show that a sack of coffee produced by free labor cost approximately half that of one produced by slave labor. The declining numbers of slaves meant that by 1880 most new coffee plantations (and many older ones as well) depended heavily on free, salaried labor. In some instances modern plantation owners were introducing labor-saving machinery. The Republican party in São Paulo, composed primarily of coffee planters, resolved in 1887 to favor total emancipation, and its members agreed to free their own slaves within a two-year period. In the same year the army, through the influential Military Club, petitioned the Crown to relieve it of the irksome and humiliating duty of chasing down runaway slaves. Slavery had lost its basis of support. Many slave owners continued to apologize for the institution, hoping more to obtain a handsome indemnification from the government than to stem the abolitionist tide.

The climax came on May 13, 1888. To cries of approval from those in attendance, the parliament passed the Golden

Law liberating the remaining three-quarters of a million slaves. The final vestiges of slavery had been eliminated in Cuba in 1886, and so with the passage of the Golden Law of 1888, slavery finally disappeared from the Western Hemisphere. Ironically it once again fell to the Conservatives to act on the matter, and it was they—as in 1871 and 1885—who passed the legislation. The law contained no provision to indemnify the owners for their slaves, although the government established a new agricultural bank to extend credit to landowners suffering from the effects of emancipation. In the absence of her father, Princess-Regent Isabel, a committed abolitionist, signed the law. The crowds shouted their approval. Band music erupted. Dazzling fireworks exploded. Speeches resounded. And people merrily danced and sang in the streets of Rio de Janeiro.

While those joyous scenes took place in the capital and other major cities, a deafening silence greeted the Golden Law in much of the countryside. Confusion, uncertainty, and concern for the future troubled those directly connected with the abolished institution. The slaveholders sulked moodily over their sudden capital loss and the threat to their economic position. They blamed the monarchy for the financial blow. If the slaves expected the rapidly penned signature of Princess Isabel at the foot of the Golden Law to transport them forthwith to a promised land, they were soon disillusioned. Life continued to be hard for them, as they lamented in this popular verse:

> Everything in this world changes,
> Only the life of the Negro remains the same:
> He works to die of hunger,
> The 13th of May fooled him!

Adjustments were necessary for all involved. Most would make the necessary transitions or adaptations within a few years.

Once during the abolitionist campaign Joaquim Nabuco warned his constituents in Pernambuco of the retrograde effects of slavery on their society, and what he said could be applied to the entire nation:

Ah! Pernambuco has a great past, but it seems that its sons do not wish it to have a great future! . . .

Slavery is an institution which destroys and degrades everything that it is the purpose of social institutions to build and develop. . . . The city of Recife has awakened from the profound sleep of many years of indifference and callousness. In this place where I now speak, the center of so many traditions and so much heroism, which were it not for slavery would today be a strong and respected republic.

Nabuco happily proclaimed the abolition of slavery as a landmark in Brazil's evolution. For him the year 1888 heralded the birth of a new Brazil. The eminent historian Sérgio Buarque de Holanda endorsed that conclusion, declaring, "The year 1888, the most decisive year in the evolution of the Brazilian people, divides two epochs." Abolition signaled Brazil's emergence into the modern world. Slavery was indissolubly linked with the colonial past. That institution was one of the trinity, together with the *latifundia* and monoculture, perpetuating the traditional agrarian society. In fact, many believed that slavery made the archaic agricultural system function since it contributed the most vital ingredient, labor, which turned the land into wealth. Hence the opponents of slavery felt that the institution was the strongest cord tying the nation to its colonial past, and slavery thus stood accused of having retarded national development. The younger generation charged it with the most heinous and unforgivable of crimes: preventing modernization. In their opinion, it inhibited the mechanization of agriculture, dissuaded Europeans from migrating to Brazil, and restricted economic development, especially industrialization, already regarded as the magic key to the future. As early as 1861 at the National Exposition in Rio de Janeiro, where a minimum of industrial products were on display, slavery bore the blame for the fact that domestic manufacturing had failed to prosper. Successful industrialization required, among other things, the capital wastefully invested in slaves. Further, the slaves earned no wages and hence constituted no market, while industrialization required a free proletariat class demanding and able to pay for the

manufactured products. On a wider plane than that, slavery and modernization were simply incompatible, indeed, contradictory. The abolition of slavery thus broke the chains of a nation linked to the past and permitted it to step toward the future. The optimistic predicted immediate change and progress on an ever-accelerating scale. The decade following abolition witnessed impressive changes. Brazil made the adjustments to embrace both modernity and capitalism.

The Middle Groups and the Military

The difference in the composition of Brazilian society between the eras of the declaration of independence and the emancipation of the slaves illustrates some of the demographic trends under way in the nineteenth century. In 1822 the new nation counted barely 4 million inhabitants, of whom probably half were slaves of African birth or descent. When Princess Isabel signed the Golden Law in 1888, roughly 750,000 slaves gained their freedom. They constituted less than one twentieth of the population of 14 million. At the opposite end of the social scale stood 300,000 large plantation owners and members of their families. The vast majority of the population fell between those two extremes. True, most of them were impoverished peasants or rural proletariat wedded to the soil, who unknowingly contributed to the maintenance of the status quo. There also was an inarticulate group cultivating small and medium-sized farms. Of greatest significance, however, within the large body between the two extremes, were the urban middle groups, already mentioned as the principal agents in bringing about the mental transformation of Brazil in the nineteenth century. Among its members the consensus grew that their well-being required the modification, if not the eradication, of many colonial vestiges that still pervaded national life. With fewer and more tenuous roots in the agricultural past, these urban-based middle groups showed a growing impatience with tradition and a fascination with innovation. Change offered them the best opportunity to improve

their status. They would soon challenge the planter elite for the power to effect the improvements they desired.

Despite modifications that took place in Brazil during the Second Empire, the colonial past still formed a significant part of the present during the 1880's. An agrarian economy characterized by *latifundia* and monoculture still predominated. Agricultural exports still fueled the economy. The dominant class continued to be the large landowners. They earned the wealth and enjoyed the prestige and power it conferred. They manipulated a patrimonial regime of their fabrication incorporating small producers and laborers held to the plantation by informally institutionalized ties. Two common means of holding them were debt and permission to use land in exchange for labor or tribute. The landed class exploited the countryfolks' ignorance and isolation to augment their power. The patriarchal chiefs of the landed gentry customarily bore the title *coronel,* a title derived from the service they or their forebears gave to the National Guard. The title augmented their control of the countryside. With their economic advantages and social prestige, they also exercised local political control. Some employed small private "armies" to enforce their will; others hired the backlands bandits for that purpose. Friendship or familial ties with local, state, and national politicians and with neighboring *senhores de terras* buttressed the power structure of each *coronel.* In contrast to the ideas held in that part of the still neofeudalistic/neocapitalist countryside, the new coffee planters of São Paulo and Minas Gerais increasingly came to represent a rural capitalist class more tightly integrated than ever into the markets of the United States and Western Europe. Their ideas as well as their agrarian practices were increasingly "modern." They favored selective change. Some believed decentralization of political power would best serve their interests. Others favored a republic. Most came to regard slavery as an anachronism. They viewed such changes as complementary to their capitalist inclinations.

Along with the capitalist coffee planters, the growing urban centers, particularly in southeastern Brazil, challenged

the neofeudalism of the countryside and the power of the moribund *fazendeiro* class. The inevitable struggle between those two sharply different elements set the tone for the future.

The gulf between the neofeudal countryside and the more progressive cities and coffee planters widened rapidly during the closing decades of the nineteenth century. Eventually the urban middle groups and progressive coffee planters realized that the emperor, revered and respected as he might be, represented primarily the entrenched landed class, whom he favored with titles of nobility and political power. Many of the city dwellers viewed the emperor as the embodiment of the planters' desire to retain much of what was colonial in Brazil's society and economy, while rejecting, in the stricter legal sense, colonial status. In short, the aging emperor symbolized the past. He did not represent the emerging middle groups or the emergent capitalism. Pedro gave every indication of being reluctant to recognize the increasing importance of the merchants and industrialists. In 1875, for example, he failed to come to the support of the enterprising Mauá and allowed his economic empire to collapse. Of singular importance, he ignored the restless military officers whose desires and ambitions often reflected those of the middle groups from whose families they came. Clearly the monarchical regime revealed its increasing incompatibility with new trends.

Removed from the new elements of society, the monarchy magnified its isolation by offending two of its staunchest supporters. The emperor's liberalism did not please many within the Roman Catholic church. The display of regal ire toward the Church and the imprisonment of two bishops in 1874 had prompted some in the ecclesiastical hierarchy to reassess their relations with the throne. While the Church did not withdraw its loyalty, many of its leaders did manifest increasing indifference toward the monarchy's fate. Still, most churchmen hesitated to embrace the republican cause since the Republican party was strongly anticlerical. One official Roman Catholic newspaper, *O Apóstolo*, sought to resolve the dilemma by calling for "the re-formation of an honest

republican party." An editorial in that paper characterized the government as "pagan Caesarism" and predicted that a new republican party would "serve as a powerful brake on this political monster." Some Catholic priests did find it possible to support the historic Republican party. While the hierarchy did not wave the banner of republicanism, those churchmen simply cooled toward the empire and displayed more interest and concern in formulating a new relationship with the civil authorities than in propping up a teetering throne.

Royal favor—and, in the case of the heir presumptive, royal fervor—for the abolitionist movement, and the Golden Law's failure to compensate the former owners for their freed slaves aroused the hostility of the old landed class. Particularly hostile was that segment, comprising the older sugar and coffee planters, that had once supported the Crown most enthusiastically. After emancipation took place some angry planters joined the Republican party. Abolition of slavery in Brazil precipitated the fall of the monarchy, just as abolition in Cuba foretold the end of Spanish dominion there.

At the same time that the base of support for the old emperor diminished, the people's psychological disposition toward a monarchy lessened. A continent of republics encircled the empire, and Brazilians, because of the uniqueness of their political institutions, felt isolated from their neighbors. The trends of the time seemed to favor the republican system of government. The intelligentsia, always conscious of what was occurring in their beloved France, watched with interest the rapid dissolution of Napoleon's monarchy in 1870. Furthermore, many began to equate republicanism with progress and, conversely, to equate monarchy with backwardness. They were fully aware of the great progress of Argentina since its unification in 1862 and of the astounding rate of industrialization of the United States since the end of its Civil War. Against those records imperial Brazil contrasted poorly. For that the monarchy bore part of the blame.

During the long process during which indifference or even hostility toward the monarchy overtook increasing numbers of the Brazilians, two philosophical currents, Positivism and republicanism, gained adherents among the middle sec-

tors of the cities. Both advocated the abolition of the monarchy. The enthusiasts for those ideas spoke out loudly and frequently, although they alone did not possess the strength to bring down the monarchy. They depended on their growing influence in the army officer-corps to persuade the military to overthrow the emperor and establish a republic.

The military as an institution made a belated appearance in Brazil. It played an insignificant role until the protracted war with Paraguay. Five years of fighting increased both its size and its importance. There were seventeen thousand soldiers in the army in 1864; by 1870 there were one hundred thousand. Restless after peace returned to South America in 1870, the officers focused their attention on politics. The Duque de Caxias, unquestionably loyal to Pedro II and the supreme commander of the army, held the military in check. His death in 1880 gave license to greater political activity among the officers. Petty disputes, considered by those in uniform as "affairs of honor," marred relations between the cabinets of government and the military. To a certain degree those differences reflected a class conflict. The cabinets represented the landed aristocracy and their traditional point of view. The bulk of the commissioned officers came from the middle groups and unconsciously spoke for them or for part of them. In another sense, as a solidifying corporation, the armed forces on many matters spoke only for itself and its interests. Many officers followed a military career because of the mobility and prestige it offered. In the military academy, they received an excellent education. Dressed in splendid uniforms and favored with the aura of victories they or their predecessors had won for the fatherland on the battlefields of Paraguay, they enjoyed a privileged social position that birth or background might otherwise have denied them. Their rank and uniforms admitted them to new opportunities and situations where they did not always feel comfortable or at ease. Increasingly inflated with their own importance, the officers often felt that the politicians—more often than not the imperial nobility or its representatives—scorned, neglected, and, whenever possible, humiliated them. Their col-

lective paranoia prevented them from maintaining satisfactory relations with the civilian, imperial government.

The military first began to debate governmental policies publicly in 1879. The officers vehemently opposed a bill to reduce the size of the military and did not hesitate to voice their disapproval. Their activities violated two regulations, one issued in 1859 and a second in 1878, prohibiting officers from criticizing their superiors or debating service matters in the press. The officers nonetheless expressed their opposition with impunity, and eventually the bill was abandoned. The civil-military conflict attracted wider national attention in 1883. Over the issue of compulsory payments to an insurance fund, the officers again debated in public questions that were related to the service and the government. When the government proscribed such discussions, reprimanding some senior officers and punishing others, the officers united to defend what they considered to be their rights. One of those who rose to defend the military's position was Marshal Deodoro da Fonseca, a highly respected officer who enjoyed considerable prestige among his colleagues and popularity in the ranks. In 1886 he again intervened in a dispute—this one between some officers stationed in Pôrto Alegre and the government—to support the military point of view. Embittered toward the politicians, Deodoro accused them of furthering their own individual interests to the detriment of the country and of neglecting, even maltreating, the army despite its sacrifices for the fatherland. The marshal decried the sad state into which the nation had fallen politically. His outspoken defense of the military in its petty quarrels with the government made him a hero to those in uniform.

After their quarrels with the government in 1886, the officers agreed that the civilians had sullied military honor and determined that the insults must be avenged. In the following year they founded the *Clube Militar* to speak for military interests and to voice military grievances. The members promptly elected Deodoro as the first club president. Thereafter the military's political activities were centered within the club's salons. All these seemingly minor incidents were indications of the army's fear of neglect and its determination

to regain for itself, at any cost, the position of prestige it once enjoyed.

Aware of the mounting dissatisfaction among the officers, the Republican party moved to exploit it. They understood that the military held the key to the establishment of a republic. Unlike any other group in Brazil, the military had both the organization and power to effect change. The young officers, concerned not only with questions of honor but with problems of national development, listened attentively to Republican party and Positivist propaganda, both of which advocated an end to the empire. The military school in Rio de Janeiro resounded with discussions of Republican ideology. In the popular classes of Benjamin Constant, the cadets heard enthusiastic lectures on Positivism. Those young officers reflected the widening distance between the class from which they sprang and the imperial government. The support of the cadets and junior officers enhanced the Republican cause, but nothing could be done without the cooperation of their seniors. In the late 1880s those ranking officers moved toward the Republican camp as the logical alternative to supporting an empire that they felt had mistreated them. When the most powerful figure in the army, Marshal Deodoro, was convinced by fellow officers and Republicans that the only method of "purifying" the political body was to replace the moribund empire with a vigorous republic, the fate of the empire was decided. Deodoro commanded the loyalty of the entire army, and with him it turned on the empire.

Under Deodoro's orders, on November 15, 1889, the army marched from the barracks, surrounded the Royal Palace, occupied the principal governmental buildings, and silenced Rio de Janeiro. In a dry, authoritative tone the marshal informed a surprised nation, "The people, the army and the navy, in perfect harmony of sentiment with our fellow citizens resident in the provinces, have just decreed the dethronement of the imperial dynasty, and consequently the extinction of the representative monarchical system of government." The empire had fallen.

The nation acquiesced in the change. The masses seemed indifferent to the events. The former supporters of the mon-

archy among the planters and the hierarchy of the Church raised no voice of protest. Of the provinces, only Maranhão and Bahia offered some minor protest and resistance, token demonstrations. Tranquillity generally prevailed throughout the novice republic. Indeed, the evidence seemed to indicate that structurally the empire had been weak and that in the penultimate decade of the nineteenth century its vitality had been sapped. Consequently, more from its own infirmities than anything else, the empire expired. The military, then, simply provided the necessary coup de grace and did so without meeting any opposition.

Despite all the talk of a republic over the years, the nation was little prepared to put into practice the elaborate and varied republican theories. The principal question after the coup was whether a republic would be established or anarchy would hold sway. The populace asked anxiously if the new regime could maintain order, ensure national unity, and offer the same comfortable liberties its predecessor had for nearly half a century. Machado de Assis' novel of the period, *Esau and Jacob,* captures well the prevailing mood of apprehension.

The military, the only institution really national in scope, organization, and program—and the self-appointed guardian of patriotism—immediately took charge of the nation. The emperor abdicated and sailed into European exile, dying in a modest Parisian hotel on December 5, 1891. Deodoro, with the unanimous backing of the army, kept command of the government as chief of state. At a military parade two months after the coup, he accepted the sonorous rank "Generalissimo of the Forces of the Land and the Sea." He was a long way from his modest childhood as the son of an army officer in provincial Alagoas. He behaved himself in the presidential palace very much as he had in the barracks, with an unquestioned reliance on discipline, order, hierarchy, and command. Military influence could be seen everywhere. Abandoning the secondary role assigned to them during the imperial period, the officers assumed a primary role in the new republic. The army increased in size from thirteen to twenty thousand. Army officers governed ten of the twenty states.

Deodoro's cabinet was essentially civilian in composition, but no one doubted that the military exercised final authority. One bizarre aspect of the military influence was the conferring of the rank of brigadier general on all civilian members of the cabinet, most of whom had never held a rifle or been inside a barracks.

Titles of nobility were abolished, and the holders of them were eclipsed at least temporarily. "Doctor" and "Colonel" were the appellations most prized as the university and service-academy graduates assumed greater political and social importance. The first cabinet of the republic evinced that trend unmistakably. Quintino Bocaiúva, a respected journalist and doctor of law, held the portfolio of foreign affairs; Manuel Ferraz de Campos Sales, a doctor of law, was minister of justice; Demétrio Ribeiro, a young engineer, took charge of the ministry of agriculture, commerce, and public works; Aristides da Silveira Lobo, a journalist as well as a doctor of law, was minister of the interior; Ruy Barbosa, yet another lawyer, assumed the portfolio of finances; Colonel Benjamin Constant was minister of war; and Vice Admiral Eduardo Wandenkolk was minister of the navy. The appointment of new officials in the states also mirrored that trend.

Since advocating a republican ideology was a requirement for the holding of office on any high level, one encountered at least nominal Republicans in all the important posts. However, those Republicans were by no means a homogeneous group. At one extreme a small group of Positivists favored a "scientific dictatorship" with the trappings of a republic. A much larger body of less doctrinaire Republicans supported a democratic, federal republic. Diverse elements composed that larger group: historic Republicans who had faithfully pursued their goal since 1870; ardent young radicals; young quasi-Positivist army officers inspired by Benjamin Constant; and senior officers who, for reasons of their own, adopted republicanism at the last minute. Such diversity inhibited the effectiveness of the Republicans and strengthened the hand of the more cohesive military.

The task of creating a republic on the ruins of the empire

was challenging. However, once again the Brazilians demonstrated the capacity to make a major change with minimal strife. In direct contrast to the experience of most of the Spanish American nations in the nineteenth century, Brazil altered its government without fighting, without bloodshed, and, even more amazing, without imprisonments. In that manner, the nation consolidated the tradition it had established in the nineteenth century of bringing about major changes peacefully—exemplifying the "conciliation and reform" theory that the historian José Honório Rodrígues has elaborated so convincingly. On the surface at any rate, compromise, accommodation, and conciliation were the mode. But in the months and years after the *fait accompli* of the military, the necessary adjustments did not always come easily. Contractual governance posed more questions than it answered, and Brazilians eventually succumbed to the political instability that had bedeviled the rest of Latin America throughout the nineteenth century.

By decree on November 16, 1889, Deodoro created a federal republic. His unchallenged position as the nation's most powerful and prestigious military figure increased the strength of the regime, which quickly displayed an ability to keep order and maintain unity. The Republicans rapidly regularized their administration.

The new republic encountered little difficulty in obtaining foreign recognition. Neighboring Uruguay and Argentina accorded it on November 20. On the same day President Benjamin Harrison instructed the United States minister in Rio de Janeiro to maintain relations with the new government. A lengthy debate in the Senate delayed official United States recognition until January 29, 1890. Meanwhile, Bolivia, Chile, Paraguay, Peru, and Venezuela had given their recognition. The remainder of the hemisphere followed suit. The European nations delayed a little longer. On June 2, 1890, France became the first of the Old World to welcome the new republic into the community of nations. Great Britain recognized the republic on May 4, 1891. Russia was the last European state to do so; the czar waited until after the death of

Pedro II. The republic, upon entering into friendly relations with the outside world, indicated that there would be no change in traditional Brazilian foreign policy.

Characteristic of his authoritarian approach to power, Deodoro decreed on January 7, 1890 the separation of church and state, an action applauded by the ecclesiastical hierarchy, which sought a freedom for the Roman Catholic church similar to that insured it in the United States. The two important institutions parted amiably and both seemed to benefit from the separation.

The government, always legalistic in its outlook, promptly gave attention to the writing of a constitution. On December 3, 1889, Deodoro appointed a special committee of five jurists to prepare the bases of a new constitution. The committee drew heavily on the constitution of the United States and also found a useful model in the Argentine constitution. Minister Ruy Barbosa, impressed by the North American document, reviewed the work of the committee for the government and made extensive revisions. As a result the proposed document assumed a strong presidential flavor. Thus revised, the proposed constitution was submitted to the Assembly, which met on November 15, 1890. The electoral machinery, well oiled in the traditional fashion by the government, had produced an Assembly composed of delegates who were mainly Republicans of one shade or another, a gathering of novices. Many of these were military officers being initiated into politics. Joaquim Francisco de Assis Brasil, diplomat, statesman, and political commentator, noted with some dismay, "The ignorance of almost all of them concerning the most elementary political questions was fantastic." The only truly coherent group within the Assembly—and one of the most vocal—was the Positivists, small in number but highly influential. They encouraged the pronounced federalist sentiments prevalent among the Republicans. Assis Brasil, himself not a Positivist, had done much to popularize the federal idea in his widely read and much-discussed book, *A República Federal*, published in São Paulo in 1887. His persuasive arguments weighed heavily in the minds of the impressionable young legislators. While the concept of federalism excited the imaginations of

many who saw in greater local autonomy the end of a stifling unitary embrace, it sent chills of fear through a minority who looked back to the disastrous experiment with it during the Regency.

The constitution promulgated on February 24, 1891, provided for a federal, republican, presidential form of government. It was the legal base for a liberal, democratic, capitalist state that in practice would permit a system of regional alliances favorable to the dynamic coffee-exporting capitalists of the Southeast. Although weaker than during the Second Empire, the central government still retained some impressive powers. It reserved for itself abundant sources of income and the right to intervene in the states. Of great importance, it could mobilize the armed forces to enforce its will. Within the traditional Latin American framework, the president was not only the chief executive but also the mainspring of all power, dominating and subordinating to his will the other branches and levels of government—and so it had to be if he was to be at all effective and maintain his authority. Essentially he served as a unifying force to balance and neutralize the many centrifugal tendencies of the nation. The national legislature consisted of the Chamber of Deputies, whose members were elected for three-year terms on the basis of population, and the Senate, composed of three delegates from each state elected for nine-year terms. Contrary to the document of 1824, the new constitution disenfranchised the illiterate. It vaguely modeled the judicial system on that of the United States. The twenty states were governed by popularly elected governors and their legislatures had power over exclusively state matters. They could enact an export tax—an extremely lucrative source of income in rich states such as São Paulo and Minas Gerais—on any of their products. The states maintained militias, which provided them additional leverage in dealing with the federal government.

In general the constitution was liberal and well written; unfortunately, it was not Brazilian. In an effort to repudiate the past, the provisional government had imported a constitution, primarily from the United States, alien to the nation's experience. The past could not be so easily forgotten or ig-

nored. Brazil quixotically hoped that its liberal, democratic institutions would somehow manage to function under the crushing weight of its traditional, patriarchal, patrimonial, agrarian structures. To the disappointment of many, authoritative, paternalistic governance continued in the disguise of an enlightened republic.

The period of time between the rebellion and its institutionalization by a constitution was comparatively short, from November 15, 1889, to February 24, 1891. It compares favorably with other hiatuses between rebellion and legitimization in Brazilian history: 1822–1824, 1930–1934, and 1964–1967. Nonetheless the interim sufficed for the establishment of a military dictatorship.

After approving the constitution, the Assembly turned its attention to the election of the first president and vice-president of the republic, both to serve until 1894. The military pressure to elect Deodoro as president minimized serious consideration of any other candidates. Still, opposition to him abounded in the Assembly. The marshal already had proved himself to be an inept administrator. With little knowledge of the give and take of politics, and even less interest in it, he preferred the barracks order, given and fulfilled without hesitation or question. He experienced repeated difficulties with Republican party leaders and with the Assembly. Some within the Assembly nominated the old-time Republican Prudente José de Morais e Barros for the presidency. Nonetheless, the Assembly felt obliged to elect Deodoro since he still commanded the loyalty of the army, and the deputies wisely realized they should not offend the military at this point. The election turned out to be closer than most predicted: Deodoro received 129 votes and Prudente 97. An extremely sensitive man, Deodoro resented his perfunctory and lackluster election, which he rightly perceived to be more the result of a sense of duty than a feeling of enthusiasm. His pride suffered a further blow when the vice-president received more votes than he did. With 153 votes Marshal Floriano Peixoto was chosen by the Assembly as vice-president. And once more the Assembly affronted Deodoro when it greeted the vice-president with more applause than

it had given him. Hence, the beginning of constitutional government under the republic was inauspicious. The constitution promulgated and the elections over, the Assembly then changed itself into the first republican legislature and began to enact laws.

Without delay the president and Congress clashed. Deodoro resented all dissent within the legislature, regarding it as a personal challenge. Affairs in 1891 closely resembled those in 1823, and the similarity did not diminish thereafter. Certain of the support of the army as well as of the indifference of the public, Deodoro arbitrarily dissolved Congress on November 3, 1891, and proclaimed a state of siege. The president rationalized his action by accusing the legislature of endangering the safety of the republic and pointing out the threat of monarchical plots afoot. The state governors, with the exception of Lauro Sodré of Pará, supported his action. However, in both Rio Grande do Sul and São Paulo strong currents of opinion vociferously opposed the high-handed action. The navy, whose officers evinced strong aristocratic tendencies and had lacked enthusiasm for the republic from the beginning, challenged the arbitrary action of the president. Led by Admiral Custódio José de Melo, the navy threatened to revolt unless Congress was reconvened. Deodoro could not resolve his dilemma: he would neither give in nor countenance bloodshed. Instead he resigned from office, bitterly convinced that the nation did not appreciate his efforts and sacrifices. The old marshal who had led the nation in its passage from an empire to a republic quickly faded from public view. He died in August of the following year and, in accordance with his wishes, the generalissimo was buried in civilian clothes and without military honors.

The multiple crises of November disturbed the republic. Vice-President Floriano Peixoto, strong and unflappable, strode to the center of the political stage and forcefully took charge of the explosive situation. He declared that Congress had never been legally dissolved, thereby returning events to the status quo before November 3. With the exception of Sodré, the new president replaced all the state governors because they had supported Deodoro's second coup. The resistance

of some to their deposition precipitated outbreaks of violence that contributed to the general unrest. Floriano, however, proved master of the situation, showing that he merited his epithet "the iron marshal." The federal government won in that early display of strength against the states.

At the same time, Floriano's enemies questioned the constitutionality of his right to the presidency. They pointed out that Article 42 of the constitution required that a new election be held if the president should leave office before the expiration of two years of his four-year term. Floriano argued that the article was invalid in this case since the Congress had elected the first president and vice-president and the special nature of the election removed it from the dicta of that article. Congress concurred with his interpretation.

The acceptance of Floriano's succession signified the continuance of direct military control of the government. In another sense—to the degree the military embodied the vague ideology of the urban middle groups—it extended their hold over the government. Floriano, like his predecessor, came from a modest background. He also surrounded himself with many university graduates who proclaimed their Republican and/or Positivist preferences. The republic, therefore, continued to be identified with the military and urban middle groups more than the monarchy had ever been.

A vision of industrialization mesmerized these new leaders. Awed by the transformation industrialization had brought to Germany, France, Great Britain, and the United States, they grandly pictured a new Brazil altered by the same process. Their Positivist ideology embraced industrialization as the panacea for Brazil's problems and as a triumph of modern capitalism. However, they never fully crystallized their ideas and failed to conceive a rational plan to industrialize their country. At best they followed a piecemeal policy with weaknesses that forecast failure in attaining their goals and that, in the long run, probably retarded rather than accelerated industrialization. Symbolic of the ambitions of the middle groups, the provisional government changed the name of the Ministry of Agriculture, designating it the Ministry of Industry. As further encouragement, the government promulgated a pro-

tective tariff in 1890 in the hope of promoting manufacturing. It raised to 60 percent the duty on three hundred items, principally textiles and food products, that competed with national output. Conversely it lowered the duty on primary goods used in national manufacturing. Even steeper tariffs were promulgated in 1896 and 1900. Fundamental to any industrialization, new engineering schools were established in Recife in 1892; in São Paulo, 1894; in Pôrto Alegre, 1894; and in Bahia, 1896. They would augment the supply of available technicians, increasing numbers of whom would be necessary to any development of industrialization.

Industrialization also required greater capital investments. The abolition of slavery seemed to encourage that. From the date of the Golden Law until the advent of the republic, there already had been an increase of 402,000 *contos* in the capital invested in corporations formed in Rio de Janeiro. It was reminiscent of a similar movement following the termination of the slave trade. The doubling of coffee prices between 1887 and 1892 further increased Brazil's supply of investment capital. The first minister of finance under the republic, Ruy Barbosa, hoped to encourage capital formation by the liberal emission of bank notes and the consequent loosening of credit. He prepared a new banking law, promulgated on January 17, 1890, that divided the nation into three regions, each with a bank empowered to emit paper money. Further, he authorized the printing of a quarter of a million dollars worth of *contos* (a considerable sum given the time and place), to be guaranteed not by gold but by government bonds. Subsequently, his plan was modified many times: gold as well as bonds later guaranteed the emissions and the policy of decentralization was abandoned for the single Banco da República. An influx of new currency created for a brief period an illusion of prosperity. Between 1888 and 1891, the amount of money in circulation more than doubled. Inconvertible paper money outstanding rose from 192,000 contos in 1889 to 712,000 in 1894. The jump from a period of difficult credit to one of easy credit animated economic activity to a feverish pitch. Speculation became the order of the day. That particular whirlwind of speculation, bogus companies, and

unsound financial practices has been dubbed the *Encilhamento*.

To the dismay of the urban middle groups and the anger of the planters—and contrary to the hopes of the government—Brazil gained little from the *Encilhamento*. The rate of foreign exchange plummeted. Unprecedented inflation robbed the money of its former value. Fiscal instability undermined the nation's confidence. At the same time and following a traditional pattern, governmental expenditures exceeded revenues, prompting the printing of still more money in order to "balance the budget." The severe economic instability of the 1890s exerted a painful pressure on the wage-earning classes in the urban areas, thereby contributing to the general unrest of the decade.

Unrest erupted into full-scale revolt in 1893, the first major challenge to the republic. For some time chaos had enveloped Rio Grande do Sul, where the so-called Federalists led by Gaspar da Silveira Martins, a politician who had enjoyed high office and prestige during the empire, challenged Júlio de Castilhos, the ultra-Positivist *caudilho* of the state, and his followers. Within the Federalist ranks existed vague monarchical sentiments subordinated to an intense hatred of Castilhos. In early 1893 fighting between the two gaúcho rivals erupted. Floriano gave his support to Castilhos, president of the state. In September of the same year, a second naval revolt broke out, this one far more serious than its 1891 predecessor. Admiral Custódio de Melo again exercised the leadership. If the myth of military unity still lingered, this schism of the services dispelled it. The jealousy between the navy and the army could no longer be concealed. The admirals immediately demanded that Marshal Floriano resign, for they long had felt that he minimized the importance of the navy. With his resignation, they hoped to diminish the vast power wielded in the republic by the army. The navy's position was strengthened in December, when the respected and cautious Admiral Luís Felipe Saldanha da Gama, commandant of the Naval Academy, joined the naval rebels, bringing his immense prestige as well as the youthful vigor of the cadets with him. The navy's motives and objectives appeared at this

point to be something more than mere jealousy and a desire to increase its voice in the government. Many of the naval officers could not conceal any longer their aristocratic disdain for the republic. Saldanha da Gama issued a cryptic proclamation to the nation that in one passage declared, "Both logic and justice warrant us in seeking by force of arms to replace the Government of Brazil where it was on the 15th of November of 1889." The degree to which his monarchical preferences represented the true sentiments of the rebellious navy has been the subject of protracted historical controversy. The navy's monarchical tendencies and its dislike of Floriano were sufficient cause for it to cooperate with the Federalists led by Silveira Martins in the South. The admirals and the Federalist chief concurred, for example, that the nation should hold a plebiscite to choose between a republic and a monarchy. The two rebel forces combined to invade Santa Catarina and in January 1894 they attacked Paraná, planning to march northward into São Paulo. But heavy fighting at Lapa in Paraná caused a delay. It gave the federal government time to gather its strength sufficiently to repel the rebels and push them back southward.

Meanwhile, the heavily armed ships in Guanabara Bay threatened to bombard a virtually defenseless capital; this menace rallied republicans behind Floriano. The situation looked grim for the government, but the president stoically faced the naval firepower and refused to capitulate. At that point outside forces intervened to strengthen his position. The commanders of foreign warships in the harbor—units of the United States, British, French, Italian, and Portuguese navies—declared for humanitarian reasons their opposition to the shelling of the capital. They also indicated their intention to protect the property, such as merchant ships, of their own nationals. Their activities restricted the movements of the rebellious fleet. In Washington the Brazilian minister, Salvador de Mendonça, a dedicated, historic republican, importuned the government of President Grover Cleveland to come to the aid of the fledgling sister republic. The United States responded by dispatching more cruisers to the harbor of Rio de Janeiro. Determined not to allow the rebel ships to

interfere in any way with commerce in the port, the American naval commander stationed the cruisers between the rebels and the capital in such a way that in order to fire on the city the Brazilian navy would have to send its shells over the American vessels, a risk the admirals were unwilling to take. Consequently the maneuver prevented the feared bombardment, and the navy's position was reduced to helplessness or at least to that of a nuisance. Floriano's government proceeded to purchase some warships abroad and prepared a loyalist fleet in Pernambuco. The rebellious naval officers then understood the hopelessness of their situation and abandoned their ships to take asylum aboard the small Portuguese warships in the harbor. With the collapse of the fleet revolt in May of 1894, the government turned its full attention to the South, where after a series of victories it confined the Federalist rebels to the interior of Rio Grande do Sul. They continued to offer sporadic resistance until August of 1895, when the last participants in the revolt surrendered.

Floriano remained unshakable during the revolt. His determination saved the republican government from collapse and the nation from threatened anarchy. The early record of the republic had been one of disturbing instability: financial chaos, the dissolution of congress and resignation of the president, two naval revolts, and a rebellion in Rio Grande do Sul. Yet the new republic managed to triumph over those challenges and prove the viability of the new regime. The effective leadership of Floriano partly accounted for that triumph.

The general instability contributed to a loss of power by the urban middle groups. Their temporary prominence had been due in part to the vacuum created by the shifting of economic and political power from the old sugar barons and coffee *fazendeiros* to the new coffee class. This class was demonstrating its vigor—principally in São Paulo, but in Minas Gerais as well. The urban middle groups had also gained a temporary prominence through their informal relations with the military. The military proved to be an unreliable ally, however, since it was torn by disunion, and jealous bickering absorbed much of its energy. Even in the Constituent Assem-

bly some of the military officers had voted against Deodoro
and for a civilian candidate for president, while two naval
revolts had displayed the enmity between its two branches.

The sudden, unexpected emergence of the middle sectors as a political force and their brief exercise of power with
the military from 1889 to 1894, was unique in Latin America, a
harbinger of what would transpire elsewhere in the early
decades of the twentieth century. The middle sectors did not
have another opportunity to wield national power in Latin
America until President José Batlle took office in Uruguay in
1903. Pushed aside in 1894, the Brazilian middle sectors nursed
their political bruises and intensified their economic complaints. For the time being, however, the dynamic coffee
interests overshadowed them and forced them to accept a
secondary role.

The disunity that plagued the otherwise potent institution of the military and disoriented the feebler urban middle
groups favored the cause of the Paulistas who sought to control the government. The prosperous coffee planters for some
decades had hoped to grasp the reins of political power in
order to insure favorable treatment for their interests. Many
of them had supported republican ideology with the expectation of gaining hegemony over a new government, and
they strongly favored federalism in order to free their wealthy
state from the burden of financing the rest of the nation.
The beginnings of the republic disappointed them. They decried the financial mismanagement, the revolts, and the instability.

The crisis of 1893 provided the leaders of São Paulo with
an opportunity to assert their authority over the republic. The
military, the only institution capable of checking their interests and control, was seriously divided. Floriano needed allies
at that crucial moment, and none would have been as effective as the Paulistas with their fat coffers and well-trained
militia. Furthermore, their strategic position between the capital and the rebellion in the South made their loyalty essential
if the federal government was to win. The Paulista politicians
carefully made their bargain with Floriano: money, militia,
and loyalty in return for the scheduled presidential elections.

The well-organized Republican party of São Paulo was confident that in such elections its candidate would win. Once in control of the government in Rio de Janeiro, the Paulistas were certain they could shape the federal system to suit their own interests and guarantee the order and stability their business and trade required to prosper. At any rate, the alternative to Floriano's success and the consequent suppression of the rebellion would—to the Paulistas' thinking—plunge Brazil into a never-ending cycle of political chaos of the type that bedeviled many Spanish-American republics.

The Paulistas reaped the reward they sought by supporting Floriano. In the midst of a tense national crisis, Floriano made no effort to keep the electoral machinery from functioning. A large group of senators and deputies led by Francisco Glicério of São Paulo organized the Federal Republican party, a loose confederation of state republican parties. The party pledged itself to implement and defend the constitution, to support federalism, and to enforce fiscal responsibility, all goals highly desired by the Paulistas. In September of 1893 the party convention unanimously nominated Prudente de Morais of São Paulo for president and Manuel Vitorino Pereira of Bahia for vice president. They won the elections that were held on March 1, 1894, and took office in November of that year.

The first civilian president had been the first republican governor of São Paulo. He understood perfectly the desires, interests, and ambitions of the Paulista coffee elite to which he gave preference. Consequently the new government often contravened the goals of the urban middle groups, whose influence waned rapidly after Floriano left office. President Prudente de Morais, for example, did not encourage industrial expansion. Rather, echoing São Paulo's preoccupation with agriculture, he maintained that the soil—with São Paulo's rich *terra roxa* for coffee clearly in mind—was the nation's chief source of wealth. Those who supported that argument considered industry as an artificial and undesirable form of wealth. Those ideas smacked quaintly of Physiocrat tradition. In order to provide the propitious conditions for the Paulistas to exploit their agricultural wealth, to increase trade, and to

attract foreign credit, investments, and immigrants, he pledged his government to political stability, financial rehabilitation, and decentralization. Thus able to orient the policies of the government, the coffee interests assumed the dominant political role to match the economic monopoly they had exercised for over a generation.

Coffee production rose spectacularly during the last decade of the nineteenth century, from 5.5 million sixty-kilo bags in 1890–1891 to 16.3 million in 1901–1902. High profits explained much of the increase, but there were other factors favorable to the expanding industry as well. Abundant suitable land was available and accessible; the credit inflation of the period made money for investments easy to obtain; ever-greater numbers of immigrants provided a ready labor force. At the same time, Asian production declined because of crop diseases that practically wiped out its coffee plantations.

Brazil's expanding agricultural activities drew inhabitants into hitherto unexploited regions of the country as economic activities increased throughout the nation. Coffee culture moved into new areas of Minas Gerais and western São Paulo. Cattle raising spread into new regions and became the dominant occupation of southern Mato Grosso. The lure of rubber attracted hardy adventurers into Pará, Amazonas, Acre, and northern Mato Grosso. The cultivation of maté increased in the South and the cacao industry expanded along the Bahian coast as far south as northern Espirito Santo. As important as each one of these economic pursuits was, no one of them—nor for that matter any combination of them—could equal the preponderant importance coffee had in the national economy.

Rapidly expanding economic frontiers, the perennial search for cheap labor, a more sharply focused capitalism, the drive for modernization, and the decline of the patriarchate alarmed many of the rural folk, still the majority of the population. They hesitated to embrace perceived changes as contrary to their own interests. A conflict between those interests and the newly triumphant economic and political doctrines erupted in the backlands of Bahia during the final decade of the nineteenth century. It constituted a major crisis.

Symbolically it represented the clash between tradition and progress, between past and future.

Incorporating Rural Folk into Capitalism

For agriculture to expand and exports to rise, landowners had to assure themselves of a regular and sufficient labor supply as well as ready access to more land as needed. No document better reveals the ruthless greed for land and the exploitation of rural labor than *The Violent Land,* Jorge Amado's master-piece of the realistic novel. Peasants, squatters, and folk communities occasionally stood in the path of capitalism's rural expansion. More disturbing to the landowners, the peasants and squatters were disinclined to work on the large estates so long as they enjoyed access to land. The destruction of the Canudos folk community in 1897 signified and symbolizes the official determination to subordinate the rural poor to capitalism's advance. It also constitutes Brazil's major folk epic.

Fleeing lives of misery in the impoverished Northeast, a region long incorporated into a sugar and cacao export economy, large numbers of rural inhabitants gathered in a remote western region of the state of Bahia between 1893 and 1897. The population figures vary widely, from five to thirty thousand, the latter certainly exaggerated. An average of the two extremes probably approximates reality. They created their own folk society or community at Canudos, "New Jerusalem," under the patriarchal leadership of Antônio Conselheiro, né Antônio Vicente Mendes Marciel (1828–1897). From mid-November of 1896 to early October of 1897, those folk confronted four attacks by government troops, until, during the fourth, the might of a large, modernized army crushed them.

At Canudos country people, part of that surplus labor pool that the plantation and ranch owners of the Northeast could leisurely exploit, drew their inspiration less from the Europeanized coastal cities and more from a rural folk past based on a commonality of language, heritage, beliefs, and means of facing daily life. A carefully mediated Indo-Luso-Afro amalgamation of traditions and influences had become

over the centuries a shared way of life, a folk culture characteristic of many people on the western frontier. The combination of folkways, folk mores, and primary institutions remained largely untouched by the enacted institutions of the
nation-state. The folk life-style provided a modest degree of
equality, security, and well-being. Canudos seemed to offer
those advantages to its inhabitants along with a dignity they
had previously been denied. By the 1890s, folk societies in
Brazil—as elsewhere in Latin America—were becoming rarer.
Canudos exemplified a revival, a viable folk society, an organized group of individuals characterized by a folk culture.

The new leaders of the recently proclaimed republic
judged the events in the Bahian interior to be a threat, a
religious plot linked to monarchists eager to resurrect the
political institutions of the imperial past. In a philosophical
sense, they were correct. The folk subscribed to genetic,
patriarchal principles of governance. God ordained the leaders, just as He had Adam. God had ordained Emperor Pedro
II and man could not overthrow him. Obviously the leaders
of the newly proclaimed republic disavowed those genetic,
patriarchal principles so patently the basis of the monarchy
that had just been overthrown. They advocated contractual
theories of government, recognized but subordinated during
the empire. Both sides in the Canudos conflict had firmly
defined ideologies that apparently left no room for compromise.

Canudos constituted no ordinary threat in the eyes of
the new republican elites. It enjoyed popular support. The
people—a term so vague that it could conjure up visions of
hordes of dispossessed humanity—were in rebellion. The
barbarians clamored at the gate of urban progress. The unlet-
tered folk of the vast interior of Brazil were perceived as
attacking the civilization celebrated in the coastal cities. They
jeopardized progress; they challenged the republic; they
threatened the new order.

Antônio Conselheiro ("Anthony the Counselor"), like
many other Brazilians, questioned that new order, finding
"progress" more menacing than appealing, sensing, perhaps
intuitively, that the burden of it would fall on the ordinary

people while the benefits somehow would escape them. The folk of the *sertão* (the backlands) felt uncomfortable with the sudden secularization imposed by the republic. Civil marriage, in their eyes, attacked a sacrament revered by them. Other forms of civil registration aroused suspicions about what type of control the new government might exercise. Some viewed the government's interest in the racial identification of its citizens as a threat to reinstitute slavery abolished by the monarchy less than a decade earlier. Antônio Conselheiro had once preached against slavery.

The election of a president rather than the coronation of a monarch disturbed those people. For them the change from hereditary monarch to elected president constituted an immense political leap from genetic, patriarchal, divinely ordained governance to contractual, secular leadership. The emperor was the great patriarch, ordained by God. The events of 1889 were seen by the folk of the backlands as cataclysmic, apocalyptic, a break with the sanctioned patriarchal past, and a defiance of God's will.

The delicate matter of new taxes to be paid under the republican political system precipitated the first clash between Antônio Conselheiro and republican officials. Republican laws permitted the municipalities to raise taxes for their own use. In Bom Conselho, Bahia, the Conselheiro pulled down and burned public notices of such taxes in 1893. While his denunciation of such taxes received a sympathetic hearing from the impoverished populations of the backlands, his words—and certainly his actions in Bom Conselho—alarmed the government. State officials dispatched troops to arrest him, but his ever-growing number of followers easily put the soldiers to flight. The leader concluded it was a prudent time to withdraw farther into the sertão. At *Canudos*, his faithful began to build their "Zion."

Isolated Canudos must have seemed a safe haven to Antônio Conselheiro, far from hostile landowners, repressive government officials, and disruptive "civilization." There the folk adapted—or reverted—to a communal life. Probably their negative reaction to experience with the individualism of expanding capitalism revived their faith in the community. They

felt uninhibited in adopting a type of folk Roman Catholicism
which provided further structuring of life in the *sertão*. They
recognized the easily visible figure of Antônio Conselheiro as
their patriarch. They unquestioningly followed him as their
folk leader. The people and the patriarch identified with each
other. In that folk society, the land belonged to the community. Each inhabitant worked at an assigned task. Apparently
the farmers produced enough food to feed the population,
trading the surplus in backland towns for arms and whatever
else the community needed but could not produce.

Such a life-style must have satisfied the inhabitants. After
all, no one was required to go there or to remain. Those who
did considered themselves the chosen ones. Canudos was
blessed. For three years it expanded. The name, reputation,
and cause of Antônio Conselheiro raced like a wind through
the interior of the Northeast. Occasionally, word of Canudos
and of the activities the *jagunços* (the term applied to the
rustic backlanders) reached the distant national capital, Rio
de Janeiro, and the coastal state capital, Salvador da Bahia.
Still, relative isolation protected Canudos, giving free reign to
Antônio Conselheiro and augmenting the strength of the *jagunços*.

In 1896 that isolation abruptly ended. Antônio had contracted and paid for lumber in a neighboring town, Joazeiro,
in order to build a church. When the lumber was not delivered the *jagunços* threatened to exact justice for what they
perceived to be a swindle. Frightened, the municipal officials
hastily requested police protection from the state. In response a detachment of one hundred soldiers commanded
by a lieutenant marched toward Canudos. The backlanders
attacked and routed the detachment. The War of Canudos
had begun.

Because neither the state nor the federal government
understood the determination of the folk community—nor,
for that matter, its strength or goals—they suffered humiliating defeats in the harsh sertão whose inhabitants thrived but
for which the soldiers from the coast were ill-prepared. A
second detachment of 550 soldiers with a major in charge
marched resolutely, also to defeat. Then, a third force, 1300

men led by a much celebrated military hero, Colonel Antônio Moreira César, met an identical fate. Coastal Brazilians looked with a mixture of amazement, horror, and frustration as the rustics routed the armies.

The "mud-walled Troy of the *jagunços*"—a phrase frequently employed by Euclydes da Cunha to describe Canudos in his eye-witness account of the war, *Os Sertões* (1902), translated later into English as *Rebellion in the Backlands*— scornfully defied the government. In April 1897 a fourth expedition of more than 8000 men, armed with the latest technologies of war and commanded this time by three generals and the minister of war himself, set out amid fanfare and patriotic hoopla for the interior. The bloody siege of Canudos lasted until early October. The folk settlement did not surrender; the cannons, rifles, and bayonets of the army leveled it and killed its defenders.

In his prolix efforts to rationalize the destruction of Canudos, the death of Antônio Conselheiro, and the sacrifice of folk and soldiers alike, da Cunha felt obliged to resolve the intellectual conflict between his admiration for the strength and resourcefulness of the native *jagunços* and his advocacy of Europeanized progress for Brazil. He decided in favor the latter. In doing so that respected intellectual faithfully echoed the strong urban sentiments of his time. He branded Antônio Conselheiro a subversive, a preacher of doctrines hostile to the republic, an advocate of insurrection, a rebel, and a monarchist. He accused the folk of—more heinous yet—obstructing progress and impeding evolution. Therefore, he said, the republic must defeat them. Da Cunha concluded, with the insistence of a Positivist, "Our biological evolution demands the guaranty of social evolution. We are condemned to civilization. Either we shall progress or we shall perish. So much is certain, and our choice is clear." In that judgment, the author summarized the social philosophy of nineteenth-century progress. That progress evinced no tolerance of tradition. The future had no room for the past.

The army's cannons had opened the Brazilian interior at Canudos. For da Cunha—and in the minds of the Brazilian military and of the urban middle sectors at the end of the

nineteenth century—the army was a prime champion of progress. Spouting Positivism, the army officers had overthrown
the monarchy to usher in a "Republic of Progress." The new,
powerful cannons imported from Europe—and their physical
destruction of Canudos—symbolized the technology that
would propel Brazil into modernity.

Throughout most of 1897 the dreams of the coastal elite
of reshaping the vast interior clashed with the stubborn realities of *jagunço* victories. They taunted the nation and wore
thin the patience of politicians and intellectuals alike. The
challenge heightened their determination that the republic
must force the backlanders into a twentieth century defined
by the Positivist motto on the new Brazilian flag: "Order and
Progress." Education and technology would reshape the inhabitants and the contours of the hinterlands.

The determination to eradicate the folk societies and
cultures of the interior in favor of Europeanization was consistent with a strong nineteenth-century intellectual current
that pervaded not just Brazil but all of Latin America. In 1845
the Argentine Domingo Faustino Sarmiento clearly defined
the struggle between the Europeanized city and the primitive
countryside in this *Civilización y Barbarie: Vida de Juan Fa-
cundo Quiroga*, translated under the title *Life in the Argentine Republic in the Days of the Tyrants: or Civilization and
Barbarism*. Sarmiento saw the Argentine cities as a kind of
funnel through which European civilization passed on its mission to tame the interior. His powerful argument, a blueprint
for the Europeanized future of Latin America, received a warm
welcome from the intellectuals and ruling elite. Emperor Pedro
II, for one, acknowledged to Sarmiento the importance he
attributed to it. The Peruvian novelist Clorinda Matto de Turner
professed similar ideas in her novel *Aves sin Nido* (1889),
translated as *Birds without a Nest*. In her judgment the city
radiated civilization. Lima bore the responsibility for redeeming the Indian majority, and education constituted the major
means of redemption. The education she envisioned, as did
Sarmiento, da Cunha, and most of their nineteenth-century
peers, drew exclusively on the European experience. None of
these savants suggested that the folk might find redemption

through recourse to their own values, past or present; they recommended a Europeanized future for them.

Traditional Brazilian historiography has approved the theme of the epic struggle of coastal urban civilization with backlands rural barbarism. Over the decades, historians explained the struggle at Canudos in terms of a harsh geography and a "degenerate" race. Religious fanaticism or blatant banditry became standard explanations for the growth of Canudos and the subsequent war. The prolific and lauded Brazilian historian Pedro Calmón exemplified that traditional interpretation, characterizing the War of Canudos as "a religious conflict generated by backlands' barbarism."

Slowly other explanations of the determination and action of the *jagunços* emerged. In the late 1950s Rui Facó observed that the increasing population of Canudos in the 1890s paralleled the deteriorating economic situation of Northeastern Brazil. Sugar exports fell. Coffee culture in the Southwest, which once had absorbed migrant workers, experienced the first tremors of overproduction. The plantations hired fewer workers. Staple foods became scarcer and, hence, more expensive. Corn prices tripled and the rise in cost of beans and rice was not far behind. Buffeted by harsh economic winds, the rural population sought a safe shelter in Canudos. Facó characterized the War of Canudos as both a "peasant rebellion" and a "class struggle." In his judgment the people of Canudos fought against the misery and exploitation perpetuated by the landlords and the government. Nelson Werneck Sodré took up those themes at approximately the same time: "Canudos was a peasant rebellion, it was a class struggle of the oppressed against the oppressors." Not by coincidence, both scholars were nationalists writing in a period of increasingly fiery nationalism. In their search for popular roots for nationalism, both examined the events at Canudos with fresh insights. About a decade later Ralph della Cava expanded upon their theme. He convincingly linked Canudos to "national ecclesiastical and political power structures." Canudos was part of "a changing nation-wide economy." The wider context revealed by Facó, Werneck Sodré, and della Cava broke down the argument that Canudos was

an isolated religious protest and integrated the war into the wider drama of a changing Brazil, notable in part for the economic and political penetration by the populous coastal band into the vast, underpopulated interior: the two Brazils in conflict. Later Walnice Nogueira Galvão credited the War of Canudos with introducing the "collective person," the poor, into Brazilian historiographical consciousness. In this arresting interpretation the individual played a secondary role. The charismatic Antônio Conselheiro was perhaps the catalyst but not the cause. Major historic forces subsumed and displaced individual motives. It was the government versus the *jagunços,* the past versus the future, progress versus tradition, and, of course, civilization versus barbarism. But, significantly, cause and effect had been reversed. The historic forces propelled the collective or the individuals, not vice versa. Robert M. Levine cast his own study of Canudos in the broadest social science framework: "Canudos was, no more and no less, borrowing E. P. Thompson's phrase, 'the institutional expression of social relationships.' "

Within the field of labor history, the Canudos experience awaits full interpretation along the lines suggested by those innovators named above. María Sylvia de Carvalho Franco and Hebe María Mattos de Castro have noted the attraction of the interior's abundant land to the coastal rural poor in the nineteenth century. Dissatisfied with their lot, the folk fled seeking better conditions. The freemen deserted the rural labor pool, to the consternation of the large landowners whose desperation mounted as slavery withered. In view of that desperation, Mattos de Castro concluded, "A question arises, as yet unanswered, and seldom even formulated by the historical literature: in what ways were the mechanisms of rural social control redefined, so as to maintain the viability of commercial agriculture for the class dominance of the rural producers who controlled it?" Surely the War of Canudos suggests some answers to that challenging question.

Two societies clashed when coastal, urbanized, export-oriented Brazil—the one undergoing rapid changes after 1888—encountered the rural backland, peopled by those who questioned the changes, their meaning, and their potential im-

pact. The War of Canudos symbolized a fundamental, perhaps inevitable clash as the pace of progress (modernization) accelerated. In extending its power, the state was capable of inflicting "structural, cataclysmic upheaval,"—to borrow the terminology used by the French anthropologist Pierre Clastres in his *Society Against the State*—in order to dominate any opposing folk society. The state's violent destruction of Canudos was based on the rationale that it was "backward," "primitive," and "barbaric."

"Barbarism," a widely accepted code word employed by Brazilian and Latin American intellectuals and politicians, signified local, traditional, folk, and/or Indo-Ibero-Afro cultures. To the degree those cultures differed from the desired North Atlantic models, they embarrassed most of the elite, the middle class, and the intellectuals. Joining with the capitalists of the export-oriented economy, they physically challenged the folk, the "barbarians" of the subsistence economy. It was the violent side of cultural clash.

Cultural clash could cut across lines. Traditionalists—or, for that matter, anyone who voiced doubts or concerns about unmediated progress—included some of the elite and intellectuals. Some landowners in the interior sympathized with the movement at Canudos. Millenarian movements often formed tacit alliances with those landowners and backlands *coroneis* [bosses]. It was not necessarily the hierarchy of power or the poor distribution of wealth the folk attacked, so much as the accelerating greed of newly imposed capitalism. In the case of Canudos, cooperation across class lines was possible and, indeed, existed in the interior. The war itself occurred along cultural lines.

The brutal War of Canudos was one of a long series of nineteenth-century cultural conflicts. Such violent conflicts continued into the early decades of the twentieth century. "Modern Brazil," the Brazil that had ended slavery, overthrown the monarchy, established a republic, separated church and state, and heralded greater urbanization and industrialization, triumphed at Canudos. The victory signified the opening of the interior to modernization, the incorporation in effect, of the land and its people into the export economy of

Brazil. When that happened folk society dissipated, although folk culture, proving more hardy and perhaps more elusive, lingered.

In important respects the War of Canudos summed up the history of nineteenth-century Brazil: the triumph of the cities and their particular view of the future. Clearly, if Brazil were to "progress"—become more like the North Atlantic models selected by the elites and approved by the nascent middle classes—then indigenous folkways would have to dissolve before the new cultural models. The twentieth century, progress, the new republican nation-state, and national viability would not accommodate the allegedly backward folk societies and could hardly tolerate folk culture.

Canudos in 1897 was the site of one of those great historical moments when the past and future interlock. It represents a clash, one of many, between two ways of life, two perceptions, two approaches to a national reality. The folk fought at Canudos to preserve their life-styles. They sought refuge in the millennial vision of the patriarchal counselor. They responded apocalyptically to outside threats. For many other Brazilians the War of Canudos symbolized the titanic struggle to escape the past. The army marched into the interior as the agent of change, unfurling the banner of the bourgeois ideal upon which the new republic had been established.

After the final cannon shot thundered into the ruins of Canudos the question remained, and remains, whether all Brazilians want to replace their own reality with another people's, whether they want to deny their own experiences to ape those of others. Nonetheless, forces intent upon changing that reality had been introduced. Inexorably they carried out their mission. Railroads and cannons destroyed Canudos. Those instruments of destruction were also instrumentalities of progress, of change. They heralded the future. The War of Canudos proved to be both a farewell to the Brazilian past and a salutation to its future. The army's victory dictated the incorporation of the folk into the capitalist economy and republic. It closed a remarkable decade of change.

Visual Documentation of the Brazilian Past

I. Colonial Architecture

1. Street scene in the old quarter of Salvador da Bahia

2. São Francisco Church, Salvador da Bahia

3. Altar of the São Francisco Church, Salvador da Bahia

4. The Rua do Ouvidor in Ouro Prêto, Minas Gerais

II. The Imperial Family of Brazil

1. Emperor Pedro I

2. Emperor Pedro II in the second decade of his reign

3. Princess Isabel (1846–1921), flanked by her father Pedro II, on the right, and her husband, the French nobleman Count d'Eu, on the left. She ruled as regent on three occasions, 1871, 1876, and 1888. The princess distinguished herself as the first female to serve as chief of state in the Western Hemisphere. She promoted and signed many laws, none more important than the "Golden Law" of 1888, which ended slavery in Brazil.

4. The royal family at the end of the Second Empire. The great patriarch, Emperor Pedro II, stands in the center. His daughter, Princess Isabel, holds his arm, with Empress Tereza Cristina seated. The Count d'Eu stands at the far left in the back row. The four young princes are the sons of Isabel and the count.

III. Coffee

1. Cândido Portinari (1903–1962) was born to Italian immigrant parents on a coffee plantation. That background influenced the creation in 1935 of his masterpiece, *Coffee*. He depicts an army of sturdy workers harvesting coffee under the direction of a single powerful owner or overseer: the many produce wealth for the few.

2. A coffee planter's house in the interior of São Paulo in the third quarter of the nineteenth century

3. The drawing room of a coffee planter's home toward the end of the nineteenth century. With cane seats and backs, the furniture, made from rich *jacaranda* wood, typified the appearance of an upper-class home in Brazil for at least four centuries.

4. A panorama of a coffee plantation in the state of São Paulo, 1962. The "big house" for the planter's family appears in the center right; housing for the workers, center left. Drying platforms for the coffee occupy the bottom third of the photo.

5.a The orderly rows of coffee trees march westward across the hills of São Paulo to the West.

5.b Men, women, and children harvest the coffee bean. In this late nineteenth-century photograph, the man in the center rear carries the beans to an oxcart for transportation to the drying platforms.

6. On this coffee-drying platform in the state of São Paulo, in 1962, a worker constantly rearranges the coffee beans so that they dry evenly on all sides in the sun before they are processed for marketing.

7. Model housing for workers on a coffee *fazenda* in São Paulo, 1935.

IV. The Brazilian People

1. Manuel Raimundo Querino (1851–1923), the first African-Brazilian historian. A founding member of the Bahian Geographical and Historical Institute, he synthesized many of his conclusions in the important essay he wrote in 1918, ''The African Contribution to Brazilian Civilization.''

2. Bahianas, the African-Bahian women of Salvador da Bahia, in festive dress, c. 1960

3. A farm family of
Minas Gerais, c. 1950

4. School children watching a puppet show in Rio de Janeiro, c. 1950

5. School children, Rio de Janeiro, 1941

7. People waiting to
see the mayor of São
João del Rei, Minas
Gerais, 1941

8. Rural folk of the state
of Rio de Janeiro, 1941

6. Farm families watching an outdoor play in the state of São Paulo, 1941

V. Brasilia

On April 21, 1960, President Juscelino Kubitschek inaugurated Brasília, the third capital of Brazil. Lúcio Costa provided the imaginative plan for the city. Oscar Niemeyer was the architect who designed the city's federal buildings that captured the imaginations of Brazilians and foreigners alike.

1. Palace of the Dawn, the presidential residence

2. The Palace of Justice on the Square of the Three Powers

3. Itamaratí Palace, the Ministry of Foreign Relations

4. The National Cathedral

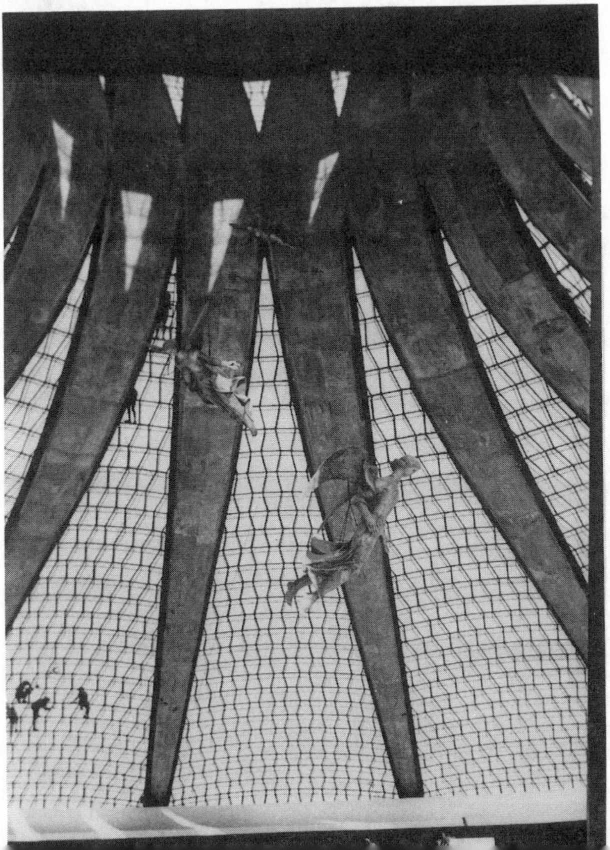

5. Two sculpted angels hover in the great dome of the National Cathedral.

6. The Congressional
buildings

7. Commercial and apartment buildings in Brasília

VI. Twentieth-Century Political Leaders

1. Elected to the presidency in 1934, Getúlio Vargas (center, wearing the sash of office) poses with his cabinet following the inauguration.

2. The inauguration of President Jânio Quadros (center), 1961. At the left stands the outgoing president, Juscelino Kubitschek. Vice president João Goulart, who within seven months would ascend to the presidency, is on the right.

VII. Painting as Historical Document

1. José Ferraz de Almeida Júnior (1850–1899) introduced ordinary people and scenes of their daily life into Brazilian painting. In particular, he delighted in depicting the lifestyles and historical role of the backwoods people from the interior of São Paulo, the region he knew best. He scandalized the art world and polite society with *The Woodcutter* (1879), first exhibited publicly in Brazil in 1884. His sensuous portrayal of a resting, half-nude male, plainly monopolizing the center of the canvas, offered discomfited viewers a new theme: the ordinary man. Almeida Júnior painted him as the true hero who opened the West and conquered it with his ax. This woodcutter was a distinctly Brazilian type. In every sense, the painting ranked as revolutionary by introducing a new theme, a new concept, a new person, a challenge to the Europeanized view of Brazil, a new emphasis on the West, and a consequent turning away from the coast and Europe. With this canvas, artistic nationalism triumphed. Brazilian art was never the same after the public exhibition of *The Woodcutter*.

2. Modesto Brocos y Gómez (1852–1936) painted his highly symbolic *Redemption of Ham* in 1895. The canvas, which hangs in the Museum of Fine Arts in Rio de Janeiro, reveals the official racial attitudes of the time: "white blood" would bleach "black blood" to create a Europeanized Brazilian. In the painting three generations—grandmother, mother, and child—portray the bleaching process. The Portuguese immigrant father looks with satisfaction on his white child. The black grandmother, framed by palms, the biblical symbol of hope, raises her hands and eyes in praise, an obvious approval accorded the bleaching process.

3. Belmiro de Almeida (1858–1935) offered a thought-provoking insight into the relations between the sexes, at least among the upper class, in *The Lovers' Quarrel* (1887). He depicted the female with flowing, curved lines, collapsed literally at the feet of the male. The symbolic crushed rose rests at her side. The lines for the male, in contrast, are angular. He sits erect, contemplating not the female but his cigar. The scene contrasts weakness (the female) with strength (the male), suggesting (or reinforcing) the dominant role of the man.

4. Tarsila do Amaral (1890–1973), an important contributor to the Modernist art movement and cultural nationalism, depicted in this painting, entitled *2nd Class* (1931), migrants leaving the Northeast, the most impoverished region of Brazil. They seek a promised land and their redemption. Quite probably they will end up in a large city, contributing to the phenomenal growth of places like São Paulo and Rio de Janeiro. They possess no skills suitable to the technologically oriented cities, so their hopes may lie in the success of their children. Yet the malnourishment of the young, who are depicted with thin limbs and overly large heads, taunt that hope. The painting links human misery with the train, the universal symbol of progress. Although *2nd Class* refers directly to the coach in which the migrants travel, the artist also implies that these Brazilians are second-class citizens. Amaral makes a strong statement about Brazilian development and the future.

Chapter Six

The New Brazil

The economy hummed. Talk of change stirred imaginations. One foreign observer of Brazil during the early years of the twentieth century lauded the "phenomenal growth and progress" in the process of transforming the new South American republic. Marie Robinson Wright remarked further,

The development of an essentially modern spirit of progress and enterprise, which has placed the people of Brazil in the front rank among the leading powers of the New World, and which so dominates the national life at the present moment that every part of the vast republic is responding to its stimulating influence, shows an awakening to new conditions and a realization of larger responsibilities such as necessarily distinguish a great nation thoroughly aroused to the importance of its high density. It is this spirit which has created the new Brazil.

The period in which "the New Brazil" emerged forms a part— a major part—of a longer political era in the traditional periodization of Brazilian history. Known as the Old Republic, it began with the fall of the monarchy on November 15, 1889, and continued to the rebellion that placed Getúlio Vargas in power in 1930. Since the years from 1922 to 1930 mark the

overt challenge to the power structure of the rural oligarchy, a challenge that triumphed in 1930, discussion of those eight years will be considered part of a longer discussion on the Vargas years in Brazilian history. The discussion of the New Brazil concerns itself primarily with the identification of a combination of significant activities visible during the early decades of the twentieth century. Coffee growth, processing, and exportation ranked high among them. The thriving coffee industry mesmerized Ms. Wright as it did most Brazilians. Its efficiency engendered impressive economic growth in the southeastern states. Its ultimate link to economic patterns established during the 1530–1560 period, and its relationship to economic development pose significant historical questions in the study of the twentieth century.

The Old Republic Ascending

The Brazilian social historian Gilberto Freyre correctly observed, "The coffee boom represents the transition from the patriarchal to the industrial economy." The reasons are many. Coffee modernized Brazilian capitalism by favoring European immigration as labor recruits, encouraging foreign investment, creating domestic capital for investment, promoting railroad construction as well as port renovation, introducing new technologies, accelerating entrepreneurial activity, investing burgeoning profits into industrialization, fostering a dynamic bourgeoisie, opening and populating the West, and accelerating integration into the world capitalist economy.

As production rose, coffee came to dominate Brazil's export trade. By 1901 it accounted for approximately 46 percent of the total exports and by 1908, 53 percent. During the first decade of the twentieth century, the Brazilian production of coffee composed approximately 77 percent of the world's total (see Table 6.1). The importance of coffee in Brazil's international trade assumes even greater dimensions when its success is compared to the fate of sugar, which once dominated Brazil's exports. In 1901 sugar barely reached 5 percent of the total exports, and in 1912 sugar accounted for only .007

Table 6.1 Brazilian Coffee Production, 1901–1940

	Index Numbers 1901–1905 = 100		Brazilian Production in Percent of Total	Percent Increase in Volume of World Consumption Over Preceding Five-Year Period
	World	Brazil		
1901–1905	100	100	76	17
1906–1910	109	113	78	14
1911–1915	105	103	74	6
1916–1920	105	99	72	−6
1921–1925	120	107	67	15
1926–1930	138	119	65	12
1931–1935	219	182	63	5
1936–1940	232	183	60	7

SOURCE: Henry W. Spiegel, *The Brazilian Economy* (Philadelphia, 1949), p. 170.

percent of Brazil's international trade. A large internal market consumed nearly all of the sugar crop. During the same period, coffee far outdistanced the second most important export, rubber. In 1901 rubber provided 28 percent of Brazil's exports, whereas in 1912, although it maintained its importance, the percentage had declined to 22. These statistics indicate the overwhelming predominance coffee assumed in the national economy during the first decades of the republic.

As had been true throughout its history, Brazil depended—or gambled—once again on a single raw product for sale on a capricious world market, repeating in the twentieth century a pattern established in the sixteenth. As long as coffee sold well the nation prospered, but provisions had not been made, as they never had been made in the past, to lessen the economy's vulnerability. The potential danger grew as the coffee planters concentrated their sales in a few countries. The United States, Great Britain, and Germany bought fully three-quarters of the coffee. The possibility was all too real that any decline in demand from those purchasers would immediately affect the price and have drastic repercussions on the Brazilian economy. Some Brazilians noted the latent threat but none did anything about it. To the contrary, the planters went on expanding, as they hoped blithely that with their superproduction they could monopolize the world mar-

ket and hence control it. And for a limited time the *fazendeiros* did manipulate it to their advantage.

The influence of coffee extended beyond the realm of economics into both national and international politics. The once-dominant sugar barons had partially set the tone of nineteenth century diplomacy. They sold their sugar to Europe and looked to the Old World as a mentor, seeking spiritual inspiration in Portugal, cultural orientation in France, and commercial and political guidance from Great Britain. The coffee producers, on the other hand, found their best market in the United States, as did the rubber and cocoa exporters. Since 1865 the United States had taken the single largest share of Brazil's coffee; after 1870, with the abolition of import duties on coffee, the United States bought more than half of the Brazilian coffee beans sold abroad. By 1912 New York had become the world's largest rubber market and nearly 60 percent of the rubber traded there came from the Amazon. Likewise, the United States consumed more Brazilian cocoa than any other country. The result was that by 1912 the United States bought 36 percent of Brazil's exports, while the second most important market, Great Britain, purchased only 15 percent. The emergence of the United States as the best customer of Brazilian exports helped to shift Brazil's diplomatic axis from Europe to the United States. By 1905 Washington had replaced London as Brazil's principal diplomatic post.

Coffee's dominance over the national economy concentrated economic power in the region best suited to coffee production. The peculiar *terra roxa* soil in the states of São Paulo, Minas Gerais, and Rio de Janeiro, because it was deep and porous and contained humus, was particularly suitable for the growing of healthy coffee trees. Mild temperatures and adequate rainfall also contributed to coffee development in that region. Consequently, for topographic and climatic reasons, the production of coffee concentrated in southeastern Brazil, giving the three coffee-producing states of that area a formidable influence over the economy of Brazil. That influence seems all the more impressive when one considers that geographically the Southeast constituted only a small

parcel of the immense national territory. Yet those states had nearly half of Brazil's population; they contributed over half the national revenue; they boasted the best transportation and communication networks in the country.

Within the tripartite control of the economy, the state of São Paulo played the leading role. Of the total exports of Brazil for 1916, São Paulo furnished 46 percent, whereas Minas Gerais supplied only 22 percent, and Rio de Janeiro 18 percent. During optimum years, the state of São Paulo alone harvested between 65 and 70 percent of all the coffee and provided 30 to 40 percent of all the revenue to the national treasury. The economic importance of São Paulo prompted a notation in an official Ministry of the Treasury report in 1912 that, "as is always the case," São Paulo held first place among the states as the chief exporter. In that year, São Paulo furnished 50 percent of the nation's exports. In striking contrast, the formerly dominant sugar area of Pernambuco contributed barely 1 percent of Brazil's exports.

In truth, a green wave of coffee trees swept westward across São Paulo, inundating the state. Moving inland by train, the traveler passed countless rows of coffee trees. At the end of the nineteenth century, Frank G. Carpenter left this description of the world's largest coffee *fazenda*, the Dumont plantation, some three hundred miles inland from São Paulo:

The estate itself comprises thousands of acres. It has over 13,000 acres of coffee fields and 2,500 acres of pasture land. It is planting more trees every year and is kept like a garden. To go round the estate one would have to travel 40 miles, and more than 40 miles of railroad track have been built upon it to transport coffee.

The estate supports 5,000 people. It has 23 colonies, ranging in size from 70 families downward. It has great stores to supply its workmen with food. It has a bakery, a drug store, a saw mill, a planing mill, and at one time it had a brewery. It has vast factories for cleaning coffee and preparing it for market, and it has offices in which there are bookkeepers taking account of every item of expense, so that they can tell you how much coffee each of the 5,000,000 trees is producing, and give every item connected with picking the coffee and sending it to the seaports.

The labourers on the estate are thoroughly organized. Each man has his own work, the employees being directed by administrators, each of whom has charge of a block of trees, ranging up to a million; these trees are divided among families, each family taking charge of from 3,000 to 4,000 trees, planting them and keeping them clean.

Owing both to foreign immigration and to internal migration, the state's population more than tripled in three decades, increasing from 1,384,753 in 1890 to 4,592,188 in 1920. The capital of São Paulo state, also named São Paulo, became the dynamic financial and managerial center of the Southeast. Santos, the port of São Paulo, shipped most of Brazil's coffee to the burgeoning markets of the United States, England, Germany, and France. Between 1900 and 1914, the annual quantity of coffee handled by Santos virtually doubled, going from 5,742,362 sacks of 130 pounds each to 11,308,784. Santos testified eloquently to the fact that São Paulo consistently harvested and exported more coffee than any other state.

The economic strength of the Southeast conferred political power on the coffee triangle of São Paulo, Minas Gerais, and Rio de Janeiro during the Old Republic and particularly on the state of São Paulo. Control of the presidency unlocked the door to economic legislation and patronage. So, throughout the Old Republic, the dynamic coffee states successfully maneuvered to gain the presidency and thus to enhance their local economies. The first three civilian presidents (who governed from 1894 to 1906) were Prudente José de Morais, Manuel Ferraz de Campos Sales, and Francisco de Paula Rodrigues Alves, all from São Paulo. The next two presidents (governing from 1906 to 1910) were Afonso Augusto Moreira Pena and Nilo Peçanha, from Minas Gerais and Rio de Janeiro respectively. With two exceptions the other presidents down to 1930 came from either São Paulo or Minas Gerais. Coming from areas in which coffee dominated, those presidents carried out programs favorable to them. The first secretary of the United States legation, G. L. Lorillard, aptly reported this reciprocity between coffee and politics:

All the Northern States are bitterly opposed to the hold the coffee planters have over the Government and complain that their legitimate needs are being sacrificed in favor of the planters. The Executive, however, clings to its purpose of doing everything to please the coffee interests. The President fully realizes that he was elected by the planters and that he must now return the favor.

It was obvious, much to the displeasure of the rest of Brazil, that the coffee interests dictated most of the policies of the government. Commenting on that situation, Lorillard wrote:

At the present time, however, there exists a group of persons which is stronger than the Executive and Congress combined. As is universally admitted here, never before has the country and especially everyone connected with the Government been so much under the influence of the coffee planters as at the present and any measure which is seriously desired by that element is sure of immediate passage by Congress.

That alliance of the coffee planters and the federal government came quickly after 1889, and it superseded all previous political arrangements, so that political control by the coffee interests was one of the principal political characteristics of the 1894–1930 period. Because São Paulo played the dominant role within the alliance, this period of Brazilian history has been designated one of Paulista control.

The coffee interests of the tripartite alliance managed to govern Brazil through agreements, cohesion, coalitions of state parties, and political maneuvering, usually with the implicit or explicit backing of the army. One of the curious aspects of the Old Republic was that no national political parties developed. The old Liberal and Conservative parties of the Second Empire disappeared without leaving heirs. The *Partido Republicano Federal* (Federal Republican party) initially held some promise as a nationally based party, but soon after the party nominated Prudente de Morais in 1894, it began to disintegrate because of internal quarrels.

A significant political pattern quickly emerged. The incumbent president, with the approval and support of the powerful states, selected the next presidential candidate. The

chosen candidate in turn dealt with the principal state governors, promising them favors in return for support. Under the system of the "politics of the states" the governors sent congressmen to Rio de Janeiro who favored the president's programs, and in return the president neither intervened nor interfered in the governance of those states. On one level, then, the president and governors depended upon each other's goodwill and cooperation. A similar reciprocity existed on another level between the governors and the *coroneis*. The latter regimented the local vote that elected the former. The governors in turn respected the local authority of the *coroneis*. Of course, some *coroneis* opposed some state governments, but that position generally lessened their authority and prestige and was to be avoided if possible. Politically, the Old Republic rested firmly on a rural base. After all, Brazil's wealth originated in the countryside, where a majority of the population still lived.

Failing to organize a strong party, the traditional republicans abdicated their brief hegemony in politics. It was not long before some of the older and more experienced imperial politicians returned to power. Both presidents Rodrigues Alves and Afonso Pena (1902–1909), for example, had been counselors of the empire.

From time to time new efforts were made to organize national parties, but the results were inconclusive at best. José Gomes de Pinheiro Machado, a Gaúcho politician, was among the most energetic in making those efforts. He organized the new Partido Republicano Federal in 1905 and later the *Partido Republicano Conservador* (Conservative Republican party). Neither party became truly national; instead, they remained organized on a state level with few links among the state organizations. The nomination and endorsement of presidential candidates remained in the hands of either the incumbent president or an informal congressional caucus. A lack of institutionalized procedures was but one of the many disadvantages the system evinced. As the system functioned in practice, federalism became regionalism and national interests were sacrificed to regional ones. However, on the positive side, that system did manage to provide a candidate for

the presidency and guarantee his election. Hence the political process was continuous. It did not break down into the chaos characteristic of the political systems of so many of Brazil's republican neighbors.

The masses, of course, played no role in the political process, their interests being subordinated, as they always had been, to the well-being of the oligarchy. For their part, the middle sectors increasingly resented their own political impotence, a condition that encouraged frustration. The gender, age, and literacy voting requirements enfranchised a minority: adult literate males. It so happened that, since the president was chosen by direct vote of those few male literates, and since the economically powerful states tended to be those with the largest populations and the best educational systems, São Paulo, Minas Gerais, Rio de Janeiro, and Rio Grande do Sul held a distinct command in the presidential elections. By 1910 slightly over 50 percent of the electorate resided in those four states, and those voters cast over half the ballots. The representative system of government proudly proclaimed in the Constitution of 1891 actually represented only the upper echelon of Brazilian society and only one limited geographic region.

Through control of the government the coffee interests sought to maintain the political stability necessary for the progress of the nation or, perhaps more realistically stated, for that of the Southeast and for profitable international trade. They succeeded remarkably well for a generation. Prudente de Morais quelled the rebellion in the South in 1895. Some local rebellions flared up periodically but they were easily handled. During the heyday of the Old Republic, civil order reigned and Brazil was generally peaceful.

Clearly it was in the best interests of the coffee class to encourage economic stability and progress. The *Encilhamento* had set in motion an inflationary and speculative spiral that disturbed the planters, who felt it essential to reestablish Brazil's international credit, strengthen the national currency, and balance the budget. The financial crisis reached its peak in 1898. To stave off disaster, President-elect Campos Sales visited European bankers and governments in order to reach

an understanding with Brazil's creditors and negotiate new loans. He obtained a funding loan of £10 million from the house of Rothschild that saved the government of Prudente de Morais from bankruptcy. A sworn enemy of inflationary policies, Campos Sales entered upon his term of office determined above all else to rehabilitate Brazil's finances. He named as his minister of finance the able Joaquim Murtinho, who shared his determination. Murtinho also shared the belief that Brazil had misspent its capital foolishly in the previous decade on an irrational attempt to industrialize. Brazil's wealth, he and the president agreed, came from agriculture, not industry. While the president judiciously balanced the budget by cutting expenses and abandoning public works projects, the finance minister halted further emission of money, increased taxes, and concentrated on the redemption of paper money. To increase revenues the government raised tariff rates in 1900—which raises were further augmented in 1905 and 1908—and encouraged greater exportation. The program showed the success the government hoped for: the amount of inconvertible money in circulation dropped, and the rate of exchange improved. The budget began to show a surplus. The government improved its international credit rating by paying off its loans. An immediate influx of foreign funds resulted. Rodrigues Alves and his own skillful finance minister continued the policies of their predecessors. The program of financial stabilization obviously required sacrifices; this did not endear it to most Brazilians.

Always with an eye on the world markets, the coffee planters continued to urge the government to stabilize the national currency and fix the rate of exchange. Early in his administration President Afonso Pena turned his attention to those problems. In December 1906, he signed a law establishing the *Caixa de Conversão* (Conversion Office). Primarily concerned with external financial transactions, it received deposits of gold and issued against those deposits convertible paper bills with a fixed exchange value. The cumulative total of the paper bills it issued always equaled the amount of gold held by the Conversion Office. The principal advantages of the plan were that a fixed rate of exchange strengthened

Brazil's links with the financial centers of the world, halted the constant rise in running expenses that weakened the planters' economic position, and improved Brazil's place in the world markets. The coffee planters endorsed the Conversion Office, and other business groups quickly echoed the praise when they saw the steady rate of exchange it maintained. The financial health of the nation continued to improve until war in Europe upset Brazil's exchange rate again.

With the encouragement of state and federal governments coffee production continued to increase. By 1900 ten million bags left Brazilian ports annually for overseas consumption. The increased supply regularly lowered the price, but the level of profits remained sufficiently alluring to attract greater and greater investment in coffee planting. In the last decade of the nineteenth century, the number of coffee trees under cultivation in São Paulo increased from 220 to 520 million. By the beginning of the twentieth century the planters realized that they faced the serious problem of overproduction.

The concerned coffee interests presented their problems to the government, which undertook to help them. In 1902 the government forbade any new coffee-tree plantings for five years. Nonetheless, because of considerable speculative planting before that date, coffee production rose at a much faster rate than did world consumption. By 1905 Brazil had 11 million sacks of coffee in warehouse storage, and productivity was rising as new trees matured. In 1906 Brazil produced a record coffee crop of 20 million sacks, and Brazil was not the only country with coffee to sell. As an economic crisis loomed the coffee alliance expected the government to come to its rescue.

In order to avoid the financial debacle created by overproduction, the government took steps to regulate the production and sale of coffee, extending the prohibition of new coffee tree plantings until 1912. By means of the Convention of Taubaté, signed on February 26, 1906, the governors of São Paulo, Minas Gerais, and Rio de Janeiro sought to control the marketing of coffee. The convention authorized a valorization scheme whereby, if coffee prices fell below a minimum level,

the state and federal governments would remove the beans from the market by purchasing and holding them until the price rose again. President Rodrigues Alves opposed it, but Congress approved the convention and pledged federal co-operation. The three coffee states exerted their influence to enlist federal support. Other states complained loudly, but ineffectively, that valorization reflected governmental favoritism.

Both the Rodrigues Alves and Pena administrations made strenuous efforts to limit the production of coffee and to withhold it from the market so that the enormous surplus could be sold at reasonable prices. With the aid of loans from foreign and national banks and the cooperation of the federal government, São Paulo alone held eight million sacks of coffee off the market in 1907. The following year São Paulo harvested one of the smallest crops in a decade, thanks to the policy of restricted planting as well as to adverse weather conditions. Between 1908 and 1912 the harvests were small, permitting the government gradually to sell its stored coffee and thus liquidate its investment. This led the government and the planters to judge the valorization scheme a success, and with various modifications it was used until 1929.

The transportation of product to market was another problem facing the coffee planters as well as other producers of agricultural exports. The 9,500 miles of railroad tracks laid in the nineteenth century were insignificant in such a large country as Brazil. Aware of the pressing need for more transportation, the republican chiefs of state accelerated railroad expansion. By the outbreak of World War I, Brazil had increased its railroad network to 16,000 miles, most of which—it should be no surprise—traversed the coffee-producing states. São Paulo, Minas Gerais, and Rio de Janeiro accounted for well over half the total national trackage. Certainly one of the most profitable of the railroad lines was the one connecting the capital of São Paulo with Santos. With a monopoly over coffee transportation, it carried so much that it frequently paid dividends of 50 percent per annum. Thus, the pattern well established during the first decades of railroad expan-

Table 6.2 Population Growth of the Capitals of the Major States, 1890 and 1920

State Capital	1890	1920
Salvador	174,412	283,422
Belo Horizonte	—	55,563
Recife	111,556	238,843
Niterói	34,269	86,238
Pôrto Alegre	52,421	179,263
São Paulo	64,935	579,033
Rio de Janeiro (federal capital)	552,651	1,157,873

sion continued: the rails linked the plantations to foreign markets, facilitating exports but also deepening dependency.

The renovation of ports received the full attention of both state and federal governments. Between the end of the century and World War I major improvements were made in the harbor facilities of Manaus, Belém, Recife, Salvador, Vitória, Rio de Janeiro, Santos, Paranaguá, Pôrto Alegre, and other smaller ports. Channels were deepened, new wharves and piers added, and more warehouses built, all with the object of facilitating the shipment of coffee, rubber, cacao, tobacco, cotton, maté, and hides.

Material progress obsessed Brazilians during the Old Republic. The nation paused in 1908 to commemorate the centennial of the opening of the ports. None of the celebrations surpassed the grandiose exposition held in Rio de Janeiro. It delighted the Brazilians, who proudly viewed the exhibits that showed the impressive progress they had made in a hundred years.

More than anything else, the cities testified to that progress. On the one hand, new towns appeared on the map. Approximately five hundred new municipalities were established during this period. In 1897, the Mineiros began to build their new capital, Belo Horizonte. On the other hand, old cities showed new vigor. Table 6.2 indicates the rapid population growth of the major cities. São Paulo recorded the most phenomenal growth, increasing at a rate above 25 percent every five years after 1895. Immigrants poured in: Italians, Portuguese, Spaniards, Germans, English, and French. The

developing industry and commerce of the state added to its notable prosperity. A rapid and constant construction program altered the physiognomy of the city. In 1906 the imposing Municipal Theater opened its doors and thereafter contributed mightily to the cultural formation of the state and nation. The new Polytechnical School (1895), Conservatory of Music and Drama (1906), and Faculty of Medicine and Surgery (1913) also made significant local and national contributions. By 1920 São Paulo ranked as Brazil's premier industrial city, a position it has held ever since.

Rio de Janeiro, too, underwent change. Shortly after his inauguration, President Alves focused his attention on the renovation of the unhealthy and underdeveloped national capital, initiating a program to beautify the city, build a first-rate port, and eliminate yellow fever. The president entrusted the eminent Dr. Oswaldo Cruz with the task of eradicating yellow fever in the unhealthy lowlands upon which parts of the capital were built. Yellow fever had first appeared in Rio de Janeiro toward the end of 1849 and in the years thereafter became the scourge of the city, making life there hazardous for both residents and visitors. Fortunately, the turn of the century witnessed scientific advances that conquered that tropical disease. Taking his cue from the accomplishments of North American scientists and doctors in Cuba and Panama, Dr. Cruz vigorously undertook a four-point program to kill mosquitoes, destroy their breeding ground, isolate the sick, and vaccinate all the inhabitants. The year he began his campaign, 1903, 584 recorded deaths were attributed to yellow fever. The following year the figure dropped to 53 and, in 1906, to zero. Cruz's energetic and effective campaign made the capital as healthy as any contemporary European city.

Concurrently, the newly appointed prefect of the Federal District, Pereira Passos, set about to rebuild Rio de Janeiro. He brutally cut a wide swath through the old business district to create the ample Avenida Central (today named Rio-Branco) and laid out the pleasant Avenida Beira Mar which skirted the seashore. He enlarged and redesigned the parks, constructed splendid new buildings, among them the Municipal Theater, inaugurated in 1909, and cleaned up the most

unpleasant parts of the capital. Meanwhile, engineers were rebuilding and expanding the capital's port facilities, for which modern equipment was purchased and installed. Aided generously by a luxuriant and verdant nature, Pereira Passos created the modern wonder of Rio de Janeiro, a source of admiration and awe for natives and tourists alike. The reconstruction of central Rio de Janeiro confirmed the the ascent of the urban middle class and, in a broader sense, of a new Brazil. The renovated city projected the image of the new bourgeoisie.

As the intellectual and political center of the republic, Rio de Janeiro vibrated with activity. The quaint colonial street Rua do Ouvidor, which threaded its narrow way through the heart of the business district, was the locus of intellectual and political discussion. Pedestrians were crowded together between the buildings—one, two, and three stories high—lining the famed street. Their walls, painted white, pink, blue, yellow, and pastel shades, were as colorful as the crowds they framed. The women paused to gaze into the elaborately decorated shop windows displaying the latest French and English imports; that they still held to the traditional preference for French styles was demonstrated by the fact that two of the foremost shops for the carioca elite were French, Madame Coulon's and *Au Printemps*. The men, newspapers in hand, ambled toward their favorite restaurant or coffee bar for yet another cup of coffee and still more conversation. The ubiquitous coffee bar was a notable and essential feature in every town or city, for Brazilians were much given to coffee and conversation, and more business was transacted over a demitasse of strong, sweet coffee in a corner coffee bar than was ever done in any office. The price for a small cup of the always freshly made beverage was a penny and a half. The steaming jet-black coffee was poured directly from a pot off the stove into the cup, already half filled with sugar by the customer. There was great truth to the Brazilian proverb that good coffee should be "as strong as the devil, as black as ink, as hot as hell, and as sweet as love." The coffee animated conversation as it relaxed the drinkers. They tarried in energetic discussion, pausing frequently to shake the hand of a

passing acquaintance and inquire after his health and that of his family. For intimates there was a warm embrace, given with genuine cheer and enthusiasm.

Poets and politicians jostled one another in the Rua do Ouvidor and its restaurants. The politicians were distinguishable by their tall, black silk hats. They held daily receptions, feeling the pulse of the populace, carrying on debates begun in the chambers. Crowded around the small circular tables, poets read and explained their works while friends and rivals complimented or criticized. They laced their conversations with French and occasionally English expressions and displayed a thorough knowledge of what European publishing houses were turning out. Such serious tones were enveloped in a symphony of cries from lottery-ticket peddlers and hucksters selling a wide variety of wares. Added to that cacophony was the babble of French, English, German, Spanish, and Italian, for Rio de Janeiro had become a gathering point for foreigners, who also showed a preference for the Rua do Ouvidor.

The cities nurtured a cultural life of ever-widening dimensions and importance. Machado de Assis had already reached a position of eminence in the Portuguese-speaking world. His pen produced *Dom Casmurro* (1900), considered by most critics to be Brazil's finest novel. *Dom Casmurro* enjoyed considerable popular success; it was a best-seller, a category that permitted the printing of 2,000 to 2,500 copies per edition and guaranteed a sale of between 600 and 800 copies in the first year. A worthy successor to Machado was Afonso Henriques de Lima Barreto, a writer of great sensitivity and insight, whose biting prose dissected the manners and mores of urban and suburban life.

The year 1902 became a literary landmark with the publication of two remarkable books. The first was Euclydes da Cunha's *Os Sertões* (translated into English as *Rebellion in the Backlands*), one of the most significant works of the new analytical school of literature, as already discussed. Critics hailed it as a classic.

The second book *Canãa* (*Canaan* in English translation), an analytical novel by José Pereira da Graça Aranha, studied

Brazilian society, examining it through the eyes of both foreign immigrants and natives. Highly critical of his society,
Graça Aranha observed that the nations of the New World
suffered from all the evils afflicting the Old. He also concluded that the only "true Brazilian" was the mulatto. Contributing to the intensifying feelings of nationalism, he bitterly attacked Brazilian dependency. In one passage, his characters debated that dependency in these sharp words:

> "You gentlemen speak of independence," observed the mu-
> nicipal judge caustically, "but I don't see it. Brazil is, and has always
> been, a colony. Our regime is not a free one. We are a protecto-
> rate."
> "And who protects us?" interrupted Brederodes, gesticulating
> with his monacle.
> "Wait a minute, man. Listen. Tell me: where is our financial
> independence? What is the real money that dominates us? Where
> is our gold? What is the use of our miserable paper currency if it
> isn't to buy English pounds? Where is our public property? What
> little we have is mortgaged. The customs revenues are in the hands
> of the English. We have no ships. We have no railroads, either;
> they are all in the hands of the foreigners. Is it, or is it not, a colonial
> regime disguised with the name of a free nation. . . . Listen. You
> don't believe me. I would like to be able to preserve our moral and
> intellectual patrimony, our language, but rather then continue this
> poverty, this turpitude at which we have arrived, it is better for one
> of Rothchild's bookkeepers to manage our financial affairs and for
> a German colonel to set things in order."

The intellectuals awoke fully to the economic, political,
and social realities of a changing Brazil. They identified and
discussed many of the problems and innovations, and thus
helped to make Brazil not only conscious of itself but better
known abroad. By so doing they contributed at the turn of
the century to the wave of nationalism inundating Brazil, a
nation confident for the first time in its new republican institutions.

The Triumph of Diplomacy

The impressive diplomatic triumphs Brazilians celebrated between 1895 and 1912 carried nationalism to a flood tide. Prosperous and peaceful at home, Brazil for the first time in several decades could turn its full attention to international affairs and concentrate its energy on the formation and execution of a constructive foreign policy. When the republic replaced the monarchy, Brazil still had not demarcated its lengthy frontiers, save those with Uruguay (in 1851) and Paraguay (in 1872). The republican ministers of foreign relations turned their full attention to the boundary questions.

The first order of business was the Missions territory disputed by Argentina and Brazil. Foreign Minister Quintino Bocaiúva had suggested that the two nations divide the territory, but the Brazilian congress adamantly refused to approve such a treaty. The two neighbors then agreed to submit their claims to an arbiter and chose U.S. President Grover Cleveland. The government in Rio de Janeiro selected Brazil's historian of the Rio da Prata (or Río de la Plata), José Maria da Silva Paranhos Júnior, the Baron of Rio-Branco, to present its case. Years of research, firsthand experience, and a reputation among Brazil's intellectuals for his studies of the Plata qualified him to head the mission. The Floriano government summoned him from his European diplomatic post. In his preparation of Brazil's case, he based his arguments on eighteenth-century documents and maps as well as on Brazilian settlement of the area. So skillfully had he mastered the material that he was able to use Argentine arguments to strengthen the Brazilian claim. When President Cleveland delivered the arbitral award on February 6, 1895, Rio-Branco won an overwhelming victory. The Missions territory, 13,680 square miles, fell to Brazil.

The government then assigned Rio-Branco to work on the troublesome boundary between Brazil and French Guiana. France made broad claims that extended all the way to the mouth of the Amazon. The two nations agreed to submit their dispute to arbitration and chose the president of Switzerland

as arbiter. Once again Rio-Branco had to write detailed arguments in which he employed history and geography as the handmaidens of diplomacy. On December 1, 1900, the Swiss president awarded the controversial territory, approximately 101,000 square miles, to Brazil. Rio-Branco had triumphed in both the north and the south, permitting Brazil to expand peacefully in both directions and to mark the frontiers that had vexed it for four hundred years. The two diplomatic triumphs made Rio-Branco a national hero. The Brazilians rejoiced to see themselves twice vindicated internationally, first with a victory over their archrival, Argentina, then with an award over a major European nation, France. After more than two decades, during which time the once-brilliant imperial diplomacy had declined to banal routine, Rio-Branco successfully projected national interests into the international sphere.

In December 1902 Rio-Branco returned to Rio de Janeiro from his post in Berlin to assume the portfolio of foreign affairs in the new government of President Rodrigues Alves. As foreign minister, he resolved to complete the task he had begun so auspiciously as a diplomat, that of marking the Brazilian frontiers. He faced at once the acrimonious dispute with Bolivia over the Acre territory in the heartland of South America. By firm pressure and adroit maneuvering, Rio-Branco caused Bolivia to negotiate the quarrel and, in 1903, to sign the Treaty of Petropolis by which Brazil acquired the rubber-rich Acre, approximately 73,000 square miles. In return, Bolivia received a small strip of territory that gave it access to the Madeira River and thus to the Atlantic (as well as a perpetual pledge of freedom of river navigation), ten million dollars, and Brazil's promise to construct a railroad on the right bank of the Madeira that would bypass the rapids and give Bolivia ascess to the lower Madeira. The Treaty of Petropolis completed the demarcation of the frontiers from the Atlantic Ocean in the south to Peru in the far west.

Peru, claiming for itself Acre as well as a large part of Brazil's Amazon basin, vociferously protested the settlement provided by the treaty. Rio-Branco then focused his attention on the Peruvian claims. Peru proved to be more difficult than

Bolivia to bring to the negotiating table. Lima persisted in using delaying tactics in the hope that somehow time would favor its case; but if time favored anyone it was Brazil. The constant change of Peruvian foreign ministers and diplomatic representatives to Brazil weakened the presentation of the Peruvian case, whereas the five years of negotiations by Brazil under one minister provided a continuity that strengthened its position. On September 8, 1909, Lima consented to sign a treaty defining the boundaries. Once again, the principle of *uti possidetis* determined ownership. Brazilians inhabited the extensive area claimed by Peru. Approximately 63,000 square miles were awarded to Brazil and the newly acquired Acre confirmed as Brazilian. The Spanish-speaking neighbor received less than 10,000 square miles. In addition, Rio-Branco defined the 972-mile frontier, thereby closing Brazil's far-western boundaries.

While the protracted negotiations with Lima were running their course, Rio-Branco attended to other frontier problems. The boundary with British Guiana was resolved in 1904 by a division of the territory in dispute. In the same year, Brazil and Ecuador (then neighbors) signed a treaty resolving their boundary problems. A treaty with Venezuela in 1905 settled the northern frontier; Brazil and the Netherlands negotiated an agreement in 1906 that determined the limits of Surinam; and in 1907 Colombia and Brazil reached an understanding which later would permit them to mark their frontiers. Rio-Branco capped the final demarcation of frontiers with the magnanimous Treaty of 1909 with Uruguay, assenting to that small neighbor's petition to redraw the boundaries between the two countries so as to give Uruguay the right of navigation on the Jaguarão River and Lake Mirim.

In fifteen years, Rio-Branco had marked Brazil's boundaries, the cause of debate and conflict for four centuries. The most obvious result of his settlements was the addition to Brazil of approximately 342,000 square miles of territory, an area greater in size than France. The Baron of Rio-Branco carried to a successful conclusion four hundred years of Luso-Brazilian expansion from the Atlantic Ocean to the foothills of the Andes Mountains. The frontier epic created the fifth

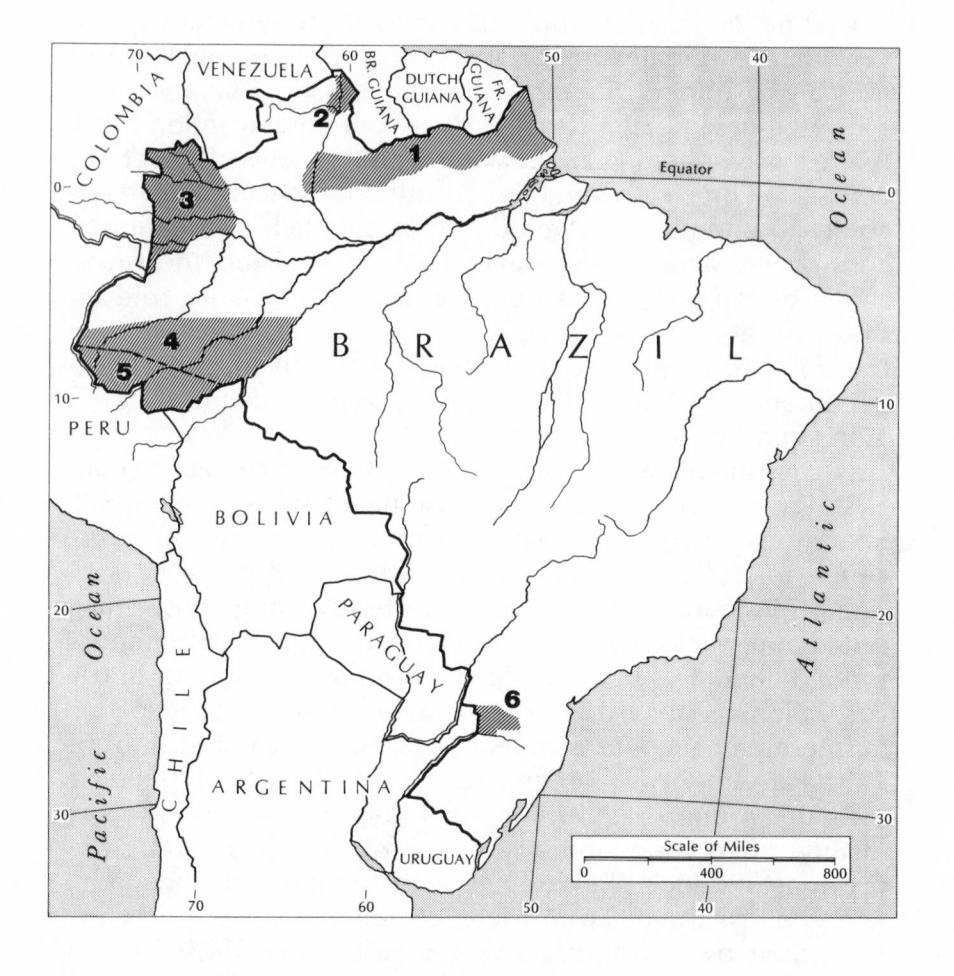

Map 4. Territorial Settlements Made by Rio-Branco

1. French Guiana, Territory of Amapá
   Arbitral Award of the Swiss Federal
   Council, December 1, 1900
2. British Guiana
   Arbitral Award of King Victor Emman-
   uel III of Italy, June 6, 1904
3. Colombia
   Treaty of Limits and Navigation, April
   24, 1907
   Clarified by the Treaty of Limits and
   Navigation, November 15, 1928

4. Peru
   Treaty of Demarcation of Frontiers,
   September 8, 1909
5. Bolivia, Territory of Acre
   Treaty of Petrópolis, November 17,
   1903
6. Argentina
   Treaty of Missões Arbitral Award of
   President Grover Cleveland of the
   United States, February 5, 1895

largest nation in the world. Somewhat more difficult to measure, and of greater importance, were the potential causes for war, misunderstanding, and dispute that he eliminated.

At the same time that he was defining frontiers, Rio-Branco was initiating new foreign policy goals that set the course for Brazil's twentieth-century diplomacy. He had the ability to attend to the mind-numbing details of diplomatic controversy and, at the same time, to envision the broad scope of diplomatic strategy. He saw a leadership role for Brazil on a larger world-stage. Such an expanded role contrasted sharply with the parochial nineteenth-century preoccupations with boundaries in general and with the Plata region in particular.

The new foreign policy consisted of four related goals. First, Rio-Branco sought to increase national prestige abroad. Sharing the invigorated nationalism of the new century, he aimed to make Brazil known and respected in the international community. The newly renovated and augmented navy called at more foreign ports to show the flag. The number of foreign diplomats in Rio de Janeiro and the number of Brazilian diplomats abroad increased, as did Brazil's participation in international congresses. Rio de Janeiro played host to the Third Pan-American Conference and the Third Latin American Scientific Congress. During the Rio-Branco ministry, more distinguished foreigners visited Brazil than had during any previous decade. The foreign minister greeted and entertained all of them. From their statements to the press and from their own writings, it was apparent that those visitors carried away with them a favorable impression of the country. In France during this period a stream of books about Brazil cascaded off the press. English, German, and North American writers joined in the literary discovery of Brazil. Meanwhile, German and Belgian universities began to offer courses in Portuguese and in Luso-Brazilian literature. The diplomat Joaquim Nabuco was speaking at civic clubs and universities across the United States, while the historian Manuel de Oliveira Lima lectured at Stanford University, Williams College, and the Sorbonne. Much to the satisfaction of the Brazilians their country was being recognized abroad.

Foreign Minister Rio-Branco foresaw the prestige that would accrue to Brazil if it were the first Latin American nation to receive a cardinalate. As late as 1904 there was not one Latin American cardinal, a curious fact when one realizes that the area was a bastion of Roman Catholicism. Pressure mounted on Rome to elevate a Latin American to that eminent position. The first Latin American nation to receive the honor would enjoy a singular distinction. The foreign minister ordered the Brazilian diplomat at the Vatican to inform the pope that Brazilian Catholics would be pleased to have a cardinal. In comparison to the rest of Latin America, Brazil had maintained good relations with Rome. Indeed, Brazilians were not reticent in pointing out that they had displayed more loyalty and consideration than other Latin Americans. They also employed the effective arguments of size and population. The reasoning was sound, and the decision of Rome was not long in coming. In the consistory of December 11, 1905, Pope Pius X created as cardinal the distinguished archbishop of Rio de Janeiro, Joaquim Arcoverde de Albuquerque. The announcement was a diplomatic triumph for Brazil. For thirty years thereafter Brazil was the only Latin American nation with a cardinal.

As a second goal in the new policy, Rio-Branco wanted Brazil to exercise leadership in Latin America in general, but in South America in particular. He began by strengthening his nation's diplomatic ties throughout Latin America. Discovering that Brazil had no representative in either Quito or Bogotá, he corrected that oversight in 1904 by dispatching resident ministers to both capitals. In 1906, Brazil accredited a diplomatic representative to Costa Rica, Cuba, Guatemala, Honduras, El Salvador, Nicaragua, and Panama for the first time. The only Latin American capitals to which he did not accredit a diplomat were Port-au-Prince and Santo Domingo. When necessary, the baron conducted his diplomatic intercourse with those insular republics in Washington. Buenos Aires, Santiago, and Lima became the most important posts in Latin America, and he assigned to those three capitals his ablest diplomats and closest associates. Recognizing the importance of Mexico in the Pan-American community, he es-

tablished a legation there in 1906, thereby separating the previously joint Washington–Mexico City diplomatic post.

The examples of Rio-Branco's and Brazil's leadership in Latin America were numerous. Nowhere is it better illustrated than in the coordination by *Itamaraty* (the name given the Foreign Ministry) of the Argentine-Brazilian-Chilean-Mexican recognition of Panama in late 1903 and early 1904, a perfect example of the foreign minister's ability to direct the international participation of the major Latin American nations. Brazil's leadership at the Second International Peace Conference at The Hague in 1907 was another cogent example. There, Ruy Barbosa spoke with the support of all of Latin America when he demanded the equality of all nations on the arbitration court debated at The Hague. Itamaraty also helped to mediate the conflict between Peru and Ecuador over frontiers, found a solution for the impasse over the Alsop claims threatening Chilean–United States relations, and urged the United States to send a permanent diplomatic representative to Paraguay. Brazil came to regard itself as the diplomatic bridge between the United States and Latin America. The Brazilians sought to interpret the United States and its actions to the Latin American community and in turn to serve as the mediator for Latin America before the U.S. Department of State. Its efforts at leadership did not go unobserved. The Chilean minister in Rio de Janeiro wrote to Santiago:

> Brazil believes itself, because of its enormous size, population, geographical position, and evident rich future, to be the country destined to exercise in South America part of the hegemony which the United States now exercises over all America. That line of thought has the publicly declared approval of the United States. Brazilian politicians do not hide their thoughts and they have stated them in documents.

As the Chilean diplomat hinted, much of the success of new foreign policy depended on Rio-Branco's skill in closely aligning Brazil and the United States. He succeeded during the early years of his ministry in shifting Brazil's diplomatic axis from London to Washington. Throughout the nineteenth cen-

tury, Great Britain enjoyed a commercial and financial monopoly over Brazil, and the British government served as the
unofficial model for the Second Empire. In contrast, the republic modeled its Constitution of 1891 upon that of the
United States, the new political mentor. Also, by the last
decades of the century, the North American market was by
far the prime purchaser of Brazil's exports. Rio-Branco clearly
understood that the newly emerged world power, if properly
cultivated, could serve Brazilian interests well. By an intimate
relationship with the United States, he hoped to tip the balance of power in South America to favor Brazil, to add to his
diplomatic strength, and to increase his international maneuverability. Washington became the "number one" post, and
the foreign minister counseled his diplomats there to maintain the closest contact with the U.S. State Department.

The United States, gladly accepting the proffered friendship of the largest Latin American republic, reciprocated Brazil's good will. The two nations exchanged ambassadors in
1905; Washington thereby received the first Brazilian ambassador, the distinguished and pro-American Joaquim Nabuco,
and Rio de Janeiro welcomed the only U.S. ambassador accredited to South America. Together the foreign minister and
his ambassador won the understanding and cooperation of
Secretary of State Elihu Root and President Theodore Roosevelt, who ensured North American support of Rio-Branco's
new foreign policy. At one point the ebullient Roosevelt,
always intrigued by the size of Brazil, was quoted as remark-
ing to a Brazilian official, "Your great country is reserved a
brilliant future toward which, as representative of this Government, I hope to be able to contribute." Root made his
own contribution in the form of an official visit to Brazil in
1906, the first visit abroad of a U.S. secretary of state. There is
every reason to believe that Root regarded Brazil as the key-
stone of his Latin American policy. Certainly his enthusiastic
reception throughout Brazil sealed the bonds of an unwritten
alliance which then seemed to unite the two giant republics
of North and South America, and the visit served notice to
the rest of the hemisphere of the special relationship existing
between them. Brazil's principal rival, Argentina, took note

of that unofficial but nonetheless firm alliance. The baron's new policies were already beginning to strengthen Brazil's hand in international politics.

For the final point of the new foreign policy, the baron placed a new emphasis on Pan-Americanism. Set apart from the rest of the hemisphere for nearly a century because of its unique monarchial institutions, Brazil joined the fraternity of republics in 1889, the same year in which the modern Pan-American movement got under way. The amicable settlements of frontier problems put to rest the major potential source of conflict between Brazil and its neighbors so that inter-American friendship could become a reality. Whatever the personal feelings of the Brazilians toward their sister republics, all responsible leaders understood the importance of friendly relations with them. The foreign minister organized the highly successful Third Pan-American Conference in Rio de Janeiro in 1906, which consolidated and gave permanence to the Pan-American movement.

Pan-Americanism, close relations with the United States, Latin American leadership, and international prestige became the four cardinal points of a new foreign policy that showed increasing vigor as Itamaraty brought the former frontier diplomacy to a successful conclusion. The Brazilians were delighted to find their country embarked upon new international policies. As they lifted their former limited diplomatic vision from the frontiers to the world scene, they determined for the first time to take their place on the global stage. An apt example illustrates their change. In 1899 Brazil, still very much engrossed in its boundary disputes, refused an invitation to attend the First Hague Peace Conference, claiming that no national interests of Brazil would be discussed. In 1907 Brazil, then engaged in its new policy of aggrandizement, not only eagerly accepted an invitation to the Second Hague Peace Conference but even requested an official position for its chief delegate, Ruy Barbosa, who played an active role in the discussions.

Only eight years had elapsed between the two conferences, but during that time the diplomacy of Brazil under Rio-Branco's guidance had changed completely. The new inter-

national attitude and the foreign policy accompanying it constituted the legacy of the Baron of Rio-Branco. In the decades following his death his policies became traditional and his successors proudly and unquestioningly carried them out. Concluding the diplomacy of the empire and setting the course for the diplomacy of the republic, his time of ministry was the decisive transitional period in Brazilian diplomacy. Furthermore, by studiously avoiding politics Rio-Branco raised foreign policy above partisan polemics, so that, instead of representing one or another party or faction, it reflected the desires of the entire nation. Foreign policy became identified with the idea of unified nationality and an external manifestation of growing nationalism.

Exploiting the Amazon

The prosperity and progress of the "New Brazil" extended even into the distant Amazon Valley, many times regarded as promising and many times failing to fulfill that promise. Hopeful of a brighter future for the valley, the emperor created the province of Amazonas in 1850. Manaus, a small collection of mud huts on the Negro River, a few miles from where it empties into the Amazon, served as the capital. Shortly thereafter steamships began to ply the waters of the "river-sea," contributing notably to the opening of the valley and to its future exploitation. Mauá's steamship line in 1853 connected Belém with Manaus, providing scheduled service on the eight-day run. In 1855, another scheduled steamship service linked Manaus with Nauta in Peru. Under foreign pressure, the imperial government opened the Amazon to unrestricted international traffic in 1867. Regularly scheduled steamship service appeared in the years thereafter on the major tributaries of the Amazon: the Purús in 1869, the Madeira in 1873, and the Juruá in 1874. Settlements all clung to the edge of the rivers, and hence a network of steamship lines could unite the inhabited regions of the Amazon quite well. Logically, then, the river dominated the lives of all the inhabitants of the North. To the shores of that great river

came a wide variety of natural products for transport: gums, roots, drugs, woods, animal skins, and rubber. Rubber transformed the Amazon.

Rubber remained unimportant until 1840 when Charles Goodyear discovered a vulcanizing process to keep it from becoming sticky in hot weather and brittle in cold. It then proved useful for rainwear, electric insulation, carriage and bicycle tires, and finally automobile tires. With the increased practicality of rubber, the demand for it multiplied. Belém exported 69,174 pounds in 1827, but by 1853 those rubber exports reached 5,214,560 pounds and showed every indication of rising. The Amazon was on the threshold of a boom.

The speculators searched out rubber trees along the courses of the Amazon and its tributaries, claiming gargantuan tracts of land with the hope that they contained the precious tree. No one thought to plant the tree, which took over twenty years to mature. Popular belief held that wild rubber was superior. Anyway, there seemed no limit to what Nature had provided. The entrepreneurs of the burgeoning industry lived in either Belém or Manaus, from which they directed their gathering operations and the exportation of crude rubber to eagerly waiting world markets. The principal problem was an old one for Brazil: a labor shortage. Dwindling numbers of Indians were pressed into service as *seringueiros* (rubber gatherers), recreating many of the seventeenth and eighteenth centuries' worst scenes of enslavement and abuse. A large percentage of the population of the Amazon during the rubber boom had come from the Northeast, driven there by the recurring droughts and held there by a cruel form of debt peonage. But those men, among the most heartless exploiters of the Indians, were forced to borrow heavily from the simple Indian civilizations in order to survive. In his short story "Hospitalidade," Alberto Rangel depicted the relations between the two groups and the necessity of the invader to adopt indigenous ways. Rubber profits also enticed many foreigners to the tropics, but they stayed principally in the two cities, Belém and Manaus. The English, French, Germans, and Portuguese arrived to direct the rubber operations, while the Spaniards, Italians, Syrians, and

Lebanese immigrated to conduct other types of business in the two state capitals. In the entire Amazonian North, the population rose from 250,000 in 1853, to 330,000 in 1872, to 380,000 in 1890, and reached nearly a million in 1910. Never, however, was there a sufficient number of *seringueiros*.

The isolated, difficult life of the exploited *seringueiro* explained the recruitment problem. Euclides da Cunha in his perceptive essays on the Amazon repeatedly stressed the theme, "Man is alone." Indeed, the rain forest engulfed the *seringueiro*. Each gatherer was assigned a path that, leading through dense undergrowth and swamps to scattered rubber trees, exposed him to all the dangers the Amazon could offer. His path might require his attending as many as two hundred trees. Early in the morning he tramped along it to tap the rubber trees. He gashed the bark to draw the milk-white fluid that he collected in a cup fastened to the trunk. The *seringueiro* returned later to gather the offering of the tree. His next task was to smoke the rubber. To produce the best rubber the sap had to be smoked the day it was gathered. The dense smoke of a palm-nut fire quickly coagulated the white fluid into the marketable black rubber ball. Those balls were then stored to be shipped later to either Manaus or Belém for export. The rich profits of the trade did not fall to the *seringueiro*, who was fortunate to earn a dollar a day. The wage was high, but the cost of living in the Amazon was astronomical. In 1910 coffee, sugar, rice, and beans, the mainstays of the workingman's diet, cost about four times what they fetched in New York City. Because the population refused to farm, nearly everything they ate was imported. In addition to the cost of transporting food into the Amazon, the federal government exacted a high tariff on foreign imports, including imports of food. The expense of importing the food naturally was passed along to the consumer. Little wonder that the *seringueiro*, no matter how hard he worked, could not rise from poverty and servitude.

Over the years the rubber gatherers fanned out along the many tributaries of the Amazon, large and small, into the most remote regions of the interior. By so doing, they not only tapped new trees and increased rubber exports but they

also carried Brazilian territorial claims into hitherto uninhabited regions of the South American hinterlands. They functioned as modern *bandeirantes;* their settlement of the Amazonian interior validated Brazil's claims of *uti possidetis,* establishing the basis upon which Rio-Branco made the definitive and advantageous settlement of the frontiers.

Along the numerous tributaries of the mighty Amazon, the rubber floated into Manaus or on downstream to Belém, leaving the interior no richer for the extraction, but augmenting the wealth and ostentation of those rapidly growing ports.

The price of rubber rose steadily, if not evenly. In April 1910 it reached a peak, $2.90 per pound, a record never again equaled. The joy of the rubber barons was brief. In May, the price began to decline just as it had risen. The sagging prices throughout the remainder of the year, however, did not prevent 1910 from setting income records. The average price for the year, $2.01, was considerably more than the $1.60 average of 1909 and about double the 1908 average of $1.18. The lucrative profits in 1910 set the record for income from rubber sales, even though more rubber had been exported during several previous years and 1912 would subsequently mark the apogee of rubber exports.

The increasing income from the rubber industry made possible comfortable budgets for the governments of Amazonas and Pará. The main interest both of those governments displayed in the industry was to levy taxes. A 20 or 25 percent export tax on each kilogram of rubber enriched the treasuries. Budgets boasted gratifying surpluses. For Amazonas in 1910, rubber provided 82 percent of income. In the previous year it had furnished 79 percent and in 1911 it would contribute 78 percent.

In many respects the prosperity extended beyond the jungle confines. All Brazil benefited. In the first decade and a half of the twentieth century rubber ranked second only to coffee in furnishing the country with foreign exchange. In the period from 1910 to 1912, coffee brought some 25 million pounds sterling, while rubber brought nearly 22 million. From 1900 to 1912 rubber made up about one third of Brazil's export trade. The taxes paid on rubber exports sustained in

grand style the states of the North and also provided prosperity for several of the states of the Northeast, many of whose citizens were directly or indirectly involved in the industry. In turn, the Southern states benefited from the lively sale of their cereals, meats, coffee, and textiles to the North. The many imports that the northerners could afford to buy also contributed to the national treasury through the high import duties collected by the federal customs service.

The mounting wealth, as rubber exports jumped from 10 percent of the national total in 1890 to 39 percent in 1910, transformed the provincial riverine capitals of Manaus and Belém into modern cities. Situated (or as some thought, imprisoned) in the midst of a vast and alluring rain forest, Manaus in the first decade of the twentieth century proudly offered all the amenities of any European city of similar or even greater size. In 1896 Manaus became the first large Brazilian city to introduce electric street lighting. An excellent system of waterworks, an efficient garbage collection and disposal system, telephone service, handsome public buildings, and comfortable private residences attested to the modernity of the city. The crowning glory of the city was the magnificent Amazonas Theater, one of the splendid opera houses of the day. Built entirely from rubber money between 1891 and 1896, it was reputed to have cost two million dollars, an astonishing figure for the period. Like most Brazilian buildings constructed in the nineteenth century before French gingerbread styles became the vogue, the theater showed a solid, simple exterior and a wildly imaginative baroque interior. Ordinary stone was the main material used in the construction but the entrances and supporting pillars were finished in Italian marble, and colorful tiles adorned the dome. The rich elaborate interior was brilliant with gold leaf and lush with red velvet. Classical Greek and Roman mythological figures vied for attention with Indian and local motifs in the decorations, painting, and sculpture. Indian heads protruded from the balustrade of the staircases, and palm leaves interlaced in the friezes. Murals depicted European gods and goddesses frolicking in the Amazon. Large gilded mirrors reflected the splendor of the chandeliers. The orchestra pit could easily

hold sixty musicians, and the stage in its day was considered immense. Elegant crowds converged on the theater for the many dramatic, operatic, and musical events it offered during the winter season.

The newly expanded harbor bustled with activity. In the port foreign flags, particularly British and German, mixed freely those of Brazil. The year 1910 set a record for ship movement, unequaled for a decade and a half thereafter. The rubber merchants were just finishing their biggest decade of export. They had shipped some 345,079 tons of crude rubber abroad, well over a hundred thousand tons more than they had sold the previous decade (or would sell the following). The rubber went to New York, Liverpool, Le Havre, Hamburg, and Antwerp, the principal world markets of that product.

Belém, a city that had grown from forty thousand in 1875 to over one hundred thousand by 1900, also bore ample testimony to the rubber riches. It too boasted electricity, telephones, streetcars, comfortable residences, splendid public buildings, and—as one contemporary North America visitor said—"an amount of vice that would shock our modern reformers." The lower city comprising predominantly white buildings possessed several fine cultural institutions as well. The Teatro da Paz opened its doors in 1878, and in 1891 the Paraense Museum, founded some decades earlier, was restored. The river harbor played host to steamships from various continents. In fact, the port in its heyday was one of the busiest in South America. Around it the very smell of rubber hung in the air. Vessels of all descriptions arrived from upriver with their rubber balls. They were carried to the warehouses, chopped up, and packed in boxes for shipment. The huge wood and corrugated iron warehouses bulged with rubber. Indians, blacks, and mulattoes carried the great boxes from the warehouses to the waiting ships.

The rubber merchants exuded confidence as they watched fleets of ships carry away their product, and the entire economy of the North vibrated with their enthusiasm. The First Commercial, Industrial, and Agricultural Congress of the Amazon, which met in Manaus in February of 1910, proclaimed, "The superiority of this country as a rubber producer is guar-

anteed for some time because of the exceptional quality of its product, and also by the possibility of increasing, one might say indefinitely, the output of the forests." Optimism pervaded this congress just as it characterized the general business attitude in the North. Still, those who were realistic and also possessed a gift of vision—and there were a few—saw clouds forming on the horizon that threatened to cast a shadow of despair over the Amazon. The governor of Amazonas, in his annual message of 1910, complained that increasing attention, energy, and investment focused on the rubber industry to the neglect of such other forest products as castanha nuts, pirarucu fish, cacao, woods, and *guaraná*. In a vain echo of an earlier message by the president of the province of Pará in 1854, he warned that such a concentration created a potentially dangerous situation—overdependence on one export. The warning went unheeded. Anyway it was too late.

Asia already had begun to produce rubber in quantity. In 1876, the Englishman Henry Alexander Wickham surreptitiously had taken seeds of the *hevea brasiliensis* from the Amazon to Kew Gardens in London. From there, seedlings were transplanted to Ceylon, where Europeans laid out well-planned plantations. Asian labor cost a quarter that of Amazonian labor, and one Asian could tend over five hundred trees on a plantation, while one Brazilian with great effort tapped two hundred trees in the jungle. The first young rubber trees flowered in Asia in 1881. Initial exports from those efficiently organized plantations were modest. In 1900 Asia exported only 4 tons but the figure grew rapidly: in 1905, it reached 145 tons; in 1910, 8,000; and by 1915, 107,000. In other words, the percentage of plantation-grown rubber from Asia entering the world market grew from 0.3 in 1905 to 9.0 in 1910 to 67.6 in 1915. By 1922, plantation rubber accounted for 93.1 percent of international sales. The sharply rising supply of rubber on the world market, together with the low overhead of the European-owned and -managed plantations in Asia brought the price of rubber down. Consequently, in May 1910, the price of Brazilian rubber began a slow and steady decline that eventually shrouded the Amazon in economic stagnation.

The falling prices pinched the rubber barons. They awoke at once to the changing realities of the world market. By the end of 1910 they were in full panic. They complained bitterly of their plight, and in pessimistic tones predicted even lower rubber prices in the years ahead. Those predictions proved accurate. The merchants were loath to blame their own haphazard and inefficient production methods for their predicament. Instead, they sought more distant causes. They accused the federal government of lavishing its attentions on coffee to the neglect of the rest of the economy. Another handy target for their ire was the United States, the world's largest rubber market. They charged "Yankee speculators" with causing falling prices. Even so staid an institution as the Amazonian Bank pointed a finger of blame at American manufacturers, whom it accused of tampering with the world rubber market for the purpose of bringing about a decline of prices—to the great advantage of their own businesses. In doing so the merchants tended to neglect or underestimate the most important cause of their plight: efficient, large-scale Asian plantations that could produce more rubber more cheaply than the Amazon. In truth, Asian rubber had succeeded in breaking the monopoly Brazil had enjoyed for so long in the world's market.

However they might diagnose their problems, the merchants realized by the end of 1910 that the rubber boom was ending and that they needed help, and needed it quickly, to prevent a further decline. They recalled that a similar problem of overproduction and falling prices had beset the coffee industry about a half-decade before. Restricted planting and the Convention of Taubaté (in addition to bad weather that diminished the crop) had caused a price rise for coffee. Since Brazil was the major producer of coffee, national action in that case *did* affect the world market.

The rubber barons, refusing to recognize that they no longer held a world monopoly in the face of Asian productivity, spoke out for a "Convention of the Amazon." This was to be signed by the states of Amazonas and Pará and the federal government, giving to rubber a valorization similar to that enjoyed by coffee. Their aim was to stabilize the price of

rubber. As an emergency measure, the state of Amazonas passed an unrealistic law for intervention in the rubber industry. The merchants, though, continued to look to the federal government as the only possible source of a solution to their problem. Rio de Janeiro vacillated. The politicians there had a wider perspective of the global scene than did the rubber merchants and doubtless understood the hopeless situation of their national rubber industry. The belated Rubber Defense Law of 1912 encouraged the creation of plantations, the improvement of transportation, the attraction of immigrants, and ordered a 50 percent reduction of export taxes. It brought no results. Valorization schemes proved equally ineffective. The Bank of Brazil nearly went broke buying rubber and waiting for a price rise which never came.

The rubber boom was over. Panic replaced prosperity. The frantic activities so characteristic of a boom subsided. Belém and Manaus settled back into somnolence. The docks and warehouses deteriorated; banks closed; foreign merchants moved away; the two great opera houses fell into disrepair. Belém and Manaus took their places beside Olinda and Ouro Preto as cities of the past, victims of export growth and dependency.

The boom and collapse of the rubber industry followed a pattern well established by dyewood, sugar, gold, diamonds, tobacco, cotton, and cacao. The story of those industries points out one of the major themes in Brazilian history, so evident throughout the colonial period and the nineteenth century, and still visible in the twentieth century: the recurrence of economic cycles during which one product of the soil or subsoil determined the well-being of the entire economy or a large part of it. The history of the Brazilian economy has been one of the rise and decline of entire industries, one after the other. The single-product economy formed a pattern followed for over four hundred years. Each cycle left residues and effects. The cycles often populated new regions of the country and the product continued to be produced, albeit in diminished amounts and for lower prices, providing at least some source of wealth.

Likewise, the rubber cycle left its impress on the Ama-

zon. Human activity stirred the slumbering river valley. The adventurous *seringueiro* criss-crossed the hinterland in search of his livelihood, and in doing so expanded the Brazilian frontiers. The skilled river pilot navigated uncharted tributaries and streams, thereby extending the effective national territory. The population increased. Belém and Manaus grew from riverside towns to cosmopolitan cities.

In retrospect, the era that began with the return in 1894 of the government to civilian rule and continued through the first decade of the twentieth century emerges as one of the fruitful periods in Brazilian history. The few revolts that marred the period were minor, localized, and swiftly quelled. They were exceptions to a general tranquillity and to the stability that characterized the period. Most historians pay tribute to the good order and material progress during the Paulista domination. Perhaps the situation was best summarized by the Mexican diplomatic representative in Rio de Janeiro who informed his government in 1910, "The development of the vast wealth of Brazil is visible. In almost every case, the progress in these last years has been greater than even the most optimistic had hoped for." Like the Mexican diplomat and Marie Robinson Wright, most observers confused outward material progress with economic development.

The Decline of the Old Republic

The proper functioning of the constitutional machinery in June 1909 elevated Nilo Peçanha to the presidency to complete the sixteen months of office of the deceased Afonso Pena. Only forty-one years old when he unexpectedly became chief of state, he was the first president who had not received his political education under the empire. A citizen of the coffee state of Rio de Janeiro and a signer of the Convention of Taubaté, Peçanha continued the policies of his predecessors. One of the most important acts passed during his administration was the creation in September 1910 of the Indian Protection Service incorporating the diminishing Indian population of the hinterlands into the national family. In

reality, the limited time for which Peçanha held the helm of state was too brief for him to demonstrate his abilities—or lack thereof. Basically he presided over a caretaker government. And the first hotly contested presidential campaign in the short history of the republic overshadowed his administration.

Afonso Pena, like the presidents before him, had indicated his successor, the astute finance minister, David Campista. The unexpected death of the president robbed that favorite of the strong support he needed to claim the election. In the novel political vacuum thus created a variety of factions maneuvered to seize the political prize of the presidency. First some young officers and then some politicians spoke of Marshal Hermes da Fonseca as a candidate. An informal caucus of a few senators and deputies officially nominated him. Hermes had served as minister of war in the Pena cabinet and, as a representative of the conservative elements of Brazilian politics, could count on the support of the government. But his election was by no means a foregone conclusion.

The nomination of Hermes da Fonseca, a native of the southernmost Brazilian state, Rio Grande do Sul, expressed the ambitions of that rich, maverick state. The economy of Rio Grande do Sul rested on cattle ranching, rice cultivation, and industry. Its interests dictated a far greater preoccupation with internal rather than international trade. The Gaúcho politicians cooperated easily with the military. Fully a quarter to a third of the army was posted in that strategically located state, and the only professional military academy outside of Rio de Janeiro was located in Pôrto Alegre. At times it enrolled more cadets than the better known academy in the federal capital. Traditionally Rio Grande do Sul contributed a disproportionate number of officers to the military. Further, ideological bonds, namely those of Positivism, tied the military and the state Republican Party together. The Gaúcho congressional delegation always defended military appropriations and interests in the federal legislature. For these reasons, it seemed logical for Rio Grande do Sul to endorse the nomination of Marshal Hermes da Fonseca in a bid to achieve

national leadership and to challenge the political power of the coffee triangle.

Protest against a military candidate rallied the opposition which nominated Ruy Barbosa of Bahia. Statesman, jurist, and orator, Ruy had earned a splendid reputation among his compatriots for his role at The Hague Peace Conference in 1907 where, according to Brazilian legend, he dazzled the world's diplomats with his erudition. As a candidate, Ruy indefatigably toured the states to arouse support. In his lengthy and emotional campaign speeches he criticized the concentration of political power in the hands of a small political clique, lamented the government's failure to represent the people, and above all else warned of the menace of growing militarism. His liberalism was of the old school, but he stated his objectives more clearly and forcefully than most of his predecessors in that school ever had. He appealed to the urban middle sectors.

In his ambitious campaign the mistake the Bahian made that perhaps cost him the victory was his oversimplification of the issues. Opposing militarism and most specifically decrying a military man as president, Ruy characterized the election as one choice between military and civilian control of the government. He heaped abuse on the military (increasingly restive because it felt politically and economically neglected during the Old Republic), labeling it a "scourge." Many military leaders had opposed Hermes, but angered by the vehement anti-military tirades of Ruy, they gave their support to Marshal Hermes as a means of self-protection. Ruy alienated the military from the middle class.

As the campaign progressed it assumed significance in Brazilian history for several reasons. It provided a blunt discussion of the role of the military in which a sizable portion of the politically aware expressed a firm opposition to the participation of officers in politics. Further, a careful reading of the platform and speeches of Ruy reveals one of the early calls for democratic reform and the purification of the political body. It was a protest, doubtless quixotic, against the traditional oligarchical establishment dominating Brazil. In that protest, Ruy attempted to present the issues to the broadest

possible constituency, and in doing so he conducted the first truly large and important electoral campaign in Brazilian history.

Marshal Hermes' campaign, on the other hand, was a lackluster one, but he counted the government, Congress, Rio Grande do Sul, and Minas Gerais on his side. São Paulo and Bahia supported Ruy. The two principal coffee states split in that election—Ruy's running mate was Governor Albuquerque Lins of São Paulo and Hermes' was Governor Venceslau Brás Pereira Gomes of Minas Gerais. The election held on March 1, 1910, generated great enthusiasm and excitement. Congress took a little less than three months to count the popular vote: Hermes received 233,882 votes to 126,292 for Ruy. Not even half a million out of a population of twenty-two million (about 2.8 percent of the Brazilians) had voted. The highly restricted electorate was a graphic commentary on Brazilian democracy. Marshal Hermes received a far lower share (64.4 percent) of the votes than had any of his victorious predecessors (Prudente de Morais, 84.3; Campos Sales, 90.9; Rodrigues Alves, 91.7; and Afonso Pena, 97.9!).

The election of a soldier to the presidency climaxed a period of growing militarism in Brazil. In late 1905 the alleged German violations of Brazilian sovereignty—when, according to an excited press, sailors from one of the Kaiser's warships disembarked in Santa Catarina to apprehend a German immigrant there—impressed upon the Brazilians their military inability to meet foreign threats. Shortly thereafter the energetic ministers Admiral Júlio de Noronha and Marshal Hermes da Fonseca reorganized the army and navy with the encouragement of Minister of Foreign Affairs Rio-Branco. Arms purchases increased. Growing rivalry with Argentina prompted Brazil to buy new warships, and soon the two neighbors were engaged in an arms race neither could afford. The Kaiser's 1909 invitation to Marshal Hermes to attend the German army's annual maneuvers proved to be the capstone. The efficiency of the German army fascinated Marshal Hermes, and he returned to South America with some grandiose ideas. Overlaying these specific causes for the rebirth of militarism in Brazil was the general military spirit abroad in a world

noisily arming itself for the Grand Conflict. Brazil simply followed the trend of the times.

Ironically, one of the major consequences of Brazil's overt militarism was a series of naval revolts, in late 1910, whose potential seriousness startled the nation.

President Hermes hardly had settled into the Palace of Catete when the sailors of the renovated navy mutinied. On November 23 the enlisted men of four warships expelled their officers, killing several in the process. The crews of seven other warships in Guanabara Bay abandoned ship. The capital waited nervously as the "black mutineers" turned landward the powerful guns of the "great white battleships." The ships fired sporadically at the defenseless capital. The revolt proved to have no political significance. The sailors, exhausted and overworked, had resolved to take dramatic steps to air their grievances. They complained of harsh corporal punishment, excessive hours of work, insufficient pay, and the bad quality of rations. A later congressional investigation substantiated the charges of overwork and frequent flogging. After an amnesty and a promise of improved conditions, the sailors surrendered meekly and allowed their officers back on board on November 25. At once the government landed all the munitions and the breechblocks of the principal guns, rendering the expensive warships as harmless as steamboats.

More trouble, however, was in store. Hardly had the battleships been disarmed when the five hundred marines stationed on the Isle of Cobras, situated just off the waterfront of Rio de Janeiro, revolted. On the evening of December 9, they began firing at the Naval Arsenal. Sailors aboard one warship mutinied and joined to the cause of the marines. The critical situation required the government to use force as well as grant another amnesty before the marines would surrender. After quelling the revolt the government announced that the uprising was devoid of any political significance but declined to give any additional explanation.

Those disquieting naval revolts contributed to the violence that erupted during this era to disturb the placidity of the nation. A renewed propensity for federal intervention in state affairs brought immediate hostile reactions. The Paulista

and Mineiro presidents had avoided those interventions, knowing that their states preferred to pursue their own courses and assuming that the others did too. Such, however, was not the case after 1909. The emerging leadership from Rio Grande do Sul, directed in the federal capital by Pinheiro Machado, was considerably less cautious in interfering in the states to impose its will. Intrigue and intervention accompanied the *riograndense* predominance in Rio de Janeiro. The North and Northeast seethed with plots and counterplots as state and federal politics intertwined. Even Rio Grande do Sul and São Paulo did not escape those intrigues. Part of the troubles can be blamed on the heavy-handed politics of Rio de Janeiro, but another part resulted from the local resentment of an entrenched oligarchy and a desire to remove those privileged few from office. In the larger sense, then, the violence stemmed from the growing desire to modernize the country by diminishing political patriarchy in order to encourage democratization.

Trouble in the backlands also convulsed the nation. The rural disturbances arose from the gross injustices of Brazilian society, aggravated by the steady expansion of capitalism inland as communications and transportation networks reached out from the ports with increasing effectiveness. Capitalism brought new cultural values that challenged the folkways of the interior. As events at Canudos amply demonstrated, two very different Brazils were coming into closer contact and on occasion clashing.

The despair of the rural masses, their rejection of the present, and their longing for a better life in the future had given rise to numerous millenarian movements in the nineteenth century. Thanks to the conceptual framework offered by E. J. Hobsbawm, it is possible to consider millenarianism as a type of popular revolution, the rejection of the present for a total restructuring of the future. The first such millenarian movement of the republican period took place in the *sertão* of Bahia, where Antônio Conselheiro had gathered his impoverished followers into the rustic settlement of Canudos. While that bloody drama was being enacted, a second manifestation of religious fanaticism rocked Ceará. A "mira-

cle" in the Cariri backlands in 1889, repeated in 1891, turned a humble parish priest, Padre Cícero Romão Batista, into one of the most powerful political figures of the Old Republic. A hard-working and dedicated servant of mankind and the Church, Padre Cícero became legendary in the Northeast after the communion wafer he administered to one of the faithful turned to blood in her mouth. Overnight, the dusty village of Joaseiro become the focal point for religious pilgrimages. The Church cast disapproving eyes on the "miracle" but never removed Padre Cícero from the interior, although it restricted his religious activities. But the peasants of the interior regarded him as their saint. Although his control in Ceará remained unshaken throughout his long lifetime (he died in 1934), some of the priest's most blatant political activity took place during the administration of Hermes da Fonseca. At one point his rural followers marched on Fortaleza and brought about the downfall of the state government.

In the southernmost part of Brazil a messianic movement among German immigrants occurred between 1872 and 1898. Jacobina Maurer, the self-proclaimed reincarnation of Jesus Christ, announced the end of the world and life everlasting for her followers. (This movement is one of the very few examples of female leadership during the nineteenth century.) Later, in the Contestado, an interior area claimed by both Paraná and Santa Catarina, a religious mystic who called himself João Maria, the Monk, agitated the simple folk. Between 1912 and 1915, he put himself above the civil and religious authorities to offer his followers a new and better life. There, as in Bahia, the state militia and police fell in defeat before the rural forces, and the federal government found it necessary to dispatch an army to wipe them out, a task that occupied a full division of six thousand heavily armed men.

Periodically small messianic movements flourished in the Amazon Basin. Deculturated by missionaries and explorers, the Indians developed a syncretic religion, part Roman Catholic, part that of their ancestors. They turned to religion for unity and hope. The messianic movements denounced "white civilization" as the source of local misery and announced a

new and perfect life in which the whites would not be present. The masses often conceived of the millennium as a world without whites, whom they universally associated with their exploitation misery. The many and varied millenarian movements revealed the spiritual and temporal needs of the people who subscribed to them, a denunciation of the society in which they dwelled, and a longing for a better life.

Banditry plagued the interior, particularly the Northeast where at times state and local officials were unable to guarantee the security of life or property. It attracted the desperate, whether they were poor or members of the impoverished gentry, who had lost out in the system. Whatever else banditry might have included or meant, it also was as much a means of protesting an injustice or righting a wrong as it was a way of equalizing the wealth or taking political revenge. To the rich and powerful bandits were outlaws meriting severe punishment; to the poor rural masses, however, they sometimes represented justice and liberation. Bandits roamed the Brazilian interior in the nineteenth century, particularly the impoverished Northeast where a few won the admiration of the poor and the respect of the wealthy (who not infrequently coopted them and utilized their services). Some scholarship correlates the rise of banditry in the late nineteenth century with the breakdown of patriarchal order in the countryside. Brazilian popular poetry abounds with tales of the bandit hero. A well-known verse sung at the beginning of the twentieth century, related the history of Antônio Silvino (1875–1944), who became a *cangaceiro* in 1896 in order to avenge the murder of his father by a police official who went unpunished by the government. Others related the adventures of Josuíno Brilhante (1844–1879), also seemingly pushed into banditry by the need to avenge local injustices against his family. He assaulted the rich and distributed their goods and money among the poor, boasting that he never robbed for himself. In 1878 such "Robin Hood" robberies and redistributions of wealth received the censure of the newspaper *O Cearense* which huffed, "These bandits loot properties in the most unrestricted fashion as if communism had already been proclaimed among us." The most famous *cangaceiro* of

the twentieth century was Lampião (Virgolino Ferreira da Silva, 1898–1938), whose adventures in the *sertão* extended over decades until he was killed. The motives and activities of the *cangaceiros* varied widely, but at least in part they could be explained as protests against the wrongs of society, as they viewed them. Because of their strength and because they often opposed the elite and the official institutions, they received the support, indeed the admiration, of large numbers of the humble classes who often hid them, lied to the authorities to protect them, guided them through strange terrain, and fed them. In short, the disturbances in the backlands were in part symptoms of the sterility of the social and economic systems that had been inherited from a distant past.

Assassination was yet another form of violence that disturbed the Old Republic. In 1897, while waiting in the Arsenal of Rio de Janeiro for the disembarkation of troops returning from Canudos, President Prudente de Morais was confronted by a young soldier who pulled out a pistol and attempted to use it. The weapon misfired. Minister of War Machado Bittencourt and several other officers jumped on the would-be assassin and attempted to disarm him, but in the scuffle, he stabbed Bittencourt to death and wounded two others.

The other high-level assassination attempt occurred in 1915. Political animosity toward the Gaúcho political "boss," Pinheiro Machado, had reached vehement proportions. One September afternoon, as the Riograndense politician entered the Hotel dos Estrangeiros, an unknown assailant who nurtured a grudge against him stabbed him in the back. Both attacks profoundly disturbed the nation.

Assassination attempts, banditry, revenging armies marching on Canudos and into the Contestado, the brutal political rivalries in many states, and the naval revolts revealed a violence that has usually been disregarded in studies of Brazil. The tendency in Brazilian historiography is to emphasize peaceful evolution. Perhaps a comparison with the historical experience of Mexico, Venezuela, or Paraguay justifies this emphasis. Certainly some momentous changes occurred in Brazil without bloodshed: independence, the abo-

lition of slavery, and the establishment of the republic. Yet, beneath the tranquil surface of Brazilian evolution, some disquieting currents of violence eddy. Taken together, the turbulent incidents raise questions about the traditionally accepted concept of Brazil as always leaning toward conciliation and compromise. This propensity is present, perhaps even dominant, in Brazilian history, but it does not exclude the possibility of violence. Beginning with the slave revolts and the *bandeirantes'* treatment of the Indians, there has been violence in Brazil, and it continues to the present day.

At any rate, President Hermes da Fonseca presided over a restive nation between 1910 and 1914 and, indeed, his actions contributed to the rising level of violence. The president did little to fulfill the growing desire of the prospering citizens of his natal state, Rio Grande do Sul, to shift the political axis of the nation southward to their state. The most powerful political figure in his administration, Pinheiro Machado, had attempted to force just such a shift. In addition to the president and Machado, Dr. Barbosa Gonçalves, the second minister of public works, Rivadávia Correia, the minister of the interior, and General Mena Barreto, the minister of war, were from Rio Grande do Sul. They formed an impressive body of leadership in the top echelon of government. But neither as individuals nor as a group did they possess the ability or strength to effect such a shift, at any rate not while coffee ruled supreme. Clearly it was still too early to challenge Minas Gerais and São Paulo successfully.

Hermes proved to be a careless administrator of the treasury. As a result, methods more characteristic of the free-spending days of the early 1890s replaced the stringent measures imposed under the Paulista presidents. The national debt mounted. In 1914 the treasury fell back on an old expediency: it issued inconvertible paper money. The government was forced to contract a second British funding loan.

Few doubted that the government of Hermes da Fonseca was inferior to those before it. Lack of ability and lack of positive action characterized it. The Brazilians became increasingly restive about their choice of a president and dissatisfied with the course of events. Lest the history of the Hermes

da Fonseca administration be represented as one of total gloom, it should be pointed out that coffee continued to sell well, and this managed to keep the economy buoyant; a large number of immigrants continued to arrive; and the railroad network continued to expand. Little else, however, was accomplished.

The gathering war clouds in Europe darkened Brazil's horizon as well, and the storm that engulfed Europe in August of 1914 disturbed Brazilians in many ways. Clearly the nation's sympathy lay with the Allies, particularly with France, the cultural mentor of the elite. There were sizable colonies of German immigrants in the South, especially in Rio Grande do Sul and Santa Catarina, and not a few Brazilians questioned the loyalty of those new arrivals. The government resolved at once to maintain a "rigorous neutrality," to use the words pronounced by President Hermes on August 4, 1914. It fell to the newly elected president, Venceslau Brás of Minas Gerais, to enforce that neutrality.

The initial impact of the conflict on Brazil's economy was staggering. In 1914 imports plummetted to half the amount of the previous year. Since the government earned a large share of its income from import duties, the national treasury suffered severely. Exports fell as well, a disaster for the state treasuries whose income derived chiefly from export duties. President Brás reacted to the emergency by cutting back on federal spending. Then, in 1915, the heavy needs of the Allies caused exports to rise spectacularly. Brazil's income mounted as it sold increasing amounts of its national products abroad.

As the war dragged on, Brazil found it ever more difficult to maintain a neutral posture. Sentiment for the Allies welled up. The government vigorously protested the German blockade of Allied nations declared on January 31, 1917. Only a few months later, on April 5, a German submarine sank a Brazilian freighter. The news stunned the Brazilians. To protest that violent act and to demonstrate its sympathy with the Allies and its solidarity with the United States, which had just declared war on Germany, the government severed relations with Berlin. On June 1, the government took further steps, revoking Brazil's neutrality and authorizing the use of Ger-

man ships anchored in Brazilian ports for its own purposes. The torpedoing of a fourth Brazilian ship on October 23, 1917, prompted the government to declare war on Germany; it was the only South American nation to do so. Participation in World War I was limited to furnishing supplies to the Allies, sending some army officers to Europe and a medical mission to France, and assigning a naval mission of two cruisers and four destroyers to patrol the South Atlantic with the English squadron.

Cooperation with the Allies enhanced Brazil's international position and augmented the prestige Rio-Branco had thought so desirable. Both Great Britain and Italy raised their legations in Rio de Janeiro to embassies in 1918. Further, Brazil, as a belligerent, participated in the peace conference at Versailles. The delegation under the leadership of Epitácio Pessôa pressed two claims against Germany. First, Brazil wanted Germany to pay at the 1914 value for the coffee stored in German ports that the Germans had sold at the opening of World War I. With the support of President Woodrow Wilson, Brazil's claim was recognized. Second, Brazil sought to keep the seventy German ships seized by the government in 1917 in its ports. The Allies, on the other hand, wanted to divide those ships among themselves in accordance with their naval losses, a formula that would have deprived Brazil of even one of them. Once again the United States intervened on Brazil's behalf to forge an agreement that permitted the Brazilians to keep all the ships.

In the organizational discussions for the League of Nations, Brazil spoke for the other Latin American states represented in Paris. Epitácio Pessôa, in a manner reminiscent of Ruy Barbosa at the Second Hague Peace Conference, enunciated Latin America's preference for equality of nations in the League with each continent represented on each committee. But Epitácio's stay in Paris was brief. Rodrigues Alves, elected president for the second time in 1918, was prevented by illness from taking the oath of office. When he died on January 18, 1919, Vice President Delfim Moreira of Minas Gerais assumed the first office of the land. In such cases, the constitution prescribed new elections. At that point, Gover-

nor Artur Bernardes of Minas Gerais and Governor Washington Luís of São Paulo came to a political agreement, which history records as the "policy of large states." They resolved to select a prominent figure from one of the small states to complete the presidency of Rodrigues Alves. Then the two major states planned to alternate the presidency between them with first a *mineiro* serving the four-year term and then a *paulista*. Recognizing the overwhelming power of the two principal coffee-producing states, the plan not unexpectedly annoyed the other states as a blatant reminder of their own political weakness. Epitácio Pessôa, a former minister, congressman, and Supreme Court justice, was selected by the two coffee governors in 1919.

Brazil won for itself a place of honor in the League of Nations. Although not a permanent member of the Executive Council, it was reelected repeatedly to a seat on that prestigious and powerful body between 1920 and 1926. Several distinguished Brazilian diplomats presided over the Council. Their position on the Council allowed the Brazilians to continue to play the role taken at the peace conference as the leader of the Latin American nations. The South American giant persistently demanded that a Latin American nation be represented on the Council with a permanent seat, a post for which Brazil, of course, felt itself eminently qualified. The European nations failed to heed that demand, to the mounting chagrin of the government in Rio de Janeiro. Then the other hemispheric republics switched their support from Brazil's demand for a permanent seat for a Latin American nation to a plan for three temporary, rotating seats. At that point, Brazil, vetoing the admission of Germany, withdrew from the League in 1926. The rationale apparently was that it would be more honorable to play no role at all than to play an insignificant one. The withdrawal signaled a return to a phase of hemispheric isolation, an isolation not unlike that of its North American ally. Thereafter, Brazil concentrated its diplomacy on affairs of the New World.

The years marking World War I witnessed changes in Brazil that tended to increase that nation's independence and self-reliance. Some of them owed little to the war itself. The

promulgation of the Brazilian Civil Code, for example, on January 1, 1916, resulted from years of study and preparation; it eradicated once and for all the many vestiges of Portuguese colonial laws Brazil had clung to. However, the war instigated some changes too. It concluded a process that had been under way since the end of the nineteenth century, when the United States began to exert its authority throughout the hemisphere: it broke Brazil's century-old financial and commercial dependence on Great Britain.

A significant economic change increasingly characteristic of Brazil during the three decades after the fall of the empire was rapid industrial growth. Industrialization expanded parallel to the phenomenal rise of Brazilian exports, particularly of coffee.

Some formidable handicaps had retarded industrialization: the lack of liquid capital, of an adequate system of currency, credits, and banking, of skilled workmen and technicians, and of a satisfactory transportation network; the failure to erect high enough tariff barriers or to meet competition from Great Britain; the inability to identify and deal with the effects of slavery, the elite's ingrained mercantilist mentality, and the self-interest of the agrarian sectors. These handicaps explain to a large extent why Brazil had been so little affected by the long Industrial Revolution that by then had transformed England, the United States, Germany, and France. However, once industrialization did get under way Brazil learned from Europe and the United States, benefiting from their experience and freely adopting their inventions.

To the degree that industrialization offered an alternative to the purchase of imported items and diversified the economy, it seemed to challenge the powerful grip of dependency. Each new factory promised some degree of local independence; each augmented the wealth of the nation. Nonetheless, reality sometimes circumvented promises. Foreign-owned or -financed factories could extract more wealth from Brazil than they infused. Nor could industrialization be expected to eradicate dependency so long as the fundamental social, economic, and political institutions went unchanged. The quicker and cheaper production of goods could

supply the needs of more people. Thus it smoothed the way for the phenomenal growth of the Brazilian population in the twentieth century. The concentration of the factories in a few cities increased both the size and the importance of those cities, and, as they grew, the nature of Brazil altered. Hence the factories and the cities contributed to the questioning of a traditional society implanted in the sixteenth century and unchallenged until the last half of the nineteenth.

At the Exposition of 1908 the national industries proudly displayed their wares, a display that afforded the nation an opportunity to take stock of its industrialization. The authorities estimated that Brazil possessed approximately three thousand industrial establishments, large and small—but preponderantly small. Just as in the industrialization of Great Britain and the United States, textiles were the first important industry. The most industrialized areas were Rio de Janeiro (the Federal District) with 35,000 workers, São Paulo with 24,000, Rio Grande do Sul with 16,000, Rio de Janeiro (state) with 14,000, and Pernambuco with 12,000. That year Brazil was in the midst of a modest industrial expansion. Between the fall of the empire and the outbreak of World War I approximately 7,000 new industrial establishments were created, a remarkable record when one considers that prior to 1889 there had been only 626.

The volume of industrial production doubled during World War I and tripled by 1923. The number of new industrial enterprises grew by 5,940 between 1915 and 1919. Two industries, foodstuffs and textiles, accounted for nearly three-quarters of the total factory production. By 1920, the industrial production was valued at $153,060,000, an increase of nearly fivefold since 1907. Table 6.3 illustrates the industrialization under way.

The processes of industrialization and modernization went hand in hand. Both made themselves felt within the citadel of traditionalism, the plantation. Once the fazendeiros had ruled their own plantations according to their will and whim and had interposed a formidable barrier between the distant government and the humble plantation worker. But now the rail and road networks had expanded, making possible a chal-

Table 6.3 The Growth of Industrialization, 1907–1940

Year	Number of Industrial Establishments	Capital Invested (1,000 contos)	Value of Production (1,000 contos)	Number of Employees
1907	2,988	665	669	136,000
1920	13,336	1,815	3,200	276,000
1940	70,026	12,000	25,000	1,412,000

SOURCE: U.S. Tariff Commission, *Mining and Manufacturing Industries in Brazil* (Washington, 1949), p. 13.

lenge to their authority and an end to the peasants' isolation. The rails and the roads led directly to the cities and ports, where the need for stevedores, service labor, and construction workers offered the ambitious rural arrivals a means of escape to a better life. Second generation migrants with some education might hope for industrial jobs. The opportunity to make a choice, however limited, was in itself a novelty. For the country folk who migrated there, the cities were symbols of a hope, often frustrated and unrealized but never forsaken.

Industrial expansion increased the size of the urban working force. Whereas the factories employed approximately 136,000 workers in 1907, they employed 276,000 in 1920. The rise in the number of workers in the two principal industries during those same years reflected that growth: the textile industry employed 53,000 in 1907 and 104,000 in 1920; the food industries, 29,000 and 41,000. By contrast, the 1920 census showed that federal, state, and local governments together employed 140,000 persons. The civil service, traditionally a big employer in Latin America, was being rapidly outranked in Brazil by industry.

Efforts to unionize labor accompanied industrial growth. The working conditions were abysmal: long hours, a pittance of a salary, dangerous machines, poor lighting, no vacations, no security—a dismal list almost without end. That women suffered worse conditions than men is well illustrated in this call for action by three São Paulo seamstresses to their co-workers in 1907:

Comrades! It is essential that we refuse to work night and day because that is disgraceful and inhuman. Since 1856 men in many

places have attained the eight-hour day. But we members of the weaker sex have to work up to sixteen hours a day, double that of the stronger sex! Comrades, think about your futures; if you continue to allow yourselves to be weakened and the last drop of your blood drained off, then, after you have lost your physical energy, motherhood will be martyrdom and your children will be pale and sickly. . . .

We too would like to have leisure time to read or study, for we have little education. If the current situation continues, through our lack of consciousness, we shall always be mere human machines manipulated at will by the greediest assassins and thieves.

How can anyone read a book if he or she leaves for work at seven o'clock in the morning and returns home at eleven o'clock at night? We have only eight hours left out of every twenty-four, insufficient time to recuperate our strength and to overcome our exhaustion through sleep! We have no future. Our horizons are bleak. We are born to be exploited and to die in ignorance like animals.

Congress passed a law in 1907 to recognize the organization of industrial and commercial employees as well as professionals. Nonetheless, the government and the elite in general looked upon union activities as subversive, probably because the socialists and anarchists paid the most attention to the workers. In fact, the anarchists dominated the labor movement until the early 1920s. A workers' congress met in Rio de Janeiro in 1906, and the delegates initiated the steps toward national unionization. The result, the Confederação Operária Brasileira (Brazilian Labor Confederation), appeared two years later. The confederation established affiliates in all the major states and in 1913 began to publish a newspaper.

The first major strike thundered across southeastern Brazil in 1907. Labor sought to reduce the workday to eight hours and to raise wages. Management met most of the demands. In an unusual show of organization and determination among rural laborers, many of whom apparently were foreign-born, workers on the coffee plantations in Riberão Preto in São Paulo struck for better wages and working conditions in April and May of 1913. Reports circulated that as many as ten thousand were on strike. Significantly, the federal government

cooperated with the coffee planters to suppress the strike. Higher prices and stagnant wages during the war years touched off a general strike in São Paulo in 1917. It affected the entire state and completely paralyzed the city of São Paulo for several days. The government attempted to use the military against the strikers but desisted when the soldiers manifested sympathy toward them. Amid a hostile atmosphere, the unions grew slowly if erratically.

Much of the capital for the new industrialization came from successful merchant-importers (who could mobilize credit) and from coffee growers-exporters (whose profits were channeled into industrialization through banks). Thus many of the coffee planters participated in the transition to industrialization, supplying, directly or indirectly, the funds for its growth. It is not surprising, then, that the principal coffee state, São Paulo, emerged as the foremost industrial region by 1920. For the first time that state seemed psychologically disposed to assume national leadership in industrialization, a role it previously had left to Rio de Janeiro.

In truth, São Paulo possessed most of the ingredients for successful industrialization. It succeeded in attracting into the labor force migrants both from abroad and from poorer states within the federation. Expanding coffee plantations provided capital. São Paulo possessed a wide variety of raw materials and considerable potential for hydroelectric power. It had developed a railroad network and a reasonably good road system. Furthermore, the state had an accessible, populous market with buying power, and an increasingly favorable trade balance enhanced its economic prowess. Little wonder then that São Paulo grew in population and wealth.

The heady days of wartime boom ended quickly after 1918. Brazil, like the other nations that had participated directly or indirectly in the war, had to readjust to a normal international peace economy. As the European nations regained their equilibrium, their dependence on Brazil for many raw materials and agricultural products lessened. Brazilian exports declined; the rate of exchange diminished; the price of coffee fell. By 1920, a trade deficit cast its shadow across the economy. President Pessôa found it necessary to reinsti-

tute the valorization of coffee in an attempt to strengthen the mainstay of the nation's economy.

Clearly the 1920s opened amid economic uncertainty, soon to be accompanied by political unrest. More pronounced than even a decade earlier, a dysfunction in which political institutions failed to speak to social needs and expectations pervaded the Old Republic. Coffee production remained basically prosperous, although not without its price fluctuations. Yet that prosperity touched relatively few people within the geographic limits of the Southeast. The nation depended more than ever on a single export to fuel the entire economy. The new political institutions proved to be as exclusive as their predecessors, marginalizing nearly all Brazilians from power. At the same time society grew increasingly complex at an unprecedented rate. Those excluded from political and economic benefits, or what they considered to be their just share of them, demonstrated impatience. Even the small but significant middle class grumbled with discontent. The stresses during the turbulent decade would test the foundations of the Old Republic.

Chapter Seven
The Challenge of Change

Gradual change in the twentieth century weakened the base of some archaic institutions long characteristic of Brazil. Emboldened by the modernization process, the critics of the established system intensified their attacks on monoculture, the *latifundia*, and the entrenched rural oligarchy. A new generation announced its intention to develop the nation—spiritually and materially—in 1922. Getúlio Vargas seized power eight years later and, in the following decade and a half, implemented some of the program the dissidents had favored. The coffee interests lost their absolute control of the nation and the urban middle class and proletariat strengthened their positions. The landed class, while still powerful, had to learn to compromise and to share some of its power with those two newly potent elements. Vargas enlisted both to support his government and skillfully identified his program with the increasingly powerful force of nationalism. Waves of nationalism, the desire for economic development, and the effects of urbanization and industrialization combined to challenge economic and political structures. Basic and well-established patterns and institutions accommodated some change but in the long run limited its impact and potential.

New Themes in History

The period embracing the late nineteenth and early twentieth centuries witnessed new historical trends. Mental attitudes underwent modification. The traditional patriarchal system withered in the growing cities, which were a fertile breeding-ground for new ideas. French influence yielded its exclusivity among the intelligentsia, who found the English language of new interest and fell increasingly under the sway of Anglo-Saxon culture. English theories of Positivism as propounded by Herbert Spencer gained adherents at the expense of the more orthodox theories of Comte. The foremost novelist, Machado de Assis, turned to England for literary models and inspiration. Brazilians admired not only the Constitution of the United States, so important in the writing of their own basic document of 1891, but they also stood in awe of the rapid industrial progress of that northern republic, progress they very much hoped to imitate. The commercial ties between the two hemispheric giants continued to grow. Brazil inaugurated a direct steamship service with New York in 1906; the National City Bank of New York, the first North American banking house in Brazil, established two branches in that country in 1915, and in the same year the American Chamber of Commerce established an office in Rio de Janeiro. Until World War I American investments in Brazil were minor, but thereafter they grew steadily. For practical reasons, then, English became a more widely spoken language among the educated, who increasingly turned to the United States as a commercial and political mentor.

An intensified interest in the United States reflected a broader concern with world affairs in general. The favorable demarcation of the disputed frontiers released Brazilian energies; lifting their eyes to wider, global horizons the Brazilians acquired a greater interest in international affairs. A grandiose foreign policy, aimed at increasing Brazil's prestige in the world and enabling it to assume the leadership of South America, absorbed the nation's attention and set the international course for the future.

The new attitudes characterized the cities, which were growing both in size and number. The ever larger urban society favored a quicker pace of modernization. The vocal middle groups concentrated in those cities spoke out to suggest reform. These restive groups savored the taste of power between 1889 and 1894. A new landed class representing the coffee interests replaced them in that year, but they continued to hunger for power and would be heard from again in 1922 and thereafter. Industrialization accompanied urbanization, accounting for some of the city's growth and contributing to the increase in the size of the middle groups. The new factories offered employment to greater numbers of workers. Industrialization centered in the Southeast, roughly in the same region where the coffee culture had predominated. That region emerged as the fastest-developing area in the country, the economic and political heartland of the nation.

A combination of prosperity and the abolition of slavery enticed larger numbers of immigrants into Brazil. In the last quarter of the nineteenth century, European immigration intensified. Between 1891 and 1900 the yearly average reached 112,500. The trend continued and reached record yearly averages just before World War I. From 1911 through 1913, about 500,000 immigrants entered. The figures for the total number of immigrants arriving in Brazil between 1820 and 1930 vary, but a conservative estimate would place the number between 4.5 and 5 million, of whom roughly 3.5 million remained. Italians composed the largest group of immigrants, 34.1 percent; the Portuguese were second with 30 percent; the Spaniards third with 12.2 percent; and the Germans fourth with 3.5 percent. The proportion of immigrants to the total population in Brazil was never very high. In 1872 3.9 percent of the entire population was foreign-born. The percentage rose to 6.4 in 1900, dropped to 4.8 in 1920 and continued to decline thereafter. However, a majority of those immigrants clustered in the four southern states, where they formed a large and influential portion of the total population.

The number of European immigrants making their homes in Brazil during the period 1820–1930 approximated the number of Africans imported between the early sixteenth century

and 1850. After the passage of the Queiróz Law and its enforcement, few if any Africans arrived in Brazil. A definite opinion against admitting them solidified. In fact, Decree Number 528 of June 28, 1890, prohibited Africans and Asians from entering without special congressional approval. That prejudice against Africans and Asians continued, while, on the other hand, the government went to great lengths to encourage Europeans.

In truth, the Brazilian intellectuals, like their counterparts throughout Latin America by the end of the nineteenth century, had fallen victim to specious racial doctrines imported from Europe. The richness of biological thought in the nineteenth century, the popularity of Darwinism, and the complex ethnic composition of Latin America aroused a lively interest in race and racial theories. Much talk circulated about superior and inferior races, and Spain's humiliating defeat in 1898 by the United States seemed to some Cassandras to be the final argument to prove the superiority of the northern European. Brazil's cultural mentor, France, provided an impressive array of pseudoscientific books attesting to that superiority. Joseph Arthur de Gobineau forcefully put forth that argument in his sociological treatise *Essai sur l'Inegalité des races humaines*. Widely read at the end of the century was the French social psychologist, Gustave Le Bon, who methodically classified all mankind into superior and inferior races with the Europeans indisputably at the top. Of particular concern to the Brazilians, Le Bon asserted that miscegenation produced offspring inferior to either parent. Another champion of the Aryan, the French anthropologist Georges Vacher de Lapouge, minced no words in his chief work, *L'Aryen, son rôle social*, published in 1899 to support the theory of racial significance in cultural development. He characterized Brazil as "an enormous Negro state on its way back to Barbarism."

Owing partly to that French influence, many Brazilians equated whiteness with beauty, intelligence, and ability; conversely, they felt the darker the people, the less possibility of their possessing those desired characteristics. Books such as Manoel Bonfim's *O Parasitismo Social e Evolução: A América Latina* (Social Parasitism and Evolution: Latin America), pub-

Table 7.1 Color Classification of the Brazilian Population, 1872, 1890, and 1940

Year	Whites	Browns	Blacks	Yellows	Total
			Population		
1872	3,854,000	4,262,000	1,996,000	—	10,112,000
1890	6,302,000	5,934,000	2,098,000	—	14,334,000
1940	26,206,000	8,760,000	6,044,000	243,000	41,253,000

SOURCE: *Contribuições para o Estudo da Demografia do Brasil* (Rio de Janeiro, 1961), p. 201.

lished in 1903, admitted the racial inferiority of Latin America. Graça Aranha's novel *Canaã* (Canaan) suggested the inferiority of people with mixed blood, even as he indicated that the future Brazilian race probably would be mulatto. The self-taught sociologist Oliveira Viana accepted the idea of the superiority of the white in his *Populações Meridionais do Brasil* (The Southern Populations of Brazil). Brazilians were well into the twentieth century before they reevaluated their racial concepts, a reassessment which fortunately corrected most of their mistaken ideas.

Meanwhile, the end of the slave trade and the influx of European immigrants, the lower life expectancy of the blacks and the higher infant mortality rate among them altered the complexion of the Brazilians. They tended to become whiter, the "bleaching process" to which some anthropologists refer. Table 7.1 illustrates that process, but it must be borne firmly in mind that much of the classification was done capriciously by census takers. According to the figures in the table, browns and blacks together constituted the following percentages of the population: 61.9 percent in 1872, 56 percent in 1890, and 35.9 percent in 1940. The figures, if roughly accurate, would seem to lend credence to the "bleaching" theory. A quaint concept of that process and the appreciation of it are superbly illustrated in the painting *Redemption of Ham* (1895) (the title itself is significant) by Modesto Brocos (1852–1936) (see A Pictorial Study of Brazil, in this book). The black grandmother with hands and eyes uplifted in thanks stands at the side of her beautiful mulatto daughter who in turn is seated next to her white Portuguese husband. On her lap sits her white child. The implication is that the family in three gener-

ations has gone from black to white. The expression of the grandmother as well as the presence of the palm branches represent the redemption acknowledged by the old woman. The presentation may be a bit dated today, but less than a century ago it represented the feeling of many Brazilians.

Of course it is difficult to speak of Brazil's large population—by 1920 Brazil was the ninth most populous country in the world—in absolute terms. The racial composition varied considerably from region to region. In the North, the Indian-Portuguese combination predominated, with a majority of the population some shade of light brown. The Northeast revealed an even wider variation caused by the amalgamation of Indian, black, and white, a characteristic of the West also. Along the coast from Pernambuco down to São Paulo the black influence predominated with the mulatto much in evidence. The white dominated in the South. Bahia was the blackest state, Santa Catarina the whitest.

While most Brazilians solemnly accepted the European racist doctrines, a few intellectuals raised their voices in protest, a prelude to later, deeper questioning. A few even began to speak in praise of a Brazilian "culture and race" to which the three races contributed. The literary critic Sílvio Romero preached throughout the last quarter of the nineteenth century and into the second decade of the twentieth that the African had made significant contributions to the creation of Brazilian culture. He concluded:

> The African race has had an enormous influence in Brazil, second only to that of the European. The African penetrated the confines of our most intimate life and in that way greatly molded our popular psychology. . . . The Portuguese alone could not repel the Indian nor till the soil, and therefore he had recourse to a powerful ally: the Negro from Africa. While on the one hand, the Indians proved themselves unproductive, fled, scattered into the hinterland, and died, the Africans, agile, strong, and able, arrived in ever greater numbers. They made possible the establishment of plantations and sugar mills, of towns and cities, and they penetrated the very bosom of the colonial families. The Indians, in general, were not up to the tasks and disappeared; the Negroes, allies of the white, prospered.

Found in nearly every part of the colony, the slaves lived closely with the families as domestic servants. From that intimate contact came a mixing of the races; the mulattoes appeared and were yet another link between the two races. The Negro worked in the fields producing the sugar, coffee, and other products known as "colonial" which Europe consumed. Just in the three factors of slavery, labor, and miscegenation, it is easy to discern the immense influence the Negroes had in the formation of the Brazilian people. Slavery, in spite of all its vices, worked as a social factor modifying our habits and customs. It enabled us to cultivate the land and to withstand in leisure the rigors of the climate. It developed as an economic force, producing our riches, and the Negro thus was a robust civilizer. The mixing of the races modified relations between the master and the slave, relaxed our customs, and produced the mulatto who constitutes the majority of our population and to a certain degree the most beautiful part of our race.

Also among the first to assign the African-Brazilians an important historical role in the development of Brazil was Afonso Celso, a contemporary of Romero, in his blatantly nationalistic *Porque Me Ufano do Meu País* (Why I Am Proud of My Country), first published in 1901 and repeatedly republished thereafter. The book was required reading in most primary schools. Celso boldly and proudly affirmed, "Today it is a generally accepted truth that three elements contributed to the formation of the Brazilian people, the American Indian, the African Negro, and the Portuguese. . . . Any one of those elements, or any combination of them, possesses qualities of which we should be proud." Celso's book contained a chapter praising the heroic resistance of the slaves at Palmares. The author lavishly bestowed the adjectives "courageous" and "noble" on the black defenders. Brazilians at first timidly explored the idea that their unique civilization was strengthened by Afro-Brazilian contributions. Inhibited by European racist doctrines, they slowly began to investigate those contributions. Their previous concepts changed, and their doubts and misgivings disappeared. The new nationalistic temper recoiled from any concept condemning Brazil to an inferior status. Clearly the racist doctrines seemed to twentieth-century Brazilian intellectuals as yet another European effort

to subjugate their country by an insidious mental colonization.

The pioneer of anthropological studies of the African in Brazil was Dr. Raimundo Nina Rodrigues, a physician born in Maranhão and trained in part at the medical school at Salvador. He worked in Bahia from 1890 to 1905, and it was at that time that he made his anthropological studies. He delved into African cultures with the intention of identifying their survival in Brazil and thus reconstituting the ethnic groups of blacks representing those cultures. He disproved the long-accepted idea that the Bantu predominated in Brazil by demonstrating the strong cultural presence of Sudanese groups, particularly the Yoruba, in Bahia. He was the first to study the Afro-Brazilian religions. After him came a small but important group of Bahian scholars, who continued research on the African contributions to Brazil.

Manuel Querino (1851–1923) maintained an active interest in labor and political affairs but, after the turn of the century, devoted increasing amounts of his time and energy to historical studies, in particular to research and writing on the contributions of the Africans to Brazil's growth. Those studies had a twofold purpose. On the one hand, he wanted to show his fellow blacks the vital contribution they had made to Brazil; on the other, he hoped to remind the white Brazilians of the debt they owed Africa and the African-Brazilians.

As Querino turned his attention to history, he hoped to rebalance the traditional emphasis on the European experience in Brazil. No black had ever given his perspective on Brazilian history before. Querino emerged as the first Brazilian—black or white—to detail, analyze, and do justice to the African contributions to Brazil. He presented his conclusions amid a climate of opinion which was at best indifferent, at worst, prejudiced or even hostile.

Querino, then, brought to Brazilian historiography the perspective of the African-Brazilian. Living in the Matatú Grande section of Salvador, immersed in and an intimate part of the black community, he knew perfectly well the habits, aspirations, and frustrations of black Brazilians. Speaking of his source material, Querino revealed that much of his informa-

tion came directly from respected black elders who spoke to him without inhibition since they recognized in him a sympathetic friend. Evidence exists that, besides writing about the African-Brazilians, he helped to defend them. He tried to bring to the attention of municipal officials the persecution inflicted on the practitioners of the Afro-Bahian religions. The police, labeling the religions as "barbarian and pagan," frequently raided the *terreiros* where the ceremonies were held, destroying property and injuring the participants. Querino's intervention on their behalf before the local government revealed once again his unique accomplishment in bridging different cultures and classes.

Historians certainly owe a heavy debt to Querino. He preserved considerable information on the art, artists, and artisans of Bahia. No one can do research on any of those subjects without consulting his works. Further, he is an excellent source for social history. His *As Artes na Bahia*, for example, includes an ample sampling of biographies of workers, artisans, and mechanics, those who qualify as "the ordinary people." Such unique biographies provide an invaluable look into the lives of the humble upon whom much of the growth of Brazil rests. He also offers in his essays abundant information on popular customs, culture, and religion.

Certainly one of Querino's chief contributions to Brazilian historiography was his insistence that national history take into account its African background and the presence and influence of the blacks. Brazil, he emphasized, was the result of a fusion of the Portuguese, Indian, and African, but the contributions of the Africans had gone unheralded. He sought to redress the balance in his suggestive essay "O Colono Prêto como Fator da Civilização Brasileira" (1918), now translated into English under the title *The African Contribution to Brazilian Civilization*. It abounded with insights, many of which later scholarship adopted and expanded—so much so that it is now difficult to appreciate Querino's originality. Subsequent scholars have emphasized, for example, that Africa provided the skilled and unskilled labor for Brazil. However, the essay suggested other significant contributions of African-Brazilians on which historians have yet to dwell. For example,

Querino assigned the black a principal role in the defense of Brazil and the maintenance of national unity.

At the same time, the literati looked anew at African-Brazilians. In the late nineteenth century, the naturalist novelists gave some attention to them. Aluísio Azevedo in his *O Cortiço* (The Tenement) (1890) and Adolfo Caminha in his *O Bom Crioulo* (The Good Blackman) (1895) described at length the black as a member of the urban proletariat. In some of his best novels, Lima Barreto raised his voice to protest the discrimination against blacks that manifested itself in Rio de Janeiro, described some of its ugliest aspects, and called for justice. In his lengthy poem "Juca Mulato" (1927), Menotti del Picchia characterized the Brazilian as mulatto, and in this work, for the first time in Brazilian poetry, a mulatto appeared as the hero. The poem received universal acclaim from the critics, both at home and abroad. The more enlightened attitudes toward the races removed embarrassments which earlier had inhibited or confused the intellectuals. Thus freed, they became increasingly proud of the nation's racial amalgamation, which they now viewed as an achievement, not a disgrace.

The more realistic appraisal of the African presence improved the blacks' position in Brazilian society. The myth has persisted that there is no racial prejudice. The facts, alas, contradict that boast. Racial prejudice did and does exist. Newspapers carried help-wanted advertisements seeking whites only. Until well after the middle of the twentieth century both the diplomatic corps and the naval officer corps remained lily-white. After World War II it was necessary to promulgate a law to punish overt discrimination. However, it must be emphasized that Brazil probably has less racial tension and less racial prejudice than any other multiracial society, past or present. The races mix freely in public places and interracial marriage is fairly common. A more formidable barrier than race is probably class. Class membership depends on a wide variety of factors and their combination: income, family history and/or connections, education, social behavior, tastes in housing, food, and dress, as well as appearance, personality, and talent. Traditionally the upper class has been

and still remains mainly white; the lower class, principally colored. The significant point, though, is that colored people can and do form a part, albeit a small part, of the upper class, just as whites are by no means uncommon among the humbler classes. Upward mobility exists and education promotes it. With effort, skill, and determination—as well as some luck—class barriers can be hurdled. But frankly it is a jump proportionately few people have been able to make.

Women began to play more varied roles in society. True, lower-class women always had worked at a variety of humble jobs and often formed a part of an economic team with their husbands and other members of the family. But now upper-class women were seen in novel surroundings, and women of the middle sectors strove to change old prejudices that confined them. The literacy rates provided by the census of 1872 revealed that there were 1,012,097 literate free males and 958 literate slave males, while there were 550,981 literate free females and 445 literate slave females. In major cities, the percentage of literate women was closer to that of males. Prior to World War I few women enjoyed the right to pursue a life outside the home on an equal footing with men. Their inferior position prompted Francisca Senhorinha da Motta Diniz to speak out in 1890 in protest. She outlined a feminist program:

> We want our emancipation and the regeneration of our customs; we want to regain our lost rights; we want true education, which has not been granted us, so that we can educate our children; we want pure instruction so we can know our rights and use them appropriately; we want to become familiar with our family affairs so that we can administer them if ever obliged to. In short, we want to understand what we do, the why and wherefore of matters; we want to be our husbands' companions, not their slaves; we want to know how things are done outside the home. What we do not want is to continue to be deceived.

Women worked but remained concentrated in relatively few occupations, especially those of the service sector, including teachers, clerical workers, and domestics. In 1872 a third of the teachers in Rio de Janeiro were female, a proportion that

rose to two-thirds by 1900. By then women also worked in railroad, telegraph, and mail offices; they entered the field of nursing in larger numbers.

The professions opened slowly to women. The Educational Reform Law of 1879 gave them access to the higher institutions of learning, and within a few years some females matriculated in law and medicine, first being graduated in the late 1880s. Dr. Rita Lobata, who was graduated from the Medical School in Bahia in 1887, was the first female physician trained in Brazil to practice medicine. Two years later a female lawyer defended a client in a courtroom for the first time. By the opening of the twentieth century, women had begun to organize—in the Feminine Republican party, for example—to express their political views.

Intellectuals expanded people's vision to include those "outside of society." João Capistrano de Abreu acknowledged the significant role of ordinary people in the forging of history. Indeed, Euclides da Cunha provided the perfect example of those people "making" history in his *Rebellion in the Backlands*. Novelists, too, took up the story of the humble, a good example being Azevedo's *The Tenement*. The painter José Ferraz de Almeida Júnior (1850–1899) rattled the foundations of the art salons in the 1880s when he displayed "The Woodcutter." His canvass featured a half-nude *caboclo* (backwoodsman), a realistic figure lounging in a romantic landscape, resting from his efforts to clear a forest. It was not the depiction of a bare-skinned proletarian that shocked the bourgeoisie: they saw such figures in daily life; they had seen such figures as part of the background in other paintings. But never had they seen a painting whose single purpose was to glorify such a lowly fellow, placing him squarely in the foreground, emphasizing both muscle and sensuality. Almeida expanded the content of Brazilian art. The ordinary person predominated, the "outsider" intruded. That reality discomfited most viewers of the period. In the final analysis, these perceptive intellectuals were simply preparing Brazilians for the twentieth century.

The Brazilians' growing understanding of themselves by

the early decades of the twentieth century, coupled with their pride in the nation's prosperity and achievements, encouraged a nationalism characterized by a literary historian of the period, Júlio Barbuda, as "the emotional synthesis of the fatherland." Nationalism ceased to be that simple defensive force that had characterized it throughout the nineteenth century. In the twentieth century it became the aggressive means of obtaining a leadership role abroad, of destroying patrimonial institutions and colonial patterns, of liberating Brazil from foreign control, and thereby of developing a modern, industrialized, indigenous society. Nationalism in its new, positive form was a powerful force described by Afonso Celso as "the incalculable dynamo of energy of our times . . . the lever which moves the world." It brought to Brazil a new self-confidence exemplified in Celso's cry: "We will grow, we will prosper. Education and perfection will come. We are still in the dawn of our greatness. We will arrive inevitably at the brilliance and full heat of mid-day . . . We will be the second or first power of the world."

Since the Paraguayan War the military had felt itself to be the embodiment of patriotic feeling, an opinion strengthened after the overthrow of the monarchy, when it became the most important single national institution. The army officers in particular—of which there were 3,352 in 1896—felt an obligation to wield the potent moderating power as Pedro II had so wisely and ably done. From 1889 to 1894, the military openly controlled political power. In the years thereafter, the officers manipulated it more discreetly. The governments of the Old Republic deferred to the ideas and ambitions of these officers. Militarism became an increasingly important aspect of political life, and the issue of the position of the military in the republic predominated in the 1910 presidential campaign. Militarism triumphed with the election of Marshal Hermes da Fonseca to the presidency.

Clearly there was much that was new in Brazil by 1922. Urbanization, industrialization, and modernization were trends well under way. Immigration continued to contribute to the change. Nationalism and militarism, both forces still in the

process of being defined, were already powerful instruments which would significantly alter the course of Brazilian evolution.

Despite the changing aspect of Brazil, the past by no means had been eradicated. It still cast a long shadow across the twentieth century. Brazil remained predominantly rural. In 1920, over 70 percent of the employed males were engaged in agriculture. A few products, among which coffee was by far the most important, dominated an economy that retained unmistakable vestiges of mercantilism. The *latifundia* and monoculture imbued the economy with the dependency patterns of the past. A privileged, landed oligarchy continued to rule, exercising its prerogatives under the cloak of constitutional provisions. Ignorance and paternalism neutralized the masses. In 1920, more than 64 percent of those over fifteen years of age were illiterate. Modernization, as it unfolded after 1850, failed to diminish dependency. Ironically it strengthened foreign control. Obviously much yet remained to be changed in order for Brazil to fulfill its ambition to develop.

Intellectual and Political Ferment

During the 1920s the intellectuals, always a potent force in the formation of Brazilian public opinion, articulated new challenges to established order and practice. As in the past they did not hesitate to import from Europe ideas that suited them or their objectives. In that tradition, a small group of young and avant-garde intellectuals introduced the latest artistic themes and expressions of the twentieth century. Returning from Europe in 1912, Oswaldo de Andrade awakened the first interest in Futurism, a radical artistic movement promoted in Europe by a group of Italians in revolt against realism. It urged a greater freedom of artistic expression. The idea of disregarding tradition and concentrating on the present and future fascinated young Brazilian intellectuals. They experimented with freer verse and literary forms. Meanwhile, in 1914, the painter Anita Malfatti had returned to São Paulo

from study in Germany and presented an exhibition of her startling paintings in the German Expressionist style. Three years later she introduced Cubism to the Brazilians. The sculptor Vítor Brecheret, who had studied in Italy, joined the courageous young painter and exhibited his own strong and novel works.

Reliance on European culture was regarded with mixed emotions. On the one hand, Europe provided a lively inspiration for arts; on the other, overdependence on Europe disturbed the young Brazilian intellectuals, who felt they had neglected their own homeland to favor foreign modes and trends, that the lure of Europe had blinded them to their own surroundings. They felt guilty that they had failed to heed the advice of Sílvio Romero and João Capistrano de Abreu, among others, to deemphasize the preference given to European values. The pulse of an intense nationalist feeling—as evidenced by the rearmament of the army and navy, the creation of the Indian Protection Service, the foundation of the *Revista do Brasil*, the organization of the League of National Defense, and the campaign in favor of obligatory military service—stirred their consciences. They resolved to reduce their reliance on European culture and to explore their own. Futurism—itself, of course, a European import—provided one formula; it freed them from restraints and patterns of the past. They turned their attention to the present and to their immediate surroundings. They set about to discover Brazil. To define and encourage national culture were their dual objectives, and in fulfilling them they intended to declare Brazil's cultural independence.

Appropriately, their activities reached a peak in 1922 during the centennial celebrations of independence. The impressive centennial exposition in Rio de Janeiro amply demonstrated the economic growth of the country in the preceding hundred years. The intellectuals in São Paulo determined to show a parallel cultural maturity by issuing a manifesto of cultural independence. The poet Menotti del Picchia phrased their goal as the "Brazilianization of Brazil." "Let us forget the marble of the Acropolis and the towers of the Gothic cathedrals," exhorted Ronald de Carvalho, "We are the sons

of the hills and the forests. Stop thinking of Europe. Think of America." Impelled by such enthusiasm, a group of intellectuals in São Paulo organized the Modern Art Week (February 11–17, 1922) during which they defined and enunciated the objectives of their Modernist movement.

The activities of the Modern Art Week centered in the São Paulo Municipal Theater. Graça Aranha, a highly respected author of the previous generation and a member of the Brazilian Academy of Letters, opened the sessions with a speech proclaiming that the intellectuals were in rebellion against the stagnant state of the arts in Brazil. The younger generation spoke through Ronald de Carvalho and Menotti del Picchia. During the week poets illustrated the revolutionary form and content of modern poetry by reading from their own works. Oswaldo de Andrade read equally novel selections from his prose. The youthful Heitor Villa-Lobos conducted his own music, based on folk themes and employing indigenous instruments. Ernani Braga contributed other compositions of a nationalistic inspiration. The precocious Guiomar Novais interpreted many of the selections, revealing a talent that soon won her international fame as a concert pianist. Modern paintings and sculpture were displayed in the foyer of the theater. In that manner, the Paulista intellectuals succeeded in introducing to a curious—at times hostile—public the latest artistic trends as well as their growing appreciation of the Brazilian environment. The intellectual excitement in São Paulo proved contagious. It spread quickly to the other major cities. Poets declaimed and writers lectured in such diverse places as Manaus, Fortaleza, Belo Horizonte, and Pôrto Alegre. New literary journals sprung up wherever the dedicated revolutionaries sowed their intellectual seeds.

True to their declared goals, the intellectuals weakened their bonds with Europe and increased their concern with national identity. A profound psychological change took place in which national values supplanted foreign ones. Perhaps Graça Aranha best summarized the historic moment in a speech he gave before the citadel of literary traditionalism, the Brazilian Academy of Letters, in 1924. In it he defined national culture as a European legacy that had been transformed by

the conditions of the New World. Brazilian culture owed a debt to Europe but it was also the creation of its own environment. Such opinions harmonized with those being expressed throughout the hemisphere, as the Latin Americans began their struggle to achieve their own cultural identity. Mexico, in particular, because of the profound and introspective Revolution of 1910, led the way for the Latin American community toward spiritual and cultural freedom. After 1922 Brazil rapidly took its own place in the vanguard of that movement.

The results of the Modernist movement were quickly apparent and nowhere more so than in letters. Speaking for his fellow intellectuals, the youthful Sérgio Buarque de Holanda argued, "Brazil has to have a national literature." The best way to create such a literature in his opinion was to respect national traditions, to obtain inspiration from national sources, and to listen to the "profound voices of our race." The writers brazenly attacked the stylistic conventions inherent in their devotion to Europe, which they alleged inhibited their own inventiveness. Freedom of form, a vigorous style rich in fresh images and vernacularisms, and originality of expression characterized the new literature.

A concern with Brazilian themes accompanied the preoccupation with new styles. To better explain Brazil, the intelligentsia probed the national psychology, questioned national motives, and reexamined the past. The number of folkloric studies multiplied. By the end of the 1920s a respectable bibliography on the subject existed. Mário de Andrade, who emerged as the dean of the scholars in the field, undertook an active campaign to acquaint his compatriots with their own folk culture and to persuade them to study that invaluable source of information and inspiration. Later he established courses in ethnography and folklore as well as a museum of folklore in São Paulo. Not surprisingly, folklore made its way into national literature, as exemplified by Andrade's novel, *Macunaíma*, published in 1928. Macunaíma, a Brazilian folk hero, has been called both the Peer Gynt and the Paul Bunyan of the tropics. He seemed to synthesize the positive qualities as well as the defects of the Brazilians. Andrade delighted in

employing numerous regionalisms and popular expressions to enliven and "Brazilianize" his prose.

In Recife in 1926 at the First Brazilian Congress of Regionalism, the young sociologist Gilberto Freyre introduced into Brazilian studies and popularized a significant theme that thereafter would exercise a powerful influence on national thought. He expanded the neglected ideas of von Martius and Romero that the uniqueness of Brazilian civilization sprang from the contributions of three races. In 1933, his ideas appeared in *Casa Grande e Senzala*, an immediate classic that was later translated into English as *The Masters and the Slaves*. The national and international acclaim given the book freed the intellectuals from many of their cultural complexes and made the themes of African contributions and of racial miscegenation more acceptable than they had been hitherto. Miscegenation, it was at last recognized, had made Brazil a more homogeneous nation, despite its gargantuan size. Freyre's cogent discussion of the creation of a unique civilization in Brazil opened vast new areas for research and study. Before then most of the works written about the blacks concerned the institution of slavery. Such was not the case after 1933, when scholars sought to emphasize the African heritage in the formation of Brazil.

The new enthusiasm for the study of the African-Brazilians reached a peak during the celebrations in 1938 marking the golden anniversary of the abolition of slavery. In Belo Horizonte, the state's Historical Institute and its Fine Arts Society jointly sponsored an "Afro-Brazilian Studies Week" that featured an art exhibit and a series of lectures. Mário de Andrade organized for the city of São Paulo an elaborate program of speeches, dances, and music. Rio de Janeiro feted the occasion in a similar manner.

The literati also gave their attention to the African influences on Brazil. At the same time that Freyre was preparing his sociological study, Jorge de Lima was writing poems on black themes. Some of his works paid tribute to the moral superiority of the black in a manner reminiscent of the treatment earlier accorded the Indian. In *Urucungo,* his short

book of poetry published in 1933, Raul Bopp treated exclusively Afro-Brazilian themes. Blacks also appeared as the protagonists in novels, not as a curiosity, as had frequently happened in the past, but as respected members of the community. José Lins do Rego's *O Moleque Ricardo* (The Young Man Richard) and Jorge Amado's *Jubiabá,* both published in 1935, illustrated that trend.

The ferment of the 1920s also stirred the intellectuals to attempt new interpretations of their homeland. From the pen of Paulo Prado came the most penetrating analysis of Brazil in the 1920s. Pessimism dominated his *Retrato do Brasil* (Portrait of Brazil), published in 1928. His opening words, "In a radiant land live a sad people," set the tone for the study. He viewed the history of Brazil as the chaotic development of two passions, sensuality and greed. In order for Brazil to progress, according to the author, it was essential to first isolate and diagnose the weaknesses of Brazilian character and then to correct them. His pessimism contrasted sharply with the buoyant optimism of other writers, such as Afonso Celso. In fact, those two represent the extremes of the views Brazilians take of their own country.

It was soon apparent that beneath the excitement of cultural nationalism swirled powerful political currents. Most of the contributors to the intellectual ferment became deeply involved in politics in the 1920s and thereafter. Their political preferences varied widely from the far right to the far left. In common, they all shared a bitter disappointment with the effete republic and a desire to reform the political structure and to reorient the nation. By the mid-1920s, a majority of the intellectuals withheld their allegiance to the republic. The mounting discontent with the governments originated not from the fact that the administrations of that decade differed from their predecessors—they did not—but rather from the fact that social and economic conditions had changed, a change the political system failed to register. The dysfunction signaled that political arrangements increasingly failed to accommodate social aspirations. The intellectuals spoke out to call to the attention of the public the need for new solutions to

old problems. Their persuasive arguments and their easy access to the press enabled them to mold as well as to express public opinion.

Their influential voices joined those of the single most powerful group in Brazil, the military, to express a dissatisfaction with the course the republic had taken. Few would deny the significant role of the military in the republic, but after 1894—and with the exception of the Hermes da Fonseca regime—the officers left the overt administration of the government in the hands of civilians representing the coffee elite. In turn, those governments scrupulously provided generous budgets for the army and the navy. As a result, for several decades relations between the republican governments and the military hierarchy tended to be harmonious. After World War I, the tacit accord between the two ended. The change began under President Pessôa who boldly vetoed a bill to increase military pay and appointed two civilians to head the Ministries of War and Navy. Since the advent of the republic, the military had been accustomed to holding those portfolios. The reaction to the unexpected appointments was immediate and negative. The navy openly, though vainly, threatened the president. The officers manifested a growing concern for their position, privileges, and honor. Offended and displeased, they drew back from the government. The situation became more complex and dangerous in 1921, when Marshal Hermes da Fonseca returned to Brazil after spending six years in Europe. He provided the prestige and leadership under which various military factions could unite. In recognition of his unique role, the officers duly elected him president of the powerful Clube Militar in Rio de Janeiro, a position that lent to his pronouncements the voice of all the military. Soon he began to make ominous statements which seemed to bode no good for the civilian government. Dissatisfied with the course Pessôa pursued, Marshal Hermes observed, "The political situations change, but the Army remains." With that veiled reminder of its stability, its continuity, and its exercise of the *poder moderador*, the military warned the government of its dissatisfaction.

With exports, coffee prices, and the rate of exchange all falling as Europe recovered its prewar vitality, the Pessôa government already had experienced its share of troubles, when, in early 1921, the question of presidential succession surfaced. In accordance with a previous agreement between the two important states of São Paulo and Minas Gerais, the young governor of Minas Gerais, Artur da Silva Bernardes, was slated to be the next president. Protest erupted from the states that had not been party to that exclusive agreement. They increasingly resented the dominance in the selection of those to hold public office exercised by those two coffee states. In disgust, they formed their own coalition, the Republican Reaction and nominated Nilo Peçanha for the presidency. That coalition allied Rio Grande do Sul, Rio de Janeiro, Pernambuco, and Bahia with the military. As a bitter campaign got under way it exposed deepening national divisions and frustrations.

The Republican Reaction exerted great efforts to woo the disaffected military. In October of 1921, the *Correio da Manhã*, a Rio de Janeiro daily long in opposition to the government, published a letter, said to be in the handwriting of Bernardes, that was offensive in its remarks about the military. Bernardes categorized the letter as a forgery. The Clube Militar insisted immediately it was authentic. Offended by the letter, most of the military officers followed the lead of Marshal Hermes and pledged their support to Nilo Peçanha. Events surrounding the election of the governor of Pernambuco further alienated the military from the federal government and hence from its official candidate. The opposition accused President Pessôa of putting local army units at the disposal of gubernatorial candidates favorable to the federal government. As president of Clube Militar, Hermes da Fonseca telegraphed the army garrison in Recife, asking it to defy the supposed orders of the federal government. The government arrested Hermes for signing the extraordinary telegram and shut down Clube Militar for six months. The presidential elections held in March 1922 did nothing to improve relations between the government and the military. Bernardes won, receiving 56 percent

of the votes. The candidate favored by the military had lost. For the first time in the history of the republic, the military was alienated from the government.

In repeating events of the last decade of the empire, alienation occurred on two levels. The highest-ranking officers, although unfriendly to the government, were reluctant to take up arms to overthrow it. More than their aroused ire was needed to entice them into action. They had to be convinced that military honor, privilege, and prestige were irrevocably compromised or at stake. The junior officers cared less for those vanities. Imbued with idealism, they sought a government pledged to reform and strengthen the nation. The apparent weakness of the republic, the pettiness and vanity of the politicians, the corruption, fraud, and inefficiency which surrounded and pervaded the government disturbed them.

The junior officers displayed little of the patience of their seniors. A small group of them resolved after the elections of 1922 to end the monopoly that the coffee interests exercised over the government and to purify it. Poorly planned and badly coordinated, on July 5, 1922, a revolt broke out at the fort in Igrejinha on Copacabana Beach under the leadership of some lieutenants stationed there. The cadets at the military academy joined the rebellion, but they were quickly brought to order. In the crisis, the senior officers gave their loyalty to the government and led their troops against Copacabana. The rebellious fort fired a few desultory rounds before it came under bombardment from both land and sea. Most of the rebels surrendered to the government forces, but a quixotic band of eighteen came onto the beach to fight it out, in vain, with the overpowering forces of the government. There most of them dramatically gave their lives for their vaguely defined cause.

As an isolated incident, the revolt at Copacabana appears to project little meaning or importance. In retrospect, however, it is possible to relate the heroics on the beach to a larger movement under way in Brazil in the 1920s. As part of a general protest against the eroding effectiveness of a nearly moribund republic, it assumes considerable importance. Fur-

thermore, it initiated a series of revolts which would end with the overthrow of the republic in 1930. Its occurrence in 1922 helps to highlight that year as the beginning of an active repudiation of the past, a manifestation of disappointment and frustration with the course Brazil had followed. The Copacabana revolt, coupled with the pronouncements culminating in Modern Art Week, were notification that a new generation, representative of the increasingly well-defined urban middle groups, challenged the nation's hoary political, economic, and social institutions and sought to propel Brazil into the future. Although vague, their plans adamantly demanded change and reform. They infused questions of social justice into political discourse, as did the Communist party and the Roman Catholic church.

Other manifestations favorable to change also occurred in 1922. In that year, the Roman Catholic church expressed a new interest and concern in the plight of the proletariat. The resourceful Sebastião Leme, later to be elevated to cardinal, oversaw the foundation of Workers' Circles, whose principal purpose was to improve the temporal lot of the working class. The Circles operated cooperatives, hospitals, clinics, pharmacies, and schools for workers, activities publicly frowned upon by the more conservative elements of society. At that time Brazilian Catholicism was undergoing a spiritual renovation.

Reflecting a small minority's desire for radical change, the Communist party of Brazil was founded in 1922. Three unique features for the Brazilian politics of that time characterized that party: it was national in scope, well disciplined, and offered a firm and identifiable ideology.

Varied forms of protest came together in the centennial year. The intellectuals issued their proclamation of independence; the Roman Catholic church invigorated its concern with the poor and proclaimed its indelible imprint on Brazilian nationality; the military initiated its physical protest against the government; and the Communist party emerged to voice a radical program of change. After 1922, Brazil would never be quite the same. New forces stirred, for the time being imperceptible in their direction and consequence.

President Bernardes proved unable to master the situation. He inherited a legacy of resentment of the domination of the coffee elite. The financial picture was "gloomy": heavy debts, budget deficits, declining exports, and the lowest rates of exchange since 1894. The political turmoil appeared equally discouraging: the Federal District and Rio de Janeiro were under a state of siege, and civil war had erupted in Rio Grande do Sul. Further, Bernardes, in order to get vengeance on Nilo Peçanha, helped to create a situation in the state of Rio de Janeiro, the political base of his opponent, which required federal intervention. Nor did Bernardes display an eagerness to win the much-needed support of the military. He refused to pardon the young officers who plotted and revolted in 1922. The government tried, convicted, and sentenced them, treatment that only increased military opposition to the president. One group that Bernardes could not afford to alienate was the coffee interests. Here he faced a dilemma. Personally he favored financial orthodoxy and thus questioned valorization. However, beholden to the coffee interests for their support, he could not neglect their appeals for guarantees that coffee prices would slip no farther on the market. He decided to turn the supervision of valorization over to São Paulo and ordered the Bank of Brazil to follow a generous policy toward the coffee planters.

Criticism cascaded over the president, who shut himself up in Catete Palace, made few public appearances, and sternly concentrated on maintaining public order. One of the few to come to the defense of the beleaguered president was Jackson de Figueiredo, a powerful polemicist and militant Roman Catholic lay leader. In his writings he assailed both the rising tide of nationalism and the restive young army officers. "Order above law," a phrase he coined, summarized part of his political philosophy. His prescribed treatment for the protesters of his day was "Club them!" He believed that threats to Brazilian nationality came not from foreign powers, as was a conventional belief among the nationalists, but from Protestantism, Masonry, and Judaism. Also contrary to the nationalistic trends of his age, he was pro-Portuguese, appreciating

and lauding those values and institutions that Portugal had transmitted to Brazil. Those opinions, forcefully stated, did little to rescue the president from unpopularity, and they serve best to represent a minority opinion expressed in the twenties by a few intellectuals.

Intensifying their demands for change, the young army officers waved the banner of rebellion again on July 5, 1924, this time in São Paulo. The rebels entrusted their leadership to a retired general, Isidoro Dias Lopes, but it was the young officers who provided the enthusiasm and impetus. The lieutenants maintained limited but significant contacts with the local laborers: by 1924 São Paulo was the major industrial city of South America. The rebels denounced Bernardes and made vague calls for the reformation of the republic. Loyalist forces converged on the city of São Paulo from all sides. After holding the city for twenty-two days, the rebels evacuated it and moved first west and then south. Meanwhile rebellion erupted briefly in Aracajú, Manaus, Belém, and, on a larger scale, in Rio Grande do Sul. In November the crew of the warship *São Paulo* mutinied in Guanabara Bay and sailed to asylum in Montevideo. Under the command of Captain Luís Carlos Prestes, rebels from Rio Grande do Sul moved northward to join the forces of Isidoro Lopes that had withdrawn from São Paulo. That unified body of rebels, which won national fame as the "Prestes Column," then began a rugged three-year odyssey (1924–1927) through the *sertão*. They marched northward into Maranhão before turning southwest and disbanding in Bolivia after a lengthy trek.

Prestes, dubbed the "Knight of Hope," exerted a strong mystic appeal to his followers and many elements of the Brazilian population who admired his bold if quixotic challenge to the government. Nonetheless, his efforts to arouse the populace to take up arms against that government failed. The peasants were still too much under the powerful sway of local *coroneis* to be enlisted into the ranks of rebellion. The countryside had never been the place to foment change in Brazil; the result of the Prestes Column demonstrated that in the mid-1920s it still was not. The discontented elements cen-

tered in the cities: the column never made contact with the urban protesters and consequently never tapped that potential reservoir of support.

The federal government scoffed at the significance of the rebellions and, as far as possible, ignored the discontent. Political maneuvering absorbed most of its energy. Coffee sales recovered from their decline of the early 1920s to rebound to new highs. The dictum that so long as coffee sold well the government could follow whatever course it preferred seemed true. Good prices and ready sales ensured the coffee interests' monopoly over the federal government.

In 1926, in accordance with a previous agreement between the two major coffee-producing states, Bernardes turned over the reins of government to the Paulista Washington Luís Pereira de Sousa, whose candidacy had not been challenged. He won 98 percent of the 700,000 votes cast. As a gesture of conciliation, the new president lifted the state of siege (an intrinsic part of the previous administration), and restored freedom of the press. Two matters dear to the hearts of the coffee planters also received his attention. First, the government encouraged the building of roads with the prompt initiation of two highway projects to connect Rio de Janeiro with São Paulo and Petropolis (the first step toward Belo Horizonte). Second, the government resolved to make financial reforms. To fulfill time-honored goals it balanced the budget. It scrupulously kept public finances in order. Similar to the Conversion Office under the Pena administration, a Stabilization Office issued a new paper currency backed by gold. By the end of the Bernardes administration, the government had embarked on a new experiment in coffee marketing, leaving the administration of it in the hands of the states. The experiment continued during the Luís government. São Paulo, with its powerful Coffee Institute, directed the marketing, limiting shipments and storing the beans, when necessary, to sell when the market was favorable. Able administration of the institute as well as optimum international conditions brought about a sharp rise in coffee prices.

The prosperity of the early years of the Washington Luís administration only thinly disguised the discontent with the

republic. Of course, some discontent had existed since the beginning of the republic. First, there had been the embittered Monarchists who assailed the New Republic. They were joined shortly by disillusioned Republicans who voiced their disappointment with the new regime. A *"complexo de remorso"* (feeling of remorse) saddened many. Afonso Celso, a Republican who by 1893 had become a Monarchist, lamented, "With remorse, I confess that I did attack, not rarely, the Emperor in the press and in parliament, attributing to him exclusive responsibility for all our ills. . . . Publicly I confess my contrition." One intellectual, Alfredo de Paiva, asked bluntly in 1891, "Where are the statesmen of the Republic?" A multitude echoed that embarrassing question during the following decades. Nostalgically men looked back to the "glories of the empire." They remembered the years prior to 1889 as ones of statesmanship, order, and liberty, and contrasted them with the passions, disorders, and repressions of the republic. Some of the literati reminisced and complained in print, further developing the literature of "remorse." Their writing reflected the deepening disappointment and frustration with the republic. The reality of the republic, they emphasized, differed diametrically from the theory and principles upon which it was based. Farias Brito, a fiery partisan for the establishment of the republic, sadly reflected in later judgment of it, "All the good of which I had dreamed, I saw transformed into anarchy and disorder, perturbation and injustice." In his *Retrato do Brasil*, the patrician critic Paulo Prado deprecated the evils of the republican political system and recommended, "We have used unsuccessfully many medicines for our malady. It remains to try surgery." Many liberal democrats concurred as they surveyed the history of coffee politics, the selfish regional monopolization of power, manipulated elections, the continuation of patriarchalism and colonialism, and the consistently impotent governments. The republic had not fulfilled their hopes.

The restive young military officers, the impatient and articulate sons of the urban middle groups, also judged the republic unsatisfactory. Their dissatisfaction, then, represented the opinions of those who felt themselves marginal-

ized politically and economically by coffee politics. Protest burst into open rebellion in 1922 and 1924 and during the Prestes march. Although their objectives were cryptic and muddled at first, the young officers gradually began to codify them. By 1926, the *tenente* (lieutenant) movement had acquired a somewhat more identifiable philosophy, even though—it must be emphasized—it never became precise. Above all else, the *tenentes* maintained a mystical faith that somehow a military revolution would alter the habits of the country and provide the impetus to propel it into the modern age. Reform, not democracy, was their primary concern. They wanted to retire the entrenched politicians and modernize the nation; then, and only then, would they consent to return the nation to constitutional rule. They correctly pointed out that fewer than 5 percent of the adult population met literacy and other qualifications to become voters. Between 1894 and 1906, an average of 2.4 percent of the population voted in presidential elections; between 1910 and 1930, participation averaged 2.7 percent. Democracy under the Old Republic played as farce. The *tenentes* proposed a government that would unite all Brazilians and thereby negate the debilitating regionalisms. A powerful central government was their goal. Believing reform incompatible with democracy, the young officers assigned the state a major role in transforming society and the economy. The change they advocated would come from above. Revealing strong "social democratic" tendencies, the *tenentes* proposed government recognition of trade unions and cooperatives, a minimum wage, maximum working hours, child labor legislation, agrarian reform, and nationalization of the mines. The magazine *5 de Julho*, which spoke for the Prestes Column, expressed many of the ideas of the young military revolutionaries:

> Reasons: financial and economic disorder; exorbitant taxes; administrative dishonesty; lack of justice; perversion of the vote; subordination of the press; political persecution; disrespect for the autonomy of the states; lack of social legislation; reform of the constitution under the state of siege. Ideals: to assure a regime loyal to the republican constitution; to establish free primary in-

struction and professional and technical training throughout the country; to assure liberty of thought; to unify justice, putting it under the aegis of the Supreme Court; to unify the Treasury; to assure municipal liberty; to castigate the defrauders of the patrimony of the people; to prevent professional politicians from becoming rich at public expense; to account strictly for public funds.

Clearly much of the program advocated by the *tenentes* favored the urban middle groups.

Returned to their secondary position in 1894, those middle groups increasingly resented the economic and political monopoly the large *fazendeiros,* particularly the coffee planters, wielded in the republic. They decried the many favors the government lavished on the planters. Burgeoning coffee harvests in the 1920s alarmed them. Between 1927 and 1929 production exceeded 21 million sacks, of which scarcely 14 million were exported. Subtracting the coffee consumed in Brazil, it still meant that the public—especially the bourgeoisie—bore the financial burden of valorizing the coffee kept in storage, and, by extension, of supporting international coffee prices. The government, faithful to its coffee backers, borrowed more abroad to make valorization feasible. A foreign debt which in 1926 reached $900 million with annual interest of $175 million in 1930 shot up to $1,181 million with a debt service charge of $200 million yearly. It was at that moment that the United States—whose rapid industrialization in the last half of the nineteenth century and whose military prowess during World War I had aroused the admiration of the middle groups—supplanted Great Britain as Brazil's major foreign investor. By 1927 North Americans owned about 35 percent of Brazil's entire federal debt. The middle groups remained spectators to all these events. In the elections of 1910 and 1922, when a possibility for change was offered, they lacked sufficient strength to seize it. Further, they failed to understand that the various military rebellions in the 1920s could have been turned to their advantage. Indicative of their weakness, the middle groups failed to coordinate their desires for modernization with the similar desires of the young officers.

People professing nationalistic inclinations also counted themselves among those disgruntled with the republic. On the one hand, they harbored suspicions of the coffee oligarchy, which seemed too intimately linked with world markets and far too international in its outlook. Consequently, its interest could hardly coincide with national interests. On the other hand, the nationalists viewed with alarm the rampant regionalism that the permissive Constitution of 1891 encouraged. In some state capitals, the state flag flew from every mast, while one searched in vain to locate the Brazilian colors. The militia of São Paulo employed its own French military mission to train it and stood at a strength and readiness capable of challenging the federal army. The nationalists favored a government which would subordinate both regionalism and internationalism to the well-being and advancement of the nation.

Few means of effective protest existed. Political parties—which could have provided some alternatives—continued to be small and poorly organized. In contrast to the system fostered by the empire, not one national party existed, with the minor exception after 1922 of the Communist party. The Republican party maintained its strength in most of the important states, but the only national link between the highly individual regional organizations was through the letters, telegrams, or telephone calls of the president of the republic to the presidents of the states. The nationalists tried at various times to organize parties to reflect their views, but their organizations always remained small and local. Consequently their message seldom extended beyond the confines of half a dozen coastal cities. Their platforms contained a variety of planks, such as the transference of the capital of Brazil from the coast to the interior, nationalization of commerce, retention of profits within the country, nationalization of the press, creation of a national theater, control of rents to limit foreign control of property, establishment of agricultural credit, closer relations with the Latin American community, and a stronger federal government. The proposal to relocate the federal capital to the interior, an old dream of patriots, symbolized their aspiration to "Brazilianize" Brazil. The desires to nationalize

commerce and to control rents, and, to a lesser degree, to nationalize the press, create a national theater, and keep profits within the country reflected Brazilians' continuing resentment of the resident Portuguese and their antipathy toward the former metropolis.

An elitist, restricted political democracy infused no social democracy and promoted scant economic progress for the majority of the citizens. From the disaffected middle groups came the rank and file as well as the leaders of the protest against the republican governments. Those groups felt most pinched and thwarted by the static political system. The masses, rural and urban, fatalistically accepted their menial position. The middle groups, through the outcries of the young military officers, the intellectuals, and the nationalists, refused to. They sought higher social distinctions and greater political power and, what is very important, they thought they saw the possibility of attaining them. Hopes for progress and social democracy energized large numbers of the discontented.

It took a grave political error and an international crisis to end the power monopoly exercised by the coffee oligarchy. Washington Luís made the political error by selecting as his successor another Paulista, the young and talented governor of São Paulo, Júlio Prestes. The old politicians bridled at the affront of one of their number being passed over in favor of a younger candidate. The noncoffee states protested that yet another president would serve the exclusive interests of the coffee producers. All literate Brazil might have laughed when Mendes Fradique wittily noted, "The twenty states of Brazil are two: São Paulo and Minas Gerais," but that laughter rang hollow in the other eighteen states, embittered by long neglect. Of greatest significance was the friction between the two coffee allies, Minas Gerais and São Paulo, caused by the selection of Prestes. Favoring alternation in office, the Mineiros claimed that the presidency should be returned to one of them. The split between São Paulo and Minas Gerais over the presidential succession offered the noncoffee states a rare opportunity to attempt to capture the presidency for themselves. It politically united disaffected Minas Gerais and ambitious Rio Grande do Sul, potentially a powerful alliance and

a challenge to the coffee triangle that had dominated the Old Republic. Still, São Paulo might have been powerful enough to enforce its will had not a deepening world depression knocked the bottom out of the coffee market, thereby weakening its economic and psychological position.

The economic debacle of North Atlantic capitalism in 1929 and 1930 sent the Brazilian economy reeling. Between 1929 and 1931 the price of coffee plummeted from 22.5 to 8 cents a pound. Between 1929 and 1932, Brazil's foreign trade fell 37 percent by volume and 67 percent by value. The substantial gold reserves disappeared by the end of 1930, and the exchange rate, relatively stable between 1927 and 1930, reached a new low. The full weight of the disaster fell on São Paulo, whose warehouses groaned with unsold coffee. In 1930, 26 million sacks lay in storage, a million more than the world consumed in 1929 and twice the amount Brazil usually exported in a year. Such an economic reverse made the coffee oligarchy vulnerable to political attack at a time when disenchantment with its rule soared. Opponents mounted the attack on São Paulo over the question of the presidential succession in 1930.

To combat the candidacy of Júlio Prestes, a coalition composed of Minas Gerais, Rio Grande do Sul, Paraíba, and by an assortment of small opposition parties, urban middle groups, young military officers, nationalists, and intellectuals took shape under the name the "Liberal Alliance." Through an agreement between the politicians of Rio Grande do Sul and Minas Gerais, the Alliance nominated the gaúcho Getúlio Vargas for president and João Pessôa of Paraíba for vice-president. Their program, announced at the end of July 1929, called for an amnesty for all participants in the 1922–1926 rebellions, new election laws, social legislation, a reorganization of the educational and judicial systems, and accelerated economic development. Those planks seemed to promise change and to further modernization.

During the campaign the two candidates behaved in the manner tolerated by the practices of the republic: they were wheeler-dealers, double-crossing each other and their allies, contradicting themselves, and freely dispensing platitudes. In

the process, Vargas made a curious pact with Washington Luís. He promised not to campaign outside of Rio Grande do Sul and to accept the results of the election in return for Luís' agreement not to support the opposition to the Liberal Alliance in Rio Grande do Sul and his promise to use his influence, along with that of Prestes, to urge Congress to seat the deputies, whoever they might be, elected from Rio Grande do Sul. Excitement engulfed the campaign as oratory built to a crescendo. Despite some minor disturbances, the election held on March 1, 1930, was generally peaceful. Prestes triumphed, claiming 1,100,000 of 1,900,000 votes cast. The rural oligarchy had succeeded in marshalling enough votes to more than offset those of the urban malcontents.

Disappointment over the results of the election permeated Brazil. Vargas, however, seemed to accept them, although he perfunctorily cried fraud, a safe enough accusation that all losing candidates were expected to make. In May the Congress refused to seat the deputies from Minas Gerais and Paraíba elected on the opposition ticket; resentment of the government candidates' victory welled up. The political situation grew tenser. It took only the crack of an assassin's pistol in Recife to set in motion a far-reaching rebellion. Personal and local matters were the principal cause of the assassination of João Pessôa on July 25, 1930, but the opposition linked the murder to the political group of Washington Luís, and the nation in general regarded it as politically motivated. The tragedy infused new energy, unity, and purpose into the Liberal Alliance and its adherents, who determinedly set about to plan the overthrow of the Washington Luís government by force.

Coordinated from three states—Rio Grande do Sul, Minas Gerais, and Paraíba—the revolt broke out on October 3. Forces from Paraíba under the command of Juarez Távora, a *tenente* from the uprisings of the 1920s, marched southward, capturing Recife and Salvador with no difficulty. Led by Pedro Aurélio de Góes Monteiro, the rebels from Rio Grande do Sul moved northward toward São Paulo. And from Minas Gerais insurgent forces invaded the states of Espírito Santo and Rio de Janeiro. The government proved unable to halt the ad-

vances. One might have expected the coffee planters to rush to the support of the Paulista president and his hand-picked successor, but many of them, troubled by the Great Depression and concerned by the government's reluctance to mobilize all its resources behind valorization, adopted a neutral if not hostile attitude toward the faltering government in Rio de Janeiro. Despite all the civilian support for the rebellion begun by the Liberal Alliance, its success would not have been possible without the support or at least acquiescence of the military. First the *tenentes* active in the 1920s revolts resolutely joined the ranks of the rebels. Then unit after unit of the army spontaneously adhered to the cause. Finally the senior officers decided that the moribund republic no longer merited further support. They seized power from the president on October 24 and established a junta of three officers as an interim government. Meanwhile, the journey of the chief of the Liberal Alliance from Pôrto Alegre to Rio de Janeiro turned into a triumphal procession. Nowhere was Vargas more enthusiastically cheered than in São Paulo. Apparently to those who shouted his "vivas," he embodied hope and promise. To a considerable number, he symbolized change. He reached the capital, where the atmosphere was already festive, on October 31. Four days later, the junta handed him the sash of office. The military had played the arbiter in politics again, and the Old Republic ended as it began, with a military movement. The military coup, a political miscalculation, and a deepening world depression were the immediate causes for the demise of the republic. More basically, industrialization, urbanization, the spread of nationalism, and a growing desire for change set in motion forces with which the ineffectual and unimaginative Old Republic could not cope.

Shifting Patterns of Power

After accepting control of the nation from the military junta, Getúlio Dórtico Vargas governed for nearly a generation, first as chief of the provisional government (1930–1934), next as

constitutional president elected by Congress (1934–1937), then as dictator (1937–1945), and finally as constitutional president elected by the people (1951–1954). His position in modern Brazilian history remains so dominant that even the governments of the 1960s fell under the shadow of his formidable legacy. Any person wielding such potent influence is bound to be controversial, and over the years Vargas has inspired paeans of praise and elicited curses of damnation.

Vargas was born in 1883 on the rich cattle estate of his family in São Borja, Rio Grande do Sul, just across the Uruguay River from Argentina. After preparatory studies in Minas Gerais, he enrolled in the military school at Rio Pardo in his natal state and, still a cadet, served in garrisons in Pôrto Alegre and Mato Grosso. He abandoned his military training to take a degree from the Faculty of Law in Pôrto Alegre in 1907. Soon thereafter he entered politics, spending the formative years of his political career under the tutelage and discipline of the perennial governor of Rio Grande do Sul, Antônio Augusto Borges de Medeiros, in an atmosphere of Comtian positivism. Once under way, his political rise was meteoric: federal deputy (1924–1926), minister of finance (1926–1928), governor of Rio Grande do Sul (1928–1930), and chief of state in 1930. Short, wiry, with a winning smile, Vargas proved to be gifted with unusually keen political intuition. Above all else he was a realist, and his political decisions generally reflected that pragmatism. Often he has been termed a *caudilho* in the Spanish American tradition, but it would require exaggerated license to compare him with contemporaneous caudilhos such as Juan Vicente Gómez of Venezuela, Jorge Ubico of Guatemala, or Rafael Trujillo of the Dominican Republic. Vargas governed more or less within the Brazilian tradition. Moderation and affability tempered his administration. Absent were the extremes of pomp, terror, and inflexibility so often characteristic of Spanish American dictatorships. He seemed disposed in most cases to follow the currents of his time, to innovate if necessary, and to experiment when required. The prospects of change did not frighten him, but he approached change cautiously.

Surrounding Vargas and urging reforms during the early

years of his administration were the *tenentes,* the radicals of the rebellion. They hoped to remove the corrupt and reactionary old-line politicians from office, strengthen the central government, discipline the local oligarchies, foster nationalism, and promote economic and social change. Those young idealists soon discovered both the strength and conservatism of the politicians and senior army officers who thwarted their drive to initiate change. Vargas had consolidated neither a strong coalition of support nor a popular base and put forth no coherent program. He wrestled with the realities of the new situation and cast about for a power base. The *tenentes* applauded Vargas as he dissolved all legislative bodies from Congress down to the municipal councils, intervened in the states, removed governors, and strengthened the central government. His hesitation to move faster, however, created anxieties among the *tenentes* and eventually prompted them to organize themselves.

In February of 1931 they banded together in the *Clube 3 de Outubro.* Their program advocated a strong presidency, an indirectly elected legislature composed of both sectoral and territorial congressmen, state-directed reforms to promote national development, harmony between capital and labor encouraged and facilitated by the state, land reform through differential taxation, state encouragement of agrarian and industrial development, and a wide range of social legislation that would include a labor code, a social security system, a public health system, universal education, and more equitable distribution of income. The program emphasized the predominance of the group over the individual, the union over the states, and national interests over international ones. It envisioned an authoritarian government capable of imposing reforms. Change rather than democracy attracted them.

A strong surge of strength in 1931 from the politicians linked to the Old Republic turned Vargas more resolutely toward the *tenentes* for support. They became mutually useful allies. Vargas needed the young officers to enhance his powers; they needed the president to enact their reforms. Vargas appointed many of them as state intervenors or as advisers. In 1931, the *tenentes* enjoyed their maximum influ-

ence. Yet, within a year it waned and within a few years had all but disappeared. Vargas often found their determination embarrassing in his delicate political maneuvering. Further, the ranks of the *Clube* fragmented into ideological factions. Finally, the civil war in São Paulo returned the young officers to military duties and removed them from politics. While the middle class had sympathized with the *tenente* movement during the 1920s, its members felt the *tenentes* shifted to overly radical ideas in the 1930s, incompatible with the "liberal reform" and "democratic" behavior sought by the ever more cautious middle class. Nonetheless, the lower ranks of the middle class continued to back the *tenentes* and their ideas in the 1930s.

Those *tenentes* bequeathed an impressive legacy. They helped to convert a regional revolt in 1930 into a national movement; they helped keep Vargas in power during some difficult years of political maneuvering; they impressed on Vargas the need for reforms; they helped bring the urban middle class and proletariat into national politics; they strengthened the role of the state in economic and social matters; they reinforced the drive toward centralization of power; they encouraged nationalism. Even after the *tenentes* as a group passed from prominence, their goals continued to attract support and in many ways served as the signposts guiding Vargas. Individually, the former *tenentes* played significant roles in the public life of the nation.

The new regime confronted severe political and economic challenges. With declining coffee sales threatening its collapse, the economy struggled under the weight of a worldwide depression. The instability of the international coffee market showed once again—and all too vividly—the reflexive nature of the Brazilian economy, dependent for its well-being, as it always had been, on the sale of one major raw product abroad. By 1935, Brazilian exports were only a third of what they had been in 1929, figures that reflect rather accurately the difference between coffee exports in the 1920s and those in the 1930s: in the decade before the crash of the stock market Brazil sold abroad 806 million pounds of coffee; in the following decade it exported only 337 million pounds.

The price of coffee between 1931 and 1937 averaged only 9.8 cents per pound, as compared to 21.7 cents in 1929. At the same time, competition for the world's coffee markets increased, so that Brazil's share fell from 60 percent in 1932 to less than 50 percent in 1937, a reflection of the mounting production of coffee in the other Latin American republics and in Africa. Through an aggressive sales campaign, Brazil brought its share up to 57 percent in 1939, but at the same time, the price slipped to 7.5 cents.

Vargas' government met the economic challenge in a variety of ways. Fully cognizant of the importance of coffee to the national economy, the government did not abandon the planters during their difficult days. The National Coffee Council (after 1933, the National Department of Coffee) proved flexible in adopting various plans to relieve the plight of the planters. At once it ordered a reduction in coffee-tree planting. The number of trees had risen from 1.7 billion in 1920 to 3 billion in 1934, a figure which receded slowly to 2.5 billion in 1939 and 2.3 in 1942. In 1931 the government initiated a program of coffee burning and before the end of the decade destroyed approximately 60 million bags of coffee. Variations of the old valorization scheme as well as international agreements with other coffee-producing states were tried with minimal success. Brazil's coffee trade only recovered with the advent of World War II. In the meantime, the government exerted every effort to diversify the economy through industrialization and agricultural expansion. Livestock raising and cotton production showed the most significant growth in the agricultural sector. Cotton accounted for 18.6 percent of the exports in the 1935–1939 period, a marked increase over 2.1 percent in the 1925–1929 period. Internal consumption of cotton rose as well. In São Paulo cotton planting increased sixfold in the years from 1933 to 1939, while at the same time coffee planting diminished. The success of the industrialization program will be treated later.

The crisis in the coffee market after 1929 and the government's determination to diversify the national economy rang down the curtain on the coffee civilization in Brazil. Responding to the economic challenges of the thirties, Brazil experi-

mented with various economic solutions. True, coffee would continue to figure prominently in the nation's economy, but the long-term trend initiated after the market crash to diversify the economy diminished its contribution.

Political problems accompanied the economic challenges. They came from the old oligarchy, dispossessed of power by the events of 1930, and the political extremists of both the Left and the Right. The coffee elite of São Paulo particularly manifested an antipathy toward the goals advocated by the nationalistic *tenentes*. In turn, Vargas harbored suspicions about the intentions of the richest and most powerful state, suspicions that prompted him to remove at once the governor installed by the junta in 1930, a general friendly to Júlio Prestes. To insure the loyalty of the state, Vargas dispatched General Isidoro Dias Lopes, the nominal chief of the 1924 revolt, to command the Second Military Region with headquarters in São Paulo. He sent João Alberto, a *tenente* from the Northeast, to serve as interventor, an appointee named by the president to replace an elected governor. The military interventor immediately earned the enmity of the Paulista establishment by decreeing a 5 percent wage raise for workers and by distributing some land to army veterans. The Paulistas accused him of being a Communist and—probably closer to the truth—of being incompetent. The elite understood that the consequences of politics and rebellion deprived them of their control of the federal government, but they bitterly resented the fact that they were not allowed to run their own rich state. If an interventor they must have, they wanted a civilian and a Paulista. At the same time, they agitated for a return to constitutional government, preferably under the lenient Constitution of 1891. Vargas was neither insensitive to their demands nor immune to their pressures. As one gesture of conciliation, he named José Maria Whitaker, a coffee banker from São Paulo, as his first minister of finance. Further, he made every possible effort to solve or ameliorate the coffee crisis. Eventually he appointed the desired civilian Paulista interventor, Pedro de Toledo, and announced elections for May of 1933 to select a constituent assembly. Instead of soothing the Paulistas, those measures

appeared to them as a sign of weakness in the national government. On July 9, 1932, under the command of General Bertaldo Klinger, the Paulistas revolted.

The significance of the revolt was readily discernible in its limited geographic and popular appeal. The rebels had counted on support from Minas Gerais and Rio Grande do Sul, but contrary to expectations those two states pledged their allegiance to Vargas, as did the rest of the union. In São Paulo the working class, both rural and urban, refused to embrace the cause. More than anything else, the rebellion seemed to be a rearguard action by the Paulista oligarchy, who looked to the past and desired a restoration of their former privileges and power, and the government treated it as such. Federal forces converged on the capital of São Paulo, and after three months of seige and desultory fighting the revolt collapsed. Understanding the necessity of a prosperous and a happy São Paulo for the well-being and progress of Brazil, Vargas wisely rejected the punishment and humiliation of the losers. He proceeded with the plans to constitutionalize the government.

On February 14, 1932, Vargas had promulgated an Electoral Code that lowered the voting age from twenty-one to eighteen, guaranteed the secret ballot and extended the suffrage to working women. (Earlier, in 1926, the state government of Rio Grande do Norte had granted women the right to vote.) Although a liberal code in most respects, it denied the vote to the illiterate, contrary to the practice in some other hemispheric republics. Under the provisions of the code the representatives to the Constituent Assembly were elected, and in November 1933 they began their deliberations. The Constitution promulgated in mid-1934 revealed the results of their labors. The new document maintained the federal system but delegated wider powers to the executive. The sections on labor, the family, and culture expanded the social consciousness of the government. It also showed a new concern with the nation's economic development. In an effort to reduce the power and influence of the rich states, in particular São Paulo, fifty corporative representatives (delegates from labor, industry, the professions, and the civil ser-

vice) were admitted to the chamber of deputies along with 250 of the more traditional representatives of areas and populations. The president was to serve for four years and be ineligible to succeed himself. The Assembly promptly elected Vargas to that office.

As the new constitutional machinery began to function, pressures on Vargas mounted. The state elections of 1935 favored the oligarchy and politicians linked to the Old Republic, intensifying the struggle between those advocating states' rights and those favoring centralization of power. At the same time, those espousing extremist political doctrines made aggressive appeals to the populace. Always vulnerable to the penetration of foreign political ideologies, Brazil did not escape the lure of communist and fascist doctrines in the 1930s. Following its foundation in 1922, the Communist party grew slowly until the economic crisis accelerated its activities and enhanced its attraction in the early 1930s. One faction of the party organized a popular front to combat fascism, the Aliança Nacional Libertadora (National Liberation Alliance), which began to take shape in 1934 but did not emerge until March 1935. With the motto "Bread, Land, and Liberty," the National Liberation Alliance (ANL) called for the cancellation of foreign debts, nationalization of foreign enterprises, full personal freedoms, a popular government, and distribution of the large estates among the rural proletariat. It remained largely an urban movement, recruiting its membership from the middle and lower middle classes rather than from the working classes. The ANL articulated nationalistic sentiments and was the first broad open challenge to the existing system. Most supporters of the ANL did not consider themselves Communists but passionately desired modernization and development, which they thought foreign exploitation retarded.

Luís Carlos Prestes, the romantic revolutionary who had led the march through the interior and then became the leader of the Brazilian Communist party, served as honorary president of the ANL. In early July 1935 he issued some inflammatory calls for the defeat of the Vargas government and the establishment of a popular revolutionary government. Vargas promptly outlawed the ANL for violation of the Na-

tional Security Laws. The Communists then discredited themselves by fomenting in Natal, Recife, and Rio de Janeiro three separate and bloody military uprisings between November 23 and 26, which outraged the public. Congress at once voted a state of seige. Federal officials arrested and jailed Communist and assorted leftist leaders. A specially created National Security Tribunal tried those implicated in the plots. From that time through 1937 the government mounted a vigorous anti-Communist campaign. Forced by Vargas to disband, the Communist party ceased to be active for a decade. The plots provided the government with ample opportunities to harass its critics. Casting its security net widely, the police arrested the distinguished novelist Graciliano Ramos in 1936 on vague charges of communist activities. His multivolume, autobiographical recollections, *Memórias do Cárcere*, chronicles the degradation and humiliation of political imprisonment in 1936 and 1937. (Published in 1953 in Rio de Janeiro, *Prison Memories* has not been translated into English.) Boldly using the opportunities provided by the revolts for his own advantage, Vargas greatly strengthened his authority, increased federal powers, and silenced his critics. The military also saw its own influence increase.

By the mid-1930s a threat from the far Right also emerged. In 1932, shortly after the São Paulo revolution, the Ação Integralista Brasileira, the Integralist party, was formed with support of conservative elements and in frank imitation of the European fascist parties of the time. Like their European counterparts, the Integralists had their own symbol (the sigma), flag, and shirt color (green). Raising their right arm in the traditional fascist salute, they uttered the word *ananê*. Although the meaning of this Indian word is obscure, its use showed that the Indian as a nationalist symbol still survived. Nationalistic and somewhat mystical in its appeal, the party emphasized order, hierarchy, and obedience. "God, Country, Family" was its motto. It proposed an "integral" state under a single authoritarian head of government. The party identified the "enemies of the nation" as Democrats and Communists, as well as Masons and Jews.

The young Paulista Plínio Salgado, an intellectual who

had dazzled Brazil with a literary best seller, *O Estrangeiro* (The Foreigner), in 1926, emerged as leading figure of the Integralist movement. His speeches, essays, and books re- sounded with nationalist phraseology. *Nosso Brasil* (Our Bra- zil), published in 1937, blindly glorified the fatherland. No official connection ever existed between the Integralist party, with its nationalistic doctrine, and the government, with its nationalistic programs, although some highly placed bureau- crats and army officers were Integralists. Nor was there any official link between the party and the Roman Catholic church, although many members of the Catholic hierarchy lent the party their support and prestige.

First the Communists and then the Integralists posed political threats to Vargas. Both were well-organized, disci- plined, national parties that professed a rigid ideology. Never before had Brazil experienced such parties. The other parties existing in the 1930s—like their predecessors during the Old Republic—were of the traditional weak and regional stripe. While they offered little effective challenge to Vargas, they did hinder his efforts to create and enforce national unity. He believed that the political parties dissipated the nation's ener- gies, and the politicking which intensified in 1937 as the pres- idential election campaign got under way confirmed him in that opinion. Echoes of the political past reverberated. Savvy observers predicted that the politicians most closely linked to the Old Republic would maneuver the election of the gover- nor of São Paulo to the presidency.

Vargas disdainfully observed the campaigning for a while and then decided to terminate it and resolve the question of presidential succession himself. The immediate cause for his action was the convenient discovery of the "Cohen Plan," a crudely forged document detailing a vast communist plan of terrorism. That fabricated threat, the general agitation caused by campaigning, and Vargas' personal desire for power moti- vated the coup d'état that Brazil confronted on November 10, 1937. By radio, Vargas explained the coup to the nation:

In periods of crisis, such as the one through which we are now passing, the democracy of parties, instead of offering a certain

opportunity for growth and progress within the framework necessary for human life and development, subverts the hierarchy, men-
aces the fatherland, and puts in danger the existence of the nation
by exaggerating competition and igniting the fires of civil discord.
It is necessary to note that, alarmed by the cries of the professional
agitators and confronted with the complexity of political struggles,
the men who do not live from such struggles but rather from the
fruits of their labor abandon the parties to those professionals who
live from them, and they abstain from participating in public life
which would benefit from the participation of those elements of
order and constructive action. Universal suffrage thus has become
the instrument of the astute, the mask which thinly disguises the
connivings of personal ambition and greed.

On that day he canceled the presidential elections, dismissed
Congress, and assumed all political power for himself. He
announced a new constitution, drawn up for the occasion by
Francisco Campos, a political philosopher whose influence
extended from the early Vargas years when he served as
minister of education through the early years of military government of the 1960s. In fact, he authored the first Institutional Act, April 1964. The Brazilians observed some amazing
constitutional hocus-pocus.

The coup represented more than an immediate political
victory for Vargas. On some levels, it signified a triumph of
Vargas' long political maneuvering, the capstone of the 1930–
1937 period; on others, it meant the emergence of—or at
least expression of—Vargas' new solutions for old problems.
The president obviously had resolved the thorny problem of
states' rights versus centralization in favor of the latter, incorporated the new urban elements into his political machine,
and formulated, at last, his ideological commitments. Proving
himself to be a master manipulator of the increasingly complex forces in Brazilian society, he had preserved national
unity, marginalized his enemies, confronted and partially solved
the tremendous problems of economic dislocation, and har-
nessed the power of rising nationalism. In the process, he
perfected the "populist" image that pleased the masses.
Drawing on a patriarchal heritage, they came to identify him
as "father of the poor."

After the coup, Vargas ruled by decree. He imposed press censorship and created a special police force to suppress any resistance to his regime. Police interrogation, torture, and imprisonment followed in due course. Possibly a hundred political prisoners were confined to the island of Fernão de Noronha, usually for a period of months. Many others found it prudent to live abroad in self-imposed exile. In December 1937, the new dictator disbanded all political parties. At no time did he make any effort to organize a political party of his own upon which he could rest his government. Terming his new government the Estado Novo (New State), he promised that it would achieve "the legitimate aspirations of the Brazilian people, political and social peace." Such rhetoric resounds through Brazilian political history.

Reaction to the sudden coup varied. The liberals, democrats, old elite, and some politicians protested. The coup outraged democrats, genuine believers in free elections and civil liberties. When the Integralists understood that they too were to be excluded from power in the Estado Novo, they made a brazen attack on Guanabara Palace, the President's residence, during the night of May 10–11, 1938. Vargas, his family, and his staff repulsed the attack; loyal troops arriving on the scene tardily finished the job. The Integralist attack was the only armed protest to the newly established dictatorship, and Salgado's motivations could scarcely be termed democratic. The masses, still passive to all political events in Brazil, accepted the Estado Novo. The military, nationalists, and large numbers of the middle groups welcomed it. They believed that authoritarian means might benefit the nation by imposing significant salutary changes. Although the *tenente* movement had died out, the Estado Novo represented the regimented, nationalist renovation for which those *tenentes* had agitated during a decade and a half. Its accomplishments fulfilled most of the goals they had sought.

In general, Vargas forged a careful and useful alliance with the military. The officers received good salaries and prompt promotion. Budgets were generous. The size of the military doubled from 38,000 in 1927 to 75,000 in 1937. As one consequence of the coup, the regional army commands ab-

sorbed the state militias, a severe blow to regionalism. Most important, the establishment of the Estado Novo accomplished the officers' goal of creating a strongly nationalistic, military-backed, centralized government. The coup underlined Vargas's dependence on the military.

The coup of 1937 seemed at first to nudge Brazil closer to the totalitarian states of Europe. The rhetoric echoed much of the phraseology current in Italy, Spain, and Portugal at the time, and the fascination with the corporative state structure momentarily strengthened the similarity. Some of the ideological motivations coincided. Certainly statements made by Vargas in the years immediately following the coup favored the corporate state structure. He announced the demise of democracy in the twentieth century: "The decadence of liberal and individualistic democracy represents an incontrovertible fact." He proclaimed the superiority of the State over the individual: "The Estado Novo does not recognize the rights of the individual against the collective. Individuals do not have rights; they have duties. Rights belong to the collective!"

At the same time, commerce drew Brazil closer to Germany than ever before. In the decade after 1928 both the United States and Great Britain reduced their purchases of Brazilian exports, while Germany increased its purchases. Germany doubled its imports from Brazil between 1933 and 1938 to become the biggest customer for Brazilian cotton and the second largest for coffee and cacao. In 1938 Brazil shipped 34 percent of its exports to the United States, 19 percent to Germany, and 9 percent to Great Britain; it bought 25 percent of its imports from Germany, 24 percent from the United States, and 10 percent from the United Kingdom. The new importance of Germany in Brazil's international trade went a long way to explain Brazil's friendly disposition toward that increasingly belligerent European power. At any rate, as long as the United States maintained an officially neutral attitude toward the European conflict, the Brazilian leaders saw no reason why they had to take a stand, particularly if such a position would cause reverses in an already unstable economy.

Once the United States entered World War II, Brazil, in company with most of Latin America, followed suit. On January 28, 1942, Brazil broke diplomatic and commercial relations with the Axis. In the months thereafter German submarines repeatedly sank Brazilian ships, a campaign that reached a climax during three days in mid-August, 1942, when five Brazilian ships went down with a loss of many lives. Rio de Janeiro reacted immediately. On August 22, 1942, Brazil declared war on Germany and Italy. It was more than a paper declaration, contrary to similar declarations made by other Latin American governments. Brazil sought, within its limitations, to play a contributory role as a responsible ally. The government authorized the United States to establish air and naval bases in the North and Northeast, strategic for the defense of the Atlantic and vital to the invasion of Africa and the subsequent campaigns in that region. The navy patroled the South Atlantic. A small contingent of the air force participated in the war over Italy. Moreover, an expeditionary force of approximately 25,000 men arrived in Italy in late 1944 and took part in the fierce fighting there. In the drive up the peninsula 451 Brazilian soldiers gave their lives and another 2,000 were wounded. Their contribution to the defeat of European fascism increased national pride, solidified Brazil's position as the leader of the Latin American community, and ensured a prestigious place for Brazil in the United Nations. The war experience particularly impressed those officers who participated in the campaign, shaping their attitudes—admiration for the United States and for technology, for example—and uniting them into a fraternity whose influence on Brazil would be momentous. Internally, the war was a mighty impetus to increased agricultural production and manufacturing.

The accelerating industrialization during the Vargas years led to an urban expansion that altered many national customs. Patriarchal families abandoned their homes in the country, or on the urban fringes, for apartments within the city, where the larger clans frequently dispersed into marital groupings. Multistoried apartment buildings began to appear, many in a refreshingly original style designed by an

emerging school of talented Brazilian architects, of whom Oscar Niemeyer is an outstanding example. They transformed the skyline of the major cities from Pôrto Alegre to Manaus. Legions of the poor migrated to the cities, in hopes of taking advantage of their promise, and settled in the squalid *favelas* (slums). Pressing close to the luxurious apartment complexes, these slums offer a vividly symbolic contrast with the extremes characteristic of Brazilian society. Desperate as the situation of the urban poor was, they probably enjoyed a better diet, health, and education than their rural counterparts. In the impersonality of the city, the paternalistic relationship between the elite and the masses eroded, although it has never completely disappeared. Still, the city had no counterpart to the "colonel" who rigidly controlled hundreds, even thousands of peasants. The city provided the workers with wider choices than the peasants ever had and, to make those choices, an independence which the peasants never felt possible. Foremost, of course, the city offered workers a hope for the future of which their rural counterparts could not even dream. Hence it was small wonder that the cities attracted ever-larger numbers of migrants. On the other hand, many of the dispossessed wandered into the city only because they had nowhere to go in the countryside. Driven from the land, they ended up in the city no better prepared to integrate into urban life than the city was to receive them.

Urban life tended to be more permissive, relaxing the traditions and habits which made a ritual out of rural life. The city dwellers enjoyed greater independence and had more opportunities to improve themselves as well as raise their standards of living. The merchants encouraged the desire for improvement. They introduced installment buying, which put within the reach of the middle groups products, luxuries even, once inaccessible. Urban women enjoyed far more freedom than their rural counterparts. The granting of the vote to working women in 1932 announced their political emancipation. The presence of the daughters of the middle class in the universities became more pronounced, and not a few took their places as lawyers, judges, professors, and doctors. The autobiographical novel *The Three Marias* (*As Tres*

Marias, 1939) by Rachel de Queiroz (1910–1978)—the first woman admitted into the Brazilian Academy of Letters—illustrates the rising expectations and frustrations of urban middle-class females of this period. The dynamic changes introduced by the complementary processes of industrialization and urbanization seemed at the time to threaten the oligarchical control and elitist politics characteristic of Brazil during both the Empire and the Old Republic.

Obviously more diverse than ever before, the cities provided Vargas with new sources of power. From this point onward, it is possible to abandon the use—liberally made—of the term "middle groups." Society by the 1930s and thereafter was sufficiently complex and developed to warrant the more precise use of the terms "middle class" and "proletariat." The middle class consisted of those economically independent of medium wealth and income and the salaried who depended mainly on their intellectual ability in business, industry, commerce, bureaucracy, and the professions. The ranks of the middle class expanded liberally. Factory managers, foremen, technicians, representatives, salesmen, office workers with a host of new skills, bank managers, tellers, accountants, university professors, and a wide variety of businessmen joined more traditional elements of that class: the doctors, lawyers, engineers, military officers, and civil servants. In his fascinating sociological study of Itaipava, an interior city with a population of approximately twenty-five thousand in the 1940s, Emílio Willems defined the middle class as "all the inhabitants who are more or less economically solvent, who assume in their relations with local authorities an attitude of relative freedom and criticism, who sell services or goods of relatively high social esteem, who, thanks to education, can participate in recreational activities which demand familiarity with certain rules of urban social etiquette, whose economic-professional position represents a 'political potential' highly appreciated by the parties." He found that 29 percent of the city's inhabitants belonged to that middle class, among whom were merchants, farmers, public officials, artisans, and some highly paid employees.

The urban proletariat included all those in inferior eco-

nomic positions whose income came primarily from manual labor. The numbers of the proletariat increased rapidly as the need for more stevedores, factory hands, and construction workers grew. Like the middle class, the proletariat grew not only in the large coastal cities, but also in the towns of the interior as well. Concentrated in the sensitive and restive urban areas, the proletariat and middle classes wielded influence and power disproportionate to their size. They never constituted a majority; most Brazilians continued to live in the countryside, but, except for the small but powerful rural oligarchy, they were politically inarticulate.

That Vargas understood and appreciated the importance of the support of the urban middle class and the proletariat to the consolidation of his power was apparent from the first days of his administration. He intended to use them to check the traditional oligarchy. They, in turn, approved Vargas' efforts to fix the locus of power in the cities. Immediately after taking command of the government he moved to reduce the authority of the *coroneis,* one of the foundation stones upon which the power structure of the Old Republic had rested. Many of the rural patriarchs had made the mistake of supporting President Luís in October of 1930. Vargas disarmed them and their followers—or he did so to the extent possible—and thus deprived them of much physical power. Further, he reduced the control of the *coroneis* over the backland municipalities by decreeing that thereafter the federal government would direct all local police forces, appoint all mayors, and supervise all municipal budgets. One historian of the Northeast, Irineu Pinheiro, concluded, "After 1930, in place of colonels of the National Guard, merchants and farmers began to dominate the municipal governments in Ceará. They were elements of the so-called liberal classes such as lawyers and doctors." The *coroneis* sometimes allied themselves with those new holders of power, but after 1930, in contrast with the past, they were more often than not the junior members of such an alliance.

As an early indication of his intention to broaden and strengthen his urban base of support, Vargas created in 1930 two new cabinet posts, the minister of labor and the minister

of education. Previous governments had either neglected or persecuted labor. They often regarded unions as a source of social unrest and political disturbance. The police commonly intervened in union activities, and a law of 1927 authorized the executive to dissolve unions considered to be troublesome or obnoxious. At the time of the fall of the Old Republic, there were approximately a quarter of a million organized workers. While hostile to strikes and manifestations, Vargas, in a purely paternalistic—and some say demagogic—manner, granted the workers more benefits than they probably could have obtained through their own organizations. The new Ministry of Labor served as the instrument through which the government dealt with the workers. A decree in March of 1931 authorized that ministry to organize labor into new unions under strict governmental supervision. By 1944, there were about eight hundred unions with a membership exceeding half a million. The government forbade strikes but did establish an elaborate set of courts and codes to protect the workers and to provide redress for their grievances. Under governmental auspices, unions could and did bargain with management. Vargas promulgated and the minister of labor administered a wide variety of social legislation favoring the workers. There were retirement and pension plans, a minimum wage, a workweek limited to forty-eight hours, paid annual vacations, maternal benefits and child care, educational facilities, training programs and literacy campaigns, safety and health standards for work, and job security. In short, Vargas offered to the workers in less than a decade the advances and benefits that the proletariat of the industrialized nations had agitated for during the previous century. In Latin America only the workers in Chile, Mexico, and Uruguay boasted of similar gains and privileges. In return for those broad advances, the Brazilian workers loyally, even devotedly, supported Vargas. It must be emphasized, however, that those benefits accrued only to privileged workers in large industries in major cities. The majority of the workers received no benefits, although they identified with the rhetoric and entertained hopes of inclusion.

The elaborate labor courts, welfare benefits, and careful

control of unions bespoke a paternalism prevalent in the Brazilian experience. Labor and the government interacted, supported, and depended upon each other. With its vision of the corporate state, the government manipulated labor into cooperating with both capital and the state to encourage industrialization. Such manipulation theoretically avoided or minimized class conflicts. It demonstrated Vargas's skills as a "populist" leader. From 1930 onward, the political role of labor increased but then so did government manipulation.

Through the Ministry of Education, Vargas reached out to the middle class, whose children predominated in the schools. Obviously, education had a crucial role to play in a developing society, particularly one in which the population was getting larger and younger. After 1930, immigration declined sharply but the population continued to grow rapidly, with birth rates exceeding 3 percent per year. When Vargas assumed power in 1930, Brazil boasted of approximately 33 million inhabitants; when he lost power in 1945, it exceeded 46 million. Observing that "Education is a matter of life and death," Vargas ordered greater attention focused on the schools, which in the last analysis would shape the future of Brazilian society. Indeed, education was the portal through which Brazilians had to pass if they were to participate in a modern society which demanded increasingly greater skills and technical ability. The first minister of education, Francisco Campos, reformed the educational system in 1931 with the intention of making it more modern and efficient. Teacher training and classroom construction received new emphasis. The first university, that of Rio de Janeiro, had been created in 1920 by joining together a number of dispersed schools—law, medicine, engineering—under a central administration. In 1934 the University of São Paulo emerged from a similar unification, and four years later the University of Brazil, with its seat in Rio de Janeiro, became the third university.

Vargas also intended to use the newly centralized school system as a means to encourage the growth of national sentiment. He decreed that all instruction be given in Portuguese, a requirement aimed at accelerating the Brazilianization of European immigrants and their descendants, particularly in

the South with its large concentrations of Germans, Poles, and Italians. The schools placed a greater emphasis on the teaching of Brazilian history; the new universities established for the first time chairs of national history. In short, after 1930 education sharpened national consciousness, thereby fostering a mentality favorable toward nationalism.

Technical advances facilitated Vargas' efforts to strengthen national unity and his own personal control. They permitted him to reach out to all the Brazilian people, even in the remotest hinterlands, with a speed and thoroughness none of his predecessors enjoyed. Radio broadcasting, inaugurated in the 1920s, expanded rapidly, and before the close of the 1930s a radio network spread across the entire nation. The government regulated broadcasting and made extensive use of it to present the official point of view. Vargas himself gave occasional "fireside chats." Movies, from the early days of the film industry, engrossed the Brazilians, who flocked to the increasing number of cinemas. The screen, through newsreels and documentaries, became an important medium to carry the government's official message. In a society in which barely a quarter of the population was literate, both the radio and the cinema were indispensable instruments of propaganda. A special agency, the Department of Press and Propaganda, promoted the official viewpoint and censored whatever the government found displeasing or imprudent to reveal, a responsibility the department did not always exercise with subtlety. One of the government's most successful controls over the press was the tax exemption permit that it could give, withhold, or withdraw on imported newsprint—and all newsprint was imported. The prestigious *O Estado de São Paulo* proved to be a particularly recalcitrant daily and occasionally refused to adopt the government's line. A cache of weapons "discovered" by the political police in the building housing *O Estado* gave Vargas the excuse he sought to close down the paper and then take it over. A result was a sycophantic news medium that permitted Vargas to get his message across to the nation both efficiently and effectively.

The air age had dawned in Brazil. Even before independence had been declared, two Brazilians, Bartolomeu de Gus-

mão in his experiments and Bishop Azeredo Coutinho in his writings, had contemplated the day when man would conquer the air. In 1901, Alberto Santos Dumont—another Brazilian intrigued with the conquest of the air—flew a dirigible balloon around the Eiffel Tower, and in 1906, duplicating the more heralded feat of the Wright brothers, he flew a heavier-than-air plane. The advantage of air travel for a country as vast as Brazil, with its limited network of roads and railroads, was obvious. Commercial aviation began in 1927 with the foundation in Pôrto Alegre of the first air transport company. By 1939, nine commercial companies were flying 81 planes over routes extending 43,000 miles. Aware of the value of the airplane for national unification as well as its value as a means to increase his control of the nation, Vargas created the Air Ministry in 1941. Brazil soon handled three-quarters of all commercial air traffic in South America.

The surface transportation network continued to expand, of course, but not so spectacularly as the air network. By 1939, there were only 21,241 miles of railroads, 65 percent of which could be found in four states: São Paulo, Minas Gerais, Rio de Janeiro, and Rio Grande do Sul. The government, either federal or state, managed over two-thirds of the railroads. By the end of the 1930s, they were transporting 195 million passengers, 4 million animals, and 35 million tons of freight a year. Vargas pushed road construction, and in 1939, with obvious satisfaction, he opened the vital road between Rio de Janeiro and Salvador da Bahia. By the end of that year, there were 258,390 miles of roads—96 percent of which were dirt, mostly unimproved—over which approximately a quarter of a million motor vehicles passed, a third of them trucks.

The expanding transportation and communication networks welded Brazil into a tighter unity than it had ever before achieved. They facilitated the strong centralism Vargas imposed on the nation. Just as the decentralization experiments of the Regency were condemned and reversed by the Second Empire, so the laissez-faire federalism of the Old Republic came under attack by those who rebelled in 1930 and later applauded the establishment of the Estado Novo. Rejecting previous federalism, Vargas enforced the suprem-

acy of the government in Rio de Janeiro. He became the strongest executive Brazil had known. He exercised more power more effectively over a larger area than any of his predecessors, emperors not excluded. The strong centralization of power imposed by the Estado Novo has characterized Brazil ever since.

All factors considered, Vargas seems to have exercised that omnipotence satisfactorily, although a group of unrelenting critics regarded the regime as the most disreputable of dictatorships and the crudest of police states. Generally Vargas seems to have listened attentively to diverse opinions; his fingers were firmly on the pulse of public sentiment. Thus oriented, he enjoyed considerable support for his programs. Certainly he understood the desire and need for reform as well as the extent to which reform could be made and accepted. Again, as had been customary in the past, reforms were handed down to the nation from above. They were not the result of popular agitation, struggle, or threat.

In introducing changes and maintaining his position, Vargas wielded new instruments of power. He recognized the potential of the middle class and proletariat and used both of them. In turn, they found Vargas to be their portal to power. Their influence grew rapidly after 1930. The rural oligarchy, battered by the effects of the depression, the collapse of the Old Republic, industrialization, and urbanization, lost its former political dominance. Vargas encouraged and guided that changing pattern of power. Under his aegis many groups—civilians and military, bureaucrats, technicians, professionals, and industrialists, bourgeois and proletariat—emancipated Brazil from the absolute control of the coffee interests.

Vargas avoided extremes in making reforms and in altering the political balance of power. Following a recognizable Brazilian tradition, he knew how to compromise. His government acquired a decidedly populist cast but at the same time won the support and cooperation—in some cases, even the enthusiasm—of the principal members of the business and industrial community. He tried not to antagonize the rural oligarchy. Land reform, for example, was neither an interest nor a goal of his government. He managed to offer something

to both the elite and the masses. In the final analysis, he owed his long tenure to his ability to hold the support of business, labor, the military, many landowners, and the nationalists. The coordination of those seemingly diverse elements into a base of support indicated that Brazilian politics had become more complex. Two forces rapidly accelerating that complexity were industrialization and nationalism.

Nationalism and Industrialization

Industrialization and nationalism accompanied one another in twentieth-century Brazil as they did throughout much of Latin America. Many Brazilians viewed industrialization as a key to the future, unlocking the door to development and hence to national greatness. Little wonder, then, that the nationalists promoted it. Their first efforts in the nineteenth century had been to criticize foreign merchants resident in Brazil and to demand laws to protect local industry. Modern economic nationalism found in Alberto Tôrres one of its earliest effective advocates. In a series of books published between 1909 and 1915, he brought together the concepts of development and nationalism and indicated the course nationalism would follow thereafter. In his view, any nation, in order to exercise "real sovereignty" or manifest "true nationalism," had to control its own source of wealth, its industry, and its commerce. He discussed that idea in detail in his *O Problema Nacional Brasileiro* (The National Brazilian Problem), published in 1914:

Above all else, the independence of a people is founded on their economy and their finances. . . . In order for a nation to remain independent it is imperative to preserve the vital organs of nationality: the principal sources of wealth, the industries of primary products, the instrumentalities and agents of economic circulation, transportation, and internal commerce. There must be no monopolies and no privileges. . . . A people cannot be free if they do not own sources of wealth, produce their own food, and direct their own industry and commerce.

The government, Torres argued, had entrusted Brazil's economic destiny to foreigners, who had sown their capital without restriction to reap an abundant harvest of profit at national expense. He urged the government to reconsider and to adopt a nationalist economic program. His ideas appealed to the *tenentes* and fitted the plans of Vargas. It was no coincidence that the second edition of *O Problema Nacional Brasileiro* appeared in 1933, just as the nationalists' campaign for economic development got under way.

In that campaign, the nationalists emphasized that only through intensive economic development with due attention to industrialization could Brazil become truly independent. They pointed to the international market crash of 1929 as conclusive proof of the vulnerability of Brazil's economy, based as it traditionally had been on one major export, always subject to the whims of foreign markets. Brazil, they lamented, still could not control its own economic destiny. In their eyes it remained an economic colony with remnants of institutions and patterns of the past, an obvious reference to those economic characteristics acquired during the 1530–1560 period. Most offensive were the residues of the mercantilist system perpetuated by the rural oligarchy in alliance with foreign capitalism. Tenacious economic continuity perpetuated dependence.

The nationalists clamored for diversification of the economy as a major step toward economic and hence greater political independence. Adopting the cogent arguments of economic nationalists like Roberto Simonsen that industrialization would diversify the economy, keep precious foreign exchange from being spent to import what could be produced at home, and raise national self-sufficiency, they urged the government to further stimulate manufacturing.

Those economic arguments of the nationalists did not go unanswered. Intellectuals like Eugênio Gudin spoke out to favor a continuation of the agricultural regime. They believed that Brazil lacked the resources and ability to industrialize. Such industry, they charged, always would produce at a high cost, dependent on the protection of the government. They counseled the continuation of the sale of its agricultural prod-

ucts abroad—like the nativists of an earlier century they delighted in cataloging the richness of the soil—and the purchase of whatever manufactured goods the country needed from the cheapest seller. More internationally minded, they would mesh the economy of Brazil with that of Europe and the United States.

Vargas inclined toward the arguments of the economic nationalists and indicated his intention to implement their program, while still encouraging the absolutely vital agricultural sector of the economy. To direct the economy and to encourage industrialization and development, Vargas expanded governmental planning and participation. In that way, the government assumed the principal leadership of the nationalist movement. For the first time, the intellectuals lost control of the nationalist rhetoric they had monopolized. The base of support of nationalist policies at the same time broadened to include larger numbers of the military, industrialists, politicians, and the middle class. The urban proletariat for the first time began to identify with the nationalist program. After 1930, it was apparent that Brazilian nationalism, like that flourishing in most of Latin America, became increasingly characterized by resentment of foreign capital and foreign personnel, suspicion of private enterprise, a growing approval of state ownership, emphasis on industrialization, encouragement of domestic production, and a desire to create or nationalize certain key industries such as oil, steel, power, and transportation.

Burgeoning industrialization after 1930 resulted from more than the encouragement of a benevolent government and enthusiastic advocates. There already existed a firm industrial base upon which further industrialization could be built; the international economic crisis served to propel the cause of industrialization. After the market crash in 1929, Brazil drastically reduced its imports. They fell approximately 75 percent between 1929 and 1932, from $416.6 million to $108.1 million. While exports declined as well, they did not fall nearly as far nor as fast as imports: from $445.9 million to $180.6 million. As a consequence, Brazil enjoyed favorable trade balances in the early 1930s. In addition, the government's valorization

scheme maintained much of the coffee production, providing the workers with their salaries and the planters with profits. Internal demand for goods thus remained relatively normal, but the external sources of those consumer goods could no longer be easily tapped because of the government's stringent curtailment of purchases abroad. At that point, local capital, a large percentage of which came from coffee, was invested in new industries that manufactured articles formerly imported, accelerating the much discussed economic trend of import substitution. Further, since prices on the domestic market had not fallen as much as those on the international market, it was more profitable to produce goods for home consumption than for export, a persuasive enticement to local investment. Various governmental policies, such as the prohibition of the planting of more coffee trees, channeled into industry money once invested in agriculture. Industrial growth further resulted from a more efficient and intensive use of the production capacity already available. The textile industry, for example, substantially increased its output in the early 1930s without expanding its facilities. Contrary to the experience of many other countries, including the United States, Brazilian industry recovered from the depression by 1933 and entered thereafter a period of expansion. In 1934, the industrial production index surpassed the pre-depression height. Vargas promulgated a host of legislation, decrees, and policies to speed it along its way. Import controls as well as depreciation of the currency discouraged purchases abroad. Import duties rose to protect new industries. In 1933 duties averaged 39 percent of the cost of goods imported. However, liberal exemptions were made for capital machinery and raw materials imported by new industries. Tax exemptions were dispensed generously. The government offered new industries direct financial assistance through long-term loans with low interest rates. Where necessary, the government supervised, operated, or owned certain industries.

Local natural resources facilitated industrialization. Fortunately, Brazil possessed an abundance of them: quartz crystals, industrial diamonds, chrome, iron, and manganese ores, copper, lead, zinc, and gemstones, although much of

this potential had not been explored, let alone exploited. In the 1920s the nationalists mounted a noisy campaign to protect the country's natural resources and prevent their exploitation by foreigners. Percival Farquhar, an adventurous North American investor in Brazilian railroads and mines triggered the campaign. The nationalists fumed when he obtained from the government in the early 1920s a concession for the fabulous Itabira iron-ore deposits. They protested the alienation of their country's riches. Thanks principally to the interest President Bernardes took in the case, the government eventually canceled the concession, a major victory for the nationalists. They capped their triumph with a significant amendment to the Constitution: "Mines and mineral deposits necessary for national security and the land in which they are found cannot be transferred to foreigners" (Article 72). An even stronger restriction on foreign exploitation of natural resources appeared in the Constitution of 1934: "The law will regulate the progressive nationalization of mines, mineral deposits, and waterfalls or other sources of energy, as well as of the industries considered as basic or essential to the economic and military defense of the country" (Article 119). The Constitution of 1937 included the same provision. Accordingly, Vargas placed restrictions on foreign companies to discourage or control their exploitation of the country's natural wealth. In due time his government turned its attention to the coveted iron-ore deposits of Itabira. In 1942 it established the Companhia Vale do Rio Doce (Doce River Valley Company) to tap their wealth. Brazil's production of iron ore quintupled between 1939 and 1951, most of the rise taking place after 1942.

After the proclamation of the Estado Novo, economic nationalism intensified. Notification of the government's fuller participation in and direction of the economy was given in January 1940 with the announcement of a Five Year Plan. It promoted the expansion of the railroad network, state steamship services, basic industry, and hydroelectric power. In 1940, foreign companies generated the vast majority of the nation's electrical power, a fact embarrassing to national pride. The military and the nationalists cited such foreign ownership as

a threat to national security and lashed out against that monopoly of foreign capitalists.

Vargas already had initiated a search for another source of power: oil. For the Brazilians, as for most Latin Americans, petroleum became a major symbol of economic nationalism. Its discovery and exploitation were not only economically desirable but promised, in the minds of the nationalists, a brighter future for the country, and indeed its achievement of the status of a world power. Vargas organized the National Petroleum Council in 1938 to intensify the search for oil. The first discovery occurred in January of the following year just outside Salvador da Bahia. To the joy of the nation, oil gushed forth from Brazilian soil. The deposit turned out to be a modest one, but everyone viewed it as the overture to greater discoveries. Calling for the creation of a national oil industry to protect the precious new resource, the nationalists opposed any foreign involvement in the search for and exploitation of petroleum. Before long it dominated their thoughts; petroleum emerged as the major issue for the nationalists. Vargas, in turn, began to appreciate the emotional importance of oil, and he too came to pay homage to it as a symbol. "Whoever hands over petroleum to foreigners threatens our own independence," he stated to the delight of the nation in general and of the nationalists in particular.

The petroleum question remained unsettled until his second administration (1951–1954), when Vargas—ever more vocal in his nationalism—resolved to bid for wider support by appealing frankly to nationalist sentiment. Honoring the symbolic significance of oil to the nationalists, he adopted the idea of establishing a national petroleum industry. In 1951, he proposed the creation of Petrobrás, a state monopoly of all activities concerned with the exploration of petroleum resources. Amid a strident nationalist campaign, the cry "O petróleo é nosso!" (The oil is ours!) echoed across the land. In response, Petrobrás was created in 1953, a major victory for the nationalists over those who argued it would be more economical and efficient to allow foreign oil companies to drill and pay Brazil a royalty on whatever was pumped out. The question, however, was not one of economics; emotions

dominated. To the nationalists and the multitudes they stirred, national sovereignty had been at stake and had triumphed. The creation of Petrobrás was a contribution to the economic independence of Brazil. In their campaign, the nationalists had been extremely successful in convincing the masses that a national oil industry represented sovereignty, independence, power, and well-being. For the first time they succeeded in arousing popular support for a nationalist cause. Petrobrás remains the major single permanent achievement of the nationalists. The passionate support accorded its creation recalls the dramatic nationalization of the oil industry in Bolivia in 1937 and in Mexico in 1938.

With equal fervor, the nationalists advocated the creation of a national steel industry. On this issue, as on the oil question, the military joined them. The officers understood and preached that Brazil could only be of military importance when it possessed its own basic industries, of which oil and steel were of primary importance. As early as 1931, Vargas pronounced, "The biggest problem, one might say the basic problem for our economy, is steel. For Brazil, the steel age will mark the period of our economic opulence." Finally, in 1940, adhering to its program of economic planning and demonstrating a willingness to play an active economic role when private capitalists hesitated, the government drew up plans to construct a steel mill. The National Steel Company was organized the following year, and work on a steel plant began at once at Volta Redonda, situated between Rio de Janeiro and São Paulo. In 1946 it went into operation. By 1955, Volta Redonda was producing 646,000 tons of steel, an annual output that doubled by 1963.

Steel and oil shone as the showpieces of Brazilian industrialization under Vargas. In broader perspective, they reflected an impressive rate of growth for industrialization in general. Between 1924 and 1939, industrial output grew at an annual average cumulative rate of approximately 6 percent. Some economists cite 1933 as the year in which the rhythm of industrialization accelerated. In the five years thereafter the volume of industrial production mounted by approximately 40 percent and the value of industrial production, taking into

account monetary devaluation, increased by 44 percent, making industrial production some 60 percent greater in value than the combined output of livestock and agriculture. In the 1930s approximately three times more new industrial plants went into operation than during the preceding decade. By 1940, capital investment in factories totaled over 700 million dollars, an impressive figure for Latin America, but of course an almost insignificant sum compared to investments in the major industrial nations. The United States, for example, in 1860, with only three quarters of the population of Brazil in 1940, had about a billion dollars invested in manufacturing. The value of industrial production in the United States at the opening of World War II was approximately fifty times that of Brazil.

A modest diversification of industry occurred during the 1930s. Textiles, long a primary industry, maintained importance but declined significantly in the total value of industrial output, while other industries, such as printing and publishing, chemical and pharmaceutical products, metals, and machinery increased to provide by 1940 a slightly more balanced industrial park. In 1941 there were 44,100 plants or enterprises employing 944,000 workers. (The figures contrasted sharply with those of 1920, when there were 13,336 plants and a little over 300,000 workers.) Most of the manufacturing was done in small plants and relied heavily on hand labor. The factories produced principally consumer goods, which they provided in sufficient quantity and quality to obviate their importation. National industries increasingly bought more local raw products and sold their manufactured goods in the local markets. Almost all of them entered that market; the industrial sector exported very little. While internal sources provided four-fifths of the materials used in manufacturing, the plants still depended on foreign sources for a large part of their required machinery, heavy equipment, and fuel. However, by the early 1940s a trend was initiated to develop heavy industry.

World War II spurred economic growth. Brazil exported at enticing profits all its products to a warring world eager to buy anything. Manufactured goods for the first time became a noticeable export item. The export of textiles rose briskly,

to the point where Brazil ranked as one of the world's leading textile exporters. The industrialized nations, with their economies geared for the war, had little or nothing to sell back. As a consequence, Brazil built up sizable foreign exchange reserves, from $71 million just before the outbreak of the war to $708 million in 1945, and further expanded and diversified its industrial parks. Growth occurred despite the difficulty in obtaining capital machinery, almost all of which came from Western Europe and the United States. The concept of the planned economy took hold, as the promulgation of a second five-year plan in 1943 demonstrated. (The success of the plans— or even of the implementation of them—can be questioned, but acceptance of the idea of planning was established.)

The industrialization of Brazil met some formidable obstacles. Certainly not all of the population of forty million by 1940 constituted a market. Large numbers lived outside the national economy. The minimum wages Vargas guaranteed the urban workers helped to expand the market, and growing industries hired more workers who in turn became consumers. The enlightened industrialists understood that Vargas's labor policies tended in the long run to increase the size of the internal market. More concerned with producing for that internal market than in exporting raw materials or importing manufactured goods, they had reason to applaud the benefits of Vargas's social legislation. Cumulative effects caused the market to grow steadily, but it never embraced the entire population. An underdeveloped transportation network further handicapped industrialization. At some times it was impossible to get raw products to interested industries, and at others it was impossible to distribute the manufactured product throughout the nation. Inadequate transportation underlined the difficulties caused by the geographical separation of certain interdependent natural resources. Further, Brazil lacked sufficient fuel, water power, capital, technicians, and skilled workers, a handicap that could conceivably be overcome with time and ingenuity.

Not all of Brazil entered the industrial age by any means. The southern and central-eastern states monopolized manufacturing, accounting for approximately five-sixths of the total

value of manufactured goods. São Paulo clearly emerged as the industrial giant. With 15 percent of the country's population, it produced 43 percent of the nation's manufactured goods in 1938 (a figure that rose to 54 percent in 1943). The other industrial leaders were the Federal District, which manufactured 14 percent of the industrial goods; Minas Gerais and Rio Grande do Sul, which manufactured 11 percent each; and the state of Rio de Janeiro, which manufactured 5 percent. Those five states employed about three-fourths of all factory workers in 1940, with São Paulo alone accounting for 41 percent of that total. Obviously, in those states most subject to the economic transformation engendered by industrialization the social structure underwent the greatest change.

Important, then, as industrialization was, it affected only a part of the nation. The rest of Brazil slumbered in the past. Previous economic and social patterns remained dominant. The Vargas government made some effort to awaken the rest of the nation, but with limited success. Adopting a theme popularized by the nationalists in the 1920s, Vargas pointed to the West as the key to the realization of the nation's potential. He often spoke of his plans for the development of the hinterlands, his "March to the West." Developing that great promised land was to be "the true sense of Brazilianism." Vargas was the first chief of state to visit the interior, and he approved plans to colonize Goiás by distributing fifty-acre plots to settlers. His administration also enacted programs for the arid *sertão* of the Northeast and the forgotten Amazon Valley. Not all his programs were carried out, but their very promulgation revealed an executive who demonstrated an interest in all of Brazil, who thought in national rather than regional terms, in sharp contrast to his Republican predecessors. Their promulgation signified a new emphasis on national integration.

Brazil remained an agricultural nation. Still, important as the soil was to the economy, only a small percentage—approximately 4 percent of the usable soil in 1945—was under cultivation. In the United States, in contrast, over ten times that amount of land fell under the plow. The areas of greatest use and productivity of the land were in the industrialized

Table 7.2 Landownership in 1940

Size of Farm in Hectares (1 hectare = 2.47/acres)	Percentage of Operators with Farms of Stated Size	Percentage of Land in Farms or Estates of Stated Size
Under 1	2.1	Less than 0.1
1–4.9	19.7	0.6
5–9.9	12.6	0.9
10–19.9	16.6	2.3
20–49.9	23.9	7.2
50–99.9	10.8	7.2
100–199.9	6.5	8.8
200–499.9	4.7	13.9
500–999.9	1.6	10.9
1,000–2,499.9	1.0	14.4
2,500–4,999.9	0.3	9.3
5,000–9,999.9	0.1	7.6
10,000–99,999.9	0.1	13.3
100,000 over	Less than 0.1	3.6

SOURCE: "Sinopse de Censo Agrícola, Dados Gerais," *Recenseamento Geral do Brasil*, 1940 (Rio de Janeiro, 1948). Reprinted in T. Lynn Smith, *Brazil, People and Institutions* (Baton Rouge, Louisiana, 1954), p. 419.

states: São Paulo, Minas Gerais, and Rio Grande do Sul accounted for about five-eighths of all the Brazilian farm lands. Coffee, the predominant export, remained the most important single crop, and São Paulo continued to harvest about two-thirds of it. Other important crops were cocoa, tobacco, cotton, rice, sugar, fruits, wheat, corn, barley, rye, cassava, potatoes, yams, and beans, most of which fed the Brazilians, but some of which, such as cacao, tobacco, and cotton, also played a significant role in the export trade. Livestock raising contributed significantly to the rural economy. The largest cattle herds roamed central Brazil, which accounted for two-fifths of the cattle in the nation. The South was the second most important area with approximately a fourth of the herds. Sheep raising was concentrated in Rio Grande do Sul.

Rural Brazil retained much from the past. The traditional way to clear the soil, the the slash-and-burn method, still prevailed. The farmers seldom used fertilizer, or used it sparsely. Those two practices resulted in quickly exhausted and badly eroded land. The farmers adhered to other antiquated agrarian practices as well. Their principal instrument was the hoe, unmodified for centuries. The plow was rare,

the tractor even rarer. In 1940 only a fourth of all the farms boasted a plow, and half of those could be found in Rio Grande do Sul, a state heavily influenced by foreign immigration. About one farm in five hundred owned a tractor. *Latifundia* predominated, although the number of large landholdings declined. The number of farms tripled from 648,000 in 1920 to 1,896,000 in 1940. The difficulties in the sugar and coffee industries, the influence of European immigrants, and subdivision through inheritance accounted for the breakdown of some large estates and the multiplication of the number of farms. Table 7.2 indicates the land-owning structure in 1940. Obviously there still existed concentrated control over the land. A total of 85.7 percent of the farm operators worked land that did not exceed one hundred hectares (approximately 250 acres) in size. Altogether they farmed only 18.2 percent of the land under cultivation. On the opposite end of the scale, 0.3 percent of the operators owned 24.5 percent of the land. Tenants throughout Brazil cultivated about a fifth of the total land, paying rents considered to be very high.

Generally the rural workers suffered under harsh conditions. They received a pittance in wages, and often were in debt to their employer. Housing was primitive, the diet inadequate, health and sanitary conditions abysmal, and education generally nonexistent, and where existent substandard. Social mobility was rare. The many benefits conferred on the urban proletariat did not extend into the countryside. Rumors of a better life wafted through parts of rural Brazil. Often the more daring left their rustic purgatory for the promises of the city. That internal migration increased in the 1930s and continued at a rapid pace thereafter. Still, as late as 1945, nearly 75 percent of the Brazilians—the vast majority subservient, illiterate, disenfranchised, and unassimilated—lived outside the cities. The accelerating industrialization, urbanization, and modernization of the nation bypassed them.

Chapter Eight

Reform, Radicalization, and Reaction

The fall of Vargas in 1945 initiated a period of democratic experiments in Brazil. Impressive economic growth encouraged by a vigorous nationalism accompanied those experiments. The pace of both industrialization and urbanization quickened. That dynamic combination of democratization, nationalism, industrialization, and urbanization created a thrust that for a brief period seemed to propel Brazil toward both political and economic development. Those who drew their power or prestige from institutions fundamentally connected with the past—*latifundia*, elitist education, social stratification, restricted suffrage—balked at the rapid rate of change. They hoped to retard it. Their opposition strengthened the resolution of the radicals, and at that point the customary political dialogue ended. Conservatives and reformers could have conversed with each other as they had many times in the past, but not conservatives and radicals. The radicals momentarily seemed to triumph, but the conservative forces in Brazil revealed both resiliency and power. On March 31, 1964, they reasserted their authority and removed the radicals from power to return Brazil to past patterns of behavior. Some see

the 1945–1964 experiment with democracy as the natural consequence of gradual political maturation, while others regard it as an aberration, an unexpected hiatus between authoritarian governments.

Democratization

The Allies' march toward certain victory in Europe in 1944 marked democracy's triumph over dictatorship. Latin America felt the consequences. In the Spanish-speaking republics, one *caudilho* after another fell. The Brazilians, more heavily committed to the struggle in Europe than any of their Latin American neighbors, questioned why they should contribute to the promotion of democracy in Europe while suffering the constraints of dictatorship at home. This inconsistency annoyed them. Intellectuals and opposition politicians voiced that annoyance, as did ninety prominent Mineiros who in October of 1943 signed a manifesto that stated, "If we fight against fascism at the side of the United Nations so that liberty and democracy may be restored to all people, certainly we are not asking too much in demanding for ourselves such rights and guarantees." The students echoed that sentiment. Caught in the inconsistency of its own role, the military applied pressure on Vargas to return the nation to democratic rule. Both Generals Eurico Dutra and Góes Monteiro, long supporters of Vargas, but also representative of the pragmatic attitude of the military, agreed that the times demanded that the Estado Novo give way to democracy. Under increasing pressure by late 1944, Vargas slowly turned his attention to provisions for some sort of elections and to the reinstitution of democracy. Accordingly the government relaxed censorship and permitted political activity. A law appeared in February 1945 to govern voter registration and the elections of the president, the governors, and the members of state and national assemblies. Vargas set December 2, 1945, as the date for presidential and congressional elections. Those were to be the first elections since 1934, and the electorate was five times larger. Women had won the vote.

Many doubted the sincerity of Vargas' intentions to re-store democracy. They suspected that after enjoying fifteen years in power he would not really hand over the reins of authority. Memories of his lightning coup in 1937 had not faded. Suspicion mounted in July 1945 when fervent followers of the wily gaúcho began to express their desires for his political continuity. The chief of state maintained a delphic silence. His adversaries scrutinized his every move to confirm their suspicions. On October 10, he suddenly advanced the date for all state and local elections to December 2 to coin-cide with presidential and congressional elections. The ad-vance meant that all those who currently held office and planned to run in the elections would have to resign their office thirty days before the election, a maneuver that would permit Vargas to appoint friends to their posts. Then, on October 25, the president goaded speculation still further by appointing his brother Benjamin, the possessor of an unsa-vory reputation, to the important post of chief of police of Rio de Janeiro. Those activities seemed to signal that Vargas was preparing something more than elections. To prevent him from staging another coup and to calm public agitation, the military themselves staged a coup and took command of the government on October 29. The military, which had as-sured Vargas power in 1930 and for a decade and a half thereafter, intervened in 1945 in such a way as to guarantee the initiation of the democratic process. The middle class, convinced that democracy would best serve their interest, applauded. Quietly, Vargas retired to his *fazenda* in Rio Grande do Sul. The officers designated the chief justice of the Su-preme Court to head the government until after the elec-tions.

The urge to democratize Brazil ended fifteen years of Vargas government. Vargas, however, attributed his downfall to foreign influence, particularly the influence of the foreign business community. In a speech given in Pôrto Alegre at the end of 1946, he stated, "I was the victim of agents of interna-tional finance who intended to keep our country simply as an exporting colony for raw materials and a purchaser of indus-trial goods." His policies of economic nationalism, he be-

lieved, united "trusts and monopolies" against him. It was an intriguing idea well phrased within the emotional framework of economic nationalism so much in vogue during the latter years of his administration. As in years past, he scorned "old liberal capitalist democracy" and recommended his own brand of "Socialist Democracy for the workers." Apparently Vargas had changed little from his heyday, but for once he was out of harmony with the democratic sentiments of many Brazilians. Further, Brazil seemed to have changed: the industrialized and urbanized Brazil of the mid-forties contrasted with the coffee-dominated and rural-oriented Brazil of the late twenties.

Brazil owed at least part of that change to the guidance of Vargas. He restored unity and assigned the nation new goals. Diminishing the power of the coffee interests, he distributed it more broadly. He encouraged industrialization, which, in turn, fostered urban growth. The middle and working classes won political recognition for themselves. During a period of political extremism in the world, he steered a course between communism and integralism. The cost of those achievements came high. Political liberty and freedom of expression were part of the price paid. Yet, it would be specious to argue that Brazil under the Old Republic had enjoyed anything more than the formalities of democracy. In reality, Vargas had substituted one elitist rule for another, but in the process, as an aspiring populist leader, he had broadened the base upon which the government rested, drawing effectively upon the support and participation of both the urban middle and proletariat classes. He did bequeath a certain legacy to the future growth of democracy. He trimmed the power of the *coroneis,* and the 1932 Electoral Code lowered the voting age to eighteen, conferred the right to vote on working women, guaranteed the secret ballot, and created a system of electoral courts. He introduced the civil service merit system, and, after 1937, most of federal appointments were made on the basis of competitive exams. While the merit system may not have worked as well as envisaged, it did establish a precedent. His impressive labor legislation improved the living conditions of the expanding number of urban workers. Bow-

ing to political exigencies, he permitted the organization of political parties during his final year in office and even helped to create two of them.

Three important national political parties took shape in 1945, and they influenced the political life of the nation for a generation. Of equal significance, they contributed to the growing democratization of the country. The *Partido Social Democrático* (Social Democratic Party, or PSD), the largest of the three (and created by Vargas), drew much of its strength from the countryside. The state political machines that once supported Vargas rallied to its banner. The vigor of the party centered in Minas Gerais, but it also enjoyed considerable support in Rio de Janeiro state, Pernambuco, Maranhão, Bahia, Ceará, and Goiás. Vargas also presided over the creation of the *Partido Trabalhista Brasileiro* (Brazilian Labor Party, or PTB), the smallest of the three, which he regarded as his own personal machine. He had been contemplating the formation of such a party at least since 1943. It frankly and aggressively appealed to the urban worker and received most of its leadership and strength from the cities. Rio Grande do Sul and the Federal District of Rio de Janeiro formed the two strongest columns of support for that party. Finally, the *União Democrática Nacional* (National Democratic Union, or UDN) united those who opposed Vargas and his political heirs. Rejecting all that Vargas stood for, the UDN seemed to look back nostalgically to the Old Republic and included such old *políticos* as Artur Bernardes. Conservative in orientation, its center of strength also rested in Minas Gerais, with strong support in Bahia, the Federal District of Rio de Janeiro, Santa Catarina, Ceará, and Pernambuco. These three parties dominated the political scene, and only candidates from them reached the presidency. Together they regularly held 75 percent of the seats in the Chamber of Deputies. Table 8.1 illustrates their relative strength in the Chamber.

A wide variety of smaller parties also appeared. On the extreme right, the *Partido de Representação Popular* (Popular Representation Party, or PRP) continued the tradition of the Integralists. Plínio Salgado, returning to Brazil in 1945 from exile in Portugal, formed the party. He maintained it was not

Table 8.1 Strength of the Three Principal Parties in the Chamber of Deputies, 1945–1962 (by percentage)

Party	1945	1950	1954	1960	1962
PSD	40.9	32.3	31.1	34.6	30.0
UDN	25.4	23.9	20.7	21.4	23.0
PTB	9.7	17.5	19.8	20.5	26.6

totalitarian, although it supported the creation of a corporative state. On the extreme left, Luís Carlos Prestes, released from prison by Vargas at the end of World War II, reorganized the *Partido Comunista Brasileiro* (Brazilian Communist Party, or PCB), which enjoyed two years of legal existence. The Communists elected one senator, Prestes, and fourteen deputies in 1945, to whom they added four more in the elections of 1947. The other minor parties—they numbered about nine by the early 1960s—were more regional in their appeal.

Concerning the political parties in general, it can be concluded that platforms, programs, and policies tended to be vague. As had been true always in Brazilian politics, the personality dominated. Men took precedence over party labels. A firm sense of party loyalty failed to develop. Voters and politicians alike shifted party allegiance with bewildering rapidity. Parties often formed alliances among themselves on all political levels with little embarrassment and little regard to incongruities.

Although imperfect, they did provide the machinery for selecting and putting forth candidates. And if they did not always provide the electorate with a clear choice of issues, they did offer a choice of personalities. Democratic elections could not have been held without their participation. At least the three largest parties were national in scope. To a limited extent they reflected and expressed public opinion. Generally the parties indicated a willingness to abide by the give and take of politics. The parties—although not always their leaders—accepted the results of the elections in good grace. They paid homage to the ideals and goals of democratic government. Considering Brazil's scant experience with popular and national political parties, the organization of those parties in 1945 and their progress, often under considerable stress, in

the years thereafter were satisfactory. In short, they contributed—at least superficially—to the growth of the democratic process in Brazil after 1945.

For the first elections, whose date of December 2, 1945,
the coup did not alter, the UDN nominated Major General
Eduardo Gomes, a former *tenente,* and the PSD selected
General Eurico Dutra, who had been minister of war throughout the Estado Novo period. Tardily Vargas put the PTB behind Dutra. His growing coolness toward Dutra sprang from
his resentment of the contact his former minister maintained
with politicians and military officers who had opposed his
regime. Dutra polled 55 percent of the vote, and the PSD won
a majority in both houses. The election proved to be a victory
for Vargas as well: he was elected senator from two states
and congressman from six states and the federal district.

The congress elected at the same time also sat as a constituent assembly. Although the constitution promulgated on
September 18, 1946, institutionalized the labor legislation of
the Vargas era, it also reacted in many respects against Vargas
in an attempt to prevent the rise of a similar *caudilho.* The
presidency remained the key institution, yet was sufficiently
circumscribed to inhibit a future holder from abusing his
powers. The new constitution carefully separated the three
branches of government, ensuring Congress of its independence and its freedom from presidential control in the election of its members, and establishing an independent court
system with sufficient power to review the actions of the
other branches. It restored the office of vice president. To
the armed forces, it assigned the responsibility to "defend
the country and guarantee the constitutional powers and law
and order." Within a federal structure, the central government predominated, but restrictions were placed on it in an
effort to prevent abusive intervention in the internal affairs of
the states. All persons over eighteen years of age, except
military enlisted men and noncommissioned officers and illiterates (a major exception in a nation with an illiteracy rate
approaching 60 percent), enjoyed the right to vote. The Constitution of 1946, the fourth of the republic, demonstrated
one more effort of the Brazilians to adjust to the challenges

of contractural governance. It temporarily resolved the fundamental questions of who should govern and how.

The taciturn military career officer who entered the presidency on January 31, 1946, had supported the establishment of the Estado Novo; but later, propelled by the currents welling up within the nation in favor of democracy, he had helped to remove Vargas from office. As president, Dutra interpreted his duties to encourage the growth of democracy as a mandate to outlaw the activities of the local Communists. He judged the PCB as a threat to the nation's nascent democracy. What annoyed him in particular was the bold declaration of Senator Luís Carlos Prestes, leader of the PCB, that in the event of war between the U.S.S.R. and Brazil, the Brazilian Communists would support Russia. The memories of the Communist uprising in 1935 burned too vividly in Dutra's mind for him to tolerate such talk. The electoral growth of the PCB, as evinced in the state elections of January of 1947, further disturbed him. The government reacted by outlawing the PCB on the grounds that its objectives were contrary to the goals of a democratic society, a move sanctioned by the Constitution of 1946. The Brazilian government broke diplomatic relations with Moscow, and Congress expelled from its ranks those members elected on the PCB ticket. The PCB remained illegal after 1947 but by no means inactive. Dutra had demonstrated, nonetheless, the limitations of tolerance in the new democracy.

Dutra presided over an essentially conservative government. The administration regarded suspiciously any opinions favorable to economic, social, or political reform, if, indeed, it did not outrightly label them communistic. As in the United States and elsewhere in the world at the time, anti-Communism became the doctrine of the status quo, and not a few of the men in positions of power had for years made a career out of being anti-Communist. They gratuitously made the charge of "Communist" against those with whom they disagreed, liberally applying the epithet to labor, students, and intellectuals in particular.

Dutra chose to ignore nationalism, a force he regarded with some suspicion, perhaps identifying it, or its goals, with

parts of the Communist program. Although avoiding the nationalist rhetoric his predecessor had perfected, he did undertake some projects the nationalists could only applaud: the construction of oil refineries, a tanker fleet, and port installations, the rebuilding and paving of the Rio-São Paulo highway, and the beginning of the mammoth Paulo Afonso hydroelectric project to provide the energy needed by burgeoning industrialization.

Superficially the economy seemed healthy. The price of coffee rose, and the quantity of coffee beans sold abroad reached new highs. Still, Brazil lived far beyond its means. When Dutra became president, Brazil held gold and foreign exchange reserves of nearly $800 million, a record high. The entire sum was used to buy imports, many of them luxuries, which during the war years had not been available. A spendthrift attitude prevailed, and more rapidly than anyone had imagined possible the reserves were exhausted, partially, it should be noted, because Brazil paid inflated prices for the items imported.

For the presidential elections of 1950, the PTB and PSD offered their support to Vargas. After ensuring that the military would not object, he accepted the candidacy and waged a vigorous campaign on a platform of accelerated industrialization and expanded social legislation. A wide variety of supporters drawn from the ranks of the industrialists, businessmen, nationalists, and the proletariat gave him 49 percent of the vote, a handsome victory over other rather colorless candidates. Thus, for the first time in his long political career, a popular electoral mandate opened the doors of the presidential palace to him on January 31, 1951.

Governing under a constitution which he neither wrote nor influenced and amid a welter of political parties, many of which were hostile, was a challenge for the former *caudilho.* Aged sixty-eight when he assumed office again, Vargas seemed less adept, less flexible. His own personal secretary observed that his chief showed "signs of exhaustion." The challenges in no way abated. Budgetary deficits, the rising cost of living, and general inflation clouded the financial horizon. The cost of living had risen on an average of 6 percent a year from 1945

to 1950, when it jumped 11 percent, a figure repeated in 1951 and doubled in 1952. The government balanced the budget but uninhibitedly printed new currency. The volume of paper currency rose from 31 to 50 billion cruzeiros during Vargas' tenure. Vargas encountered some difficulty with the military over his labor policies. In 1951 he raised the minimum wage, the first such raise since 1943. In 1954, his minister of labor and political disciple, João Goulart, tried to double wages. The officers charged Goulart with demagogy and criticized him for using his office, its powers and finances, to enhance his own political position. A bitter "Manifesto of the Colonels" demanded his dismissal, and a cautious Vargas removed his young protégé from office—but later he enacted the wage increase and praised Goulart in the process.

Vargas faced some crucial decisions that proved extremely difficult for him to make (as they were for his successors). While it was not difficult to sustain the momentum of growth—simple numerical increase—it was challenging to pursue genuine development—the utilization of Brazil's potential for the greatest good for the largest number of citizens. Basically the governments faced a series of choices that revolved around reforms of the institutional structures as opposed to encouragement of additional investments, part of which originated abroad. Repeatedly the presidents opted for the latter, and the forms the investments inevitably took did more to promote economic growth than to foster development. Since growth favored the privileged at the expense of the impoverished majority the long-term result of the governments' economic policies was to exacerbate social injustice. However, growth can disguise the inequities or cloak them with euphoric hope, at least for a time, creating the illusion of well-being or improvement. The governments became masters of creating economic illusions. Presidents performed with smoke and mirrors as accomplished magicians to conjure up images of economic miracles. In reality, few steps toward development were taken and those which might have encouraged development—increased hydroelectric power and expanding road networks, for example—were used so that

they contributed primarily to growth. In fairness, it must be reemphasized that under Vargas the government's commitment to first create a vast steel producing complex and later to institute an oil monopoly further expanded the role of government. It became actively and inextricably involved in the vital economic questions of planning, industrialization, modernization, and development.

President Vargas was not without his detractors, particularly within the UDN. They attacked relentlessly. In the vanguard of the attack marched the vitriolic Carlos Lacerda, editor of the *Tribuna da Imprensa,* who wielded a poisoned pen unrelentingly hostile to Vargas. Under the censorship imposed by the Estado Novo, he would have been silenced at once, but under the new democracy it seemed impossible to stop him. An attempt to do so precipitated the end of the Vargas administration, and indeed of Vargas himself.

In the early hours of the morning of August 5, 1954, Lacerda returned to his apartment in Copacabana accompanied by Air Force Major Rubens Florentino Vaz, one of a series of volunteer military bodyguards. As their car pulled up in front of the apartment building, shots rang out, one slightly wounding Lacerda, another killing the major. Indignant, the air force, in addition to the police, undertook an investigation to apprehend the assassin. Clues pointed to the presidential palace. Soon investigators confirmed that the chief of the president's personal guard, an intimate of Vargas, had planned the crime. The political repercussions were tremendous. First the air force, then the navy, and finally the army demanded the resignation of Vargas. It was not constitutional principles but rather an elusive and pervasive military honor that dictated their actions. On the morning of the 24th, the president was informed that the military—for the second time— had deposed him. Upon receipt of the news he retired to his bedroom, from which a shot shattered the gloomy silence of Catete Palace. Those who rushed into his room found him dead, a bullet in his heart. A stunned nation paused. It read with bewilderment the cryptic and emotional suicide note Vargas left behind:

Once more the forces and interests against the people are newly coordinated and raised against me. . . . I follow the destiny that is imposed on me. After years of domination and looting by international economic and financial groups, I made myself chief of an unconquerable revolution. I began the work of liberation and I instituted a regime of social liberty. I had to resign. I returned to govern on the arms of the people. A subterranean campaign of international groups joined with national groups revolting against the regime of workers' guarantees. . . . I have fought month to month, day to day, hour to hour, resisting a constant aggression, unceasingly bearing it all in silence, forgetting all and renouncing myself to defend the people that now fall abandoned. I cannot give you more than my blood. . . . I offer my life in the holocaust. I chose this means to be with you always. When they humiliate you, you will feel my soul suffering at your side. When hunger beats at your door, you will feel in your chests the energy for the fight for yourselves and your children. When they humiliate you, you will feel in my grief the force for reaction. My sacrifice will maintain you united, and my name will be your battle flag. . . . I fought against the looting of Brazil. I fought against the looting of the people. I have fought bare-breasted. The hatred, infamy, and calumny did not beat down my spirit. I gave you my life. Now I offer my death. Nothing remains. Serenely I take the first step on the road to eternity and I leave life to enter history.

The note highlighted the president's role as a populist and nationalist leader. His personality was many-sided, but the Vargas who wrote that farewell was the one who had served as the promoter of the rights of workers and of the creation of Petrobrás.

The unexpected crisis generated by the suicide put the democratic experiment in Brazil to a severe test. The very military which had just deposed Vargas stepped forward to guarantee the constitutional process. Vice President João Café Filho, a marked contrast to Vargas in his conventional economic outlook and lack of nationalistic orientation, took the oath of office to complete the last seventeen months of Vargas' five-year mandate. For the first time, the declared enemies of the Estado Novo achieved power. Café Filho himself had vehemently attacked the establishment of the Estado Novo and had been exiled. In his new government, he assigned the

key cabinet posts of Finance, Justice, and Foreign Affairs to stalwarts of the UDN. His administration proved to be a caretaker one, since the maneuvering for the 1955 presidential elections got under way almost at once.

The PSD and PTB, the two parties founded by Vargas, jointly put forth Juscelino Kubitschek, the highly successful governor of Minas Gerais, for the presidency and João Goulart, heir to the Vargas mantle, for the vice presidency. They campaigned on an alluring platform promising economic progress for all. The UDN endorsed General Juarez Távora, former *tenente* to bear its standard. Acrimony characterized the campaign. Military leaders expressed their concern about the dangers of a violent electoral campaign in the midst of serious political and social crises, which to them seemed threatening. They harbored suspicions about the suitability of Kubitschek for the presidency and made no effort to hide their dislike of Goulart, who had earned the enmity of the officers during his brief tenure as Vargas's minister of labor. Rumors of a military coup circulated. In early October of 1955, Kubitschek and Goulart won the elections. Goulart received even more votes than the presidential victor. A month later President Café Filho, entering the hospital after a mild heart attack, turned over the duties of his office on November 8, 1955, to his legal successor, the president of the Chamber of Deputies, Carlos Luz, a declared adversary of Kubitschek and Goulart. Most observers believed that he would prevent his two political enemies from taking the offices to which they had just been elected. At that point, Marshal Odílio Denys and Minister of War Henrique Teixeira Lott, in alliance with other officers who formed the *Movimento Militar Constitucionalista* (Constitutionalist Military Movement) staged a preventive coup on November 11, removing Acting President Luz from office to guarantee the inauguration of Kubitschek and Goulart. Congress cooperated and swore in the vice president of the Senate, Nereu Ramos, as the interim president. In due course and with no further difficulty the democratically elected Kubitschek and Goulart took office on the prescribed date, January 31, 1956. Despite tribulations and stress, the democratic process survived, and in this particular

case the military seemingly contributed to its success. However, increasingly frequent military interventions signified trouble in the long run for democracy. They revealed the fragility of contractural governance. They also suggested the difficulties of integrating larger numbers of humble citizens into a traditional society structured for the benefit of an elite and a privileged middle class.

One measure of the successful democratization was that the elections in 1945, as well as all subsequent ones held under the Constitution of 1946, were generally honest. This contrasted sharply with the characteristic chicanery of elections during the Old Republic. An elaborate system of electoral courts removed the control of the elections from those in power and guaranteed the voters complete freedom at the polls and an accurate tabulation of the votes cast. Those special courts supervised the registration of parties, candidates, and voters; they also bore responsibility for the supervision of the balloting, the counting of ballots, and the investigation and prosecution of electoral fraud. An electoral reform in 1955 ended the custom by which each party printed and distributed its own ballots, substituting an official ballot made available through the Supreme Electoral Tribunal. The regional electoral tribunals appointed three poll-watchers at each polling place, and each party assigned one poll-watcher. The vote was secret: the voter marked the official ballot in the privacy of an enclosed booth and then dropped it in a box in the presence of the poll-watchers, who then accompanied the ballot box to the district electoral board where they oversaw the counting. Minimal opportunities for fraud existed.

Most charges of fraud originated in remote rural areas where the inspection system tended to be less rigorous or, in some cases, nonexistent. In some rural areas the *coronel* still held sway and he could regiment the local vote for his preferred candidate. Beholden to the *coroneis*, candidates so elected did not represent the voters, of course, but rather the interests of those men who had delivered the vote. Fortunately for the future of democracy in Brazil, that system was on the decline.

One means of effectively reducing the power of the *co-roneis* and the traditional ruling families was to create new political subdivisions, principally new municipalities, often created as the result of commercial or industrial growth in a particular area. The *coroneis* and the traditional families often continued to control the old municipalities, but other, more progressive forces—such as a middle class, an educated working class, and a general atmosphere favorable to change and modernization—dominated in the newly created municipalities. Their number burgeoned. The increase of municipalities in Minas Gerais serves as an excellent example of this growth. That wealthy captaincy was divided into 16 municipalities during the colonial period. During the imperial period, Minas Gerais province boasted 95 *municípios*. In 1948, there were 316; in 1953, 388; in 1958, 405; and in 1963, 722. In those same years, after the promulgation of the Constitution of 1946, the number of municipalities throughout Brazil doubled. Corruption, nepotism, and poverty characterized many of the local governments, but, on the other hand, examples of good government, efficiency, and grass-roots democracy could be found too.

The judicial system as it evolved under the Constitution of 1946 provided another bulwark for democracy. Elaborate provisions of that document protected the courts' independence, an independence enjoyed to a degree unique in Latin America. The federal Supreme Court, composed of eleven justices appointed by the president with the approval of the Senate (the number of judges could be increased only at the request of the court itself), had jurisdiction to rule on the constitutionality of all legislation, federal, state, or local. The bench boldly exercised its power of judicial review. Although the court never attained the power of its North American counterpart, it inhibited, checked, and, at times reversed arbitrary actions of the executive or legislature.

A further indication of the growth of Brazilian democracy was the steady increase in the size of the electorate. Despite the large segments of the population restricted from voting by the constitution, the number of voters mounted steadily as the population grew and literacy rose. The percentage of

the population registered to vote increased from 16 in 1945 to 25 in 1962. The number of voters increased rather steadily during that period at the rate of approximately 20 percent every four years. Two new groups, the urban proletariat and the industrial middle class, took important positions in the political spectrum. The growth of the urban electorate cut the power and influence of the rural coroneis to a fraction of what it had been during the Old Republic. The careers of Getúlio Vargas and others amply illustrated that politicians could successfully base their support on a mass popular following rather than on the support of the elite. Vargas appealed directly and openly to the workers, informing them of their power and advising them how to use it. As the new groups realized and exercised their power, the control of the urban elites and rural coroneis declined proportionately.

One of the major blocks to popular democracy in Brazil was the lack of education. A faulty educational system likewise retarded modernization. Good schools were essential to prepare the Brazilians to accept technological progress as well as to participate in that progress, to encourage students to higher goals, and to equip them with the means of achieving those goals. Unfortunately, about half the adult population did not even know how to sign their names. Thus they were excluded from participation in both the political and the modernization processes. Although more students were enrolled in schools than ever before, the statistics were still bleak. In 1940, there were 3¼ million students enrolled at all levels from the primary through the university level; in 1965, the total reached 11¼ million. At the same time, of course, the population had grown from 41 to 72 million. The sad result was that although the illiteracy rate fell the number of illiterates grew. In 1965, of 1,000 students matriculated in primary schools, only 13 reached secondary school and only 4 completed some form of advanced education. The dropout rate during the four years of primary school was exceptionally high, higher than that of Liberia or the Philippines, for example. In theory, primary education was both free and compulsory, but in reality impoverished parents found it an eco-

nomic hardship to send their children to school. They needed them to contribute to the meager family income or to take care of their younger sisters and brothers while both parents worked. The government never provided enough of schools or a way to enforce compulsory attendance. For these reasons most school-age children either didn't enroll or dropped out.

Like everything else, the educational situation varied widely from region to region. In the affluent state of São Paulo the budget for education equaled that of the rest of the states combined; the city of São Paulo city budgeted for educational purposes more than the rest of the local governments combined. Nearly 80 percent of the adult population of São Paulo state was literate in 1965. In the depressed Northeast, only 33 percent of the children of primary school age were in school, and only 6 percent of those of secondary school age attended any classes. Barely 30 percent of the adults were literate.

The educational system was archaic. The classical curriculum, which educated the children of the elite for further education in the universities, belied the desire for modernization. A rapidly developing nation with industrial pretensions required technicians of every sort, yet most of the population was excluded by lack of training from contributing to their nation's technical development. Modern educators realized the need for a structural change in the educational system. As a result, educational reforms in the early 1960s emphasized ambitious literacy campaigns to prepare the masses for technical and vocational training. A noticeable rise in enrollments for vocational training occurred: 124,000 vocational students in 1954 increasing to 275,000 in 1962, but the numbers fell pitifully short of the need.

The number of universities increased modestly. There were more than thirty universities by the mid-1960s. But in a population well over 70 million, barely 155,000 students matriculated in them. Those that did represented the elite in every sense of the word, since only 5 percent of the university students came from proletarian families. Law remained, as it always had been, the preferred field of study of those privi-

leged students. Of a total enrolment of 110,093 students in 1962, nearly a quarter—25,856—studied law. There were 13,325 in engineering, 13,160 in the social sciences, 10,919 in medicine, 5,548 in education, 4,274 in fine arts, 3,388 in natural sciences, 2,447 in agriculture, and 1,048 in the humanities. Extreme regional disparities in both quantity and quality of university education existed. The five states of São Paulo, Guanabara, Rio Grande do Sul, Minas Gerais, and Paraná enrolled three-quarters of the students and hired three-quarters of the professors. The universities in São Paulo and Guanabara enjoyed reputations as the best in the nation.

All Brazilians paid at least lip service to the value of education for the future of the nation. Mário Pinto Serva wishfully wrote in his *O Enigma Brasileiro* (The Brazilian Enigma), "In twenty years Brazil will be literate and then it will take its position as the second or third power of the world." (Optimism has been an enduring Brazilian characteristic.) Shining through the dismal data, however, is the one reassuring statistic that the literacy rate did continue to rise slowly, thereby expanding the electorate and the base of democracy.

Developmental Nationalism

Intensifying nationalism accompanied the democratic experiment. It displayed four major characteristics. First, it veered leftward. The Integralist party had exerted the last major effort of the right to manipulate nationalist feelings. After its suppression in 1937, the left dominated nationalist thought. The reliance on Marxist phraseology often exposed the movement to criticism that the Communist party guided or dominated it. Such an accusation was not only false but also oversimplifed the complexities of Brazilian nationalism and obscured efforts to understand it.

Second, nationalist leaders criticized ever more boldly foreign economic domination. They blamed enervating dependency on foreign manipulation. Their campaign to oppose foreign ownership found its modern roots, as noted, in

the writings of Alberto Tôrres and in the opposition to Percival Farquhar. The nationalists termed foreign ownership "economic colonialism," which drained, impoverished, and enfeebled the underdeveloped nations to further nurture the industrialized states. Despite nationalist rhetoric and agitation, the inflow of foreign investments continued at a rapid pace throughout the decade of the 1950s. By 1960 foreigners owned 69 percent of the automobile industry, 62 percent of the pharmaceutical industry, 57 percent of the auto parts industry, 38 percent of the chemical industry, 28 percent of plastics production, 22 percent of the cellulose industry, 17 percent of steel manufacturing, and 15 percent of the paper industry. They continued to repatriate handsome profits that cumulatively exceeded their investments.

Third, the nationalists concentrated their strongest attack on the United States, an obvious target since the United States was the single largest investor in Brazil. Its investment jumped from $28 million in 1914, to $577 million in 1950, to $1.5 billion in 1960—about half of the total foreign investment in Brazil. Logically any campaign undertaken against foreign investors assumed anti-Yankee tones. Furthermore, the nationalists thought they detected links among their own oligarchy, the United States government, and U.S. investors, all beneficiaries of Brazilian dependency. All three favored the status quo in Brazil and opposed change. In several respects, then, the nationalists depicted the United States as an enemy whose influence and presence had to be challenged and defeated if nationalism was to triumph. They cultivated anti-Americanism as a convenient and certain means to arouse national feeling.

Finally, the nationalists paid ever greater attention to economic development. Defining nationalism as "the political consciousness of development," they advocated it as the single force capable of modernizing the nation. Developmental nationalism, springing from the program of the *tenentes* and the policies of the Estado Novo, received new emphasis from 1951, when Vargas returned to power, until the military coup of 1964. Its doctrine called for governmental control of natural resources, limitations on foreign capital, accelerating

industrialization, and greater commerce with all nations. It emerged as the only way to liberate Brazil, to unchain it from the past and propel it into the future. Such a concept attracted many who did not necessarily support all hard-core nationalist causes.

For nearly a decade (1955–1964), the focal point of the developmental nationalist movement was the *Institutio Superior de Estudos Brasileiros* (Superior Institute of Brazilian Studies, or ISEB), established by the federal government as an autonomous agency responsible to the Ministry of Education. The institute offered courses and conducted research on the problems of economic development. It also undertook the task of formulating ideological doctrine for developmental nationalism. Its members agreed that a vibrant economy required national planning; they further agreed that the state would have to oversee and guide such planning and development. However, they differed as to whether a basically socialistic or a capitalistic economy would best serve Brazil's interests. The disagreement eventually split the ISEB, just as it did the nationalist movement itself. The moderate nationalists were more tolerant of foreign investments and less enthusiastic about government ownership or control. The radical nationalists urged state ownership of the principal industries and control of foreign investments. Winning control of the ISEB in 1959, they imposed their ideology. Meanwhile, the officers in the Escola Superior de Guerra (Superior War College) fretted about the ideas propagated through the ISEB. They believed the orientation to be too hostile to the United States and too receptive to Marxism.

As industrialization intensified after World War II, the program gradually gave up some of its emergency or stopgap aspects. Brazilian leaders adopted better plans and carried them out with more resolution. They intended to alter the basic structure of the economy by reducing the nation's customary dependence on exports, encouraging import-substitution industries, and creating heavy primary industries. Companies proving they could produce an imported item received high tariff protection, a policy that proved particularly effective in encouraging the production of consumer

goods. As late as 1950 those goods still accounted for 9.7 percent of the imports, a figure that fell to 1.5 by 1961. The consumer industries concentrated on the manufacture of goods of primary necessity: food, beverages, clothing, and textiles. The factories were small. On average they employed sixteen workers. To these basic industries the government gave new attention by making loans available on reasonable terms to potential entrepreneurs and by creating or helping to create some heavy industries. Volta Redonda in the 1940s and Petrobrás in the 1950s were excellent examples of those governmental efforts, as was the growing activity of the government in the development of electrical energy resources.

An unexpected impetus to industrial expansion was the rapid exhaustion of Brazil's foreign exchange reserves after World War II. In the emergency, the government imposed import controls. Discouraging the importation of consumer items on the one hand, those controls favored the purchase of capital goods and raw materials on the other. The controls worked in such a fashion that the price of imported capital goods and raw materials remained nearly constant. At the same time, the domestic prices charged by the manufacturers of consumer products rose steadily. Good business sense prompted the purchase of capital machinery so that more goods could be manufactured internally. Following that pattern, a host of new industries appeared. More often than not, they became each other's customers, illustrating the self-propelling nature of industrialization once under way. By the time Vargas took command of the economy for the second time, the drive for industrialization was characterized by encouragement of the importation of capital goods, discouragement of the importation of items domestically manufactured, high premiums on foreign exchange, and inflation. The industrial output in 1954 doubled that of 1945. Giant industrial strides were being made despite monumental handicaps: a poorly developed transportation network, an illiterate population untrained for technical jobs, an inefficient use of the land, and insufficient national economic integration.

In pursuit of development, President Kubitschek envisioned a rise in the production of hydroelectric power, ex-

Table 8.2 Average Annual Economic Growth Rates, 1947–1961

Period	Agricultural Production	Industrial Production	Gross National Product
1947–1961	4.6	9.6	6.1
1957–1961	4.8	12.7	7.0

pansion of road building, rehabilitation of the railroads, encouragment to basic industries, increases in both steel production and oil refining capacity, the establishment of a vehicle industry, and accelerated agricultural production. In his campaign for the presidency, he had promised his compatriots "fifty years of progress in five," and to a large extent he fulfilled that promise. The day after his inauguration he created the National Development Council to oversee his program for economic development. He drew up a "Program of Targets" both for the government and for private industry. In his speeches, he reiterated his belief that economic development was the key to national independence. Under his dramatic leadership, from 1956 to 1961, Brazil experienced unparalleled economic growth. Industrial production grew 80 percent; steel, 100 percent; mechanical industries, 125 percent; electrical and communications industries, 380 percent; transportation equipment, 600 percent. By 1960, industry accounted for over 20 percent of the gross national product. By that time, Brazil manufactured fully half of its heavy-industry needs: machine tools, motors, transformers, mining and transportation equipment, turbines and generators, etc. Although the rates of growth for the 1947–1961 period were impressive, as Table 8.2 indicates, the rates during the Kubitschek administration were nothing short of spectacular.

Agricultural output increased 52 percent during the decade of the fifties and industrial output 140 percent, reflective of the priority given industrialization. During the 1950s Brazil's rate of economic growth was three times that of the rest of Latin America. In fact, it was one of the most impressive growth records in the Western world. Economic growth kept far ahead of rapid population increases, which averaged 3.2 percent a year, the highest rate among the heavily populated

nations of the world. By 1960, 71 million people inhabited Brazil, 19 million more than a decade earlier.

Brazil achieved its economic miracle without foreign "doles." It applied for and received "hard" loans from the Export-Import Bank. Despite nationalist rhetoric, the inflow of foreign capital accelerated rapidly after 1955, attracted by the political stability, the potential of the nation, and the lack of restrictions. Kubitschek frankly encouraged foreign investment. The banks received their interest on the loans; the foreign capitalists, their profits. At the same time, domestic investment also reached new highs.

During the decade of the fifties, the number of industrial plants grew by 33 percent and the labor force by 40 percent, so that in 1960 there were 110,339 industrial establishments employing 1,796,857 workers. São Paulo and Guanabara states hosted a majority of the industries. By 1960, São Paulo alone boasted a third of the nation's factories, half of its workers, and half of its output.

To supply the desperately needed power for industrialization, the president urged the exploitation of the nation's hydroelectric potential, estimated to be the sixth largest in the world. He authorized the construction of the gigantic Furnas Hydroelectric Project and the impressive Três Marias Dam on the São Francisco River. During the Kubitschek years, hydroelectric power increased from 3 to 5 million kilowatts. Whereas Brazil lagged considerably behind the United States and Canada in electrical energy production, it far outdistanced its two closest Latin American industrial rivals, Argentina and Mexico.

Kubitschek will probably be best remembered for his most audacious scheme, which realized one of the nationalists' oldest dreams: he moved the capital from the coast to the interior. Brasília, located in the state of Goiás, became the symbol of the opening of the vast interior to modernization and the unification of all regions of Brazil. Kubitschek referred to it as the "capital that will unite the whole nation." In 1956, with the approval of an incredulous Congress, he created the *Companhia Urbanizadora da Nova Capital* (Ur-

banization Company of the New Capital) to take charge of building the new city. Lúcio Costa prepared a daring "airplane design" plan for the new capital, which Oscar Niemeyer matched with imaginative designs for the federal buildings: the eleven ministry buildings, the Praça of the Three Powers with its Senate and Chamber of Deputies complex, Palácio do Planalto (executive office building), and Supreme Court, the Palácio da Alvarada (presidential palace), and Itamaratí. One of his major monuments was the cathedral. Taken as a group, those magnificent and ingeniously designed buildings stand as a tribute to one of the most visionary architects of the twentieth century. His motifs and designs became commonplace throughout the world as other architects adopted them. Indeed, the world recognized his achievements and influence when his international colleagues bestowed the coveted Pritzker Architectural Prize on Niemeyer in 1988.

Work on Brasília began in 1957 and continued at a frantic pace, twenty-four hours a day, seven days a week. On April 21, 1960, an ebullient Kubitschek inaugurated the new capital, Brazil's third, some six hundred miles from the coast. The former Federal District of Rio de Janeiro then elected to become the union's smallest state, Guanabara. Brasília was an expensive but magnificent gesture to demonstrate that Brazil at last was going to develop its untapped hinterland, so long a promised land. The population of the new capital was 140,000 in 1960 and grew phenomenally in the years thereafter. The daring futuristic city with its exceptional architecture captured the admiration of the world.

To connect Brasília with the rest of the nation, the government undertook an ambitious program to build "highways of national union." New roads radiated from Brasília to Belém, 1,400 miles to the north, to Fortaleza, 1,060 miles to the northeast, and to Belo Horizonte, 400 miles to the southeast, where that road met others leading to Rio de Janeiro, São Paulo, and the south. In total, the Kubitschek administration opened approximately 11,000 miles of new roads and highways—over a third of which were paved.

Vehicular traffic increased proportionately. The number

Map 5. The Plan for Brasília by Lúcio Costa

1. Plaza of the Three Powers
2. Ministries
3. Cathedral
4. Cultural district
5. Amusement center
6. Banking center
7. Business district
8. Hotels
9. Television tower
10. Sports center
11. Municipal square
12. Barracks
13. Railroad station
14. Assembly plants and light industry
15. University
16. Embassies and legations
17. Residential zone
18. Single-family housing
19. Horticulture, floriculture, and tree nursery
20. Botanical garden
21. Zoo
22. Golf club
23. Yacht club
24. Presidential residence
25. Jockey club
26. Area zoned for fairs, circuses, etc.
27. Airport
28. Cemetery

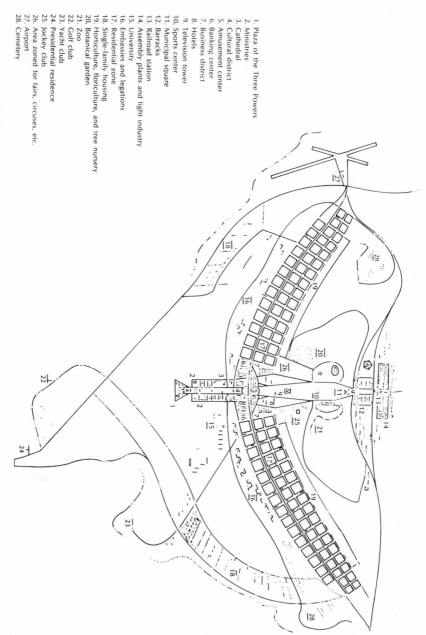

of trucks and automobiles doubled and the number of buses tripled during the decade of the 1950s. Kubitschek authorized and encouraged the creation of a national automotive industry, one of the major industrial achievements of his administration. Within a five-year period, that is by 1962, that new industry was turning out 200,000 units annually to make Brazil the world's seventh-largest automobile producer. By May 1967, 1.5 million cars had rolled off the assembly lines of the ten automobile manufacturers. Trucks, buses, and tractors also went into production. Brazil not only produced enough of these vehicles to satisfy its own market, but soon began to export them to its neighbors.

Kubitschek's programs bore a price tag. Being grandiose, they were expensive. To meet part of the costs, the government simply turned on the printing presses and let the currency flow out. In 1955, there were over 60 billion cruzeiros in circulation; in 1961, approximately 200 billion. Inflation, which, despite a hopeful hesitation in 1957, had plagued the country since the end of World War II, continued to mount, spurred on by wage increases, the high rate of investment, and budget deficits on all levels—local, state, and federal. In five years living expenses tripled. The International Monetary Fund expressed dismay over the situation and threatened to withhold loans until the government adopted more orthodox financial methods. The nationalists regarded inflation as a catalyst for industrialization; they also resented outside interference no matter how well intentioned. The president too felt that the stabilization policies urged by the IMF would retard his development plans. To the delight of the nationalists, he denounced the IMF for trying to delay the industrialization of Brazil, and in June 1959, he broke off negotiations with that international organization. Inflation spiraled upward.

The growth of Brazil after World War II was much more than material. National pride, spirit, and culture grew just as prodigiously. The world at long last began to recognize Brazilian achievements, and such recognition excited national pride. The Brazilian soccer team won world championships in 1958, 1962, and 1970; those victories were occasions for na-

tional holidays. The Brazilians celebrated with exuberant dancing in the streets. Pelé, the adored soccer ace, became a national hero and enjoyed international fame and recognition. Brazil thrilled to other athletic victories, such as that of tennis star Maria Bueno, who won the Wimbledon Ladies' singles championship in 1960. Brazilian beauty was also heralded abroad; there was hardly a Miss World or a Miss Universe contest that did not include a Miss Brazil among the finalists. The news media gave those pageants detailed coverage, and in 1963 and again in 1968, when Miss Brazil triumphed as Miss Universe, the nation rejoiced.

Brazilian music, art, and literature also burst their national frontiers. The works of composer Heitor Villa-Lobos received applause in concert halls around the world, and the composer himself conducted the major symphony orchestras of Europe and the United States until his death in 1959. Critics heaped accolades in particular on the haunting music of the "Bachianas Brasileiras," his pleasing combination of Bach and Brazilian folk music. He composed more than 1,400 works. The bossa nova invaded the field of popular music. Musicians such as João Gilberto, Antônio Carlos Jobim, Sérgio Mendes, and Edú Lobo played before international audiences. "The Girl from Ipanema" became a hit song in the United States. Later, "The Band," composed by the young Chico Buarque de Holanda, climbed to the top of the world's hit parade.

Brazil's film industry, under the inspiration and direction of the movement called Cinema Nôvo, began in the late 1950s to focus attention on national themes and problems. The Cinema Nôvo films looked sharply into the two areas of greatest poverty and injustice: the *favela* (urban slum) and the *sertão* (the arid backlands). Carlos Diegues studied the drama of the poor in the city in his *Grande Cidade* (*The Big City*, 1966), emphasizing its brutalization of the rural migrant, who, full of hope, came to the city only to be plunged into conditions worse than those he fled. Doubtless still the masterpiece of the Cinema Nôvo is *Vidas Sêcas* (*Barren Lives*, 1963), directed by Nelson Pereira dos Santos. He brilliantly transferred to the screen the powerful novel of the same name by Graciliano Ramos. Rural poverty, dependency, and underde-

velopment were depicted with unflinching accuracy in that extraordinary document of how an impoverished family survives in the backlands. Of the many young directors at work in the Cinema Nôvo movement in the 1960s, Glauber Rocha stands out as the most productive and imaginative. He imposed a heavy symbolism on his films concerned with Brazilian reality. Possibly still the best of Rocha's films is *Deus e o Diablo na Terra do Sol* (*Black God, White Devil*, 1963), which introduced the viewer to the principal human types found in the *sertão* as well as to some of the persistent causes of the poverty characteristic of that region. The invigorated film industry reaped a rich reward in the early 1960s when Anselmo Duarte's film, *Pagador de Promessas* (*The Given Word*, 1962) received the best film award at both the Cannes and San Francisco film festivals. In 1968, the Museum of Modern Art in New York City sponsored a retrospective festival of Cinema Nôvo films.

Brazilian literature received greater international recognition as the works of Graciliano Ramos, José Lins do Rego, Érico Veríssimo, João Guimarães Rosa, Rachel de Queiróz, and Jorge Amado were translated into many languages. Amado's novel, *Gabriela, Clove, and Cinnamon* became a best seller in the United States in the mid-1960s. Quite belatedly Machado de Assis received acclaim abroad as his major novels were translated. Their publication in English occurred during the 1950s and 1960s, accompanied by several critical studies.

Brazilian scholars enjoyed an increasingly favorable international reputation. As a group, they were probably accorded greater recognition than their predecessors or their contemporaries from other Latin American republics. The sociologist Gilberto Freyre, the economist Celso Furtado, the historian José Honório Rodrigues, and the literary critic Afrânio Coutinho lectured in many universities in the United States and Europe and saw their books translated into a variety of foreign languages. Institutes of Brazilian studies were established in the United States, Japan, and a number of European nations, and chairs in Brazilian history and literature were set up at the major universities in those countries.

The international recognition given Brazilian achievements invigorated national pride. Nebulous as it might be, that pride contributed significantly to the growth of Brazilian nationalism.

Growing Pains

Modernization placed heavier responsibilities on the cities, whose roles expanded and became more varied. Their primary functions were governmental, administrative, commercial, and industrial. They served as transportation hubs, and many of them became the centers of complex transportation networks. The cities provided many services as well as recreational, cultural, and educational advantages. Of the various functions of the Brazilian city by the mid-twentieth century, the industrial gave considerable impetus to urban growth. Jobs related directly or indirectly to the factories seemed to promise more social mobility. At least in the large industries salaries were comparatively high, and the workers enjoyed the benefits of the labor legislation decreed by Getúlio Vargas. Few of the untrained and/or illiterate from the countryside could compete for those jobs. However, the construction industry, based partially on the employment of the unskilled but strong, offered some hope of employment and improvement of socio-economic status to rural migrants in the city. Those migrants also performed low-skill service work. In contrast to the attraction exerted by the cities to some rural dwellers, the grinding poverty of the countryside pushed many desperate peasants into urban areas. The roads from the *sertão* to the city were well traveled. Approximately 60 percent of the increase in urban populations resulted from internal migration.

The rate of urban growth spurted after 1940. Urbanization became a salient characteristic of Brazilian development in the decades thereafter. During certain periods, some of the largest cities increased in population at the rate of 10 percent a year. In 1920, approximately 25 percent of the population lived in urban areas; by 1940 that proportion had

Table 8.3 Urban Population Growth, 1900–1960 (in thousands of inhabitants)

City	1900	1920	1940	1960
São Paulo	299	579	1,308	3,825
Rio de Janeiro	800	1,157	1,781	3,372
Recife	113	238	348	707
Belo Horizonte	13	55	211	693
Salvador	205	283	291	655
Pôrto Alegre	73	179	275	641
Fortaleza	48	78	174	514
Curitiba	49	78	142	361
Niterói	53	86	143	245
Manaus	50	75	107	175

SOURCE: Delgado de Carvalho, *Organização Social e Política Brasileira*, 2nd ed. (Rio de Janeiro, 1967), p. 51. Extracted from the *Anuário Estatístico do Brasil, 1965*.

reached 31 percent. From there it climbed rapidly to 36 percent in 1950; 45 percent in 1960, and 50 percent in 1970, or nearly fifty million. In the decade between 1950 and 1960, the number of cities with populations between 100,000 and 200,000 increased from 9 to 19 and those between 20,000 and 100,000 from 90 to 142. Table 8.3 indicates the growth of some of Brazil's major cities in the twentieth century.

On the other end of the scale, during the mid-twentieth century more than 2,000 of the 2,763 cities had populations of less than 5,000. Altogether, they accounted for a quarter of the urban population. São Paulo and Rio de Janeiro ranked as the two metropolitan giants. Yet, spectacular as their growth had been, their combined populations accounted for only about 10 percent of the nation's population. Brazil thus had no urban concentrations comparable to those in other Latin American republics. For example, Montevideo contained 50 percent of Uruguay's population, Buenos Aires 30 percent of Argentina's, and Santiago 25 percent of Chile's. Of the four major Latin American nations, Brazil was by far the least urbanized.

Urban growth represented a swell in the ranks of the middle class and the proletariat. Indeed, most of Brazil's middle class inhabited the cities. Estimates of their proportion in the national population during the 1960s varied from a modest 15 percent to a more liberal 40 percent. The middle class counted among its members the formulators of public opinion. It was

the group most acutely aware of the restrictions imposed by the traditional oligarchy and most able to express its disapproval or resentment. The urban labor force grew at an even greater pace. The number of factory workers increased by 51 percent in the forties and by 28 percent in the fifties. Vargas and his lieutenant Goulart already had seen their political potential and had attempted to awaken them to it. The literacy rate was much higher in the cities than it was in rural areas. Hence the literacy requirement for voting increased the voting power of the urban population proportionately. Little wonder then that political power gravitated toward the city with its larger, more vocal electorate.

The urban dwellers tended to be activists or at least more so than their rural counterparts. Reading newspapers, attending the movies, watching television, listening to the radio, they were aware of change and of opportunities and they were willing to strive for them. Eagerly they busied themselves making plans for the future and executing them. They sought to control the course of their own lives rather than to rely on fate. They paid less heed to traditional values—the closely knit family unit, for example—than did the rural inhabitants. They sought the rewards modern society gave to efficiency, initiative, and responsibility. The broadly stratified urban society, which blurred the distinctions between classes, facilitated social mobility. Bored by routine and tradition, they became increasingly more individualistic. Such was true of the urban dwellers wherever they lived: the great metropolises of Rio de Janeiro and São Paulo; the smaller capitals of Manaus, Goiânia, or Florianopolis; the cities of the interior, Londrina, Corumbá, or Crato. The inhabitants of all the cities knew what was going on in the rest of the world. They cared about it and they participated in it—even if, at certain times and places, that participation was vicarious.

The modernization the cities encouraged brought benefits to some inhabitants. The population more or less doubled between 1930 and 1960, whereas, during the same period, the number of pairs of shoes sold yearly quadrupled, the number of radios sold increased twelvefold, and the number of tubes of toothpaste sold increased sixfold. The urban dweller enjoyed more education, better health, and a longer life than

his rural counterpart. Elegant apartment buildings, expensive specialty shops, chic society clubs, modern cinemas, trim parks, honking automobiles—all applied a veneer of glitter to urban life. Of course that tinsel often masked misery and degradation, just as it did in Lima, Calcutta, New York, and Naples.

For the illiterate, the inexperienced, and the technically untrained, jobs were hard to find; those fortunate enough to find them earned the minimum salary. Those with the minimum wage struggled to keep their families housed and fed; those with less than the minimum wage were the scavengers of society. In the larger cities, those marginal people lived in the *hospedarias,* the flophouses providing a bed for one night, the *cabeças-de-porco,* the rooming houses in whose tiny cubicles lived entire families, and the *favelas,* the shanty towns crowded with flimsy shacks of one or two rooms. They began to appear on the hillsides of Rio de Janeiro by the end of the nineteenth century and spread rapidly after 1930. By 1957, fully a quarter of the inhabitants of the capital lived in the *favelas.* Life in one of the São Paulo *favelas* was poignantly portrayed by one of its residents, Carolina Maria de Jesus, in a diary that by chance reached print. Its Portuguese title, *Quarto de Despejo,* was rendered *Child of the Dark* when it appeared in English in 1962. The initial entry in the diary set the tone of despair:

July 15, 1955. The birthday of my daughter Vera Eunice. I wanted to buy a pair of shoes for her, but the price of food keeps us from realizing our desires. Actually we are slaves to the cost of living. I found her a pair of shoes in the garbage, washed them, and patched them for her to wear. I didn't have one cent to buy bread.

Bitterness surfaced more than once in the pages of her unique diary. At one point, disgusted by the resignation preached by the Church, she wrote

I thought: if Brother Luiz was married, had children, and earned the minimum wage, I would like to see if he would be so humble. He said that God blesses only those who suffer with resignation. If the Brother saw his children eating rotten food already attacked by

vultures and rats, he would stop talking about resignation and rebel, because rebellion comes from bitterness.

Other cities had their counterparts to those *favelas*. In Salvador, they were the *alagados,* miserable conglomerations of one-room hovels. There Brazil's most precious resource, its people, wasted away with bloated bellies, underdeveloped bodies, dysentery, fever, and an untold number of diseases. In his novel *Suor* (Sweat), Jorge Amado portrayed the degrading existence of the dwellers of a tenement in Salvador. Linked by a common poverty, they lived an anonymous life eking out an existence as best they could. Although no one would write of them as heroes, these people, Amado reminded his readers, "perfectly symbolized proletarian humanity."

The blight of Manaus was its curious Cidade Flutuante (Floating City), 2,100 small huts picturesquely built on rafts crowded together on confluents of the Rio Negro. The inhabitants were, by and large, illiterate, ignorant, and ill. Manioc meal and fish composed their diet, and these were seldom available in sufficient quantity to keep hunger at bay. Sometimes families with eight or ten members inhabited huts that seemed hard pressed to serve as sleeping quarters for two persons. In addition, animals and fowl shared the quarters. Promiscuity was total. Sanitary facilities were unknown. When the rivers were at flood stage, the waters kept clean, but the rest of the year they were cesspools of disease.

Despite such dismal urban conditions, it was not possible to stem the tide of migration from the countryside to the cramped cities. They still represented hope, and, viewed from a distance, the glitter of their tinsel blinded the beholder. After all, rural life was no paradise for the peasant. In a frank report to the Chamber of Deputies in 1962, a special committee composed of representatives of all the major parties commented on the abject poverty in the countryside and the need for reform. These excerpts summed up the alarm the committee sounded:

One truth is evident: the problem of hunger in the countryside of Brazil offends human dignity, is explosive, and will lead to

turmoil. The facts explain the problem. The last census, taken in 1960, showed the rural population of our nation nearing 40 million. And what is the living standard for that immense population? Unfortunately it is among the lowest in the world in its level of poverty, chronic hunger, social waste, chronic illness, illiteracy. . . . In the Northeast the average life span is 27 years. In Brazil a child dies every 42 seconds, 85 per hour, 2,040 per day. . . . Forty million Brazilians vegetate in our countryside like pariahs. Scarcely 4 percent own land.

The rural institutions resisted change more than any others. They seemed inflexible in their refusal to adapt themselves to the twentieth century.

Rural workers had nothing comparable to the unions, social legislation, and labor courts that protected and aided their urban counterparts. Either as tenant farmers or menial farm hands, the majority of the workers lived at the mercy of the large landowner. *Latifundia* predominated. Approximately 1.6 percent of the farms embraced over 50 percent of the land under cultivation. Contrasting sharply with the *latifundia* and their monopoly over the best lands, the *minifundia*, those minuscule plots of land, more often than not of marginal agricultural value, struggled to grow subsistence crops for immediate consumption and local markets. About 22 percent of the farms occupied only 0.5 percent of the land.

As in the past, the large estate, the *fazenda*, continued to characterize rural Brazil. Life on the *fazenda* still revolved around the "big house," just as it had for centuries. Within the archaic social structure, the rural worker looked to his *patrão* for protection, security, and guidance, and in return pledged labor and loyalty. Many of the *fazendas* were practically closed economies, confining their contacts with the outside to the sale of one cash crop, often coffee, cocoa, sugar, cotton, or tobacco. Ignorance held the peasants to their miserable existence at barely the subsistence level and all too often debt peonage enforced their immobility. As long as the peasants owed money to their employers, they could not leave the estate for other employment. That debt was easy to acquire but nearly impossible to liquidate. Hereditary debt

servitude was not uncommon. The anthropologist Claude Levi-Strauss left this candid description of contemporary debt peonage in the interior of Brazil:

The fazenda's sales-counter was, in effect, the only provision-store for sixty or seventy miles in any direction. The *empregados,* or employees—workers or peons—came and spent there with one hand what they had earned with the other; an entry in the books sufficed to turn them from creditors into debtors,and it was rare, in point of fact, for money actually to change hands. As most things were sold at two or three times their normal price—such was the accepted practice—it would have been quite a going concern if the shop had not occupied a merely subsidiary place in the whole venture. It was heart-rending to watch the work people on a Saturday. They would arrive with their little crop of sugar-cane, press it immediately in the fazenda's *engenho* . . . evaporate the juice in a hot iron pan, and pour what remained into moulds, where it turned into tawny blocks, granular in consistency. *Rapadure,* these were called; and they would hand them in to the adjacent store. When the evening came they would re-present themselves, this time as customers, and pay a high price for the right to offer their children their own product—refurbished, by then, as the sertão's only sweetmeat.

The critics of the system customarily applied the emotional adjective "feudal" to the land structure and its accompanying social institutions. They resented the power of the landowner, his interposition, as it were, between the government and the rural masses. They pointed with disgust to the difference between the modernity of the cities and the tradition of the countryside. They warned that a closed society, with no hope for evolutionary change, would breed revolution in time. Ceará symbolized the gross rural inequities and inefficiencies. In 1960, some 66 percent of the state's population resided in the countryside where a few owned most of the land. There were only 316 tractors and 1,305 plows for a labor force numbering 816,720. Food production, except for fruits, did not satisfy the needs of the inhabitants, forcing the importation of staple crops. That occurred in a region fully capable of producing food surpluses. The main reason was

simple: the few who owned the land held it fallow as investment or did not work it efficiently.

Immediate reform of the rural economic and social structures, the critics advised, was essential. In the words of Minister of Agriculture Oswaldo Lima Filho in 1963: "It is urgently
necessary by means of an agrarian reform, which will bring
prosperity and well-being to the people, to end the feudal
structure which imprisons the rural population." A statement
entitled *Pacem in Terris and the Brazilian Reality* issued that
same year by the Roman Catholic bishops called attention to
the plight of the rural population and advocated a reform of
land structures:

> The majority is deprived of the exercise of many of the fundamental
> and natural rights which are mentioned in the encyclical Pacem in
> Terris: the right of existence and to a decent standard of living, the
> right of human liberty and dignity, the right to participate in the
> benefits of culture; in other words the right to live as a person in
> society. . . . No one can ignore the situation of millions of our
> brothers and sisters living in rural areas who cannot share in the
> development of our nation, who live in conditions of misery which
> are an affront to human dignity. . . . The expropriation of land in
> such situations is in no way contrary to the social doctrine of the
> Church.

That powerful call for social and economic justice reflected
the growing social consciousness of the Roman Catholic church
in Brazil. The more enlightened members of the urban middle
class favored rural reforms, among them a redistribution of
the land. For one thing, they recognized that the inefficient
fazenda kept food prices high. For another, they desired to
reduce further the power of the coroneis and the rural aristocracy which generally was wielded to retard modernization
and to oppose the interests of the urban classes. Further, the
economic development coveted by urban dwellers would be
unattainable without rural reforms and a consequent improvement in agricultural support. Real economic development could not be expected if it excluded the rural population.

Growing efficiency and hence productivity characterized a few farms, particularly in the South and Southeast. In the fifties, the number of tractors in use rose an impressive eightfold, from 8,000 to 63,000. Predictably, about 70 percent of those tractors were in the two states of São Paulo and Rio Grande do Sul. A tractor could cultivate four acres of rice land in Rio Grande do Sul in thirteen hours and twenty-five minutes; to accomplish the same task by the customary hand labor required fifty-four days. Farmers, particularly those in the South and Southeast, increased their use of fertilizers. In 1958, they spread 42,000 tons of nitrogen fertilizer. Two decades before, they had used only 2,000 tons. The average use of fertilizer was a little over a pound per acre, about a third of the world average. Although its increase was far below that of industry in the fifties, agricultural growth outpaced population growth by 52 percent versus 36 percent. However, that growth reflected more an increase in export crops—still the dynamic part of the economy—rather than the subsistence crops which could have fed a malnourished population. The growth in production was due primarily to an increase in land utilization, from 40 million acres in 1948 to 65 million in 1960, rather than to an increase in productivity. Fortunately Brazil was immense, with much land unused. As late as 1961, only slightly more than 2 percent of the land was under cultivation, and of that only about half produced foodstuffs. Productivity remained low because of the system of land tenure and use, low technical and educational levels, lack of capital, poor transportation facilities, unsatisfactory marketing systems, limited scientific research, and lack of technical assistance to agriculture. Principally—and this point cannot be overemphasized—the problem lay with the land structures: they withheld land from the dispossessed, who could have been useful and efficient producers on a small scale.

In 1960, Brazil ranked among the world's foremost producers of cacao, sugar, and cotton and was one of the largest livestock raisers. Coffee was still the dominant crop, accounting for 17 percent of the area under cultivation, 15 percent of farm income, and 50 percent of the exports. Brazil remained the world's major producer and exporter of coffee. However,

that crop no longer reigned as king. During the last half of the century, as exports increasingly diversified, coffee's contribution declined.

A hopeful sign of change for the countryside was the steady, albeit slow growth of a rural middle class, which as a group seemed to avoid many of the weaknesses and disadvantages of both the *latifundia* and the *minifundia*. In 1960, there were 1,494,548 land holdings between 25 and 250 acres in size, a growth in number of 157,954 since 1920. Somewhat more impressive was the growth during those four decades of the proportion of the total agricultural area which those holdings occupied, from 8.9 to 17 percent. Not all the medium-sized farms were located in the South and Southeast by any means. Many could be found in the more tradition-bound regions as well. Whereas Minas Gerais counted 199,405 and São Paulo 139,620 such farms, Bahia contained 161,673 and Pernambuco 50,850. Agriculture definitely had progressed in the twentieth century, but its steps were measured, in comparison to the giant strides of industrial progress.

The different geographical regions further reflected the contrasts which historically characterize Brazil. In the opening chapter, five such regions were designated: the North, Northeast, Center West, East, and South. A glance at the accompanying map, titled *Regions of Brazil,* will indicate the variety among them in size, population, electorate, and income, as of 1965. Whereas the North was by far the largest region in size, it had the smallest population, electorate, and income. In diametric contrast, the South was the smallest region and yet it boasted the largest population, electorate, and income. The North was chiefly rural. It possessed only two cities of any size, Belém and Manaus. About 51 percent of the population of the South could be classified as urban and it contained such modern cities as São Paulo, Pôrto Alegre, Curitiba, Santos, Santo André, and Campinas. The South was also the most industrialized of the five regions. The state of São Paulo generated over 700,000 kilowatts of electric power. Pernambuco in the Northeast barely generated 50,000. In addition to its remarkable industrial record, the South also boasted the highest agricultural production.

Perhaps another way to view the disparities among the regions is to compare the state budgets. (These budgets for the year 1967 are given in old cruzeiros at the exchange rate of Cr$2,200 to US$1.) As was so often the case, São Paulo led the other states with a budget of Cr$3¼ trillion, while at the other end of the scale stood Acre with barely Cr$20 billion budgeted. Only five states were able to budget more than half a trillion cruzeiros: three of them were in the South, São Paulo, Paraná, and Rio Grande do Sul, and the remaining two were in the East, Minas Gerais and Guanabara. The territorial giants of Amazonas and Pará operated on budgets which totaled less than Cr$100 and Cr$50 billion respectively.

All statistics unmistakably pointed to the South and East as the dominant regions of Brazil. Well populated and with satisfactory transportation networks, they had urbanized, industrialized, and modernized to an extent far beyond that of the rest of Brazil. The largest numbers of well-fed and well-educated Brazilians lived in those regions.

The situation of the Northeast, one of the major underdeveloped areas of the hemisphere, was less fortunate. With 11 percent of the territory and 21 percent of the population, it contributed less than 10 percent of the national product. That contribution was about a third of what it was a generation earlier. Unemployment and underemployment plagued the adult male population. The peasants lived in rude clay huts with dirt floors, without illumination or sanitary facilities. Chances were they did not own their lands, for the dominant land pattern was one of large estates concentrated in the hands of a few owners. Their diet consisted mainly of manioc flour and black beans with occasional jerked beef. Hunger was common. Not surprisingly, life expectancy was less than thirty years. About the Zona da Mata, one of the most depressed areas of Pernambuco's backlands, Professor Nelson Chaves, director of the Nutrition Institute of the Federal University of Pernambuco, after a year's research in the town of Riberão, related, "The minimum that a man must eat in order to work is 2,600 calories. Our research into the diets of 100 workers of Ribeirão shows their daily consumption to be 1,323 calories, half of the minimum. They cannot work. They

Map 6. Regions of Brazil

SOURCE: *Brazil Election Factbook*, no. 2, September 1965 (Washington, D.C.: Institute for the Comparative Study of Political Systems, 1965), p. 2. Reproduced with the permission of the publisher.

live in a state of chronic hunger, one of the most serious in the world." An article published in the *Jornal do Commércio* of Recife on June 7, 1969, reported that workers of the Salgado sugar mill and their families were in a perpetual state of hunger and that the owner dealt with complainers by firing them. In Ribeirão, the infant mortality rate was twenty-five times greater than that of Denmark. In the Zona da Mata, 40 percent of the children died before they reached school age. Over 95 percent of the population suffered from intestinal worms. The rate of tuberculosis was ten times greater than in more developed areas. The workers and their families probably lived worse than did the slaves in the same area a century ago.

Ignorance characterized the population in these backward areas. The illiteracy rate in the Northeast soared over 70 percent, high above the dismal national average of 50 percent. In the sugarmill settlement of Taimberé, for example, about 80 percent of the inhabitants were illiterate; only 1 percent had primary educations. In 1968, of the six hundred families living there, only one sent its children to school. Statistics in other parts of the Pernambucan backlands were no better. Ponte dos Carvalhos, just twenty miles from Recife, was a decrepit eyesore with eleven thousand inhabitants. Half of them were children under sixteen years of age. Of these, only six hundred attended school. Over five hundred prostitutes plied their profession. Intestinal worms plagued 99 percent of the population. Of the 340 who died in 1967, 226 (67 percent) were less than a year old. The town grew because the peasants flocked to it, attracted by its industries, medical facilities, and television. In other words, whatever its drawbacks, they found it preferable to life in and around the sugar mills. In the midst of the misery of the Northeast, the extremes between poverty and wealth stood out more noticeably.

For many decades, the common explanation given for the plight of the Northeast was the droughts which periodically flagellated the *sertão*. The solution thought proper for the problem was hydrographic: dams and irrigation. But various hydrographic projects did little to alleviate the problem.

Anyway, poverty and backwardness continued through the long periods when rainfall was sufficient, proof that something more than droughts caused the problems of the Northeast. In the fifties, economists suggested that much of the poverty resulted from low capital investment in the region. In response to that suggestion, the federal government sought to encourage investments and industrialization. Focusing his attention on the difficulties of the region, President Kubitschek created the Superintendência do Desenvolvimento do Nordeste (Superintendency of the Development of the Northeast, or Sudene) in 1959. Under the direction of Celso Furtado, Sudene prepared a comprehensive development program, which encouraged industrialization, a reorganization and intensification of agriculture, and a relocation of population surpluses.

The Center West—composed of the states of Goiás (containing the new Federal District) and Mato Grosso,—was the fastest growing region of Brazil. It offered abundant opportunities in agriculture, cattle raising, mining, and timber. Income in the region soared. During the decade of the fifties, the rural population doubled and the urban population tripled. Brasília and Goiânia, both new captials, experienced impressive growth records. Founded in 1933 to replace Goiás Velha, the old capital of Goiás, Goiânia was not officially inaugurated until 1942. It is a well-planned city with broad, tree-lined avenues, zoned in three distinct districts in addition to spacious residential areas: one district is for government, another for commerce, and a third for industry. By 1960, the population of Goiânia exceeded 132,000.

The West attracted inhabitants from all regions of Brazil as well as foreign immigrants. It became a true melting pot, in a tradition long established for the interior. Vargas helped to popularize the idea that the West held the key to the realization of the national potential. On a number of occasions, he announced plans to penetrate definitively the hinterlands, the "March to the West." More than anything else, the establishment of Brasília focused attention on the West. The roads radiating from the new capital brought in pioneers. Linked more closely than ever with the rest of the nation, the

West showed every indication of maintaining its position as the fastest growing of the five regions. The existence of a vast interior, much of which was unexplored, most of which was unexploited, imparted to all Brazilians a certain optimism and faith in the future as well as a belief in the inevitability of progress.

Great advances in communication and transportation in the past century did much to unify Brazil and to break down regional barriers. Within that unity always existed—still exists—an immense variety which the regions exemplify. A theme underlying Brazilian history has been the conflict between the forces of unity and diversity, that is, between centralism and regionalism. The scales at one time or another have tipped both ways. In the long run, however, the two forces have maintained a certain balance. The essential fact is that despite stress and threat the Brazilian union remained intact. National unity and homogeneity are achievements of which Brazilians can be justifiably proud. However, so long as different levels of development characterize the regions of that union there will still be a great deal of diversity and considerable stress.

A Political Surprise

Political stress gripped Brazil in late 1960 and throughout 1961. In the election of 1960 the Brazilians elected Jânio da Silva Quadros, candidate of the UDN, to the presidency. Promising to eliminate corruption and inefficiency from government—his campaign symbol was a broom—he won 48 percent of the vote. His principal opponent, Marshal Henrique Teixeira Lott, the minister of war during the Kubitschek administration, ran on a combined PSD–PTB (Social Democratic-Labor party) ticket and received only 28 percent of the vote. The significances of Quadros' victory were many. It marked the first time the conservative, anti-Vargas UDN had captured the presidency, although it would be incorrect to identify Quadros too closely with that party. A maverick, he campaigned on his own personal platform. The UDN, hungry for victory, recognized a winner and supported him. Quadros

had no links with Vargas or those associated with him, another quality which endeared him to the UDN leadership. His election constituted a break with the Vargas legacy. Finally, his victory put a Paulista in the presidential palace for the first time since the collapse of the Old Republic. Running on the PTB ticket, João Goulart was re-elected vice president with 36 percent of the vote.

On the whole, the new president seemed to view internal affairs rather conventionally, although he did believe in restrictions on foreign capital. In foreign affairs, however, he displayed a flair for the experimental, which he demonstrated in his efforts to increase Brazil's independence in foreign relations. Since the era of Rio-Branco, Brazil had closely identified its international policy and behavior with that of the United States. The intensified drive to industrialize Brazil had brought the nation face-to-face with the question of the role of foreign investments in Brazil. The nationalists argued that those investments in the long run harmed Brazil and resented such investments in natural resources and primary industries. They accused the foreign investors of imperialism, and since the North Americans were the principal foreign investors, the United States bore the brunt of the attack on imperialism. The nationalists struggled to wrest their country from the suffocating embrace of the "imperialistic" United States. One method of doing so, they thought, would be to disengage Brazil from its close diplomatic alliance with Washington. Further, such a move seemed to promise a greater freedom of trade. The nationalists saw untapped markets in the socialist nations of the Eastern Bloc awaiting Brazil's products.

Public opinion indicated its desire for Brazil to play a larger role in world affairs. After all, Brazil had contributed troops to the Allied campaign in Italy and had sent men with the United Nations forces into the Middle East and the Congo. That Brazilians aspired to play an even greater role in international affairs was indicated by the titles of such books as Manuel Meira de Vasconcelos' *Brasil, Potência Militar* (Brazil, A Military Power) and Pimentel Gomes' *O Brasil entre as Cinco Maiores Potências ao Fim deste Século* (Brazil among the Five Major Powers by the End of the Century). The popu-

lar press often predicted the rise of Brazil to a world power status, an ambition that had motivated Ruy Barbosa at The Hague, as well as Brazil's behavior in both the League of Nations and the United Nations. In reassessing their international interests and strengths, the Brazilians became more aware of their country's advantageous geopolitical position. The giant of South America, it comprised half of the continent's territory and population and bordered on all but two of the nations of that continent. With an extensive coastline, it dominated the South Atlantic and was strategically located vis-à-vis Africa. Its racial diversity gave it a unique position in the world community.

The foreign policy which Quadros formulated with the assistance of his minister of foreign relations, the able Afonso Arinos de Melo Franco, pursued the basic goals of encouraging economic development and of displaying greater diplomatic independence. To carry out that new foreign policy, Quadros thought it necessary to remove Brazil as far as possible from the Cold War battlefield. Rigid adherence to the Western bloc and subservience to the leadership of the United States had seemed—at least to Quadros and the nationalists supporting his foreign policy—to inhibit Brazil's scope of action. Quadros affirmed that the doctrines of neither the West nor the East served the nation's best interests. Brazil wanted to develop; one way to develop was to trade; and trade knew no ideology. He wanted to preserve traditional markets, but he hoped to find new ones as well. Quadros sent a trade mission to China and initiated the steps to reestablish diplomatic relations with Moscow and other Eastern European countries. Trade was obviously only one of the reasons for this recognition. The desire to exert independence of action was a compelling motive too. Augmented prestige through increased diplomatic representation both abroad and at home cannot be overlooked as a motive either.

Disengagement from the Cold War not only brought Brazil closer to the East but it also put Brazil in closer contact with the neutralist countries of Africa and Asia. Those Third World nations shared the view that development should take precedence over alliances that encouraged the polarization

of the world into two armed camps. Brazil had much in common with those underdeveloped countries. United in their common desire for development, they could demand—so their reasoning went—a fair price from the industrial nations for their raw products. United, they also could regulate foreign capital investment more to their own advantage. At the same time, Brazil also envisioned for itself an excellent opportunity for leadership among the underdeveloped Third World nations.

In particular, Quadros saw an opportunity to exert Brazilian leadership among the newly emergent African states. Geography and history provided a convincing rationale for this hope. The Brazilian subcontinent juts out into the South Atlantic, providing the closest point of physical contact between the Western Hemisphere and Africa. Furthermore, during the three centuries in which the slave trade flourished between the two areas, Africa supplied a large percentage of Brazil's population. As a consequence, African blood flows in the veins of a majority of Brazilians. In every sense the African presence is very much a part of contemporary Brazil. Anyone who reads Gilberto Freyre's study *The Masters and the Slaves* will understand fully the African contributions to the new tropical civilization. Based on these considerations, Quadros found in Africa a new dimension for Brazilian foreign policy. He wanted Brazil to serve as a link between the newly independent Africa and the rest of the world. Accordingly, he recognized the new states, exchanged ambassadors with them, dispatched trade missions, offered fellowships to African students, established an Afro-Asian Institute, and denounced Portuguese colonial policies in Africa.

Brazil made its independence felt in the Western Hemisphere through its treatment of Cuba. As a presidential candidate, Quadros made a leisurely visit to the island at a time when the United States was putting pressure on the Latin American governments to break relations with the government of Fidel Castro. Later, as president, he welcomed to Brasília Ernesto "Che" Guevara, whom he decorated with the nation's highest honor, the Order of the Southern Cross.

Seemingly Quadros was maneuvering to play the role of mediator between Havana and Washington.

Acceptance of the new foreign policy was by no means unanimous. Many asked whether Brazil's best interests could be served by closer association with Yugoslavia, Egypt, and India. The critics argued that Brazil needed greater capital investments and despaired of seeing any forthcoming from either the Eastern or the neutralist countries. They agreed that new markets were desirable but pointed out with irrefutable statistics that most of the nations of the Southern Hemisphere exported the same or similar raw products. The fact was that, as the world's economy was structured in the mid-twentieth century, the underdeveloped countries were more competitors than potential customers of Brazil. One of the fiercest critics of the policy was Carlos Lacerda, no longer the fiery editor but now the querulous governor of Guanabara. The first break between the president and the governor came on April 16, 1961, over the U.S.–sponsored invasion of Cuba, the ill-fated Bay of Pigs. Quadros denounced it; Lacerda defended it. The relations between the two men deteriorated thereafter.

The new president experienced other difficulties as well. His efforts to halt inflation proved to be unpopular, and Quadros himself began to doubt the wisdom and desirability of his measures. His campaign against corruption elicited screams of protest from Congress, where the PSD and PTB held a majority. Congress charged the president and his UDN backers with seeking political revenge against those who had held power. Quadros soon regarded Congress as the major impediment to his reforms. In fact, to the new president's way of thinking, the very political structure of the nation prevented good and effective government.

The Constitution of 1946 seemed to institutionalize a basic conflict detrimental to effective government. On the one hand, the presidents were elected by popular vote. Since the majority of the literate citizenry lived in the urban, industrialized East and South, those two regions in effect elected the presidents. In fact, in the four presidential elections after

World War II, 1945, 1950, 1955, and 1960, the four states of Rio Grande do Sul, São Paulo, Minas Gerais, and Guanabara cast between 50 and 60 percent of the votes. Their vote was thus decisive in electing the president. On the other hand, Congress was elected by a restricted vote in which rural power dominated. Each state had an equal number of senators— three. The four heavily industrialized, urbanized, and populated states could raise but a weak voice in the Senate compared to the eighteen rural and largely underdeveloped states, where in most cases the *coroneis* and landed aristocracy still wielded influence. Hence the traditional rural oligarchy dominated the Senate. In the Chamber of Deputies, the situation was somewhat similar. Representation there was proportionate to the population of each state. However, only literates could vote. It is easy to see that the vote of a literate citizen in a state with a high percentage of illiteracy, Sergipe for example, outweighed that of his counterpart in a state with a low degree of illiteracy, Guanabara for example. Since the traditional rural oligarchy exerted more control in the states with high illiteracy rates, it meant that they exercised a power in the Chamber of Deputies disproportionate to their numbers. Obviously illiteracy and the requirement that voters be literate were props supporting the traditional rural oligarchy and perpetuating their influence and power. While the urban voters could elect the president, rural interests could control Congress. This created two centers of power, by their very nature antagonistic to one another. Such certainly was the case after 1950. Great tensions developed between the two opposing branches of government, which often brought the government to a standstill. A popularly elected president, under these conditions, could suggest reforms that appealed to wide segments of the people, only to have their enactment stalled or refused by the representatives of the rural oligarchy. This situation created mounting frustrations.

Quadros confronted a particularly recalcitrant Congress. As he began to organize his program in the months after his inauguration, he encountered increasing obstinacy and hostility from that body. The president proved to be an impatient man. He had expected his federal experience to mirror his

experience during the years in which he governed São Paulo and dominated the state legislature; instead he met delay and frustration.Understanding the constitutional basis for the conflict between the executive and the legislature, he thought in terms of a basic constitutional reform to rectify the situation. But just at that moment, on August 19, 1961, he stepped on the toes of his foremost critic, Lacerda, by awarding the Order of the Southern Cross to Che Guevara. Lacerda, a rabid enemy of Castro, howled in protest. On August 23 he appeared on television in São Paulo to denounce a coup d'état that, he claimed, Quadros planned in order to dismiss Congress and decree some basic reforms. The following day, the governor spoke on television in Rio de Janeiro to repeat his charge. The next afternoon, August 25, 1961, President Quadros suddenly resigned and left Brasília.

The president's abrupt departure after less than seven months in office met with disbelief and astonishment among the people. His cryptic letter of resignation, an eerie echo of Vargas' suicide note, spoke of those "forces"—"foreign" and "terrible"—that opposed and hindered him. "I wanted Brazil for the Brazilians," he wrote, perhaps proving that his conversion to the nationalist cause had been complete.

The reasons for the precipitate resignation are still not clear; interpretations vary and conflict. The following interpretation is based upon Quadros' own explanation. In São Paulo, as he paused on his way into voluntary exile, Quadros reflected on the situation in Brazil and concluded that Brazil needed three things: authority, hard work, and courageous and rapid decisions. The political structure of the nation, in his opinion, was not viable. The lack of cooperation between Congress and the president prohibited progress. Quadros resigned purposefully, to create a crisis. He believed that the nation would not accept Vice President João Goulart. He was convinced that the military would not. He fully expected the senior military officers to block Goulart, whom they suspected to be demogogic, populist, and dangerous and whom they had opposed on previous occasions. Vaguely he envisioned the military establishing an authoritarian regime under which he would be returned to the presidency with greater

powers, or, if he was not, he expected that another president would receive the powers to enable him to govern effectively. On only one point did Quadros figure correctly: his resignation plunged the nation into a crisis. However, the resolution of that crisis did not follow his script.

Dismay was the dominant popular reaction to the president's resignation. In their disappointment over his abuse of his mandate, the majority of the citizenry turned away from Quadros. In the midst of the resignation crisis, public opinion firmly advocated the constitutional solution: the elevation of Vice President Goulart to the presidency. That respect for the legal solution reflected the success of the democratization process during the previous decade and a half.

At that moment, Goulart was far away in China on a trade mission. In his absence, the legal formality called for the president of the Chamber of Deputies to assume the role of interim president, and Pascoal Ranieri Mazzilli stepped into that office. Simultaneously the military cabinet officers led by Minister of War Odílio Denys voiced their opposition to Goulart and indicated their refusal to honor his constitutional elevation. Denys represented those senior military officers who viewed politics since 1945 in terms of a titanic struggle between communism and democracy. In Denys' own words during the constitutional crisis: "The situation obliges us to choose between democracy and Communism, and the armed forces have already decided: they will carry on to the end in the defense of our democratic traditions." What the military officers meant by "democracy" remained unclear. Perhaps the cryptic reference to "our democratic traditions" explained the military's extra-constitutional insistence that it possessed the *poder moderador,* that old imperial perogative to intervene in politics. Increasingly frequent interventions by the officers suggested how fragile political contractural agreements were in the twentieth century. They certainly bespoke military impatience with, not to say disdain of, the civilian politicians.

Obviously Denys and those of similar opinions judged Goulart as part of some vague communist threat to alter Brazil and a threat to their brand of democracy. The military's dis-

like of Goulart extended back into the second administration
of Vargas, when Goulart as minister of labor settled a maritime strike in favor of the stevedores, encouraged unions
with radical tendencies, and proposed a 100 percent increase
of minimum wages. His activities, both as labor minister and
as chief of the PTB, hinted that he had learned much about
using labor as a political base of support from his mentor
Vargas as well as from Juan D. Perón, when the latter governed Argentina (1946–1955). The military hierarchy, as well
as their allies among the conservative political elements, regarded such politics as pure demagogy, to be avoided if at all
possible.

Instant and vociferous popular reaction countered military intervention in the democratic process. People with no
brief for Goulart rushed to defend the constitution. The news
media and many congressmen proved to be strong bulwarks
of the democratic process, and they seemed to reflect public
opinion accurately. The unexpected crisis divided the military. Lott, in retirement, supported Goulart's elevation and
appealed to his former comrades-in-arms to observe the order of succession provided by the constitution. For a moment, civil war threatened. Fortunately cooler heads prevailed. In a time-honored Brazilian custom the two sides compromised. The military agreed to permit the investiture of
Goulart; Congress agreed to amend the constitution to change
the presidential system to a parliamentary one and thus diminish some of the new president's power. In the new government, a Council of Ministers named by the president would
be drawn from and responsible to the legislature. That council would share executive powers with the president. As a
result of that compromise, approved by Congress on September 2, 1961, Goulart, who had entered Brazil at Pôrto Alegre
the previous day, took office officially on the seventh. He
acquiesced in the compromise as the only way to get the
presidency, but the dilution of the powers of that office clearly
disappointed him. From the start, the new president determined to end the new parliamentary system as quickly as
possible. Nor did all the public accept the amendment. The
Brazilian Socialist party and the National Student Union, to

mention two groups, promptly denounced it as unconstitutional. The crisis awoke genuine sympathy for Goulart, who emerged from the whole affair as a true democrat abused by military arbitrariness.

The Promise or Threat of Reform

The crisis provoked by the military enhanced the person and position of President João Goulart. He began his administration with far wider support than he had ever enjoyed in his career. Entering office modestly and treading carefully for the next few months, the new president thereby won, at least temporarily, the acceptance of the moderates and even of some conservatives. But after a period of grace, he alienated many of those supporters with his nationalistic and "radical" programs, as they were considered within the conventional and conservative Brazilian political experience.

In foreign affairs, Goulart followed the path cut by his predecessor. His scholarly foreign minister, San Tiago Dantas, spoke often of the nation's "independent foreign policy" that "corresponded to the permanent interests and aspirations of our nationality." As the Goulart government interpreted them, those interests and aspirations prompted the withdrawal of Brazil from the political-military blocs. The new government courted Cuba. Goulart welcomed a Chinese trade mission to Rio de Janeiro and reestablished relations with most of the eastern European states. Diplomatic missions were dispatched also to such diverse countries as Algeria and Sri Lanka. If Rio-Branco had once weakened Brazil's ties with Europe in favor of a closer friendship with the United States, the nationalists of the mid-twentieth century were ready to deemphasize those connections in favor of a new alliance between the underdeveloped nations of Latin America, Africa, and Asia.

In domestic affairs Goulart lacked the firm and clear commitments that characterized his foreign policy. Opportunism rather than conviction often seemed to guide him. Perfecting his nationalist rhetoric, he leaned ever more heavily

on the nationalists for support. Since their programs assumed a more radical ring in the sixties than previously, Goulart became associated with their drive for far-reaching changes. The nationalists, in turn, regarded him as an unreliable—they questioned his commitment—but nevertheless effective ally. After all, he did say the right things: he condemned foreign economic imperialism, encouraged economic development, and promised to carry out basic reforms. In truth, he supported and enacted two measures long advocated by the nationalists.

After years of frustrated efforts, a new national agency, Electrobrás, was finally created in 1961 to coordinate a system of state and private electric power plants. Its objective was to undertake studies of and projects involving the construction and operation of generating plants and transmission lines, and the distribution of electric energy. The government undertook vast new hydroelectric projects in an attempt to meet the insatiable demand for more electric energy, a key to future industrialization. Electrobrás gave the government authority over a power resource vital to the future development of the country, a resource the nationalists were loath to see in the hands of foreigners.

The second measure enacted at the urging of the nationalists limited the profits that foreign companies could withdraw from Brazil. Foreign investment was high, growing vigorously in the fifties. The nationalists charged that foreign investors received higher profits from their Brazilian investments than they did from similar investments in the United States or Europe. The statistics were confusing, but the charge probably was valid. One North American economist, Eric Baklanoff, concluded that during the period from 1947 to 1953, when there was a profit remittance law, the inflow of venture capital averaged only $15 million a year, while profit remittances averaged $47 million. In the period from 1954 to 1961, when there were no restrictions, venture capital inflow reached $91 million a year, while profit remittances were $33 million—a sharp decline but still a healthy return. For their part, official governmental figures for the period from 1947 to 1960 recorded an alarming capital outflow. The inflow for the period

amounted to $1,814 million in new investments and loans; at the same time, the outflow of $2,459 million in profits and interest and of $1,022 million in payment for "services" totaled $3,481 million. Such figures excited and annoyed Brazilians, who saw their nation in the same role as the "mulch cow" that once had fattened Portugal. The nationalist case against foreign profiteering had wide popular appeal. It offered a simple and understandable explanation for low wages, high prices, and poverty, all of which could conveniently be blamed on foreign exploitation. Goulart relied heavily on the foreign-profits issue to win popular support.

On September 3, 1962, the president signed a law limiting profit remittances. According to the provisions of the law, all foreign capital was to be registered with the Brazilian government and, in effect, no profit remittances in excess of 10 percent of invested capital were permitted. The most immediate result of the law was a drastic drop in foreign investments, from $91 million in 1961 to only $18 million in 1962. The nationalists rejoiced at the promulgation of the law, a major victory for their cause. In their opinion, nationalism clearly was in ascendancy in Brazil. How could it be otherwise when one president after another enacted policies from the nationalist program and spoke in increasingly nationalistic tones? Those presidents thus lent their power and prestige to the nationalist movement, and, on certain key issues, even provided a welcome leadership for the otherwise heterogeneous nationalist group, which by this time included large segments of the intellectuals, politicians, students, urban proletariat, and middle class, as well as certain elements among the military and the industrialists.

Brazil boasted of phenomenal industrial achievements by the early 1960s. An impressive world-class industrial park manufactured all Brazil's consumer goods and about 87 percent of its capital goods. Alas, a major economic thundercloud soon eclipsed that economic sunshine. The Industrial growth rate fell, reaching zero by the end of 1962. An old dilemma confronted the government: to welcome more foreign investments or to reform economic structures. Heady

nationalistic rhetoric could not disguise the gloom for long. The situation required decisions and actions.

Committed to economic development, President Goulart admired the exhilarating economic performance of the Kubitschek administration, despite the inflationary upsurge experienced during the last half of the fifties. Goulart had to face a daunting reality: as the purchasing power of the cruzeiro plummeted, more and more Brazilians found themselves economically marginalized. The rise in the cost of living exceeded the rise in the minimum wage, and the two spiraled upward with numbing regularity. Budget deficits became habitual. To meet expenses, the government printed mountains of cruzeiros. The international value of the cruzeiro, never strong, collapsed. The economists who had the president's ear convinced him that inflation encouraged development. Their policies certainly persuaded Brazilians to withdraw their depreciating cruzeiros from the banks in order to spend or invest them. Real estate and industry were popular investments—but so also were bank accounts in the United States and Switzerland. The rapid advance of prices over wages enticed investors in production who hoped to reap a rich harvest of profits. The economists further convinced the president that a major cause of inflation was scarcity of goods. According to their analyses, as soon as there were enough factories to sufficiently supply demands for goods—or enough houses and apartments to meet the requirements of a growing population—prices would fall and the inflation would taper off. Those convincing arguments explained and justified the inflation. Goulart accepted them and eventually abandoned any serious effort to control the situation. He thus disregarded the concern of large numbers of the population over galloping inflation. His failure to bridle it alienated the moderates, whose support in 1961 switched to opposition by 1963.

Although still capable of wielding considerable power, the president protested that the parliamentary system minimized the ability of his government to handle Brazil's problems. To contain inflation, which frightened the conservatives

and moderates, and to enact basic reforms, so desirable to the working classes, Goulart insisted that full presidential powers be restored to him. Confident of a growing popular desire to end the governmental lethargy—not to say outright confusion—he agitated to place before the electorate a choice between presidential and parliamentary government. Backing him were the labor unions, well coordinated by the powerful *Comando Geral do Trabalho* (General Labor Command, or CGT, created in 1962, and by late that year known as the General Strike Command). That central labor organization operated without legal status but with the support and approval of Goulart. Many critics accused it of being run or at least dominated by communists. Goulart had a long history of good relations with labor, and as president he received from labor what proved to be his strongest and most consistent support. The urban workers were well organized (thanks in part to Goulart's past efforts), increasingly vocal, and sufficiently literate to possess the vote. Correctly used, labor could be a potent force for any politician, and Goulart did not hesitate to make use of it. The highly political and pro-Goulart CGT called for strikes to propel the drive for a return to presidential government. The labor unrest added to the turmoil disturbing the nation and contributed to the argument that a stronger government was needed. Popular support swung behind Goulart and demanded a plebiscite to resolve the question. Even members of the UDN read the handwriting on the wall and favored giving their bête noire of the PTB his full presidential powers. Congress set the date for a plebiscite. On January 6, 1963, more than twelve million voters went to the polls to voice their opinion. By a 5 to 1 majority they restored to Goulart those full presidential powers contained in the Constitution of 1946. On January 23, 1963, Brazil officially returned to the presidential system. The people quite understandably then expected effective government and an end to the crises that had plagued the nation for a year and a half.

Goulart still had to deal with a recalcitrant Congress, no more cooperative than it had been with his predecessor. The legislature flatly refused to back the reforms the president

suggested. Goulart spoke out in favor of a land reform that would expropriate large estates, pay the former owners with bonds,and redistribute the land. Such a reform would entail a major restructuring of Brazil's archaic rural structures, a change, if effective, of revolutionary proportions. In March of 1963, he submitted an agrarian reform bill to Congress. It required a constitutional amendment to enact it, that is, a two-thirds approval from Congress. The legislature defeated the proposed reform in early October. The president's efforts at tax reform, anathema to the middle class and elite who did not bear their proportionate share of the tax burdens, met no greater success. The dialogue between those favoring reform and those protecting the status quo ceased. On the one hand Goulart watched his support from the moderates dissipate, and on the other he witnessed rivals wooing labor. His articulate brother-in-law, Governor Leonel Brizola of Rio Grande do Sul, emerged as a major political rival. Brizola had expropriated a local subsidiary of ITT in January of 1962, to the undisguised joy of the nationalists and the working class. To preserve his leadership over labor Goulart became increasingly more radical. The conservatives and moderates watched with foreboding as the government swung farther to the Left. The middle class, whose members for some time had encouraged and spoken for nationalism, watched with apprehension as Goulart roused the urban masses. He promised them fundamental changes; he exploited their latent nationalistic sentiments. A trend noticeable since the late 1940s accelerated: Labor, socialists, and reformers gained strength, while conservatives and moderates became more befuddled. Furthermore, radicals were strongest in the most-developed states and in the largest cities. The specter of a popular revolution frightened the middle class for the first time.

In February of 1964, Goulart presented his "Package Plan," the basic reforms demanded by his government of Congress. It called for fundamental economic and political changes that would benefit the lower classes. The elite and the middle class perceived them as restrictions, potential and actual, on their privileged positions. The plan sought the vote for illiterates, eligibility of noncommissioned officers and enlisted men

to participate in politics, legalization of the Communist party, tax reforms, periodic wage adjustments, state monopolies over coffee and ore exports, revision of all mining conces- sions, and, as a means of initiating agrarian reform, immedi- ate expropriation of all but small properties bordering high- ways, railways, and water projects. Such expropriation might seem a curious way to begin the much-needed land reform, but it was the simplest, since the government enjoyed some residual powers over lands adjacent to means of public trans- portation.

The concern of the moderates and conservatives mounted as radicalism manifested itself in the countryside, that bul- wark of elitist privilege. The rural land and labor structures had served to deflect any meaningful change and to minimize the impact of urbanization, industrialization, and moderniza- tion. Accustomed to urban agitation, the rural oligarchy—and for that matter the urban elite and middle class as well— panicked at the sight of peasant unrest, no matter how slight. In the miserable Northeast, the lawyer Francisco Julião had been organizing the peasants since 1955 into groups known as Peasant Leagues. From modest initial requests that their members receive a decent burial, the peasants turned to de- mands for an agrarian reform to restructure the rural eco- nomic system. The Leagues represented the peasants in land- tenancy courts. It politicized the peasants, making them aware of the possibility of mitigating their misery. Still, the Leagues operated in a limited area and never reached the largest por- tion of the dispossessed. At the same time, other groups advocated rural changes. Some courageous and vocal clerics within the Roman Catholic church also called for rural re- forms and the modest advent of Liberation Theology oc- curred. But the Peasant Leagues attracted national and inter- national attention, partly because it was difficult to deny the injustices of the impoverished Northeast but mainly because of the political potential embodied in the Leagues. To the hemispheric elite, reacting against the Cuban Revolution di- rected by Fidel Castro, the exhortations of Julião awoke real fears. In October 1960, Julião identified the enemy of the peasants and suggested revolution as a means to change the

system: "Your cruel enemy, the large estate, will die as it died in China . . . and in Cuba, where the great Fidel Castro handed a rifle to each peasant and said, 'Democracy is the government that arms the people.' " On other occasions, Julião boldly called for strikes.

Goulart lent his support to demands for rural change. Both the president and Julião attended a Peasant Congress in Belo Horizonte in November 1961, whose slogan was "We Want Land by Law or by Force." Goulart called for a far-reaching land reform at the congress. In March 1963, the president promulgated the "Statute of the Rural Worker," whose aim was to provide for the rural laborer what Vargas had achieved for the urban. The threats and rhetoric of reform alienated the increasingly frightened rural oligarchy. They manifested a particular hatred of Julião who, to peasant and landlord alike, symbolized the potential for pervasive changes. The landowners vilified the Leagues, labeling them communistic. Their tactic was an old one, even then: better to confuse the public with labels than to recognize legitimate need for change.

Although distressed by the course of events, neither the middle class, nor the elite, nor a combination of them seemed able to slow the radical momentum. Frustrated, the civilian political opponents of Goulart turned to the military to persuade the armed forces to act, a recourse they had used in other historical circumstances. In Brazilian history, military involvement in politics more often than not occurred when cohesion among the political elite was low. As in the past, the elite and middle class provided the military with a "legitimacy" to intervene. The press, mounting a campaign to involve the military in politics, to exercise its "moderating power," reminded the military of its "duty."

Goulart facilitated the alliance between the military leaders and his civilian opponents by alienating the officer class, a group always suspicious if not outrightly hostile to the PTB chief. A decision of the Supreme Court that sergeants could not hold seats in the legislature sparked a spontaneous rebellion of six hundred enlisted men in Brasília on September 12, 1963. The senior officers quickly put down the rebellion, but

only after the enlisted men had paralyzed the government, holding Congress and several high administrators prisoner. The incident revealed two significant factors. First, the enlisted men had allied themselves with the radical left. The CGT and the National Student Union, among others, defended their action. Second, Goulart refused to commit himself, neither condemning nor condoning the rebellion, an ominous sign to most of the officers. It seemed to indicate that the president's sympathies had swung to the radical left. The officers waited for a confirmation of that suspicion.

Goulart confirmed it during an emotional political rally directed by the CGT in Rio de Janeiro on March 13, 1964, to initiate the drive for "basic reforms." About 150,000 people, the majority of them of the working class, gathered to cheer the president on that fateful Friday. Expectation and excitement ran high. The charismatic orator Leonel Brizola, then an extremely popular federal deputy from Guanabara, spoke first. He reminded his audience that the president represented the people and that he was prevented from enacting his reforms by a reactionary Congress, representatives of the oligarchy. "Congress will give nothing to the people because it does not represent the aspirations of the people," he shouted. The alternative to a hostile Congress, he suggested, was to take matters directly to the people so that they could act. He called on the president to organize a strictly populist and nationalist government. With the crowd thus brought to a highly emotional pitch, Goulart came to the microphone and in his speech further identified his government with the people. As a climax, he signed there in public two decrees, one iniating a modest land reform expropriating lands within ten kilometers of federal highways, railways, and water projects, and another nationalizing all oil refineries. Two days later, in a message addressed to Congress, the president again challenged that body: "I have chosen to fight the privileged and to take the initiative for basic reforms." He had in mind two such reforms: a redivision of the land and the extension of the vote to illiterates and enlisted men, two powerful blows against the oligarchy. Apparently he no longer intended to compromise with the moderates and conservatives. Concilia-

tion seemed out of the question. Carried forward by the support and enthusiasm of the Left, the only political base he had, Goulart sought to radicalize the nation.

His opponents reacted. They organized rallies, and none surpassed the mammoth "March of the Family with God for Liberty" in São Paulo on March 19, 1964. Largely organized by upper and middle class women with the backing of the Roman Catholic church as well as conservative and moderate political parties, the march of several hundred thousand signaled the determination of significant social groups to stem the tide of projected reform. Like the newspaper editorials of the day, those demonstrators helped persuade the military officers to take political action, particularly as they witnessed a growing insubordination within the enlisted ranks.

Many of the politically inclined enlisted men approved the course the president took. The Sailors and Marines Association decided to call a special meeting to pledge their support to Goulart, an act the minister of the navy forbade. Admiral Sílvio Mota categorized the Association as "subversive." Nonetheless, on March 25, over two thousand sailors and marines met. To shouts of approval from the youthful gathering, the president of the Association denied the accusation of subversion and added, "The ones in this country who are trying to subvert order are those allied with the dark forces which caused one president to commit suicide, another to resign, and which tried to prevent Jango [Goulart] from taking office, and who now try to prevent basic reforms." The minister of the navy dispatched troops to arrest the participants in the meeting. At that point, Goulart intervened to grant an amnesty to the marines and sailors. The enlisted men rejoiced. Later, Goulart indicated his intention of investigating the conduct of certain admirals whom he accused of precipitating the mutiny. The officers sullenly interpreted the president's action as an endorsement of insubordination. In their eyes, military discipline had broken down. The morale of the officers slumped. Their honor had been besmirched.

Awaiting the officers was yet a stronger rebuff. On March 30 the president addressed an assembly of the Military Police

Sergeants Association in Rio de Janeiro, and his words were carried by television to the nation. He appealed emotionally to the sergeants for their support and charged the officers—those who had tried to prevent his legal accession to the presidency in 1961—with lack of discipline.

In the broadest sense, the mounting crisis of late March reflected the more fundamental tensions generated by economic development—or lack of it. Neither Quadros nor Goulart had provided the dynamic and positive leadership that had characterized the Kubitschek administration. Economic growth had slumped, a circumstance guaranteed to provoke crises because it forced the government to make difficult decisions. Usually governments opted to encourage greater foreign investments to stimulate the economy. This time, however, Goulart had frightened away the capitalists with the profit remission law. He was left with the alternative of implementing some basic reforms, a decision certain to arouse the ire of the small but potent privileged classes. Growing fiscal instability, hyperinflation, and the default on international debts further frightened the upper and middle classes. Predictably, the public complained of the upwardly spiraling cost of living. Political uncertainty caused by frequent labor strikes and pronouncements, rumors of a presidential coup, and demogogic appeals and threats further agitated the nation.

The military watched solicitously from the wings, but until the night of March 30 hesitated to stride onto the political stage. Goulart's attack on the military hierarchy during his televised speech that night excited an immediate and unified response from the officers. They yielded to the exhortations of the *"linha dura"* (hard-line) group within the military to intervene in and control the political process. Accusing the president and his government of being Communists, the military moved to overthrow Goulart. As one apologist of the coup, Juracy Magalhães, explained it, "The Brazilian Revolution was born out of the indomitable will of the people not to allow themselves to become dominated by Communism or by the corruption which was undermining our national life." On March 31 army units marched on Rio de Janeiro from Minas Gerais. The forces ordered from Rio de Janeiro to

oppose them joined them instead. The key Second Army in São Paulo adhered to the rebellion on April 1.

Surprised by the swiftness and extent of the revolt, Goulart flew from Rio de Janeiro to Brasília and thence to Pôrto Alegre in the hope of stirring up support for himself. Few stepped forward to defend the president. A small number of labor leaders, politicians, and intellectuals called for the people to rush to the barricades. Silence answered that call. With no appreciable support, on April 4 Goulart quietly slipped out of Brazil into exile in Montevideo. As a president, he had revealed many serious defects, but he had actively favored reform throughout his political career and in no way had limited the democratic process during his administration.

The Brazilian military received approval in their planning and execution of the coup from the U.S. government and the large U.S. military mission in Brazil. So committed was Washington that it dispatched warships to Brazil at the end of March in case they were needed. A U.S. naval unit with an aircraft carrier, a helicopter carrier, six destroyers, and oil tankers was ordered to take positions off the Brazilian coast near Santos. The top secret orders to the naval commander were: "Purpose of Carrier Task Force Group is to establish U.S. presence in the area when so directed and to be prepared to carry out tasks as may be assigned . . ."

Washington considered Goulart to be far too radical, unfriendly to foreign business and investment, and a potential danger to hemispheric security. Revolution in Cuba was more than enough challenge for Washington. The fear of similar events overtaking the South American giant consternated U.S. officials, who once again confused the need, desire, and thrust for change with Communism. The United States had stopped most aid and cut off sources of loans for Brazil in an effort to deepen the economic woes of the Goulart government. The Central Intelligence Agency had financed a major covert political campaign to deny Goulart control of Congress in the 1962 elections. In mid-March of 1964, Assistant Secretary of State for Inter-American Affairs Thomas Mann announced that the U.S. government would not oppose the establishment of military governments in Latin

America, a clear signal to the Brazilian military leaders that they could expect prompt approval from Washington if they toppled the Goulart government. How prompt that approval would be amazed even the Brazilian generals. Within four hours of taking power, even before they had formed a government, and while President João Goulart was still in Brazil, the officers who executed the coup d'état received a telegram from President Lyndon B. Johnson congratulating them on their maneuver. The U.S. ambassador to Brazil, Lincoln Gordon, then judged the military takeover "the single most decisive victory for freedom in the mid-twentieth century." If any further approval from Washington was needed, it came in the form of generous aid and loans that virtually inundated the new military government. Clearly involved in the military overthrow of the constitutional and democratic government of Brazil, the United States became intimately associated with the military dictatorship that followed.

Chapter Nine

The Past as Present

Contractual governance collapsed in 1964. The experiment with democracy gave way to military dictatorship. A succession of generals with technocratic advisers prescribed increased investments, capital accumulation at the expense of workers' salaries, rapid industrialization, and unquestioned obedience. They solicited foreign loans, accelerated the dependency on exports, and adhered to the dictates of the International Monetary Fund. The governments never hesitated to resort to violence to achieve their goals. During a period of impressive economic growth, from 1969 to 1974, a temporary euphoria disguised the brutality, but by the mid-1970s it became apparent that while solving none of Brazil's old problems the military government had created new ones.

In 1985 Brazil returned to the masquerade of democracy, form without content, rhetoric without meaning. The democratic governments failed to address major economic, social, and political problems. The disastrous exploitation of the Amazon and the shocking degradation of children and youths revealed the civilian governments to be as morally bankrupt as their military predecessors.

Military Dictatorship

A dark night of brutal military dictatorship descended. Having pushed Goulart from the presidential saddle, the military seized the reins of political power. For purposes of constitutional decorum, President of the Chamber of Deputies Ranieri Mazzilli once again served as acting president, the sixth time in his career he had occupied that office, but it proved to be a purely honorific position. This time the three military ministers, headed by Marshal Artur da Costa e Silva and collectively bearing the sonorous title "Supreme Revolutionary Command," exercised power. The Command reflected the dissatisfaction many officers felt about the course democracy had taken in Brazil during the previous two decades. To those officers, democracy seemed to permit and even encourage corruption, subversion, chaos, and demagogy. Twice they had removed Vargas from the presidential palace, only to see the voters return him or his heirs. Such an electorate, concluded the military in disgust, could not possibly understand its own best interests and certainly not those of the nation.

The voice of the *"tenentes,"* now tottering generals and marshals, spoke out again. Juarez Távora seemingly echoed the sentiments of many of his military contemporaries when he expressed a reluctance on the part of the armed forces to turn the government over to civilians. They were not reliable; in the past they had betrayed the military. Távora affirmed, "In 1930 we exercised restraint by not taking direct control of the government. We planned to put civilians in the government and influence them. It was an illusion. They soon pushed us aside and proved incapable of doing any of the things we had planned." Other officers shared that complaint, indicating that the military would not suffer a repetition of the politicians' perfidy this time.

In the twentieth century prior to 1964 the officers had intervened in politics with increasing frequency to change the chief executive, in 1930, 1945, 1954, 1955, and 1961, thus exercising a function comparable—in the military mind—to the *poder moderador.* They changed presidents much as the

emperor had arbitrarily alternated the Liberals and Conservatives in power during the Second Empire. The key military figure in promoting or coordinating the military coups was the chief of staff. This officer was likely to be much more attuned to and representative of the sentiments and opinions of the officer class than was the minister of war, an officer appointed by the president because of his loyalty. The officers who plotted were, in the vast majority, men from areas outside the traditional triangle of economic and political power, that is, outside São Paulo, Minas Gerais, and Rio de Janeiro. Quite often they came from Rio Grande do Sul or the Northeast. In that respect, they represented a widely felt frustration over the narrow base of political power in Brazil.

The military plots originated in other frustrations as well. Officers have been notably unsuccessful in winning presidential elections in contemporary Brazil. In 1945 two military candidates ran with the support of the three major parties, so logically one had to win, and General Dutra did. However, in 1950, Vargas defeated General Eduardo Gomes at the polls; in 1955, Kubitschek triumphed over General Juarez Távora; and in 1960, Quadros overwhelmed Marshal Henrique Lott. Apparently officers did not appeal to the electorate. Hence the ballot box seemed unlikely to serve as the portal through which the beribboned generals could enter into political power.

It is difficult to establish a pattern for the military interventions. At times, they favored the growth of democracy; 1955 serves as an excellent example. Yet at other times they threatened constitutional development; 1961 represents that aspect of the interventions. A volatile emotionalism often seemed to prompt the interventions. The concept of "military honor" that emerged so menacingly during the last decade of the Empire continued to influence the decisions of the officers; their attachment to that concept cannot be described as a force buttressing democracy. The overthrow of Vargas in 1954 illustrated their emotionalism in action, indeed, in control. The military considered neither the constitution nor public well-being. Certainly the preservation and encouragement of democracy were far from the officers' minds. Had the military shown political maturity and confidence in the constitutional

process, they would have awaited the presidential elections, only a few months away, and the change those elections could have brought about democratically. But the urge to vindicate that illusory honor took precedence in 1954, as it did on other occasions.

The military seldom acted alone. A pattern reaching back to 1889 shows that the armed forces were called into action by civilian groups, often the middle class with its close links to the officer class. In fact the military sometimes served as the surrogate for the frustrated middle class when it felt helpless or threatened in the political process. It had developed the habit of relying on the armed forces for short-run solutions to political problems. Those solutions consisted principally of forestalling any social, economic, or political reforms of consequence. The middle class seemed to resort to those patterns in calling forth the military to overthrow Goulart, but the military threw aside the traditional script on that occasion.

In 1964 the military radically altered its behavioral pattern. The soldiers did not retire to the barracks after the coup. The Supreme Military Command resolved this time not to return the government to the civilians at once. Influenced by the teachings of the Superior War College (Escola Superior de Guerra), the commanding officers espoused a common ideology. They believed that the military fostered national unity and that the best way to ensure national security was to encourage economic growth through stable government. They were determined in 1964 to involve the military more intimately in national life. The Command indicated the direction the new government would take when it issued, on April 9, 1964, the First Institutional Act, drawn up by none other than Francisco Campos, intellectual mentor of the Estado Novo and author of the Constitution of 1937. The Ato Institucional significantly modified the Constitution of 1946. Basically, the Act enlarged the powers of the president at the expense of the judiciary and the legislature. It called for the immediate election of a president who could propose constitutional amendments that Congress had to consider within thirty days and that needed only a majority vote for their passage. The president could also propose expenditure bills that Congress

could not increase, declare a state of siege, and deprive citizens of their rights for a period of ten years.

The military officers in control of the government selected General Humberto de Alencar Castelo Branco for the presidency and the subservient Congress complied with their votes. The son of a military family of the Northeast, he had served in the army since 1918 and had seen action in Italy with the Brazilian Expeditionary Force during World War II. Like many of his contemporary fellow officers, he had received advanced military instruction at the Superior War College. The officers were confident that Castelo Branco would deal firmly with the Brazilian Communists, whom they blamed for the chaos, corruption, and subversion in the nation. The members of Congress thought of the laconic general as a highly cultured officer and a defender of the democratic process. There was no difficulty, then, in electing him president on April 11.

General Castelo Branco and his military successors increased the centralization of political power. They limited or eliminated political freedoms and liberties. Until around 1980, they depoliticized the nation, repressing any opposition. Those policies contrasted sharply with the political openness of the preceding democratic experiment.

However, those two periods of twentieth-century Brazilian history had some arresting economic similarities. Neither leadership changed the basic structural foundations of the economy. Both emphasized industrialization over agriculture and left unaltered the rural patterns of land ownership and labor recruitment. Both emphasized import substitution policies and encouraged the export of manufactured goods. Government policy in both periods favored economic growth over economic development, demonstrating faith in a diffusionism that both thought would permit a trickle-down of economic benefits. Despite rhetorical differences both governments favored capitalism and, in fact, strengthened state capitalism. Both struggled unsuccessfully against inflation while augmenting the government's economic power. During the two consecutive periods highly trained technicians and highly regarded economists drew up and executed economic poli-

cies. Many of those who held influential posts prior to 1964 retained them or held similar positions after the fall of Goulart.

The government of Castelo Branco, primarily one of military officers and technocrats, pursued two primary goals: to put the nation's finances back in order and to combat the spread of communism, both internally and externally. Association of reform with communism characterized the mentality of those responsible for the coup, and, in fact, was a common association convenient for the Brazilian elite to make. It became immediately evident that the new president represented the wing of the *linha dura,* whose main concern was to eradicate communism anywhere it could be found. The opposite wing, while no less implacable toward communism, placed its emphasis on a very fundamental nationalism, more reminiscent of the Integralist variety than of the nationalism that had held sway from 1951 until April of 1964. Castelo Branco's definition of communism was very broad and tended to include any movements, parties, ideas, or persons to the left of his own position. He showed a strong suspicion of the nationalists who had dominated the previous governments. In his thinking, they were associated with if not equated to the Communists. Their economic policies, he feared, would stifle private initiative and open the door to socialism and thus to communism. The nationalists' foreign policy, with its emphasis on the Third World and its friendship toward the Eastern bloc particularly annoyed him. He viewed the international scene as a struggle between East and West in which there could be no neutral position. Acknowledging the United States as the unquestionable leader of the "free world," he vowed to follow the international leadership of Washington. Brazil at once broke diplomatic relations with Cuba and began voting against the seating of the People's Republic of China in the United Nations. The government expressed its solidarity with the United States intervention in Viet Nam. Brazilian troops participated in the intervention in the Dominican Republic in 1965, a decision defended by one officer in the following words: "The Armed Forces brilliantly stopped Communism from taking over Brazil. Another brilliant ex-

ample is their participation in the Dominican Republic in the operation initiated by the American marines, where they also stopped Communism from taking over that country." The military government actively supported the controversial Inter-American Peace Force, a fig leaf designed by Washington to disguise its interventions throughout the hemisphere, and the minister of foreign relations even visited most of the South American capitals to urge the support of that force, a mission that proved to be a notable failure.

Internally the government's hand fell heavily on the leftists and nationalists, although whim and caprice often dictated the definition of those two vague terms. Fifty-five Congressmen were expelled from the legislature and lost their political rights, thereby increasing the conservative proportion of Congress. Castelo Branco removed the democratically elected governors of Amazonas, Pará, Pernambuco, Sergipe, Acre, Rio de Janeiro, and Goiás. He deprived former presidents Kubitschek, Quadros, and Goulart of their political rights for ten years. He fired approximately 4,500 federal employees. The military ranks were purged and several hundred officers either retired or were dismissed. The hastily created Military Courts of Inquiry summoned more than 9,000 persons to answer charges of corruption or subversion. The Superior Institute of Brazilian Studies was closed, the National Student Union disbanded, labor unions purged, and the Peasant Leagues outlawed. A book-burning mentality predominated—not only figuratively but literally. In Rio Grande do Sul, the commander of the Third Army, General Justino Alves Bastos, ordered the burning all books that he branded as subversive. His capricious list of dangerous literature included Stendhal's *The Red and the Black*.

At the same time, Castelo Branco struggled to put an end to corruption in government, of which there had been a considerable amount, and to stem the tide of inflation. The latter task proved to be both difficult and unpopular. Inflation did not abate following the coup. The cost-of-living index for 1964 continued to rise, taking a record-breaking 86.6 percent jump, a six-point increase over the previous year. Wages failed to keep pace with prices. In 1965, wage earners lost 14

percent of their purchasing power; in 1966, 22 percent. After the coup and until December 31, 1964, the government emitted an unprecedented amount of currency. The cruzeiro sank even lower in international value. If business and industry had expected an immediate miracle from the military coup, they were disappointed. Both exports and production fell. Business interests complained that the government kept too tight a rein on the economy and accused the administration of showing preference to foreign capital. Indeed, both foreign capital and foreign control of Brazilian firms increased in the years after Goulart's fall. Foreign investment by 1968 reached $3.5 billion, approximately 8 percent of Brazil's total capital stock. The United States, with about $1.22 billion, remained the single largest investor, followed by France, Britain, Switzerland, and Germany. Further reflecting its distance from the nationalists, the government sold the Fábrica Nacional de Motores, the only Brazilian company manufacturing vehicles, to Alfa-Romeo of Italy and also sold to foreigners Loide, the national coastal shipping company; it reversed a previous prohibition of foreign exploitation of iron ore deposits.

During the first two years after the coup, the economy stagnated as the government turned its attention from encouraging growth to stabilizing the economy and fighting inflation. Throughout his tenure, Castelo Branco rigidly maintained a severe fiscal policy. Beginning in 1965, he restricted the new issues of bank notes. He slowed the rise in the cost of living. By the end of his administration, the economy showed signs of recovery from the lethargy into which his fiscal measures had plunged it, but nothing like the heady growth rates of the fifties and early sixties. The year 1967 ended with a trade balance of $200 million in Brazil's favor. Coffee maintained its customary primacy, still accounting for 44 percent of Brazil's exports. Significantly, manufactured goods, everything from ships to television sets, ranked as the second most important export item.

The government's monetary policies did not appeal to or benefit most of the population, which remembered the dramatic development projects of the past and the previous re-

cord of wage increases. Complaining of the official austerity, many questioned government priorities that favored foreigners over Brazilians, businessmen over workers, and the financial agenda of the International Monetary Fund over Brazilian development. In their thinking, the budgets had not been drawn up in the best interests of a nation eager to develop rapidly. The allocations, however, did reveal at least one new priority. In the last civilian budget, that of 1963, some 7 percent had gone to the military, while 19 percent had been set aside for education. In the first full-year's budget drawn up by the Castelo Branco government, that of 1965, the military received 11 percent, while the amount allotted for education was cut to 9 percent. The military establishment was small, only about 250,000 men under arms in a population of 80 million, but the cost to maintain that establishment was disproportionately high. That cost rose spectacularly. Using a 1967 constant price base, the amount spent on the military went from $386 million in 1962, to $756 million in 1967, to $1,102 million in 1971, at which time Brazil was spending nearly 50 percent of the total arms expenditures of the six Latin American nations with the largest military budgets. At the same time, Brazil received from the United States the most military assistance of any nation in the hemisphere, a reward from the metropolis to its military clients. The taciturn Castelo Branco enforced a balanced budget and brought inflation under better control. Still, legions of unemployed, illiterate, hungry, and ill Brazilians, deprived even of the solace of reform rhetoric, much less actual reforms, found nothing to celebrate under the stern military disciplinarian. The government proudly labeled itself "revolutionary" but failed to undertake any basic structural reforms that would benefit the majority. Although the omnipotent military government could have promulgated a land reform overnight if it had so desired, it ignored any such consideration. Industrialization, not farming, mesmerized the military.

Dissatisfaction with the military regime appeared quickly and grew rapidly. The workers complained that prices rose while their wages remained frozen. In late 1968, Minister of Labor Jarbas Passarinho conservatively estimated that the

workers' real wages had fallen between 15 and 30 percent in the previous four years. The intellectuals lamented the loss of their liberties. Democrats despaired as the government grew more authoritarian. Young Brazilians began to express their dissatisfaction through the medium of music. They abandoned the bossa nova for protest songs based on ethnic and folk music. The lyrics called for a return to freedom and decried the hunger, misery, and social injustice in the country. One of the most popular themes was the plight of the impoverished Northeast. A hit song of 1965, "Carcará," lamented the poverty and hunger of the Northeast that forced the poor to abandon their homes. To standing-room-only audiences, the students of São Paulo's Catholic University presented the musical drama *Vida e Morte de Severino* (Life and Death of Severino), a poem of João Cabral de Melo Neto set to music by Chico Buarque de Holanda. The drama told of the peasant Severino, the personification of the rural poor, who wandered through the arid backlands of the Northeast observing unhappiness, misery, and death. At one point, during the burial scene of a peasant, the chorus sang: "This land where you lie is just the right size—not too long, not too wide. Here is your share of the *latifundium*." Blared forth from the ubiquitous transistor radios, protest music provided a most effective form of communication in a land where half the population was illiterate.

Dissatisfaction also existed within the military itself, which was by no means unified in its political orientation. On one level, the decision of the senior officers to hold the reins of political power divided the military, many of whom did not favor the extreme ideas of the *linha dura*. Following a long tradition in the services, many officers held that the military should play at most a restricted role, one which did not include the actual governing of the nation. They advocated returning the military to its traditional and historic role as the *poder moderador*. On another level, the issue of nationalism divided the military. The nationalistic officers of moderate or liberal tendencies favored intense economic development directed by the state, basic structural reforms, an independent foreign policy, and restrictions on foreign influence, includ-

ing capital, in Brazil. The right-wing nationalists of the *linha dura* took a chauvinistic stance. But Castelo Branco and the officers who surrounded him maintained their suspicions of nationalism. They preferred fiscal stability to economic development, foreswore an independent foreign policy in order to align Brazil closely with the United States, shied away from basic reforms, and welcomed foreign investment and influence in Brazil.

Elections scheduled for 1965 offered Brazilians the opportunity to express their reactions to military governance. In the March mayoral elections of São Paulo, the candidate endorsed by Jânio Quadros won, to the obvious chagrin of the military government. The crucial test of confidence, however, was the October gubernatorial elections held in eleven states. The candidates favored by the government lost in nine of those states, including the key states of Minas Gerais and Guanabara.

Disappointed with what it considered an ingrate electorate, the government reacted swiftly. On October 27, 1965, Castelo Branco promulgated the Second Institutional Act, which further strengthened the powers of the president in matters of legislation, states of siege, and intervention in the states; dissolved all political parties; instituted indirect elections for the president and vice president; conferred on the government the power to cancel the political rights of those considered to be security risks to the state; increased the number of judges on the Supreme Court from eleven to sixteen; exempted certain actions of the government from judicial review; and authorized military courts to try individuals accused of subverting the state. The Third Institutional Act, promulgated on February 5, 1966, ended the popular elections of governors of the states and of mayors of the state capitals. Thereafter the state legislatures selected the chief executives of the states, and the governors appointed the mayors of the capital cities. Those two Institutional Acts administered the coup de grace to the democratic experiment in Brazil.

The government replaced the political parties with two official parties: the *Aliança Renovadora Nacional* (the Na-

tional Renovating Alliance, referred to as ARENA), the official government party, and the *Movimento Democrático Brasileiro* (the Brazilian Democratic Movement, or MDB), an official opposition party. One wag noted that the difference between the two parties was that the first answered the government with a "Yes, Sir!" while the second just answered "Yes." In 1972, the leader of the MDB, Oscar Pedroso Horta, labeled both officially sponsored political parties a farce since they were artificially created, tightly controlled, and devoid of "the slightest possibility of discussion."

The purge of Congress accompanied by the substitution of official parties for the disbanded ones made of the legislature a rubber stamp. The packing of the Supreme Court did the same thing to the judiciary. The government wielded censorship and the threat to cancel political rights as weapons to reduce criticism and opposition. The Constitution of 1967, which centralized the power of the nation in the hands of the president, glorified authoritarianism.

Marshal Castelo Branco reaffirmed his intention to relinquish office in March of 1967, as he had promised he would. The achievements of his three-year administration contrasted sharply with the previous evolution of contemporary Brazil. The rate of industrialization slowed, the experiment in democracy ended, military rule replaced traditional civilian rule. While the inflation was checked, so was economic development; and while a political drift to the Left was halted, so was the thrust toward basic reforms. A few Communists and their sympathizers had been removed from power, but at the same time so had many able Democrats and nationalists. Where once the positive policy of development had dominated government councils, the negative and sterile policy of anticommunism held sway.

The military government of Castelo Branco set patterns of political and economic behavior that succeeding general-presidents followed. Those governments imposed a high degree of centralization of all powers into the hands of the chief executive. State and local governments, as well as the federal legislature and judiciary, witnessed the steady erosion of their

responsibilities and authority. The goal was to depoliticize the nation and, in accomplishing it, every form of liberty and freedom was repressed, at times brutally. Extensive documentation details, between 1964 and 1979, more than 283 types of torture inflicted on "dissidents," at 242 clandestine torture centers, by 444 individual torturers. Victims still remain uncounted and unidentified, but many who lived through the military terror have since publicly described their ordeal.

Economically those governments concentrated on efforts to reduce and control inflation, but those efforts fell far short of success. The military governments pursued whatever policies might promise economic growth, regardless of whether it might mean neglect of agriculture or denationalization of industry. Faced with an old dilemma, those military governments opted to open the doors to foreign investment as a "safe" means of encouraging growth rather than to undertake basic reforms which might not only stimulate growth but foster development. Reform and development suggested change, a prospect the military and their backers judged as negatively as they did communism.

Castelo Branco picked as his successor Marshal Artur da Costa e Silva and arranged for Congress to elect him president. The new chief of state marched into office on March 15, 1967, for a four-year term, and began to govern under Brazil's sixth constitution. He conveyed the impression of being more affable than his predecessor, and that appearance of humanness, in contrast with the aloof demeanor of Castelo Branco, gave the people hope of a relaxation of national tensions. He certainly showed a concern for public opinion that his predecessor never had. Questions of a balanced budget, sound financial practices, and "purification" of the body politic concerned him less. He seemed more inclined to support industrialization, economic growth, and an independent foreign policy. The nationalists, momentarily repressed and demoralized by the March coup, gathered their strength again to encourage developmental nationalism. They criticized the government's conservative economic policies, particularly the favorable attitude toward foreign capitalists exemplified by

the repeal of the profit remittance law, the concession of new mining privileges to foreigners, and deference to the dicta of the International Monetary Fund (IMF).

Under the military presidents, that deference emerged as a major indicator of Brazilian dependency. To attract foreign investments and, most particularly, loans, Brazil needed the fiscal approval of that powerful international capitalist organization, tightly controlled by the major North Atlantic industrial nations, dominated by the United States. The IMF routinely required nations to subscribe to a standard economic formula in order to receive its endorsement and/or support: 1) the reduction of controls on trade, finance, and public enterprise; 2) restrictions on spending, above all in the public sector (i.e., education, health care, housing and welfare-related projects); 3) the stabilization of wages—more often than not the freezing of them; and 4) an emphasis on exports to earn the hard currencies needed to repay debts. Brazilian nationalists argued than the IMF terms weighed most heavily on the poor, hindered change, deflected reform, overemphasized exports, and imposed a dependent status on Brazil. Indeed, the omnipresent concern with exports reinforced those old patterns imposed by Portugal during the key period from 1530 to 1560. The nationalists bemoaned the strengthening of export orientation and dependency during the final half of the twentieth century. A combination of the IMF dicta and an escalating debt crisis highlighted a modern version of an old reality: the power of external forces in the shaping of Brazil.

Costa e Silva listened attentively to the pleas of the national business community, which, jealous of the privileges bestowed on foreigners under Castelo Branco, had been resorting to some of the traditional nationalist arguments against foreign capital. In due course he announced that his government was "restudying" the agreement signed by Castelo Branco with the United States to guarantee American investments in Brazil. His government enacted regulations to prohibit investment by foreign capitalists in the new petrochemical industry. He and his foreign minister spoke of an external policy in which Brazil would be aligned only with Brazil. He reversed

the position of his predecessor with regard to the Inter-American Peace Force. Announcing that Brazil had definitely abandoned the idea of a hemispheric police force, he reasserted Brazil's traditional respect for the principle of nonintervention in the affairs of other nations. Whether out of political conviction or simply because he was of a more easygoing nature, Costa e Silva permitted a wider latitude of action in Brazilian political life. The influence and power of that wing of the *linha dura* obsessed with anti-Communism seemed to decrease. The sudden death of Castelo Branco in an air accident in July 1967 doubtless gave Costa e Silva greater freedom and maneuverability than he might otherwise have enjoyed.

Both the Left and Right pressured the government of Costa e Silva, and both sides resorted to terrorist tactics. The far Right advocated undisguised dictatorship. The far Left called for a socialist revolution. Between the two extremes a genuine desire for a return to civilian, democratic government increased. As that desire went unfulfilled, frustration mounted. Student riots against the government erupted across the nation. The young demonstrators advocated a variety of basic reforms as well as the restitution of lost freedoms. In the words of one of the officers of the Student Federation of the University of Brasília, "The government must do away with the old structures. We demand reforms. We demand them now. Talk is nothing. We want action." Under the banner of the Brazilian Mothers' Union, the matrons of Rio de Janeiro and São Paulo allied to protest the government's harsh treatment of the students and to proclaim the right to assemble and to speak freely. Many of the leading intellectuals added their voices, where and when censorship permitted, to the cries of dissatisfaction. Some leaders of the Church likewise spoke out. Unofficially led by Monseigneur Helder Câmara, the archbishop of Olinda and Recife, the clerics reproved the military government and advocated a wide range of social, economic, and political reforms. This mounting criticism and unrest took place even while the economic situation of the country improved. Inflation was under control, prices remained relatively steady, and production rose.

Ineffectual and indecisive, Costa e Silva lost support on

all sides. The anti-Communist wing of the *linha dura* felt that his leniency encouraged the left. Yet, on the other hand, the students, intellectuals, laborites, and nationalists pleaded in vain for basic reforms. To the extent censorship permitted, the press criticized the government. Finally, despite heavy controls, the other two branches of the government, whose members were practically all handpicked by the executive, made a sudden and surprising demonstration of independence. The Supreme Court granted a writ of habeas corpus for three student leaders who had languished in jail for over two months. Congress emulated that display of independence on December 12, 1968, with the rejection by a vote of 216 to 141 of a request from the government to lift the immunity of Deputy Márcio Moreira Alves so that he could be tried on military charges of abusing his position. Alves had been a vehement critic of the military. A year earlier he had published a book exposing military brutality toward political prisoners. To protest the storming of the Brasília University campus some months before, he had spoken in the Chamber of Deputies to urge his countrymen to boycott the Independence Day parades as a sign of their disapproval of the campus invasion. Complaining that the outspoken deputy had besmirched military honor, the senior officers sought to punish him. Congress, usually compliant, showed an unusual degree of independence when it refused to surrender Alves to the wrath of the military.

The growing unrest, capped by the defiance of the military first by the Supreme Court and then by Congress, united many officers behind the anti-Communist wing of the *linha dura*. The far-rightist officers seized command of the situation and demanded that Costa e Silva crack down at once. In what amounted to a coup d'état on December 13, 1968, Costa e Silva promulgated the Fifth Institutional Act, which conferred on the president dictatorial powers in "defense of the necessary interests of the nation." The act disbanded Congress, closed down the state legislatures, suspended the constitution, imposed censorship, cancelled the political rights of many, and suspended writs of habeas corpus. During a wave of arrests, the military police took into custody Juscelino Ku-

bitschek, Carlos Lacerda, and a host of newspapermen, among others. A brutal military hand reached out to snuff the last flickering flame of liberty in Brazil. The dark night of dictatorship deepened. Washington did not protest the destruction of democracy. Quite the contrary, the United States lavished aid and training on the military.

As a result of the rigid censorship, none of the news media could report those December events. The newspapers published following the coup contained a queer assortment of information that brilliantly reflected the indomitable Brazilian sense of humor. The staid *Correio da Manhã* bore the glaring headline, "Rich Cat Dies of Heart Attack in Chicago." The *Journal do Brasil* prominently carried a wry weather report, "Weather black. Temperature suffocating. The air is unbreathable. The country is being swept by a strong wind." Censorship extended to the international press media. Foreign correspondents had to submit all their cables for governmental approval before sending them.

The government explained its own coup by saying that subversives were trying to overthrow the regime, a frequently used and much-abused rationalization that surprised no one. Costa e Silva seemed almost embarrassed and apologetic when he announced to the nation:

The promulgation of Institutional Act Number 5 after 24 hours of intense discussion and meditation did not seem to the President of the Republic as the best solution but as the only solution. Intensified to high levels of drama which had the possibility of humiliating, belittling, and provoking the Armed Forces, the crisis of insignificant dimension was headed for an unfortunate outcome whose consequence made it imperative for the Chief of State to act in order to save the nation the pain and agony of fratricidal struggle.

He informed his listeners that the coup had saved them from both corruption and subversion. It was apparent that he had been reduced to functioning as a compliant mouthpiece for the anti-Communist wing of the *linha dura*. Further evidence of the triumph of the *linha dura* was the resignation in January 1969 of Minister of the Interior Afonso Augusto de Albuquer-

que Lima, who was known to favor agrarian reforms and social welfare legislation. The militaristic, anti-Communist hardliners did not look with sympathy on such goals.

Apparently what the government mistook for subversion was a genuine desire among all classes of the population for a return to democracy. At that very time, a song entitled "Walking," by a young composer, Geraldo Vandré, gained unprecedented popularity throughout the nation. Sung in the streets of the city or in the lanes of the country, the lyrics not only protested against the unpopular military government but challenged it:

> There are soldiers who are armed but not loved
> Mostly lost with their weapons in their hands.
> In the barracks they learn the old lesson
> Of dying for the country and living for nothing.
>
> There is hunger on the great plantations
> And desperation walking through the streets.
> But still the people take the flower as their strongest weapon
> In the belief that flowers can overcome the cannon.

General Luís de França Oliveira, in charge of public security in Rio de Janeiro, classified the lyrics as "subversive" and cautioned that the song was "a musical cadence of the Mao Tse-tung type that can easily serve as the anthem for student street demonstrations." But the song, like the protests and demonstrations that preceded it, only indicated once again the estrangement of the government from the people.

While most Brazilians adopted a policy of passive resistance to the government, a tiny band of urban guerrillas intensified their activities in the major cities to oppose the military regime. They robbed banks to finance their campaign of protest and struck at police or military armories to obtain weapons. They made international headlines on September 4, 1969, by kidnaping the U.S. ambassador to Brazil. In return for his life, they made two demands to which the government quickly agreed. First, the radio and TV stations had to read and the newspapers had to print an antigovernment manifesto written by the urban guerrillas. Second, the government had to free fifteen political prisoners and fly them to sanctu-

ary in Mexico. When those demands were met, the abductors freed the ambassador.

In the meantime, an unforeseen event had once again rocked the nation's political equilibrium. On August 30, 1969, President Costa e Silva suffered a cerebral hemorrhage that left him partially paralyzed on his right side and unable to speak. The three military ministers seized power. Almost at once the crisis of the abduction of the U.S. ambassador confronted them, and they saw themselves outwitted by the imaginative guerrillas. The junta reacted by restoring the death penalty—outlawed for three-quarters of a century—for acts of violence and subversion.

When Costa e Silva failed to recover from his stroke, the junta deliberated to pick a new president for Brazil. Their search initiated a debate within the armed services between the conservatives, who concerned themselves with continuing the search for subversion and Communist party members, and the reformists, who evinced more interest in economic and social reform. On October 7, the junta named to that office General Emílio Garrastazú Médici. Revived for the occasion, ARENA, the official progovernment party, endorsed the choice. The junta then called a purged Congress back into session on October 22, to dutifully voice approval of what the military had already done. Inaugurated in the presence of Congress on October 30, 1969, Médici was to serve a full term of office, another victory for the "linha dura," which wanted the new president to have a full term of his own rather than merely serve out the unfinished term of Costa e Silva. October 30 also witnessed the promulgation of a new constitution.

President Médici presided over some years of phenomenal economic growth, the rate averaging around 10 percent per year. To many observers, that heady boom seemed to announce that finally Brazil had reached the "economic take-off." A host of Third World nations looked to Brazil as a kind of economic model. But at the same time, the government's sobering record of torture and abuse of political prisoners received growing international attention and condemnation. The repressive apparatus detracted from the economic eu-

phoria. The government resented any criticism. For example, students arrested during demonstrations in early 1972 were promptly and routinely branded as subversives by the police. Yet, the students had largely limited their actions to appeals for more schools, pointing out that the government regularly spent more money on military hardware than on the nation's education.

In consultation with top military officials, Médici selected his successor, another general, Ernesto Geisel, a selection which the compliant congress seconded. Taking office on March 15, 1974 President Geisel promised the nation a *distensão,* a gradual relaxation of authoritarian rule, and a restoration of civilian constitutional government. One logical consequence of the implementation of *distensão* was the questioning, even challenge of executive absolutism. While there were periods in which a greater measure of freedom was tolerated, Geisel demonstrated that on occasion he could crack down when executive fiat was challenged. In April of 1977, he closed Congress for two weeks purportedly because the MDB delegation had refused to pass a government-sponsored judicial reform bill; but that was really an excuse for the government to rule by decree. Geisel then issued his "April Package," a group of measures to weaken Congress still further and to guarantee that the government, through ARENA, would dominate any future elections. Still, during his term of office, Geisel did ease censorship and restrain the military's repressive apparatus, including the use of torture. The government confronted escalating economic problems: a declining growth rate, a rising rate of inflation, the high cost of imported oil, and a national debt of nearly $40 billion and rising rapidly. As the period of rapid growth slowed, the economic problems challenging the nation loomed ever larger. A faltering economy promoted political reactions.

During the Geisel administration, opposition to military government mounted, some of it emanating from unexpected sources. The Roman Catholic church, through the leadership of men like Dom Helder Câmara and Cardinal Ernest Arns, the archbishop of São Paulo, raised its voice

against social injustice and demanded economic opportunities for the masses and freedom for all. Labor showed a
renewed independence. In May of 1978, a strike in São Paulo
involving some fifty thousand workers was the first in a decade. Those workers sought higher wages and the government responded with adjustments. The students, too, became vocal again. In 1977, they organized a number of important demonstrations. More surprising, the business community
voiced criticism. In November 1977 some two thousand businessmen gathered in Rio de Janeiro called for democratic
liberties, and in July of the following year a document signed
by eight wealthy industrialists advocated a more just socio-
economic system. The document stated that full democracy
was the only way to insure economic development. Businessmen, particularly middle-level capitalists, had suffered since
1964 from the competition of the powerful multinational corporations and blamed the government for allowing those giant
firms to dominate. Finally, within the ranks of the military,
reform sentiment grew, and it became increasingly difficult
for the governing generals to disguise the cracks in the facade
of unity they wanted to project.

Unlike his military predecessors, Geisel did not consult
his colleagues to select a consensus candidate to replace
himself in the presidency. Arbitrarily he selected General João
Baptista Figueiredo, a relatively unknown figure who formerly
had directed the National Intelligence Service. A reduction of
political repression allowed a mild opposition, the National
Front for Redemocratization (FNR), to nominate a presidential
candidate, General Euler Bentes Monteiro. The FNR denounced the violations of human and civil rights, opposed
the government's economic policies, supported the strike
movements of students and workers, and decried the arbitrary powers of the president. It drew wide public support.
Clearly its success revealed a political crisis: the rupture of
the former consensus of the bourgeoisie and armed forces.
The failure of the military dictatorship to solve any basic problems was increasingly apparent to even its supporters. The
government needed all its considerable force to win the elec-

tions even though it managed the electoral machinery. While the Electoral College gave Figueiredo 335 votes, it cast 266 for Bentes Monteiro.

Assuming the presidency for a six-year term on March 15, 1979, President Figueiredo expressed a hope to preside over the political transition from dictatorship to democracy. He announced, "I intend to turn this country into a democracy . . . I hold out my hand in conciliation." True to his word, the president initiated at once the *"abertura"* (opening) to democracy. He proposed an amnesty for all those who since 1961 had been accused of political crimes, had their political rights suspended, and had been punished as a result of the various arbitrary institutional acts. Congress promptly approved that major act of justice both to ease past political bitterness and to facilitate the transition to the liberal, though controlled, democracy the military promised. He authorized the formation of new political parties, fitting instrumentalities to carry out the *abertura*.

ARENA promptly became the Democratic Social Party (PDS), while the MDB easily transformed itself into the Brazilian Democratic Movement Party (PMDB). A small Partido dos Trabalhadores (Party of the Workers, or PT) emerged. Growing slowly, it became a major political force within a decade. Other parties appeared but without a national base of support. As censorship ended, free speech flowered. The *abertura* pleased most Brazilians. The hard-line officers fretted. Change unnerved them, requiring President Figueiredo to test all his powers to control them. The national mood favored conciliation; it succeeded.

The gubernatorial and congressional elections slated for 1982, the first since 1965, signaled the success of the *abertura*, indeed its irreversibility. In a pattern complementary to the political past, the more conservative PDS triumphed in the rural areas, while the more liberal PMDB captured the cities. The PMDB won ten of the twenty-two contested gubernatorial races, celebrating victories in the three most important states: São Paulo, Minas Gerais, and Rio de Janeiro. The opposition won important victories in the races for the Senate

and the Chamber of Deputies, but the PDS hung onto its majority in both houses of the legislature.

Assessments of the political record of the military dictatorship award it very low marks. Nonetheless, the military steered a savvy political course through the *abertura* and cleaned up an otherwise dismal performance during the six years of the Figueiredo administration. Assessments of the economic record of the military dictatorship remain more controversial.

During the early years of the military dictatorship, the government concentrated on the stabilization of the economy, which grew very slowly. From the end of 1967 to the end of 1974 the growth rate for both domestic and export production soared, often exceeding 10 percent a year. Exports quadrupled. Manufactured goods replaced coffee as the principal export. Heady economic performance boasted Brazil's confidence and won converts to the "economic miracle" wrought by the generals and their technocrats. In the mid-1970s, however, Brazilians experienced the international oil crisis accompanied by rising prices for imports, falling prices for Brazilian raw materials, and spiraling global interest rates. A deteriorating trade balance troubled Brazil. Between 1971 and 1983, Brazil spent $20 billion more on imports than it earned from exports. Growth slowed and the economy soured. The government sought to circumvent the economic problems by increased borrowing abroad. Foreign debt multiplied: from $5.5 billion in 1970, to $22.2 in 1975, to $60.8 in 1980, and to $95.8 in 1985. The debt service alone on borrowings of those proportions drained abroad huge chunks of Brazil's export earnings, rising from 33 percent in 1974 to 80 percent in 1982, then falling to 40 percent in 1986. The inflation inherited by the military in 1964—90 percent a year—temporarily fell, only to rise like a phoenix after 1975, reaching 230 percent by 1984. Throughout the period, the government planned, managed, and directed the economy, even owning much of it. For example the government owned nine of Brazil's ten largest industrial firms.

The military government subscribed to the idea that a

growing economy would diffuse benefits. So long as growth occurred, it buoyed up the hopes of much of the population that they, somehow, some way, would share its benefits. Growth remained most visible in the southern and southeastern regions of Brazil, already the most privileged. To an unhealthy degree, external demands promoted a high percentage of the economic growth. Thus, true to traditional patterns, the export sector remained the most dynamic part of the economy, and foreign investments and loans further charted the course of that growth.

Like so many of the Latin Americans, the Brazilian generals and their civilian technocrats believed in the panacea of industrialization as the certain solution to most national problems, even though planners had become increasingly skeptical of the "magic solutions" attributed to it. Industries proliferated as Brazil emerged as one of the world's ten most industrialized nations. Production mounted impressively. Between 1967 and 1980, steel production rose from under 4 to over 15 million tons; electrical production from less than 10 million kilowatts to 135; and automobile production from 200,000 vehicles to over a million. Much of that industrial growth was concentrated in consumer industries catering to the demands of the middle and upper classes. Much of it also responded to a preference for production for export. In 1968 industrial goods accounted for 20 percent of Brazilian exports; in 1980 they reached 56.5 percent; in 1985, 65 percent. In general, the industrialists followed their private short-run interests rather than a clear theory or plan of national development. They opted to encourage foreign investment rather than to insist on the reforms and changes required to initiate meaningful economic development. Transnational companies penetrated at alarming rates. By 1971 they accounted for 70 percent of total net profits in five important sectors of the economy: rubber, automobiles, machinery, household appliances, and mining. Profit remittances abroad exceeded investments. The ten largest foreign companies in Brazil invested $98.8 million but remitted $774.5 million abroad between 1965 and 1975. One specific example during that decade:

Anderson Clayton, a huge international agribusiness firm, invested $1.6 million in Brazil, while taking out $16.8 million in profits and dividends. *Business Week* advised its readers that the South American giant offered the highest level of profits in the world. Brazil, in reality, provided capital for the capitalist world rather than absorbing it and utilizing it in development.

As industries became more capital-intensive, they hired proportionately fewer workers. The number of workers entering the job market annually far exceeded the number of new workers being employed by the expanding but capital-intensive manufacturing plants. This process increased the number of unemployed, conservatively estimated at 20 percent by the mid-seventies. It also promoted regressive income distribution. In most cases the interests of the local industrialists paralleled those of the powerful international investors and corporations. They deflected development for the immediate gains of growth.

Despite the hoopla of modernization, the agrarian sector followed traditional patterns. An emphasis on export agriculture concentrated labor, technology, capital, and land in the production of items for the foreign market rather than of food for the Brazilians. Witness the rush to grow and market soybeans, at the expense of producing basic foods for Brazilians. Soybean production leapt from 350,000 tons a year in the mid-1960s to 12,200,000 tons in 1977. In 1988 soybeans accounted for nearly 20 percent of exports, earning Brazil $3.5 billion. The government encouraged the production since it complemented the drive to augment exports.

While Brazil triumphed by 1978 as the world's fifth largest exporter of agricultural products, food became scarcer for the majority of its population. Annual agrarian growth rates often lagged behind rates of population growth. Per capita production of such dietary staples as rice, black beans, manioc, and potatoes fell 13 percent from 1977 to 1984, in contrast to the 15 percent rise in per capita production of such food exports as soybeans, oranges, and peanuts. In accordance with the capitalist law of supply and demand, the prices of

staples for the table items inexorably rose. To further complicate the economic situation of average Brazilians, their purchasing power plummeted.

The degree of land concentration accelerated. By the
1980s, less than 2 percent of the landowners held 50 percent
of the land. The cumulative acreage of 126 giant estates of
more than 240,000 acres each exceeded the total area cultivated by a million small farmers. Having one of the highest
concentrations of land ownership in the world did more to
hobble than to promote Brazilian development.

A strong corollation existed between farm size and food
production for national consumption. While modest-sized
farms of less than 250 acres occupied only about 20 percent
of the arable land, they produced most of the food Brazilians
consumed. Those farms boasted relatively high productivity.
Such statistics argued persuasively, but without effect, in favor of agrarian reform.

All efforts to reform the land ownership structure by
division and redistribution of land came to a halt in the 1970s.
In fact, the governments of that period believed large estates
should replace small farms on the principle that size increased efficiency, a conclusion reached without factual basis. One minister of agriculture concluded, "The solutions
adopted for industry will also be good for agriculture." Such
an idea did not augur well for the working class. A generally
inefficient and highly export-oriented agricultural system
foretold high food prices that would force Brazilians to spend
a disproportionate share of their income on food. Little remained for them to spend on the consumer items produced
by a more efficient industrial sector. The Brazilian situation
offered a striking example of the problems raised by imposing industrialization on antiquated agrarian structures. The
emphasis on the agrarian export sector, the increasing participation of multinationals in the exploitation of the countryside, and the further marginalization of the rural poor
prompted another minister of agriculture, Luís F. Cirne Lima,
to resign in 1973 in protest against those trends. He complained that the exporters were "likely to be foreign" and the
nation's prosperity "less and less Brazilian."

Table 9.1 Brazilian Income Distribution

	1960	1970	1980	1990
Percentage of national income going to top 10% of population	39.6	46.7	50.9	53.2
Percentage of poorest 50%	17.4	14.9	12.6	11

(These figures vary among sources. No agreement exists. Therefore these figures must be accepted as approximates. All sources do agree, however, on the increase for the top 10% and the decrease for the poorest 50%.)

The absolute control of the military over the nation permitted the technocrats to promote economic growth without any consideration of social or political costs. Consequently, a relentless wage squeeze afflicted laborers. Wages seldom kept pace with price increases. Between 1960 and 1978, years that encompassed the "economic miracle," fully 80 percent of the population suffered an income decline. Labor paid for much of the economic growth without garnering benefits. Table 9.1 provides the figures to illustrate the increasing concentration of income. By the mid-1970s, the most affluent 20 percent of Brazilian households averaged thirty-three times the income of the poorest 20 percent. (In the United States, by contrast, the difference was twelve to one.) Because the government tightly controlled the unions and because no political parties existed to defend the workers' interests, they lacked the means to protest their declining quality of life. Soon enough, the middle class also discovered that the "miracle" marginalized them as well.

The decision-making process, emphasis on growth, rising indebtedness, and concentration of resources on exporting strengthened hoary dependency patterns. On June 21, 1974, the English periodical *Latin America* concluded, "One fact which is not disputed by either the admirers or the critics of Brazilian economic management is that the country has become an integral part of the world trading community, more dependent or interdependent than it was before 1964."

Increasingly lethargic growth rates after 1975 signified real trouble for the government. Growth stood as the ideological base of the military dictatorship. Thus, a crisis in economic growth was in reality a crisis in political legitimacy. Many Brazilians would tolerate the dictatorship so long as

they benefited, or perceived they would benefit, from economic growth. Tolerance waned as those prospects dimmed.

By the mid-1970s, the more perceptive of the bureaucrats within the military government correctly assessed the problems highlighted by the reality that the military and technocrats possessed no economic formula for successful development. In the growing crisis, the military resolved to borrow still more money to meet the challenges of failure and to avoid any structural reforms. That decision postponed but compounded disaster. Eventually understanding that they had not addressed the economic challenges or were unable to, they saw that the time to withdraw from overt political control had arrived. The political *distensão* began as the economic situation deteriorated. Figueiredo directed the nation's return to democracy but he also witnessed its economic decline. Just as economic boom had consolidated the military dictatorship, economic bust contributed to its demise.

As the economy stumbled and fell in the early 1980s, the quality of life for most Brazilians diminished. *The Times of the Americas* reported on October 26, 1983, "Two-thirds of the population consume less than the 2,480 daily calories which is considered the minimum intake necessary for a normal life by the FAO, the United Nation's Food and Agriculture Organization. In the Northeast of Brazil only two out of ten people were considered to be well fed. . . . Every year the Armed Forces reject about 45% of those called for military service because of physical deficiencies." In that same year food riots exploded in São Paulo, Brazil's richest state, as well as in Rio de Janeiro and Salvador. The *Los Angeles Times* carried a front page headline on March 16, 1985, announcing, "Brazil's Poor Untouched by Trickle-Down Theory." The article reported, in part,

For the past 20 years, Brazil's military regime and its technocrats have invested billions of dollars in programs that have tripled the production of goods and services. But these spectacular increases in the gross national product have not produced income redistribution and benefits for Brazil's poorest people that were supposed to be a necessary consequence. . . . Despite a 50% increase in

lands sown in crops, the number of Brazilians who don't get enough to eat by medical standards has increased both in the cities and in the countryside. Foods produced for export, such as soybeans and orange juice, have shown spectacular gains. Sugar cane production for alcohol plants that provide fuel for automobiles, in place of gasoline, has been subsidized generously. But production of basic foods, such as beans, rice and mandioc root, has declined on a per capita basis.

Assessments of the economy during the military governments echoed the response given by President Emílio Médici when asked in 1972 about the state of the economy: "The economy is going well; the people not so well."

A historical argument can be made that from the mid-1930s to the mid-1960s some feeble and ineffectual efforts were made to promote economic development. Whatever the accomplishments, they were reversed by two decades of military rule. The military, as the surrogate of the elites, middle class, and foreign interests, stood guilty of strengthening the patterns of the past. The military appropriated an exciting word, "revolution," and applied it to their coup d'état of 1964, but calling it such does not a revolution make. The coup was rather a reaffirmation of the past, a strengthening of a pattern that bestowed privilege on a small, frightened upper class and a very nervous middle class, a pattern that prevented the majority from gaining access to power and from enacting reforms. To term the strengthening of past patterns a "revolution" revealed either cynicism or ignorance. Even the economic growth the military boasted so loudly of was temporary, elusive, and beneficial only to a privileged few; of economic development there was very little.

To consider Brazil under military rule as a model for development or as the beneficiary of an "economic miracle," as many did, revealed other semantic confusions. During some years Brazil recorded a remarkable growth, a quantitative increase, without the realization of the nation's vast potential to improve the quality of life of the majority of the inhabitants. Pursuit of an even higher Gross National Product (GNP) is never a search for social objectives but a blind chase of

numbers that can be expanded to infinity without social change resulting. Brazil, during the twentieth century, provides a perfect example of rising GNP without much development or resultant social benefits. Brazil's GNP reflected to a depressing degree the increasing affluence of the few, the overprotection of consumer luxuries, the growth of export agriculture at the expense of subsistence agriculture, and the handsome sums paid to foreign investors and creditors in the form of royalties, patent fees, interest rates and profits. The generals and their apologists spoke glowing of an "economic miracle," an assessment based almost entirely on the high growth rates of the 1969–1974 period. The more sober might question what was miraculous about the rich getting richer. The diffusionist approach to economics within a traditional, dependency-oriented structural framework plunged the majority of the Brazilians into economic disaster.

Whatever its record of material growth—and most agree it was exceedingly impressive—the "miracle" left an overwhelming negative legacy in the forms of increasing monopolistic tendencies, denationalization of the economy, mounting foreign debt, and a deepening dependency on: foreign investments and loans, the International Monetary Fund, expansion of foreign markets, and increasing exports. From the long-range view, the military governments between 1964 and 1985, frustrated the attempts to reform basic institutional structures, attempts that the governments of Vargas and Goulart—and to a certain extent of Kubitschek—had made, however ineffectually. In so doing, the military strengthened those iniquitous institutions whose roots burrow deep in the colonial past. In terms of historical continuity, a link exists between the years from 1964 to 1985 and two previous periods emphasized in this history: 1530–1560 and 1888–1897. The three periods, although diverse in many ways and widely separated by time, share some fundamental and significant characteristics. They focused on the affirmation and reaffirmation of: 1) an obsession with exports; 2) a strengthening of economic dependency; 3) a concentration of land holdings; 4) a concentration of wealth; and 5) governmental structures favorable to rural institutions complementary to the

large land owners and unsympathetic to labor. Continuities prompted the Brazilian poet Romano de Sant'Anna to pen his poem "What Kind of Country Is This?" in 1980, a poem the military censor refused to allow to be published. In it he observed,

> I live in the twentieth century.
> I'm off to the twenty-first,
> Still the prisoner of the nineteenth.

He exhibited historical modesty. He might just as correctly have written "Still the prisoner of the sixteenth."

The Masquerade of Democracy

Born anemic, the New Republic nurtured itself on the very institutional diet that condemned its political forefathers to an early demise during the twentieth century. The highly important elections for a civilian president in 1985 highlighted old patterns of political behavior. An electoral college composed of 686 members, congressional delegates and state assembly members elected in 1982, cast the vote for the chief of state who would guide Brazil back to civilian governance. The Social Democratic Party (PSD) nominated an able if colorless technocrat, Paulo Salim Maluf, governor of São Paulo. The Brazilian Democratic Movement Party (PMDB) put forth the governor of Minas Gerais, Tancredo Neves, whose roots sank deeply into the political past. He once served as minister of justice for Getúlio Vargas and as a prime minister under João Goulart, providing continuity at a time when perhaps the nation required novelty. With those two prominent southeastern states dominating its political debut, the New Republic could easily be confused with the Old. The party platforms lacked content. The PMDB assuaged the military with its moderation; the PSD hoped to distance itself from the generals without abandoning the military program. The two exhibited more similarities than differences. While political pacts, concessions, compromises, alliances, and plain old back-room deals linked these elitist parties and bespoke ac-

commodation to testy times, they also suggested that neither would address the real issues troubling the economy and preventing political stability. In short, the political caravan bumped along a familiar road.

Tancredo Neves held the advantage of being less associated with the generals and the military dictatorship. Further, economic hard times dimmed the chances of Maluf. Politicians from the PSD scurried to the opposing political camp to wave the banner of Neves. A deft compromiser, he selected José Sarney, once a political supporter of the military dictatorship, as his running mate. He won an overwhelming victory in the electoral college in January of 1985. Then tragedy struck.

On the eve of his inauguration, Neves underwent an emergency operation on an intestinal complication. He died. That unexpected turn of events stunned Brazilians, casting a pall over the rebirth of the democratic process. Vice President Sarney, a former president of the PSD, took the oath of office as president of Brazil on March 21, 1985. He liberally appointed PSD members to high office and included six active-duty military officers in his cabinet of twenty-four members.

Sarney confronted three crises. He had to provide the leadership to continue the redemocratization process. Debt, inflation, recession, unemployment, and hunger challenged any economic planner. Domestic consumption fell 25 percent between 1982 and 1987. By its own standards, the government classified 60 percent of the population as "desperately poor" and malnourished. A social crisis of poverty, misery, and injustice taunted the nation. Sarney recalled his thoughts when the sudden and unexpected death of Neves thrust the presidency on him:

The poorer half of the population of Brazil, which in 1960 had only 15 percent of the national income, today has less than 13 percent. The wealthiest 10 percent that held, at that time, 39 percent of the national wealth, now hold 51 percent. In rural areas, 1 percent of the landed population own 45 percent of the land. When I took office, the minimum wage was $25 a month. Thirteen million people were unemployed. Where should I begin?

No one doubted the formidable task before him.

The problems appeared all the more frustrating because of the enormous potential of Brazil. The sixth most populous nation on the globe in 1985, its population equalled those of Mexico, Argentina, Chile, and Venezuela combined. With the exception of the People's Republic of China, its economy was the largest in the Third World. It exported more agricultural products than any nation except the United States. It exported more industrial products than any developing nation except Korea. It manufactured more steel than Great Britain.

The formalities of democracy functioned, even flourished. Also, the Brazilians cherished and exercised the freedoms returned to them in the 1980s. The government enfranchised illiterates—they could have been as many as 40 percent of the adult population—thereby impressively expanding the ranks of those able to participate in the democratic process. Lively elections took place for mayors of state capitals in 1985 and for governors and members of congress in 1986. A surprising political comeback occurred in 1985, when voters of the city of São Paulo elected Jânio Quadros their mayor. If old politicos returned, some new faces also appeared. Women achieved higher elective office, particularly as mayors of major cities, and the first African-Brazilian woman, Benedita da Silva, won a seat in the Chamber of Deputies. She emerged from the poverty of a Rio de Janeiro favela to become not only the first Afro-Brazilian congresswoman but the nation's most visible black woman political leader.

President Sarney maintained the independent foreign policy forged during the last half of the military dictatorship. In need of oil as well as markets, Brazil had intensified its relations with Iraq, Iran, Lybia, and Angola despite frowns from Washington. In June of 1986, Sarney also reestablished relations with Cuba, broken by the generals twenty-two years earlier. His determination to protect new national industries, the computer industry for example, aroused the ire of the U.S. government, which wanted to gain wider access for its citizens into the potentially lucrative Brazilian markets.

Linked to the defeated political party and compromised by an association with an increasingly discredited military

past, the president faced daunting political odds and deteriorating economic conditions. Debt, inflation, and unemployment spun out of control. By 1988, the foreign debt exceeded
$115 billion and required annual interest payments of $10 to
$11 billion. Since 1971, Brazil had sent abroad $123 billion to
pay interest rates only, a sum, ironically, in excess of the debt
itself. Those interest payments had helped cripple the economy—and still the principal remained unpaid. Social unrest
gave rise to violence. Riots over increased food prices and
bus fares rocked São Paulo and Rio de Janeiro in May and
June of 1987. Street violence increased in Rio de Janeiro and
São Paulo, indeed in all cities, during the decade between
1980 and 1990. Economic disaster and political ineffectiveness
eroded public confidence. The institutions failed to address
the needs of the majority.

Sarney understood that to begin to address those needs
Brazil required an agrarian reform. Containing 26 percent of
all the cultivatable land in the world, Brazil could boast that
fully 56 percent of its land could be cultivated, an exceedingly
high figure. Yet, despite such vast potential, the fundamental
and challenging reality remained to taunt logic: Brazil did not
feed itself! Statistical evidence of hunger and malnourishment grew. At the opening of the final decade of the twentieth century, the Food and Agricultural Organization of the
United Nations estimated that fully 52 percent of Brazilians
did not enjoy an adequate daily consumption of calories.

Either Brazil was not cultivating its arable land, or was
ineffectively farming it, or was placing too much emphasis on
export agriculture and not enough on foods for local consumption. Furthermore, traditional inequities of access to land
persisted. As in the past, the privileged few who owned size-
able estates often held their un- or under-used land as an
investment as well as a means to control the labor supply. A
large landless rural population—estimates varied between ten
and twelve million day laborers, tenant farmers, and settlers—wanted land to work. The relatively few large landowners blocked their access. Brazil ranked globally as the nation
with the highest concentration of land in the fewest number

of hands. Statistics for 1988 revealed that less than 5 percent of the landowners controlled more than 66 percent of the arable land. About 1 percent owned 50 percent of that land, while slightly more than 50 percent of the landowners possessed only 2.4 percent of the land. Much of Brazil's persistent poverty originates in this high concentration of land ownership.

Land, one of Brazil's most precious resources, did not make its full contribution to national development. Some even claimed that misuse of that resource actively thwarted national development. One agrarian expert, José Eli da Veiga, observed in 1988, "Land as a resource is not a consumer good; it's a productive good; and it has to be used by society in the most productive manner in terms of production, job creation, tax revenues, and conservation of natural resources."

Sarney pushed for reforms that would provide more rural inhabitants with land and put more land into production. Fiery debates raged in the media and in congress. The conservative Rural Democratic Union, an organization uniting the largest landowners, leveled the customary charge of "communist" against anyone who suggested even the most toothless of agrarian reforms. The highly emotional charges and countercharges embedded within any issue of changing land-owning structures sparked rural violence, as emboldened landless people invaded empty lands and were repulsed by landowners with private armies. The Rural Democratic Union won. The Constitution of 1988 restricts the possibility of land reform far more stringently that did the generals who ruled during the military dictatorship. It protects "productive" land from expropriation, thereby effectively deflecting meaningful change. The constitution is very vague on the definition of "productive," but the slippery term has been interpreted in such a way that a few cows roaming vast acreage can validate a claim of productivity. In sum, the campaign to alter the oldest and most inefficient institutions, those controlling the ownership and use of land, failed. They remained unaltered. Sixteenth-century institutions still dominate the economy as

the twenty-first century approaches. Unable to fulfill promises to reform the countryside, a weak president became weaker. The political process marginalized him before the end of 1988, in order to concentrate on the 1990 elections.

Increasingly the Roman Catholic church, or at least a significant portion of it, voiced its concerns over the glaring economic and social inequities. Some of the clergy spoke eloquently the language of liberation theology, the religious concern with temporal social justice. They believed that the Bible provided the faithful with a means to effect changes on earth to implement greater social and economic justice. One of the leading theologians of Brazilian liberation theology, a Franciscan priest, Leonardo Boff, affirmed, "The current structuring of society cannot please God, because most people are excluded; there is little participation and much oppression of the poor." Brazil's Paulo Evaristo Cardinal Arns set the tone of the Church's social concerns in the 1980s in his *Suggestions for a Social Policy*. He condemned the social inequities exaggerated by industrial growth and denounced "decreased autonomy and growing dependence on the economies of the industrialized world." Using his powerful position as archbishop of São Paulo, he pointed to the obligation of the Church to help change society. He proclaimed, "The most important challenge for today's church in Brazil is to build a just society." The Vatican supported the archbishop's call for social justice. Pope John Paul II visited Brazil, the world's largest Roman Catholic country, in 1980. While denouncing any involvement in politics, he confirmed that the Church must "serve the cause of justice" by using its voice to "summon consciences, guard people and their liberty and demand the necessary remedies." The pope warned

The persistence of injustice threatens the existence of society from within. This menace from within really exists when the distribution of goods is grounded only in the economic laws of growth and bigger profit, when the results of progress reach only superficially the huge levels of the population, when there persists a large gap between a minority of the rich on the one hand and the majority of those who live in want and misery on the other.

When Pope John Paul II returned to Brazil in late 1991, he lamented the lack of progress toward greater social justice. On that occasion, he spoke out in favor of land reform, saying "The high degree of land ownership in Brazil demands a just agrarian reform." But he had given his vocal support too late. For all intents and purposes the Constitution of 1988 had silenced, at least for the time being, discussions of agrarian reform.

The inequities and most particularly rural inequities added to the burdens of urban Brazil. Uneducated, unprepared, and malnourished rural people continued to flow into the cities, which were without the infrastructure needed to receive them. Between 1977 and 1987, approximately fifteen million rural inhabitants trudged into the cities. The causes for their migration remained the same. Without lands to farm, without hope, they were either pushed or pulled toward the cities whose growth seldom faltered. By the early 1990s, well over 75 percent of the population were urban dwellers. Fully 57 percent of the population dwelt in cities of 100,000 or more, and there are twenty cities in Brazil with more than one million inhabitants.

The most predominant of those cities on every level was São Paulo. Brazilians ranked greater metropolitan São Paulo, with its population in the neighborhood of twenty million, as the world's largest city, a distinction contested by Mexico City, Tokyo, and, occasionally, by New York City and Buenos Aires. That phenomenal city contained fully 32 percent of Brazilian industry operated by 45 percent of the nation's labor force turning out something like 50 percent of the national production. It hummed with modernity. Reflecting a Brazilian reality, it had a youthful population. Fully half the residents were under twenty-one years of age. Yet among the major cities of the world it suffered the highest infant mortality rates: 56.1 deaths per 1,000 births. And the *Book of World City Rankings* characterized São Paulo as "one of the most industrially polluted cities in the world."

Foreign immigrants have always played a significant role in that burgeoning metropolis. They have come from every continent. More Italians live in São Paulo than in Venice;

more Lebanese than in Beirut; the Japanese community is the largest anywhere outside of Japan.

Among the newest immigrants to Brazil, the Japanese first arrived in 1908 to work on the coffee plantations. By the 1990s, there were nearly a million Brazilians of Japanese descent. From humble beginnings as farm workers, the Japanese-Brazilians have risen to positions of intellectual eminence, wealth, and economic and political power. Shigeaki Ueiki served as minister of Mines and Energy and later as president of Petrobrás, for example.

On quite a different level, Japan's economic relations with Brazil ballooned from the 1960s onward. Direct investment totaled $140 million in 1970, but by 1987 it surpassed $2.6 billion, ranking Japan as the third largest foreign investor, after the United States and Germany. Japanese banks hold about $12 billion of Brazil's foreign debt. Brazil has maintained a highly favorable trade balance with Japan, which has eagerly purchased iron ore, soybeans, cotton, coffee, steel, and a few airplanes. Japan also served as an economic model for many Brazilians. They admired its economic development and marvelled at its rapid ascent to the position as a major economic power by the end of the twentieth century.

Brazil's political situation remained shaky for a variety of reasons: voter apathy, frustration, and cynicism; the stultifying influences of the old regime elites and military; and the weaknesses of the political parties still dependent on personalities rather than platforms. The two dominant parties of the 1985 elections, the PSD and the PMDB, did not even make it into the final round of the presidential election in December 1989. The two final contenders were Fernando Collor de Mello, whose National Reconstruction party was more a personal vehicle for the candidate than anything else, and Luiz Inácio da Silva, universally called Lula, the candidate of the Party of the Workers (Partido dos Trabalhadores, or PT). While Lula was a candidate with a powerful personality, the PT itself, an anomaly in Brazilian politics, evinced a well-articulated platform and ideology and exercised an uncommon political discipline among its members.

Lula was an autoworker, a rare presidential candidate

with proletarian roots anywhere in the hemisphere. Born in Pernambuco, he arrived in São Paulo at age four with his parents. He completed six years of primary school and worked on the streets as a youngster. Later he rose through the ranks of the metal-workers union, leading strikes in 1979 and 1980, for which the government jailed him. The PT platform in 1989 called for the suspension of all debt payments, land reform, wage raises and price freezes, and a civilian head of a reorganized defense department. It touched upon some very sensitive matters and threatened some of the hoariest of Brazil's institutions. In contrast, the handsome, debonair, forty-year-old scion Collor had no identifiable platform. Mouthing the usual collection of platitudes in favor of economic growth and modernization and in opposition to governmental corruption and inefficiency, he won the election. He received 43 percent of the first popular vote for president since 1960; Lula garnered 38 percent. Fully 19 percent of the votes cast were abstentions or were nullified. Collor won, in part because he was vague and radiated a kind of attractive popular appeal, but principally because Lula frightened the elite and the middle class. They knew he had a program; they distrusted reform.

President Collor took his oath of office on March 15, 1990. He repeated solemn promises of profound and rapid economic changes to promote steady economic growth and arrest inflation. He had no political constituency in the congress, or anywhere else for that matter. Disaster ensued. Within a year, the purchasing power of the minimum wage had fallen to its lowest level on record. Unemployment reached astronomical levels. The economy shrank 4 percent. Inflation galloped along at 16 percent a month, reaching 25 percent by 1992. The public education and health systems disintegrated. On September 8, 1991, the *Los Angeles Times* described Brazil, after fifteen months of the Collor government, "weakened and demoralized by its worst depression on record, suffering the region's highest rate of inflation, desperately needing stability, leadership and hope for the future." Later that year, the Brazilian economist Paulo Rabello de Castro said, "Collor has failed because he has been outright incompetent in the diagnosis and treatment of the economic prob-

lem. The country is drifting." Meanwhile, the foreign debt
exceeded $120 billion. During 1991, the economy grew at 1.2
percent; farm production at 2 percent; industrial production
remained stagnant, having shrunk 8 percent in 1990.

A disastrous political blow struck in mid-1992. Brazilians
reeled under the revelations of corruption on the highest
levels, reaching into the presidential palace. President Collor
had profited personally from the influence peddling of his
friend and former campaign manager, Paulo César Farias.
Tens of millions of dollars flowed into secret bank accounts
of the president. A scandal of unprecedented proportions
unfolded to the displeasure and disgust of the Brazilian people. Congresswoman Benedita da Silva summed up public
opinion when she concluded, "Fernando Collor is the profile

of power in Brazil: a white, educated, privileged man. And he
turned out to be the biggest bandit in Brazilian history." The
streets of the major cities thundered with the popular voice
of outrage. Millions marched to demand the removal of Collor. On September 29, 1992, the House of Representatives
voted 441 to 29 to suspend the president from office and
institute impeachment proceedings against him. As required
by the constitution, Vice President Itamar Franco, an older
politician long admired for his moral probity, and more attuned to Brazil's social needs, became acting president. When
the Senate opened the impeachment trial of the president on
December 29, 1992, Collor resigned, elevating Franco to the
presidency. Brazil achieved the dubious distinction of being
the first nation in the Western Hemisphere to impeach a
president.

On the positive side, the constitution and the democracy
it fostered seemed to function: public opinion triumphed;
Congress removed a president; the president stepped down
peacefully; the vice president ascended to the presidency.
Nonetheless, no one denied that these achievements exacted
a heavy toll on the New Republic. For the second time in as
many administrations, a vice president took over the presidency. In both cases the men were little known, represented
a political party different from the president's, and evinced
little mandate to govern.

A political circus marginalized the pressing, fundamental problems troubling Brazil. Meanwhile, those problems festered. In the mid-1990s, economic growth, industrial production, and the incomes of the overwhelming majority of the Brazilians continued to decline. Inflation relentlessly rose. The distinguished Brazilian political scientist Hélio Jaguaribe warned, "Social problems are very close to unmanageable." The stormy seas of political chaos and economic disaster propelled a rudderless Brazil into the twenty-first century. It was a measure of the remarkable tolerance of most Brazilians that so many of the economic, political, and social injustices of the past pervaded the twilight years of the twentieth century. "Democracy" remained a tiring charade, a cruel masquerade.

Frontiers of Challenge

At the dawn of the twenty-first century, the development of Brazil—if, indeed, it will occur—rests partly on two significant but thus far underutilized, even abused, resources: the Amazon and the young. The first constitutes a challenging geographical frontier, only partially explored, little understood, shrouded in a mystic of hope and potential, threatened by greed. The second, potentially both Brazil's greatest challenge and resource, promises much: beauty, energy, intelligence, vision, and, above all else, hope. In both cases, size boggles the mind. The Amazon encompasses 1.3 million square miles; fully 50 percent of Brazil's 155 million inhabitants are under twenty-one years of age.

The vast Amazon beckons to Brazilians and foreigners alike. Three groups responded in different ways to the lure of this El Dorado, the world's largest tropical rain forest.

First, the military fretted about "national security" questions raised by the underpopulated and underexplored region. On the one hand, they feared that the combination of low population density and potential wealth would attract foreigners, threatening vaguely marked and generally undefended national boundaries. On the other, they envisioned a

kind of "Balkanization" of the nation through the recognition of Indian nations whose territorial claims might weaken national sovereignty, eventually leading to a future breakup of the remote interior into smaller nation-states. During its dictatorship, the military energetically advocated the construction of roads to integrate remote regions with the coast and the exploitation of the Amazon's resources to enrich Brazil. In the 1990s an impressive modern highway system penetrated the Amazon Basin; it carried migrants into the region and wealth out.

Second, national and international capitalists focused attention on the immense and varied mineral deposits of the Amazon region: gold, diamonds, tin, bauxite, copper, iron ore, and manganese. They also financed cattle raising and logging, both on gargantuan scales. An economic boom built upon the export of raw materials attracted their capital into pristine rain forests.

Third, the landless and the dispossessed peasants hoped to establish farms or encounter other means of livelihood in the Amazon, their gateway to a better future. With equal force, hope and greed propelled that population into the interior.

Symbolically, the inauguration of Brasília in 1960 opened the West and the Amazon. Thereafter, pushed by the military and the capitalists, roads steadily crept westward and migration followed. The last half of the twentieth century witnessed a slow but impressive population shift. In the middle of the twentieth century approximately 90 percent of a population of 52 million lived within a band less than one hundred miles wide along the Atlantic coast. By 1992 approximately 80 percent of a population of 155 million lived within a band twice that wide. The state of Rondonia and the western region of the state of Mato Grosso, for example, experienced an unprecedented population explosion between 1975 and 1985: more than 1.5 million people arrived to claim and clear millions of acres of virgin forest. By the 1990s the Brazilian West and the Amazon region together had a larger population than any of Brazil's Spanish-speaking neighboring nations.

Machete, ax, fire, and bulldozer felled the forests. By

1992 approximately 160,000 square miles of rain forest had
disappeared, an area equal in size to the nation of Paraguay
or to the five nations of Central America. In 1988, a disastrous
year, destruction of the Amazon rain forest claimed 6 million
acres. Then, it slowed, at least temporarily. In 1991, it was
down to 3.5 million acres. Destruction declined due to increased government concern and control, the cancellation of
subsidies for cattle ranching, the greater awareness of people
in the Amazon of the necessity to conserve the forest, and a
severe economic crisis.

Human invasion and destruction of the rain forest threatened its delicate ecology. Clearing the land exacted a heavy
toll on its topsoil, 75 percent of which was too deficient in
nutrients to sustain traditional agriculture. Tropical rains both
leached the exposed soil of its nutrients and eroded it. The
sun compacted the naked earth. Within a very few years,
cleared areas became useless for agriculture or even grazing.

Violence against the forest begot other forms of destruction. As the ecologist Susanna Hecht pointed out, "In the
Amazon, when trees fall, people die." Indians fought against
ranchers, loggers, and miners. The poor immigrants clashed
with large landowners. With impunity, the military and the
capitalists imposed a blood-stained "order" complementary
to their goals. Land conflicts in the decade of the 1980s claimed
the lives of more than one thousand rural workers, a statistic
that excludes the number of Indians killed. Few of the impoverished migrants found their "promised land" in the Amazon.
One sobering migratory cycle traces impoverished people
from their original rural poverty to city slums and thence to
the Amazon in quest of work, subsistence, and a minimal
quality of life. At each stage further hardships and disappointments greeted them.

Westward expansion decimated the Indians. Comprising
180 tribes, they numbered between 200,000 and 225,000 in the
last decade of the twentieth century. Those numbers have
declined monthly. The advancing frontier incorporated some
of the Indians, the inevitable victims of "progress," into miserable, marginal existences. The government gathered others
into reservations, frequently relocated and always reduced in

size. Manoel Gomes da Silva, a Caxinaua Indian, explained the plight of the indigenous to Pope John Paul II during his visit to Mato Grosso in 1991:

In the name of modernity, technology and progress they criminally invade our territories, kill our leaders, poison our rivers, destroy our environment and treat us as sub-races, turning us into foreigners within our own country. . . . If they exterminate the Indian nations, they are exterminating the forests and environment—and life on the planet will become unsustainable.

To this day the westward tide of migration has not crested and it threatens to inundate the remaining indigenous population.

The events in the West and the Amazon follow to a disappointing degree the well-established historic pattern of economic boom and bust. The vast interior remains locked into an exploitative export economy. It perpetuates old class patterns and economic inequities. Many toil; few benefit. Whatever momentary economic growth exports have promoted, they have not contributed thus far to development. In the long run, foreigners profit more than Brazilians.

Yet there exists at least one solution, albeit a difficult one, to the complex problems raised by increased human habitation in the rain forests. It requires that new inhabitants harmonize with their environment. In one effort to attune them to their unique surroundings, ecologists and agronomists at the University of Rondonia in Pôrto Velho advise the farmers to turn from the cultivation of traditional Brazilian crops such as corn, beans, and rice to cultivate plants and trees complementary to local Western or Amazonian conditions. They urge the planting of mahogany and other hardwood trees, of bananas, acai and purpunha palms, and of coffee bushes and legume plants that not only provide food harvests but protect and enrich the fragile soil at the same time. The imagination and willingness to break with old and imported patterns and to adapt to new realities not only could save much of the Amazonian rain forest, but it could also ensure profitable production as well. The difficult step from greedy to rational exploitation constitutes the only way for

Brazil to substitute economic development for the destruction wrought by the boom and bust cycles of sheer economic growth.

The achievement of such development also requires better care of Brazil's youth, who number approximately seventy-five million. In the final analysis, they are the nation's primary resource. Their treatment shapes the future. The inescapable conclusion is that Brazil has neglected its youth and thereby limited its future. Of all the challenges confronting Brazil in the twenty-first century, the education, health, and well-being of its children and youth loom as the most daunting.

In *Captains of the Sands,* Jorge Amado in 1937 called Brazil's attention to "abandoned children who lived by stealing." An early, sensitive, and polemical fictional treatment of a growing urban problem using Amado's native Salvador da Bahia as the locale, the novel regarded the homeless children as victims of social and economic institutions. Pursued by disease, hunger, and death, a few of the well-delineated characters of the novel nonetheless managed to integrate into the society that had victimized them. Significantly, two of them challenged that society, one as a labor leader and the other as a bandit. Through those two characters, Pedro Bala and Dry Gulch, Amado romanticized a link between impoverishment and rebellion: "The fists of the Captains of the Sands are raised."

The sixteen-year-old mulatto Dry Gulch resolved to return to his roots in the arid interior of the Northeast: "The backlands were calling him, the struggle of the bandits called him." He joined the followers of Lampião, a "bandit hero" of mythic proportions:

Lampião freed the brushland, drove the rich men out of the brushland, made the brushland the home of the *cangaceiro* bandits who fight against the plantation owners. Lampião, the hero, the hero of all the backlands of five States. They say he's a criminal, a heartless bandit, murderer, rapist, thief. But for Dry Gulch, for the men, women, and children of the backlands he's a new Zumbi of Palmares, he's a liberator, the captain of a new army.

Thus, Amado equated Lampião with rebellion, the backland *cangaceiro* with the struggle for freedom—one response available to the dispossessed.

The response differed for Pedro Bala. He found a common cause with the urban workers: "They're the ones who are lifting their arms and shouting, the same as the Captains of the Sands." He heard the cry of revolution beckoning: "The voice calls him. A voice that makes him happy, that makes his heart beat. Helping change the destiny of all poor people." The struggle changed the youth's destiny.

Critical of a society mistreating its youth, Amado posited two means of altering the situation: one by working within the society, the strike leader; the other by violence against society, the bandit. In both cases in *Captains of the Sands*, youth provides leadership and force. Thus, Amado portrays youth both as victim and avenger.

The situation facing a significant portion of Brazil's young, as described by Jorge Amado in the mid-1930s, changed by the end of the century: it grew worse. Sixty years after the publication of that novel of social realism, all statistics paint an even grimmer social picture for Brazilian youth.

Brazil's infant mortality rate hovers at 85 out of 1,000 live births. In South America only Bolivia and Peru suffer a higher ratio. No more than 15 percent of the children complete primary school. Less than 8 percent enroll in secondary school. About 2.5 percent enter universities or institutions of higher learning. Hunger tortures the young. Every day approximately one thousand children die from hunger-related causes. One child in ten suffers a debilitating handicap, such as blindness, deafness, or mental retardation, attributable to malnutrition in early childhood. The Brazilian Bishops National Conference estimates that thirty-six million children, about a quarter of the national population, are ill-fed, poorly clothed, badly sheltered, unable to attend school, and exploited as the most vulnerable members of the work force. Somewhere between seven and eight million of them live on the streets, where they fall victim to crime, promiscuity, and often violent death. Between January and May of 1991, 411 children were killed in the streets of urban Brazil, a high percentage of that num-

ber at the hands of death squads that specifically target the young. Héctor Babenco's powerful film *Pixote* (1980) illustrates this brutal reality. Clearly deprivation and danger stalk Brazil's children. These children are Brazil's future; to waste them constitutes a decision to forego development. More than that, it records a tragic moral decision reprehensible in any society.

In its treatment of its extensive geography, particularly the Amazon, and its legions of children, Brazil shapes its future. The potential tantalizes; the reality frightens. A presidential candidate in 1990, Luís Ignácio da Silva soberly observed,

The Third World War has already started. It is a silent war, but no less sinister. The war is crushing Brazil, Latin America and practically the entire Third World. Instead of soldiers, children die; instead of millions wounded, there are millions of unemployed; instead of the destruction of bridges, there is the destruction of factories, schools, hospitals, and entire economies.

Like other nations of the vast and varied Third World, Brazil faces the challenge of economic and social development. Unlike most of those nations, Brazil possesses the potential for development. To realize that potential requires a honest assessment of the institutions implanted during the period from 1530 to 1560 and strengthened during the periods from 1888 to 1897 and from 1964 to 1985. In the case of Brazil history not only illuminates the past; it also contains suggestions for the future.

Appendix I

Chiefs of State of Brazil

Name	From	To
FIRST EMPIRE		
Pedro I, Emperor of Brazil	9/7/1822	4/7/1831
SECOND EMPIRE		
José Joaquim Carneiro de Campos, Marquês de Caravelas Nicolau Pereira de Campos Verguerio General Francisco Lima e Silva	4/7/1831	6/17/1831
José da Costa Carvalho, Marquês de Monte Alegre João Braúlio Muniz Francisco Lima e Silva	6/17/1831	10/12/1835
Padre Diogo Antônio Feijó	10/12/1835	9/19/1937
Pedro de Araújo Lima, Marquês de Olinda	9/19/1837	7/23/1840
Pedro II, Emperor of Brazil	7/23/1840	11/15/1889
REPUBLIC OF BRAZIL		
Marechal Deodoro da Fonseca	11/15/1889	11/23/1891
Marechal Floriano Peixoto	11/23/1891	11/15/1894
Prudente José de Morais	11/15/1894	11/15/1898
Manuel Ferraz Campos Sales	11/15/1898	11/15/1902

Name	From	To
REPUBLIC OF BRAZIL (cont.)		
Francisco de Paula Rodrigues Alves	11/15/1902	11/15/1906
Afonso Augusto Moreira Pena	11/15/1906	6/14/1909
Nilo Peçanha	6/14/1909	11/15/1910
Marechal Hermes da Fonseca	11/15/1910	11/15/1914
Venceslau Brás Pereira Gomes	11/15/1914	11/15/1918
Delfim Moreira	11/15/1918	6/?/1919
Epitácio Pessôa	6/?/1919	11/15/1922
Artur da Silva Bernardes	11/15/1922	11/15/1926
Washington Luís Pereira de Sousa	11/15/1926	10/24/1930
Getúlio Vargas	11/3/1930	1/29/1945
José Linhares	10/29/1945	1/31/1946
Marechal Eurico Gaspar Dutra	1/31/1946	1/31/1951
Getúlio Vargas	1/31/1951	8/24/1954
João Café Filho	8/24/1954	11/8/1955
Carlos Luz	11/8/1955	11/11/1955
Nereu Ramos	11/11/1955	1/31/1956
Juscelino Kubitschek	1/31/1956	1/31/1961
Jânio da Silva Quadros	1/31/1961	8/25/1961
João Goulart	9/7/1961	3/31/1964
Ranieri Mazzili	4/2/1964	4/15/1964
Humberto Castelo Branco	4/15/1964	3/15/1967
Artur da Costa e Silva	3/15/1967	8/30/1969
Aurélio de Lyra Tavaros		
Mácio de Souza e Mello	8/30/1969	10/7/1969
Augusto Rademaker		
Emílío Garrastazú Medici	10/7/1969	3/15/1974
Ernesto Geisel	3/15/1974	3/15/1979
João Baptista de Oliveira Figueiredo	3/15/79	3/21/85
José Sarney	3/21/85	3/15/90
Fernando Collor de Mello	3/15/90	9/29/92
Itamar Franco	9/29/92	——

Appendix 2

A Chronology of Significant Dates in Brazilian History

COLONY

1494	Treaty of Tordesillas divides the world beyond Europe between Spain and Portugal.
1500	Pedro Alvares Cabral discovers Brazil.
1502	King Manuel licenses Lisbon merchants to export brazilwood from the New World.
1530	Expedition of Martim Afonso de Sousa to colonize.
1532	Founding of São Vicente and Piratininga. First sugar mills built.
1534–1536	King grants Brazil to twelve donees.
1538	First known shipment of slaves arrives from Africa. ✓
1540–1542	Francisco de Orellana explores the Amazon.
1549	Centralized government instituted under Tomé de Sousa in Bahia. First Jesuits arrive.
1551	Creation of the bishopric of Brazil.
1555	The French establish a colony in Guanabara Bay.
1565	Foundation of Rio de Janeiro.
1567	Mem de Sá expels the French and occupies Guanabara Bay.
1580	The unification of the Iberian crowns.
1604	The India Council is established to oversee the admin-

COLONY

istration of the Portuguese empire. (In 1642, the name will be changed to the Overseas Council.)

1616   Belém founded.

1621   Creation of the state of Maranhão.

1624–1625 The Dutch capture Salvador da Bahia.

1630   The Dutch seize Recife and begin their conquest of the Northeast.

1637–1639 Pedro Teixeira explores the Amazon and founds Tabatinga.

1640   Portugal declares its independence from Spain.

1654   Treaty of Taborda signed; the Dutch withdraw from Brazil.

1680   Colônia do Sacremento founded to ensure Portuguese access to the Plata River.

1695   Gold discovered in Minas Gerais.

1697   Luso-Brazilians destroy Palmares, one of the largest fortified settlements of runaway black slaves.

1709   Creation of the captaincies of São Paulo and Minas de Ouro.

1710–1711 War of the Mascates, a clash between the planter class of Olinda and the merchant class of Recife, in which the latter emerges victorious.

1720   The governors-general of Brazil are henceforth known as viceroys. Brief revolt in Minas Gerais against the governor.

1724   Foundation of the Brazilian Academy of the Forgotten, the first of the European-type academies of the Enlightenment.

1727   Introduction of coffee into Brazil.

1750   Treaty of Madrid marks the abandonment of the Treaty of Tordesillas and the adoption of *uti possidetis* to settle boundaries.

             Pombal begins to rule in Portugal.

1759   Pombal expels the Jesuits from the Empire.

1761   Treaty of El Pardo annuls the Treaty of Madrid.

1763   The capital is transferred from Salvador da Bahia to Rio de Janeiro.

1772   The state of Maranhão ceases to exist.

1777   Treaty of San Ildefonso redraws the Portuguese-Spanish frontiers in South America, and confirms Spain's possession of the Banda Oriental and Portugal's possession of the Amazon Basin. Pombal dismissed.

COLONY

1789	The *Inconfidência Mineira,* a conspiracy to establish a republic, is exposed.
1792	Tiradentes, a leader in the Inconfidência, is executed.
1798	The outbreak of the Bahian conspiracy—the "Revolt of the Tailors."
1808	The Braganzas arrive in Rio de Janeiro.
	João VI opens the ports to world trade and lifts restrictions on manufacturing.
	Brazil's first printing press established.
1810	Treaties signed with Great Britain giving that nation commercial dominance over Brazil.

KINGDOM

1815	Brazil raised to the status of a kingdom.
1816	Luso-Brazilian troops occupy Uruguay. French artistic mission arrives in Rio.
1817	The republican revolution in Pernambuco fails.
	Princess Leopoldina of Austria, future empress of Brazil, arrives in Rio de Janeiro.
1818	Land grants to Swiss and German settlers.
1819	First steamship in Brazil put into operation at Bahia.
1820	First organized colony of non-Portuguese immigrants established at Nova Friburgo, after their arrival in 1819.
1821	Uruguay annexed as the Cisplatine Province.
	João VI returns to Lisbon.

EMPIRE

1822	Prince Pedro declares Brazil's independence and receives the title of emperor.
1824	Pedro promulgates the first constitution.
	The United States recognizes Brazil.
1825	Great Britain and Portugal recognize Brazil.
	War breaks out between Argentina and Brazil over Uruguay.
1827	By treaty Great Britain consolidates its commercial dominance over Brazil.
	Establishment of laws schools at Olinda and São Paulo.
1828	Argentina and Brazil agree to the creation of Uruguay as an independent nation, thus ending the war between the two Platine rivals.
1831	Pedro I abdicates. A three-man regency assumes control.

EMPIRE

1834	Additional Act to the 1824 Constitution institutes federalism and a one-man regency.
1835	Outbreak of the Farroupilha Revolt in Rio Grande do Sul.
1840	Interpretive Law ended the experiment with federalism. Proclamation of the Majority ends the regency. Pedro II ascends the throne.
1843	A steamboat navigates the Amazon for the first time.
1844	Anglo-Brazilian Treaty of 1827 expires and is not renewed. Alves Branco Tariff raises duties.
1845	Caxias puts down the Farroupilha Revolt.
1850	The Queiroz Law abolishes the slave trade.
1851	First regular steamship line to Europe inaugurated.
1852	Mauá founds the Amazon Steam Navigation Company. Brazil intervenes in Argentina to help overthrow Rosas.
1854	Beginning of the railroad era.
1857	Publication of José de Alencar's novel *O Guaraní*.
1865	Argentina, Brazil, and Uruguay ally against Paraguay.
1867	Opening of the Amazon to international traffic.
1870	The Triple Alliance defeats Paraguay. The Republican party issues its manifesto.
1871	The Law of the Free Womb frees all children born to slave mothers.
1873	The number of Italian immigrants arriving begins to surpass the number of Portuguese.
1874	Transatlantic cable put into service.
1873–1875	Conflict between Church and State over the privileges of regalism.
1885	The Saraiva-Cotegipe Law frees all existing slaves at the age of sixty.
1888	The Golden Law abolishes slavery.
1889	The emperor is dethroned by the army, and the republic is established.

REPUBLIC

1890	Church and State separated.
1891	A new constitution promulgated.
1893	A naval revolt threatens the republic.
1894	The first civilian president takes office.
1895	The Missions Territory award settled in Brazil's favor the frontier dispute with Argentina.

REPUBLIC

1897	Destruction of Canudos, and the death of the religious mystic, Antônio Conselheiro.
1900	Amapá boundary dispute with French Guiana settled favorably for Brazil.
1902	Publication of *Rebellion in the Backlands* and *Canaan*.
1903	Treaty of Petropolis cedes Acre to Brazil.
1906	The Convention of Taubaté institutes valorization of coffee.
	The Third Pan-American Conference meets in Rio de Janeiro.
1907	At Second Hague Peace Conference, Brazil participates in its first worldwide conference.
1910	Indian Protection Service established.
1917	Brazil declares war on Germany and joins the Allied powers.
1920	The first university is created to replace scattered faculties.
1922	Modern Art Week initiated a new phase of introspection in national culture.
	Copacabana revolt: *tenente* movement begins.
1924–1927	March of the Prestes Column through the backlands.
1930	Rebellion brings Getúlio Vargas to power.
1932	The rebellion of São Paulo brings civil war.
1937	*Estado Novo* is established.
1942	Brazil declares war on the Axis powers.
1944	An expeditionary force is sent to Europe.
1945	The military deposes Vargas.
1946	A new constitution promulgated.
1950	Vargas reelected president.
1954	Vargas commits suicide.
1960	The capital is moved inland to Brasília.
1961	The election and subsequent resignation of Jânio Quadros.
	A parliamentary system is established.
1963	Parliamentary system extinguished by national plebiscite.
1964	The military deposes João Goulart. A purged Congress elects Humberto Castelo Branco president. First Institutional Act passed.
1965	The legal guidelines for political parties are imposed by the Second Institutional Act.

REPUBLIC

1967	A new constitution promulgated. General Artur da Costa e Silva is inaugurated president.
1968	A military coup gives Costa e Silva dictatorial power. Fifth Institutional Act passed.
1968	New constitution promulgated
1974	Economic growth falters and decline begins; foreign debt starts to soar.
1978	Popular agitation for a return to civilian government and democracy mounts.
1979	Political amnesty decreed.
1985	The military steps down from political power, returning the government to the people. Democracy restored.
1988	New constitution promulgated.
1992	President Fernando Collor de Mello impeached.

A Glossary of Portuguese Words Used in the Text

Aldeia: a village. It frequently refers to the Indian settlements administered by the religious orders in the colonial period.

Bandeira: an armed expedition in the colonial period that penetrated the interior to explore, to capture Indian slaves, or to search for gold.

Branco: a white person, phenotypically Caucasoid.

Bolas: a kind of missile weapon consisting of balls of stone attached to the end of a thong or rope, used by gauchos for hurling at and entangling an animal.

Caatinga: the stunted, spare forest found in the drought areas of northeastern Brazil.

Caboclo: either an Indian who has been Europeanized, or a Brazilian of Caucasian and Indian parentage.

Candomblé: a Brazilian folk religion of predominantly African influence.

Cangaceiro: a bandit or outlaw of the *sertão.*

Capitão-mor (plural, *capitães-mor*): a military rank formerly given to commanders of the local militia.

Carioca: native of or pertaining to the city of Rio de Janeiro.

Casa grande: the large plantation house, residence of the rural aristocracy.

Caudilho: a strong leader, often referring to a party or government chief who exercises complete authority over his subordinates.

Colégio: a three-year preparatory course of secondary school; the second phase of a seven-year high school education.

Conto: a unit of money equal to one thousand cruzeiros, written thus: Cr$1.000.00. Prior to 1942, it equaled one thousand *milreis.*

Coronel (plural, *coroneis*): a civilian political boss of a municipality. The system of political control founded on the political bosses came to be known as *coronelismo*.

Correição: an official inquiry into the conduct of a public employee.

Côrtes: Portuguese parliament.

Crioulo: a black person born in Brazil.

Cruzeiro: the Brazilian monetary unit which replaced the mil-reis on November 1, 1942.

Degredados: criminals exiled to serve out their sentence. Frequently the term refers to those minor Portuguese criminals sent to Brazil in the sixteenth century as their punishment.

Devassa: an inspection or inquiry into the conduct of a public official.

Distensão: a term used after 1974 to signify gradual relaxation of authoritarian rule and a restoration of civilian constitutional government.

Emboada: a pejorative term used by a native of an area to refer to an outsider. In eighteenth-century Minas Gerais, the local inhabitants used this term for the adventurers who came from Portugal or the coast in search of gold and diamonds.

Encilhamento: from the verb meaning "to saddle," this is the term used to designate a period of frantic financial speculation during the early 1890s.

Entrada: a penetration by a band of explorers from the coast into the hinterlands.

Favelas: city slums, a term used most frequently in Rio de Janeiro.

Fazenda: a plantation, ranch, or farm.

Fazendeiro: the owner of a *fazenda;* a planter, farmer, or rancher on a large scale.

Gaúcho: a native of Rio Grande do Sul, but literally a cowboy of the southern plains.

Homens bons: literally the "good men," those who belonged to the upper echelon of Brazilian colonial society. Their prestige, power, and position permitted them to vote for members of the town council.

Inconfidência: a conspiracy among the Brazilians for independence. Often it is used to refer to the *Inconfidência Mineira,* the plot in Minas Gerais in 1789 to declare Brazil's independence from Portugal.

Irmandades: a lay religious order or brotherhood.

Lavrador: a small landholder.

Linha dura: meaning "hard line," it refers to a small group of right-

wing military officers who believe the military must rule to "purify" the nation.

Macumba: a Brazilian folk religion of predominantly African influence.

Mameluco: the offspring of Caucasian and Indian parents.

Maranhense: an inhabitant of Maranhão.

Mascate: literally, "peddler of wares"; the term was used, sometimes pejoratively, in the eighteenth century to refer to the incipient merchant class.

Massapê: a fertile, clayey soil very suitable for sugarcane growing found in northeastern Brazil.

Mazombo: a Brazilian born in the New World of Caucasian, European parents.

Mineiro: an inhabitant of the state of Minas Gerais.

Município: an administrative division including a town and its surroundings. It corresponds roughly to a county.

Ouvidor-mor: the office of chief justice in the governments of colonial Brazil.

Pardo: a brown person, a general catch-all color designation.

Paulista: an inhabitant of or referring to the state of São Paulo.

Poder moderador: the fourth branch of government provided by the Constitution of 1824. It empowered the emperor to oversee the three traditional branches and to balance them. After the fall of the monarchy, the military took upon itself the extralegal responsibility to exercise that power.

Prêto: a black person with physical characteristics of the African.

Procuradores dos mestros: representatives of tradesmen found on a few of the city councils in colonial Brazil.

Provedor-mor: the office of treasurer in the governments of colonial Brazil.

Quilombo: a colony of runaway slaves; such colonies existed in the Brazilian interior until 1888, when slavery was abolished.

Rancho: a rude hut where herdsmen or travelers may find rest or shelter.

Reinol (plural, *reinóis*): a Portuguese born in the Old World who resided temporarily or permanently in Brazil during the colonial period. The term can be contrasted with *mazombo*.

Relação: a high court in Portugal or in colonial Brazil.

Residência: a formal inquiry into the conduct of a public official at the end of his term of office.

Riograndense: an inhabitant of or referring to the state of Rio Grande do Sul.

Senado da Câmara: the municipal government, in particular the town council.

Senhor de engenho: the owner of a sugar mill and often by extension a plantation owner.

Senhor de terras: the large landowner.

Senzala: plantation slave quarters.

Seringueiro: a rubber gatherer.

Sertanejo: one who lives in the *sertão,* a frontiersman.

Sertanista: a person who knows the *sertão* well. Often in the North sertanistas employed that knowledge for purposes of trade and commerce.

Sertão: the interior, backlands, or hinterlands of Brazil. The term refers particularly to the hinterland region of northeastern Brazil.

Sesmaria: a land grant in Portugal and colonial Brazil.

Tenente: an army lieutenant.

Tenentismo: a reform movement among junior army officers which began in the early 1920s and played a significant role in bringing Vargas to power.

Tropas de resgate: men who hunted and captured Indians in the interior to use or sell as slaves.

Tropeiro: a driver of pack animals. Often he was a wandering merchant carrying his goods throughout Brazil on muleback.

Vaqueiro: a cowboy; this term is used most frequently in the Northeast.

Visitação: an official inquiry into the conduct of a public employee.

Xango: a Brazilian folk religion of predominantly African influence.

The Novel as History:
A Bibliographic Essay

From the mid-nineteenth century to the present Brazilian novelists have recorded and explored their society. Their work provides a rich legacy documenting Brazil's social environment and its people's adaption to it or rebellion against it. While providing descriptions and analyses, their novels also reveal emotions and attitudes. These reflections of reality offer historians valuable, even unique, insights into the past and evince the vision and sensitivity necessary to understand and interpret the Brazilian experience. Concentrating only on novels translated into English, this essay recommends twenty-four works infused with that vision and sensitivity. The selection is neither exhaustive nor exclusive. To those who read Portuguese, an even richer treasury of novels awaits discovery and exploration.

This essay concentrates on novelists who have recorded their society and surroundings at a specific time. A majority of them, unlike historians, did not seek to recreate the past; they wrote instead about their present. Of course, those writings later serve as testimonies of and from the past. Delving beneath the surface of society, they illustrate individual life patterns and the relationships of people with each other and with their society's institutions. Often the individuals depicted symbolizes larger societal forces, and such symbolism opens these novels to varying, useful, sometimes provocative interpretations. The novels have often turned out to be the only contemporary record of the daily life of people, their interaction and their emotions—abundant in detail, fraught with meaning. Certainly the novels discussed here provide specifics about the local setting of personal experience, adding a welcome dimension to the institutional history of Brazil emphasized in this work.

This essay also recommends a few novels representative of the genre wherein novelists recreate the past in order to explore some (then) contemporary issue they deemed socially or politically significant. Those novelists uninhibitedly employed the past to illuminate their present.

Brazilian novelists seem always to understand the importance of their vision of society. Indeed, they have spent considerable time and energy discussing their role in chronicling, examining, and even shaping Brazilian reality. While pleased to entertain, they perceive a higher mission for themselves: to instruct. No novelist pursued higher goals than José de Alencar (1829–1877). In three essays, at least, he outlined his social objectives as a writer. Prolific, he consciously set out to define, through novels, national history, national consciousness, and nationalism. Annoyed by the menace to Brazilian values of "foreign ways and customs," he tried to draw attention to and strengthen "true national taste" through creating a literature "inherently Brazilian in inspiration and in form." The national literature he heralded sprang from the unique beauty of Brazil, its distinctive life styles, and its traditional virtues. He detailed them in four series of novels on the Indian past, rural life, urban life, and great historical moments. Those novels are set in locales ranging from the South to the Northeast, and span the history of Brazil from colonization to the mid-nineteenth century. Alencar's rich legacy of fifteen novels enlivened discourse on national self-perception and identity.

Unfortunately, only one of Alencar's novels, *Iracema,* appears in English translation. First published in 1865, the English translation bears the date 1886 (London: Bichers & Son); there is a 1978 reprint. This brief, seemingly simplistic novel focuses on various themes the author judged significant in the formative process of the Brazilian nation: the creation of a "new race" through miscegenation; the cultural dominance of Europe and the triumph of European ideology; the role of the Indian; the transformation of the state of nature into the nation-state; and the marginalization of the female in the new, male-dominated society. Clearly, transcendental themes of nationality, nation-state, and nationalism preoccupied the prolific Alencar. No one should read this suggestive novel without first consulting the perceptive essay by Ria Lemaire, "Re-Reading *Iracema:* The Problem of the Representation of Women in the Construction of a National Brazilian Identity," in *Luso-Braziian Review,* 26, no. 2 (Winter 1989), 59–73.

Jorge Amado (1912–) has been no less preoccupied than Al-

cencar with history and historical methodologies in his novels published throughout much of the twentieth century. He consciously records "the life, the customs, the language of my State [Bahia]." In order "to set down in novels the life, the picturesque qualities, the strange humanity of Bahia," the affable Amado mingles intimately with all classes of his fellow Bahians. For example, to write his novel on tenement life, *Suor* (*Sweat,* 1934), he lived in one of the tenements in the old section of Salvador da Bahia. In fact, Amado brags of his dedication to "collecting material," the stuff of reality with which he saturates his imagined plots. He once noted, "In order to put these novels of mine (which may have many defects, but which have one quality: the absolute honesty of the author) together, I tried to seek out the people, I went to live with them, ever since my childhood on cacao plantations, my adolescence in cafes in the capital, my trips all through the State, crossing it in all manner of conveyances, listening to and seeing the most beautiful and strangest parts of Bahia's humanity." Amado's marriage of fact with imagination does not contradict the methodology of the conscientious historian who must employ imagination to extract the maximum meaning from the "facts." Amado's novels store a wealth of social detail difficult, if not impossible, to find in other writings.

Novels, many of them engagingly translated into English, have streamed from the pen of Amado. An inhabitant of the city with the largest Afro-Brazilian population—and, consequently, a city permeated with African influences—he dwells on Afro-Brazilians and, in particular, on mulattoes and their place within Brazilian society. *Jubiabá* (1935; English translation; New York: Avon, 1984) relates the life of a street child, Antônio Balduíno, who becomes a circus boxer, a balladeer, a laborer, and a union activist. A mulatto, he symbolizes most Brazilians: impoverished, undereducated but able to come to understand their own interests and strengths. On their backs rests the weight of production; they provide Brazil's labor. Balduíno reasons, "When black people go on strike, everything stops, the cranes stop, the streetcars quit, where's the lights? . . . Black people are the light, they're the streetcars. Black people and poor white people, they're all slaves but they have everything in their hands. Folks, let's go on strike, because the strike is like a necklace. If we all hang together, it's something pretty." A third of a century later, Amado wrote his finest novel on race relations, *The Tent of Miracles* (*A Tenda dos Milagres,* 1969; English translation, New York: Knopf, 1978), a tour de force, based loosely but unmistakably on the life of the remarkable Manuel R. Querino, the first

African-Brazilian historian. Race relations, urban poverty, and labor unionism weave a part of the background for *Captains of the Sands* (*Capitães da Areia,* 1937; English translation, New York: Avon, 1988). The major theme concentrates on homeless children, one consequence of an urbanized Brazil lacking both a sufficient number of jobs for parents and adequate social services for youths. The problem alarmed Amado in the second quarter of the twentieth century; it permeates urban society in the final quarter of the century.

The Violent Land (*Terras do Sem Fim,* 1942; English translation, New York: Knopf, 1945, with numerous reprints) ranks as Amado's most significant novel. It treats fundamental institutions: those that encompass the ownership and use of land and the regulation of labor. The plot concerns the struggle between Horácio Silveira and Juca and Sinho Badaro over land whose fertile soil nourishes the cacao tree—a source of chocolate, a source of export wealth. The novel details how land holdings are acquired, expanded, maintained, exploited, and lost, and describes the political, social, and economic institutions involved in all these processes. It concentrates on cacao lands, but it could have just as accurately depicted sugar plantations, cattle ranches, or coffee estates. Themes involving the grandeur of nature, relations between the sexes, patriarchy, labor systems (debt peonage, particularly), conflicts of cultures, and the expansion of frontiers cascade through its pages.

Amado's preoccupation with folk cultures fits snugly in the well-delineated tradition of Brazilian novelists' depictions of ordinary people—one of their major contributions to our better understanding of the past. Their concerns contrast markedly with the historians' preoccupation with the elite. Two early novels initiated that pattern. In *Memoirs of a Militia Sergeant* (*Memória de um Sargento de Milícias,* 1852–1853; English translation Washington, D.C.: Pan American Union, 1959), Manuel Antônio de Almeida (1831–1861) focused on the adventures of his picaresque hero, Leonardo, in Rio de Janeiro, circa 1820. He enlivens the pages with detailed descriptions of local customs and charming urban insights into life in the booming imperial capital on the eve of Brazilian independence. Alfredo d'Escragnolle Taunay (1843–1899) offered similar insights into rural folk customs in *Inocência* (1872; English translation, New York: Macmillan, 1945). Describing daily life in the remote interior of Mato Grosso, this novel illustrates the pervasiveness of patriarchy—with its emphasis on "honor," tradition, and the secondary, subservient role of women. The author also introduces the challenges of change with scant indication of their success. Inocên-

cia herself rebels against tradition with death as her only reward. The past persists.

Mario Vargas Llosa (1936–) is not a Brazilian. Yet his epic novel *The War of the End of the World* (*La Guerra del Fin del Mundo,* 1981; English translation, New York: Avon, 1985) ranks as the most perceptive document on the conflict at Canudos, 1896–1897. The Peruvian author demonstrated an unusual understanding of the folk community and its significance. He divided the novel between events occurring inside the "New Jerusalem" and outside: in Rio de Janeiro, in Salvador da Bahia, and within the attacking armies. With deep concern and sharp perception, Vargas Llosa addresses the historical questions of why Canudos came into existence, what it signified to its folk inhabitants as well as to the political and economic elites of Brazil, and why the government determined to destroy it. Few have spoken so eloquently and knowledgeably about this intriguing historical epic—and tragedy!

Three of the novels of José Lins do Rego (1901–1957), *Menino do Engenho* (1932), *Doidinho* (1933), and *Bangüe* (1934), have been translated and incorporated into one volume entitled *Plantation Boy* (New York: Knopf, 1966). Through the experiences of a boy maturing into a young man, Lins do Rego introduced the reader to lifestyles on a sugar plantation and in a provincial city just as modernization challenges both rural and urban traditions in the early twentieth century and triumphs.

Coffee facilitated the triumph of modernization. Cecílio J. Carneiro discusses such important themes as life on the coffee plantation and immigration in his novel *The Bonfire* (*A Fogueira,* 1941; English translation, New York: Farrar & Rinehart, 1944). In the novel, Elias Arbe, a Syrian, migrates to Brazil in the early twentieth century. He both makes a fortune in coffee and loses it. In reality, the author's parents immigrated from Syria, although he was born in the interior of Minas Gerais. As is true in many of these novels, the plots incorporate autobiographical elements.

The classic novel of the Brazilian interior remains *The Devil to Pay in the Backlands* (Grande Sertão: Veredas, 1956; English translation, New York: Knopf, 1963) by João Guimarães Rosa (1908–1967). An innovative study of the backlands, on one exalted level it philosophizes on human destiny, courage, and relationships; on another, more mundane level it describes the flora, fauna, and daily life of bandits in the interior of Minas Gerais.

A masterful examination of the lives of rural folk comes from the hand of Graciliano Ramos (1892–1953). Outwardly, the action of

his novel *Barren Lives* (*Vidas Secas,* 1938; English translation, Austin: University of Texas Press, 1969) is spare. Fabiano, his wife, Victoria, their two sons, and their dog, Baleia, flagellated by the drought in the dry interior of northeastern Brazil, take refuge in an abandoned hut and are saved by the rains. Later, another drought and oppressive conditions start them on another journey. Beyond that, it provides penetrating insights into the lives, routines, and beliefs of the impoverished rural masses. Two themes predominate: the relationship of the folk to the land, and the common person as a victim of institutions he or she did not create, cannot influence, and apparently cannot change. The characters are partially shaped by their environment and partially by the institutions that weigh upon them. Fatalism, the sinew of tradition, permeates them. Fabiano faces three opportunities to rebel against those institutions that oppress him. On one occasion he has a confrontation with his boss, the landowner; on another he encounters in the thickets the policeman who tormented him in the town; and on the third some bandits invite him to join them. He backs away from each opportunity. Ramos painted an unforgettable portrait of the peasant.

Urban growth also attracted the attention of novelists. Two very important novels appeared within five years of each other to jointly comment on a trend that would reshape Brazil in the twentieth century. The first, *A Brazilian Tenement* (*O Cortiço,* 1890; English translation, New York: Robert M. McBride, 1926), by Aluísio Azevedo (1857–1913), reflected the city of Rio de Janeiro at a time of agitated change. The novel attracts attention partly because of the author's concern with social problems, but mainly because of the insight provided into the routines of daily life of ordinary people. He used this novel to alert his readers to the changing urban environment as well as to its complexities. One aspect of the city was its pervasive poverty; another was the social mobility it permitted. The novel treats both themes at length. However, a careful reading of the novel reveals much information about and insights into other subjects: life-styles, nationalism, social conflict, the roles of women, the dehumanizing aspects of poverty, race relations, for ex•mple. Some of the novel's characters play major symbolic roles. Rita Bahiana, for example, incarnates "Brazilian character." The African-Brazilian Bertoleza represents Brazil's past, while the white João Romão, the future. The process of the Brazilianization of Jeronymo, the Portuguese immigrant, provides yet another set of character symbols to enrich the novel. Azevedo offers a useful

insight into the major Brazilian city at the end of the nineteenth century, indicating the problems and stresses caused by accelerating urbanization.

The life of the proletariat in Rio de Janeiro at approximately the same time also appears as major theme in *Bom-Crioulo. The Black Man and the Cabin Boy* (*Bom Crioulo*, 1895; English translation, San Francisco: Gay Sunshine Press, 1982) by Adolfo Caminha (1867–1897). An innovator, Caminha introduced two unique themes: first, the African-Brazilian as the major protagonist; second, overt homosexuality. The relationship between the black sailor and the white cabin boy takes place partly on a naval vessel, thus affording an unusual insight into military life (Caminha served in the navy), and partly in the port of Rio de Janeiro, affording representation of a broader range of life-styles of ordinary people.

Joaquim Maria Machado de Assis (1839–1908) still bears the reputation as Brazil's greatest novelist. His so-called three minor novels and five major ones enjoy English translations and high critical acclaim. Any of his novels affords a useful insight into the upper classes—and those with upward aspirations—of Rio de Janeiro in the nineteenth century. *Epitaph of a Small Winner* (*Memórias Póstumas de Brás Cubas*, 1880; English translation, (New York: Noonday Press, 1956) depicts *carioca* bourgeois society during the first half of the nineteenth century, while *Counselor Ayres' Memoirs* (*Memorial de Aires*, 1908; English translation, Berkeley and Los Angeles: University of California Press, 1972) condemns the irresponsibility of the elite during the last half of the century. It constitutes a kind of rite of passage, a farewell to the past. The most historically oriented of the major novels, *Esau and Jacob* (*Esaú e Jacó*, 1904; English translation, Berkeley and Los Angeles: University of California Press, 1965) takes place in the capital during the years from 1869 to 1894, thus covering the period of the emancipation of the slaves as well as the transition from empire to republic. In this political allegory, identical twins, Pedro, a Monarchist, and Pablo, a Republican, struggle for the affection of the same woman, Flora, a symbol of Brazil. David T. Haberly adroitly explores the complexity of the world Machado de Assis saw around him in his thoughtful interpretive essay "A Journey through the Escape Hatch: Joaquim Maria Machado de Assis" in his *Three Sad Races: Racial Identity and National Consciousness in Brazilian Literature* (Cambridge: Cambridge University Press, 1983), 70–98.

What was the "new Brazil" emerging in the late nineteenth century and the early twentieth? Was there anything significantly

new at all? The Brazilian literati could not agree. Their anguished debates of the early twentieth century pull back the curtains of reserve to permit glimpses inside the troubled minds of the intellectuals. *Canaan (Canaã*, 1902; English translation, Boston: Four Seas, 1920) by José Pereira da Graça Aranha (1868–1931) exposes the ferment of ideas and contradictions. The novel's meaning depends heavily on the reader's perception of the three principal characters: Milkau, Lentz, and Mary. The first two are rather easy to understand: they are opposites. Milkau can be seen as representing evolution, progress, compassion, understanding, and harmony; Lentz stands for tradition. Milkau represents and idealized future; Lentz recalls the past. Milkau embodies the New World; Lentz, the Old. Mary, the daughter of immigrants, seems to symbolize Brazil, poor, dispossessed, and even confused. Roman Catholic symbolism pervades the text. The names Mary and Canaan are a biblical reference. Somewhat more subtly, the notion of redemption plays a significant role in the novel, most specifically in the concept of redeeming the Brazilian masses.

As an intellectual and a nationalist, Graça Aranha maintained a lively interest in ideology. One preoccupation was with defining Brazilian civilization. He interpreted the Brazilian past as a history of struggle, between "conquerors and vanquished under the form of masters and slaves," the struggle of classes, "the ruled against the ruling." In the mixing of the races across time, he discerned in this novel the modification of struggle and the creation of nationality: "It was necessary that out of our conflicting races there should emerge a half caste type which, adapting itself to its surroundings and possessing the average qualities of the other peoples, should vanquish and eliminate them all. . . . Those who tend to govern us more acceptably, and with greater success than any others, belong to the same mulatto type. In fact, Brazil belongs to them." Acutely aware of the problems bedeviling Europe, Graça Aranha looked inward for solutions to Brazil's problems rather than toward Europe.

Two decades after the publication of *Canaan*, Graça Aranha participated in the Modern Art Week. On that occasion, he stated

Civilization here emerged from a melting pot. The blending produced a "civilization" which is not exclusively European, having been created by our physical environment and the mixed races that populate it. This civilization still exists in mere outline, with no definite character, but it is a point of departure for the creation of true nationality. European culture should not serve to impose European domination nor as a pattern to imitate, but

rather as a tool to build something new out of the elements of the land, the people, and the primitive wildness that still persists. Our desire for cultural liberation is a sign that this new civilization is already present in us.

This statement summarizes ideas that appeared in *Canaan*. The continuity emphasizes the intensifying preoccupation of the intellectuals with questions of national identity and perception during the twentieth century. It constitutes the heart of the vitality and viability of the nation. Marshall C. Eakin suggests further insights into Graça Aranha and his novel in his useful "Race and Ideology in Graça Aranha's *Canaã*," *Ideologies & Literature*, 3:14 (September–November, 1980), 3–15.

The seminal Modern Art Week fathered one of the most challenging and unusual novels in search of national character, *Macunaíma* (1928, English translation, New York: Random House, 1984) by Mário de Andrade (1893–1945). Blending folklore with allegory, this classic "novel"—Andrade termed it a rhapsody—searches for the roots and structures of Brazilian life. A "hero without character," Macunaíma incorporates all the races, all national traits, all periods of Brazilian history. Perfectly summarizing the goal of Modern Art Week, Andrade pursued cultural originality and denounced cultural dependency. Most readers will require an intellectual road map through this short and complex novel. David T. Haberly provides an excellent one, "The Harlequin: Mário de Andrade" in his *Three Sad Races*, 135–60.

Unlike historians, novelists have always included women in their works. Women exist on the pages of novels with an equality denied them in history texts. A great deal can be learned about the roles of females in Brazilian society across time by consulting them. The engaging *The Diary of "Helena Morely"* (*Minha Vida de Menina*, 1942; English translation, New York; Ecco Press, 1977), contains a detailed daily account written by a young girl in the small town of Diamantina, Minas Gerais, from 1893 to 1895. The classification of this document raises some questions. After all, it is a primary document, a diary kept by a young lady. The action and conversations, however, flow in a style reminiscent of the autobiographical novel. "Helena Morely" contains a wealth of detail about daily provincial life from the female point of view.

Rachel de Queiroz (1910–1978) wrote the stories of three young Marias reaching womanhood during the 1920s and 1930s in a provincial city, Fortaleza, capital of Ceará, in *The Three Marias* (*As Tres Marias*, 1939; English translation, Austin: University of Texas Press,

1963). The three feel the frustrations of women facing inequality, educational and career restrictions, and the definition of their own sexual feelings. Through the eyes of Queiroz, the reader sees a Brazil at a specific time, as the women do. Nearly forty years later she published *Dora, Doralina* (1975; English translation, New York: Avon, 1984), whose heroine exudes fulfillment and satisfaction, in contrast to the sentiments of the earlier autobiographical novel. This change is doubtless a tribute to some changes in the status of females during the intervening decades.

In *The Hour of the Star* (*A Hora da Estrela*, 1977; English translation, New York: Carcanet, 1986), Clarice Lispector (1925–1977) sensitively told the tale of the young Macabéa, who migrates from the Northeast to the city of São Paulo. She is totally unprepared for the modernity she encounters, an experience that further marginalizes her. On one important level, Macabéa represents the isolated female in a modern society; on another, she serves as an historical metaphor for Brazil itself.

Finally, in the realm of the political novel, Lêdo Ivo (1924–) offers a study of contemporary totalitarian governance in his *Snakes' Nest or A Tale Badly Told* (*Ninho de Cobras*, 1973; English translation, New York: New Directions, 1981). While the novel views the government of Getúlio Vargas from Maceió, the capital of the state of Alagoas, that ruse serves only to circumvent the censors. The story is really an allegory based on the military dictatorship imposed in 1964.

These Brazilian novelists knew their nation and its past; they empathized with their compatriots' emotions and aspirations, disappointments and triumphs; they were intelligent and insightful; and they wrote well. They have contributed significantly to a better understanding of Brazil. Their novels complement and, indeed, enrich the study of history as they conduct the reader on that "marvelous journey" through the Brazilian past.

Index